Stone

Stone

An Ecology of the Inhuman

JEFFREY JEROME COHEN

University of Minnesota Press

Minneapolis • London

Portions of "Geophilia: The Love of Stone" were previously published as "Time out of Memory," in *The Post-Historical Middle Ages,* ed. Elizabeth Scala and Sylvia Federico (New York: Palgrave Macmillan, 2009), 37–61, and as "Stories of Stone," *postmedieval* 1 (2010): 56–63, reprinted by permission of Palgrave Macmillan. Portions of "Time: The Insistence of Stone" were previously published as "Pilgrimages, Travel Writing, and the Medieval Exotic," in *Oxford Handbook of Medieval Literature in English,* ed. Elaine Treharne and Greg Walker (Oxford: Oxford University Press, 2010), 611–28, reprinted by permission of Oxford University Press, and as "The Future of the Jews of York," in *Christians and Jews in Medieval England: Narratives and Contexts for the York 1190 Massacre,* ed. Sarah Rees Jones and Sethina Watson (Suffolk: Boydell and Brewer, 2013), 278–93, reprinted by permission of Boydell and Brewer and York Medieval Press. Portions of "Force: The Adventure of Stone" were previously published as "The Sex Life of Stone," in *From Beasts to Souls: Gender and Embodiment in Medieval Europe,* ed. E. Jane Burns and Peggy McCracken (Notre Dame: University of Notre Dame Press, 2013), 17–38, reprinted by permission of the University of Notre Dame Press, and as "Queering the Inorganic," in *Queer Futures: Reconsidering Normativity, Activism, and the Political,* ed. Eveline Killian, Elahe Haschemi Yekani, and Beatrice Michaelis (Farhnham: Ashgate, 2013), 149–64, reprinted by permission of Ashgate, and as "Green Children from Another World, or The Archipelago in England," in *Cultural Diversity in the British Middle Ages: Archipelago, Island, England,* ed. Jeffrey Jerome Cohen (New York: Palgrave Macmillan, 2008), 75–94, reprinted by permission of Palgrave Macmillan.

Published by the University of Minnesota Press
111 Third Avenue South, Suite 290
Minneapolis, MN 55401-2520
http://www.upress.umn.edu

Library of Congress Cataloging-in-Publication Data
Cohen, Jeffrey Jerome.
　　Stone: an ecology of the inhuman / Jeffrey Jerome Cohen.
　　Includes bibliographical references and index.
　　ISBN 978-0-8166-9262-0 (pb)
　　1. Nature—Religious aspects. 2. Stone—Miscellanea. 3. Ecology—Philosophy.
　　4. Literature, Medieval—History and criticism. I. Title.
　　BD581.C64 2015
　　113—dc23   2014045916

CONTENTS

Stories of Stone

Three Geonarratives

1. Like a Rock

Bereft of family, home, and health, Job wonders how to survive the world's catastrophes. "My strength is not the strength of stones," he laments, "nor is my flesh of brass."[1] Rocks and hard metals hold an endurance no mortal flesh can own. Nothing like stone, Job submits to sorrow and speaks a story of unbearable humanity. A vertiginous perspective shift unfolds when God intervenes, invoking geological time and demanding where Job was when the foundations of the earth were laid (Job 38:4). Does Job know the thunderous activity of the elements: rain that cascades for no witness, ice that hardens like stone, stars that course the heavens, the secrets of the whirlwind, the yawn of the submarinal abyss? Can he discern the force of the inhuman world, the long sweep of its eons? Job's complaint is rebuked through the invocation of a scale that diminishes him, reducing the human to its vanishing point.

A rock's endurance is not Job's. Yet Adam was fashioned "de limo terrae," from mud or clay (Genesis 2:7). Like stone, human flesh mingles dry earth with binding water: an unsettled union of wet and dry, cold and warm, fire and tears. Stone's materiality belongs equally to Eve (created from bone, the lithic within the corporeal) and to Job's unnamed wife, who suffers just as profoundly but without full story. Through God's breath men and women have a living soul ("animam viventem"). That difference perhaps makes Job's lithic inheritance irrelevant, even as it renders his complaint more complicated: he is in fact suffused with stoniness. By the thirteenth century, moreover, the philosopher and scientist Albertus Magnus had to refute the idea that stones possess souls, so lively do rocks appear when examined not simply in comparison to humans but in their native thriving. Stone is primal matter, inhuman in its duration. Yet despite its incalculable temporality, the lithic is not some vast and alien outside. A limit-breaching intimacy persistently unfolds.

Hurl a rock and you'll shatter an ontology, leave taxonomy in glistening shards.

2. Like a Mountain

In a seminal work of environmental theorizing Aldo Leopold introduced to the ecological lexicon the resilient phrase "thinking like a mountain."[2] Leopold begins with a wolf's howl, an "outburst of wild defiant sorrow" that reverberates in sonic progression down a wooded slope. To deer the cry is a warning of mortality; for pines, an augury of blood upon snow; to scavengers, an announcement of the feast to arrive; for ranchers the bay is loss; for hunters, the call of prey. The wolf's bonds to each human and nonhuman are varied and deep, constituting a knowledge both aeonic and recondite: "Only the mountain has lived long enough to listen objectively to the howl of a wolf . . . mountains have a secret opinion about them."[3] Leopold learns of this withdrawn relation when, dreaming a huntsman's paradise, he shoots a wolf and her pups. The peak without its pack quickly becomes a barren expanse. The deer proliferate to devour every leaf, impoverishing the ecosystem. Eventually the "starved bones of the hoped-for deer herd, dead of its own too-much" join the denuded undergrowth.[4] Because a mountain persists so much longer than pines, wolves, bucks, and people, its rocky expanses hold the profundity of a long past. A meshwork of connection, the mountain entangles every struggling life and imbues even stone with vitality.

At the summit, perspective. Leopold performs a rhetorical move familiar in environmental writing, employing a strategic anthropomorphism

2

to deepen human sensitivity to ecological precariousness. "Thinking like a mountain" stresses the stabilities achieved by diffuse biomes and the dangers of their disruption. Yet Leopold's range is too small. A mountain is something more than an allegory for Edenic nature, a figure in a human story of balanced inhabitance and expansive earthly interconnection.[5] Relations do not create things like rocks and mountains; things like rocks and mountains are what enable relations to flourish.[6] Writing in the twelfth century, Marie de France labeled such inhuman agency *aventure,* future-laden "arrival" or "adventure." In her lays *Guigemar* and *Yonec* she describes women imprisoned in towers of cold marble. Escape into a wider world arrives only upon the hurling of the self out from stony enclosure and into rocky mobility: a leap through an open window, the trying of a door thought bolted, a wandering from immurement across companionable landscapes. A road plunges deep into a barrow and emerges at a city fashioned of silver. A crag sought for suicide is where a ship awaits, conveyance to a distant life. A grandiose tomb offers not tiresome instruction in human brevity but an invitation to an unexpected future, to changed story.

Climb a mountain to seek a vista and its native prospect will give you ontological vertigo. To think like a mountain requires a leap from ephemeral stabilities, from the diminutive boundedness of merely human tales. In the geological frame within which mountains exist, pinnacles rise and fall in fearsome undulations. Peaks ascend when tectonic plates push against each other, crumble as water wears granite to dust and carries to estuaries silt for the making of new rock. Continents smash against each other then break to wander the sea. Blunt and inscrutable, stone does not offer itself as metaphor for natural harmonies, for systems in lasting balance. The tracks of living creatures are the barest of archives, their howls and speech the most fleeting of traces. "Thinking like a mountain" extends the ambit of critical inquiry by yoking two figures neither settled nor fully known: a geologic formation that does not remain still and a creature of unstable history, easily undone.

3. Like a Rolling Stone

Bruno Latour writes of the objects that crowd laboratories, rain forests, cities, and houses, their compliance or resistance when humans form alliances with them, and their collaboration in composing the narratives that become, at least for a while, facts. A progenitor of actor network theory (ANT), a mode of inquiry that details the powerful agency of nonhumans, Latour argues that objects are energetic mediators rather than passive tools.[7] The object-oriented philosopher Graham Harman likewise describes things as "actants, forever lost in friendships and duels."[8] Their marvelous stories are ignored when we reduce objects to a deeper play of forces or dissolve them into overarching context. Every object holds unfathomable reserves and cannot be equated to anything else as a way of depleting its possibilities. "Miniature trickster objects turn the tide without warning," Harman writes, so that even the smallest stone can trigger consequences disproportionate to its scale: "a pebble can destroy an empire if the emperor chokes at dinner."[9]

By invoking an imperium-toppling pebble to emphasize the power of the nonhuman, Harman participates in a long tradition of mining the philosophical from the lithic. Stones are the partners with which we build the epistemological structures that may topple upon us. They are ancient allies in knowledge making. A rock discovered at the shoreline opens an adventure in deep time and inhuman forces: slow sedimentation of alluvium and volcanic ash, grinding tectonic shift, crushing mass and epochal compaction, infernal heat, relentless turbidity of the sea. The philosopher Michel Serres argues that stone is the foundation of story at every archeological layer of human history: the Wailing Wall, ruin of a dismantled temple ("not one stone left standing upon another stone"); Thaleäes inventing geometry through his study of the pyramids, time travellers from centuries as remote to him as he to us; the Black Stone of the Kaaba in Mecca, magnet for pilgrims; the birth of modern science through the careful study of falling stones in the Renaissance; Jesus establishing a church on Peter, whose name means "rock."[10] Stone becomes history's bedrock as lithic agency impels human knowing. Neither dead matter nor pliant utensil, bluntly impedimental as well as collaborative force, stone brings story into being, a partner with language (just as inhuman), a material metaphor.[11] A conveyance device that is at once linguistic, story-laden, thingly, and agentic, a metaphor is an ontological sliding, a tectonic veer, materiality coming into and out of figure, "matterphor."[12] Like stone. Whether a pebble or a volcano,

A piece of the volcano Hekla in Iceland.

a mountain or a meteor, the lithic offers passage into action, a catalyst, a cause. The Greek myth of Sisyphus and his frustrated labor of pushing a boulder up a Hadean hill has long fascinated. From an allegory for proper subservience to the gods Sisyphus becomes an existential hero, his embrace of the world's absurdity a triumph of the human will. As Serres wryly observes, however, no one relates the tale of the endlessly tumbling stone that accompanies him into aeonic time.[13] Stone abides at the origin of story, but a narrative in which it might figure as something more than an ancillary device, a protagonist rather than prop, has yet to appear. There opens between Sisyphus and his boulder a space of peril and beauty, of the mundane become mythic, a complicated dance of touch and withdrawal. What if the tale of Sisyphus is not only about a human and a stone, each in its solitude, vying for the status of chief character, but a multifaceted narrative of cross-taxonomic relation: a human who attempts to grasp a boulder that never ceases to tumble, hands upon hard surface, rock against hands, an epochal embrace?

Set in Stone

This book is something of a thought experiment, attempting to discern in the most mundane of substances a liveliness. Despite relegation to a trope for the cold, the indifferent, and the inert, stone discloses queer vivacity, and a perilous tender of mineral amity. Stone aggregates, attracting to itself disparate matter, varied rhetorical devices and narratives, especially of the compound and dilatory sort: catalogue poems, encyclopedia entries, biographical digression, etymological impulses, lapidaries arranged alphabetically or by color to mask their disorder, wonder-filled romance. Because of its ardor for unconformity, stone sediments contradiction, there to ignite possibility, abiding invitation to metamorphosis. It offers a stumbling block to anthropocentrism and a spur to ceaseless story. Something of my project's impetus may be glimpsed in a question posed by the environmental phenomenologist David Abram. After enjoining contemplation of our entanglement within a dynamic biome that includes skies, pines, birds, and houses, Abram hesitates at a stony limit:

> What of stones—of boulders and mountain cliffs? Clearly, a slab of granite is not alive in any obvious sense, and it is hard to see how anyone could attribute such openness or indeterminacy to it, or why they would want to.[14]

Lapidary texts and lithic architectures from the Middle Ages provide an excellent response to Abram's query. Medieval writers knew well that the world has never been still, that humans may dream a separation from nature, may strive to exalt themselves from the recalcitrance of stone, but remain earth formed from earth, living upon the earth through alliance with earthen matter, returning at death to earth again. Such are the punning, almost untranslatable words of a poignant fourteenth-century lyric known by its resonant first line, "Erthe toc of erthe erthe wyth woh" (Earth took from the earth earth with woe). "Erthe" in the poem denotes person, living body, corpse, soil, minerals, planet, world, possessions, and grave.[15] Rich in lithic transit, the lyric insists upon the inherent metaphoricity of the material as well as the sheer materiality of metaphor: "erthe" insistently conveys but does not surrender to figuration. "Erthe toc of erthe" succinctly articulates human-lithic enmeshment, making clear an ecological consciousness that suffuses language even when we turn away from that awareness.[16] "If nature is to matter," Stacy Alaimo argues, "we need more potent, more complex understandings of materiality."[17] We need models from as many times as possible for thinking about the inhuman, nature with our art and art with our science. With its romances and lapidaries, its histories that do not exclude magic and other complicated systems of mapping nonhuman agency, with its astonishing narratives written on, with, and by stone, the Middle Ages proffer a rich store of such potent and complex apprehensions of what materiality does.

As Julie Cruikshank demonstrates in her work on local modes of environmental knowing, an important lesson of postcolonial studies is that the Enlightenment divorce of nature from culture demands repeated interrogation. Indigenous epistemologies often frame worldly relations in ways productively different from contemporary Western scientism.[18] Yet conceptualizing the human as separate from nature did not take seventeenth-century science to achieve, and difficult entanglement subtends supposed separation at every turn. Because the book of Genesis told them that humans have been granted earthly dominion, "literate medieval Europeans" assumed that they were "separate and distinct" from nature, even if both were part of a sublunary realm.[19] Because humans are a microcosm, because medieval writers were creative and intellectually restless, because the world is complicated, that supposed distinctiveness is actually quite a tumult. Other structurations were possible. Alternate models are most evident in textual performance. We learn as much about nature from history, chronicle, and romance as we do from the technical discourses of theology, philosophy, and natural history. A firm distinction between science and art in the Middle Ages would, moreover, be exceedingly difficult to maintain.[20]

This book excavates some "local knowledge" about lithic ecomateriality in the late Middle Ages, especially in Britain.[21] Adopting a medieval practice, I will often speak about stone in generalities: the allure of the diamond, the radiance of the carbuncle, the mobility-within-recalcitrance of what we might now know as dolerite but what in medieval Britain was simply called *lapis, ston,* or *pere.* Yet stones arrive with specific histories attached: the diamond that John Mandeville palms in India, the carbuncle that shimmers in the shield of Geoffrey Chaucer's comedic Sir Thopas, the gemmed ring that the lady Laudine entrusts to the knight Yvain in *Le Chevalier au lion,* the errant bluestones from which Stonehenge was fashioned.[22] A universal and a specific entity at once, of a certain time and yet a materialization of time out of memory, stone challenges small segment, contextualizing history. Fixing analysis within a synchronic totality, historicism proceeds through the nuanced emplacement of an object (physical or textual) within contemporary political events, literary traditions, law, cultural context. Because the Middle Ages seem so distant, so disjunct, historicism offers a surety of truth in explication, a promise that the comprehension of what is temporally remote is not distorted by anachronism, transforming dense heterogeneity into explicable slices.[23] Yet stone is difficult to contain within bounded spatial and temporal scales. Lithic materiality pushes story into expanses too large to be contained by periodizations like "classical," "medieval," "postmodern." Stone arrives with particular histories attached, of course, but carries also a past surpassing human enframing. Excavation risks inundation: stone is thick in its compaction of possibility, explosive in its release. Case study (exploring the figuration of Stonehenge in Wace's *Roman de Brut,* ca. 1155) opens immediately to epochal sweep (Stonehenge as a multimillennia sojourner; sarsen stones as matter wandering out of place through forces cultural, glacial, tectonic). Through abiding alliance humans become stone's time travelling companions, with the lithic offering multiple, noncoincidental modes of worldly inhabitance, a dizzying multiplication of prospect. Because of its density, extensiveness, tempo, and force, there is something in rock that is actively unknowable, something that will not surrender itself to stabilities, a truth behind the trope that stone rebukes epistemology. In that reproach inheres a trigger to human creativity and a provocation to cross-ontological fellowship.

A substantial force that exists outside of particular humans and often bluntly disregards their intentions, shaping and working and using and making with a startling autonomy, language responds to stone as matter to matter.[24] Compounded of sediments and telluric cogencies, a maker of heterogeneous aggregates, stone accretes, contains, conveys. This book is therefore full of litanies, varied collocations, recursive wanderings, dilatory romances, roving histories, unexpected collaborators, appositives, lists, personal excursus, accurate and false etymologies, juxtapositional compendia, strange bedfellows, temporal disjunctions. An attempt to accompany Sisyphus and his vagrant stone rather than a quest for the mountaintop barred to both—an attempt that is to delve into the stone-embraced spaces detailed by authors like Marie de France in her lays *Guigemar* and *Yonec*—*Stone: An Ecology of the Inhuman* does not offer a progress narrative in which medieval myths, misprision, and occult knowledge (alchemy, natural philosophy, astrology, lithotherapy) build a foundation for chemistry and geophysics or yield to medicine, geology, and plate tectonics. Nor am I arguing for a return to the search for the philosopher's stone, or positing that crushed gems relieve the symptoms of gout and ward against inebriation. But I do insist that medieval writers thought about materiality in ways worth investigating for the challenge they pose to those who would disenchant the world— where enchantment functions (in Jane Bennett's smart gloss) as an "affective force" that might "propel ethical generosity," a way of thinking that contests dreary and destructive modes of reducing matter to raw material, diminishing objects to uses.[25] Enchantment is estrangement and secular enmeshment, sudden sighting of the world's dynamism and autonomy, the advent of queered relation. Inhuman agency undermines our fantasies of sovereign relation to environment, a domination that renders nature "out there," a resource for recreation, consumption, and exploitation. Pondering the medieval use of petrifying tropes applied to people and to matter invites us to examine the persistence of these modes of thought, as well as to discern the wondrous beneath every still surface. Thinking geologically brings the medieval and the modern into unaccustomed proximity and reveals how, when imagining deep time, a shared vocabulary of cataclysm reveals an abiding inclination to stories of rocky entanglement, to the making of exigent and unexpected art.

The ecological project of thinking beyond anthropocentricity requires enlarged temporal and geographical scales. Yet expanded frames risk emphasizing separations at the expense of material intimacies. In both eco-theory and object studies, much critical writing on the inhuman is animated by an ardor for an unpeopled world. While the project of this book is disanthropocentric, assuming a world irreducible to its human relations and not existing for any particular purpose, its methods stress alliance, continuity, and mutual participation over elemental solitariness and human exceptionalism. The stories we know of stone will always be human stories, even if the cosmos they convey makes a problem of that category rather than celebrates some specious natural dominion. Rock formations like the Salisbury Crags (where the physician James Hutton glimpsed deep time) and lithic architectures like Stonehenge (where the historian Geoffrey of Monmouth discerned a tale of healing and remembered war) transport narrative. Mapping spaces of emergence and confederation, this book plumbs the petric in the human and the anthropomorphic in the stone. Catastrophe limns the investigation, but companionship propels its trajectory. I speak therefore of the "inhuman" to emphasize both difference ("in-" as negative prefix) and intimacy ("in-" as indicator of estranged interiority).[26] In Britain in the twelfth through fourteenth centuries, the provenance of many of the primary texts examined, stone's favored genres are sedimentary, alluvial, aggregative: the encyclopedia, the lapidary, history, and the exuberant tales of aristocratic life and intensified possibility known as romance. Speculative modes of writing, these genres investigate matter's agency, revealing its invitations to find in the ordinary a capacity to astonish. Desire suffuses their narrative structures: erotic yearning, sometimes, but also a diffuse magnetism and mundane movement toward relation. Romance, history, encyclopedias, and the medieval science of stones are modes of writing in which things speak, story-filled encounters with the inhuman. As genres they overlap. Romance is intimate to history; indeed, history forms its matter in the sense of both substance as well as subject (following medieval precedent, romance is often divided into the three "matters" of France, Britain, and Rome).[27] The burgeoning of romance from within history is easily discernible in Geoffrey of Monmouth's seminal account of King Arthur, a narrative of tumbling stone towers, rocks within which dragons slumber, and the peregrinations of Stonehenge. Romance seeps at strange moments into medieval scientific texts, including lapidaries, the popular compilations of lithic lore that amount to astonishing lithic biographies. Romance and lapidary rumination both know that the world is full of forces and objects that proliferate disruptive connections and possess uncanny vitality. Although inherently anthropocentric, such narratives unleash ecologies-in-motion that subtly challenge that perspective, that offer alternative visions in which a gem of cold gleam touched by water explodes in sudden storm, or a rock that calls out to be held burns the hand that grasps its heft.[28]

Unturned

A stone is that mundane object on which a philosopher might perch in order to think, ideation's unthought support; or in the palm, a spur to affect, cognition, and contemplation. Foundation of the inhabited world and its most durable affordance, stone is the material of our earliest tools, a lasting substance for our architectures, an intellectual ally ("calculate" derives from *calculus,* a pebble used for reckoning; *abacus* is related to the Hebrew word for "dust"), a communication device that carries into distant futures the archive of a past otherwise lost. Such are its story-laden activities, and yet lithic federation seldom merits its own tale. The reason for such stony silence is suggested within an early, prescient contribution to the environmental humanities. In a widely anthologized essay, medieval historian Lynn White Jr. argued that "all forms of life modify their contexts."[29] Coral polyps rearrange the seafloor into new biomes, while for six millennia the banks of the lower Nile have been reconfigured out of their swampy natural state into human usefulness. Even though integral to both these modifications, stone is not a "form of life" and is therefore relegated to ecological substrate. Despite White's privileging of biological activity, however, material "contexts" are seldom passive, leaving a tangible impress as they intensify, curb, or break relations. The lithic has for too long served as an allegory for nature stilled into resource.[30] If stone trips us up, challenges, intensifies, remediates, and thwarts, if stone demands certain genres and figures of speech and modes of narrative approach, if stone materially defeats the separation of tenor from vehicle that propels metaphor, then these effects derive from its evident force and epochal insinuation. Medieval writers knew this power well. They described thunderstones that drop with fire from the sky, rocks that emerge through the subterranean lovemaking of the elements, rubies that tumble along river beds from Eden, diamonds that travel the world in the holds of ships, lodestones exerting irresistible pull, gems that cure diseased bodies and pulse with astral energies. To examine a quarry from the eyes of a miner, a marble block as a mason or sculptor, a veined boulder as a climber, an amethyst as a lithotherapist or geologist, a fossil as a theologian or paleontologist is to behold a dynamism the Middle Ages knew well. To tell a story with stone is intensely to inhabit that preposition *with,* to move from solitary individuations to ecosystems, environments, shared agencies, and companionate properties.[31] In the interstice between boulderer and granite escarpment, between ecologist and mountain, between Albertus Magnus as he composes a magisterial treatise about rocks and the mines he explores to better know stone's ways, mineral life emerges. This vivacity is, to use Jane Bennett's apt word, *vibrant*: pulsing, radiant, thrumming with possibility.[32] Albertus writes that he could not find the fabled *Lapidary of Aristotle* and so "became a wanderer, making long journeys to mining districts, so that I could learn by observation the nature of metals" (*Book of Minerals,* 3.1.1). To wander in search of stone's stories is to wander in its enduring company. When stones are examined as something more than fixed and immobile things, as partners in errantry, then facts likewise begin to ambulate. After the bedrock of reality reveals its unrelenting slide, then perception, cognition, and environmental sensibilities shift. The nature of nature changes.

"Nature" is a difficult word. It names something at once "everywhere and nowhere," leading some critics to argue that we are better off without the term.[33] If nature, refracted through the geological, is understood as interfactual (knowledge arises within mediated spaces), transcorporeal (a phenomenon of bodily crossings and ontological hybridities), transmaterial (forces and things that may at times be utterly indifferent to *Homo sapiens* but not to other nonhumans, with whom a multitude of relationships are composed), our ethical connectedness to the nonhuman would become more tangible.[34] If stone is not just that of which we are certain (foundation of thought systems as well as houses, an imperturbable solid upon which we build our truths), but a material inexhaustible in its mystery and provocative in its vitality (a substance and force so much more ancient, so much denser and more powerful than parvenu humans), then shouldn't our relations to stone move beyond the utilitarian and the dominating to become at once more hesitant and gregarious?

Stone does not carry story passively forward, tractable surface for inscription. The lithic is tangled in narrative: prod as well as hindrance, ally as well as foe, a provocative and complicit agency. In medieval exegesis stone's story often ends once it becomes a symbol for the divine, so that like all created substances rock yields a reminder of "a God beyond human categories . . . beyond the world in unimaginable and unanalyzable darkness or light." Though this formulation is taken from Carolyn Walker Bynum's summation of the theology of Nicholas of Cusa, faith that the purpose of earthly matter is to reveal supernal might is a medieval Christian commonplace.[35] At its most acute, this yearning to behold traces of the celestial in the secular leads to water, wood, earth, cloth, wax, oil, and bone that shimmer with saintly power as relics.[36] Yet to resolve all material agency in divine providence ends its narrative in foregone conclusion and human-centered story (even if the purpose of such story is to draw listeners toward the heavenly). In the Middle Ages matter exists to reveal something about God, certainly, but it also divulges something about itself, something that cannot be wholly subsumed into allegory or wrested from the mundane.[37] Medieval writers were reverent enough to believe that all creation owes its genesis to deity, and perceptive enough to realize that this origin did not necessarily resolve into a wholly satisfying order or neatly finished story stone's palpable agency.

Such material insistence is especially evident in unworked stone. *Stone: An Ecology of the Inhuman* focuses on raw or minimally refined rock rather than the totalized products of human shaping, such as statuary and the dressed blocks of cathedrals. Stone in the careful hands of a sculptor or mason is as plastic a substance as wood, and a favorite material for transformation into sumptuous effigies, tombs, and churches. These metamorphoses demonstrate the power of human impress more than the virtues of stone itself.[38] Lithic sculpture tends toward the anthropomorphic. A cross, a cathedral, and a carved saint are all versions of the human figure. Art also offers an invitation to think beyond familiar forms. The lithic archive bequeathed by the Middle Ages includes engravings that dance with their viewer into nonhuman realms: the kineticism of Pictish hybrid creatures, Anglo-Saxon interlace, Irish vortices and whorls, all the petroglyphs and patterns that surface stone's lithe motion. This book, however, takes as its focus stone that may be hewn but has generally not been domesticated into cornerstone or sculpture, into a display of human craft. Affixed to its earthly origin as cave wall or slope, such material was called by Roman authors *vivum saxum* (living rock), while *vivus lapis* (living stone) had been detached from its source but not incorporated into a human project.[39] Both terms were inherited into the Middle Ages and used to convey stone's enduring vivacity. We still speak of "living rock" to designate stone "growing" from the ground or embedded within a cliff. We also retain in our vocabulary the Latin idea of mountains possessing subterranean "roots," as if peaks were mineral plants of gargantuan scale. The stones examined in this book are not unrefined. The pages that follow are full of gems worked by skilled hands to intensify their glimmer. The rocks of the Holy Land are intimate to human and divine history. In the end, though, I am interested not in stone as a well-crafted and symbol-laden solidity but in lithic alliance, invitation, and advent; not stone as a malleable substance that can be shaped into desired forms so much as stone as active partner in the shaping of worlds.[40] Appearing in every chapter is Stonehenge, a lithic architecture that has been under perpetual construction for five thousand years (and counting: a new visitor center opened just as this book was completed). The ancient circle, first recorded in medieval texts, materializes this book's open, recursive, wheeling structure, leitmotif for an errant argument. Perhaps inspired by natural formations in the Preseli Hills, the immense ring upon an earthen bank, surrounded by a complex array of topographical features and megaliths, is an aeonic collaboration among disparate artists, including stone itself. Numerous rocks, pebbles, mountains, and ruins have been my partners in writing this book, but none with the compositional force of Stonehenge, that ring of ceaseless invitation.

I will sometimes use the words "stone," "rock," "mineral," "gem" and their related adjectives "lithic" and "petric" interchangeably in this book, even if they are not exactly synonyms. Medieval geological designations were likewise more precise in theory than practice. Thus Middle English *ston* could designate any lithic chunk from the smallest pebble to a towering menhir. The *Middle English Dictionary* defines the noun along an ascending scale: "A discrete piece of rock, esp. one of small or medium size; a stone, pebble; also, a large discrete piece of rock, a boulder; a standing stone, monolith." Geological terms were variably differentiated among classical and medieval writers. Lithic substance was in general given an origin that repeats some version of Aristotle's formulation: earth (an arid, powdery, restless element, one of the four from which the world's materiality was composed) admixes with water and coagulates into stone.[41] Just as in modern geology, medieval lapidary science held that each stone bears a story about the time and place of its creation. The paleobiologist Jan Zalasiewicz examines a pebble that "contains time itself" to tell a story of "thousands of corpses" from the Silurian sea compressed within its grey hardness, while the thirteenth-

century polymath Albertus Magnus beholds in *saphirus* a narrative of sand-
banks in ancient India and mines in Provence, of swirling clouds suspended
in translucence, and of the calm the gem yields to those who gaze upon
its depths.[42] For medieval writers the traction of remote stars and wheeling planets, fluctuations of heat and cold, and the peculiarities of local environment leave an ineluctable impress upon stone at its formation, with
a gem indicating an especially precious instance of lithic genesis. Cosmic
and ecological imprinting imbues a stone with its *virtus* (Latin) or *vertu*
(French and English), its inherent powers and the primary source of its
agency. Many objects that classical and medieval authors listed as stones
we would now separate as organic products (seashells, gastroliths, fossils).
Medieval lapidary inclusiveness makes clear that rocks and gems were fas-
cinating not because they offered a changeless substance but because they
are engendered through long processes and trigger wondrous effects as
they move through the world. For the etymologist Isidore of Seville (ca.
560–636), all lithic substance is dense earth, but stones *(lapides)* tend to be
smooth and scattered (that is, they are individuals), while rocks *(saxa)* are
rougher and must be quarried (*Etymologies,* 16.3). For the Latin encyclopedist Bartholomaeus Anglicus (ca. 1203–72) and his English translator John
Trevisa, stone is cold, dry, stable, dense, and always "moving downwards
through its own heaviness and weight."[43] Metals are intimately related to
stones and are often described as an especially watery version of the petric.[44] Stones and metals are, for Albertus Magnus, the two types of minerals.
Albert writes that all stone is formed of a combination of earth and water,
with the former element dominating in the densest stones and the latter in
the most crystalline, yielding translucent gems (*Book of Minerals,* 1.1.2–3).
The Islamic philosopher known in English as Avicenna (Ibn Sīnā, 980–
1037) insisted that "pure earth does not make stone," and Albertus quotes
this pronouncement approvingly: stone is a durable record of the elements
in union.[45] Origin in earth's embrace of water holds true for Albert no matter
if the stone should originate in a volcano, a hot spring, subterranean depths,
an oyster shell, or the bladder of a sparrow. Bartholomaeus Anglicus repeats
the declaration of Saint Ambrose that stones are the bones of the earth, for
they make the world stable and prevent its fabric from fragmenting (*On
the Properties of Things,* 16.74). Without rock, Bartholomaeus insists, humans could not endure. Stones are "nedefulle" for the making of houses,

walls, pavement, bridges. They keep us safe from enemies, wolves, hounds, and "oþere euel bestes" (other evil beasts). They draw out metals and cure illnesses. They are the foundation of the courts of kings and the fabric of cities, towers, castles, the substance of mundane dwelling (16.74). This vision of lithic activeness is, in the end, not all that dissimilar to Manuel De Landa's use of "geological" to designate the "dynamical elements (energy flow, nonlinear causality) that we have in common with rocks and mountains and other nonliving historical structures," a commonality that belies our "organic chauvinism."[46]

Stone's time is not ours. For many, this disjunction will never be noticed, triggering neither affect nor insight. For those for whom rock's alien intimacy becomes palpable, however, its temporal noncoincidence is profoundly, productively disorienting. A climber faces the face of the mountain, and in that interface relation unfolds, bringing each into intimacy: fraught, perilous, fleeting, familiar, suspended above the certainty of ground. Something happens in such interfacial zones: anarchic irruption (*arche* is origin, grounding: what happens when *arche* is impossibly distant, geologically adrift?), generative encounter, an erosion of secure foundation, an ethical moment of connection-forging. Lithic-induced perspective shift triggers an ontological and temporal reeling, a rocky movement of affect, cognition, horizon. This book simulates that seismic effect by intermixing the medieval and the modern, the theoretical with the blunt, the linguistic and textual with the ecomaterial. Vertigo is the book's intent rather than an accident of its rhetorical excess. Reading it may induce dizziness, but there are handholds along the steepest slopes and, with luck, some pleasurable wayfaring along the way. This book is an interlocutor in some lively critical conversations: ecotheory and environmental studies, posthumanism, medieval studies, and the new materialism (including vibrant materialism, the "geologic turn" of cultural studies, speculative realism, and various object-oriented philosophies).[47] As a primal materiality, stone is a symbol for that which is bluntly real, a synonym for mere thingness, a figure for recalcitrance, even silence. Stone therefore enters these discussions as an unlikely—and all the more valuable—participant. This turn to the inorganic may seem surprising to readers who know that my previous work has examined such topics as the cultural work of the monster; the precariousness of human embodiment and its dependence upon animals, objects, dreams; the creativity and violence that explode in contact zones; the complications of race; the vexing multiplicity of time; and the inextricability of the human from an enmeshment within a material world. *Stone: An Ecology of the Inhuman* continues these investigations but brings them to a limit case.[48]

Seismic slide topples houses onto their builders. Jesus tells a parable about how seeds, yearning for fecundity, fall upon stony ground *(in petrosa)* and wither from its impassivity (Matthew 13:5). The Roman scientist Pliny was smothered by the fumes of Vesuvius, the volcano he had been studying, the mountain that entombed Pompeii and Herculaneum. In *Sir Gawain and the Green Knight,* the wasteland of "naked rokkes" among which the wandering hero must sleep manifests the precarity of his life. Hung with icicles, devoid of shelter, these cold crags are the elements at their most uncaring, a stony indifference to human suffering. Yet the chapters that follow discern in stone not just a rebuke to our habitual anthropocentrism but an aeonic companionship of the ephemeral and the enduring, the organic and the material, fellow travellers of a difficult road.

Life with Stone

The pines, craggy shores, gneiss, and gray granite of New England are my home ecology, but one stone in particular forcefully impressed itself on my childhood sense of world. Dense with houses, the neighborhood where I grew up was cut from drained swamp, scraps of farm and forest, and the roll of a barren hill. No house topped the mound around which this topography arranged itself: its rippled blue and white strata rendered the crest impervious to foundation. Three quarters of the way to the top of the anomalous barrow perched a trunk-sized boulder, its flecked whiteness nothing like nearby geology. Later in life I would recognize in the Big Rock (as children called this obvious intruder) a glacial erratic, swept southward and stranded by ancient ice. Even in winter the stone absorbed sun and radiated warmth.

For friends and siblings I wove an elaborate mythology around the Big Rock, tales of how its enduring solidity entangled distant pasts with far futures. The stone was primordial, eyewitness to apatosaurus before the marshes shrank. Its freckled density would persist into an age when earthbound creatures roam the skies in ships. The rock was transportive: to perch upon its heft was to risk the opening of a portal to storied lands. When I was given a telescope for my birthday, I set up the tripod nearby, not simply for the height of the hill but because the stone at night was luminous, good company for mapping lunar oceans. The worlds this rock opened were the dreams of a child who lived in a place too small.

Without the Big Rock's invitation to think the past and future beyond the limits of the humanly possible, without its advent of lithic possibility, the astonishing intrusion of the erratic, I could not now offer you (fellow traveler with me and that glacial stone) this story, this book. Medieval writers knew well what geologists reaffirm: undiscovered kingdoms attend every pebble. No more than basaltic plains, the dusty leavings of volcanoes, the *Mare Ingenii, Mare Nubium,* and *Oceanus Procellarum* do not roil the barren moon. Yet even that dry satellite is rich in stormy oceans once we realize the force that pulses in stone.

Geophilia

— —

The Love of Stone

Love and Strife

The love of stone is often unrequited.

An intimacy of long unfolding fails to be apprehended, and the story concludes in familiar solitudes, human exceptionalism and lithic indifference. Withdrawal and remoteness are inevitable themes within any romance of stone, since rock outlasts that which it draws close, that which draws it close, that to which it is strangely bound. Humans respire, reproduce, invent, desire, dream. The lithic inhabits the secret interiors of the earth. What could be more cloistered? Inorganic, nothing like the familiar animals we conditionally welcome into community, an everyday material that surfaces blunt rebuke to assimilation, stone remains aloof. Yet a mutuality is always possible, some narrative of companionship and concurrency. This chapter maps geophilia, a pull, a movement, and a conjoint creativity that breaches ontological distance. Even if born of a general principle of matter, geophilia's mobility and clasp possess their own rocky effects, in the quadruple sense "effects" carries of aftermath, agency, production, and belongings. These effects are palpable even in my prose, an aggregate matter that moves by slide and shift. An elemental geophilia surely exists outside

Reliquary.

human experience. Yet to us nonlithics its force will be most evident in the relations that enmesh us over long scales of time and in the "storied matter" these confederations of the human and inhuman divulge.[1]

Monstrous child of the meeting of incompatible scales, queer progeny of impossible taxonomic breach, geophilia is the lithic in the creaturely and the lively in the stone. Humans walk upright over earth because the mineral long ago infiltrated animal life to become a partner in mobility. Vertebral bone is the architect of motion, the stone around which the flesh arranges itself to slither, run, swim, fly. Had the organic not craved durable calcium as shield and conveyor, numerous types of sedimentary rock would never have arrived. A common mode of petrogenesis (creation of stone) unfolds when tiny ocean dwellers settle in their mortuary billions to the subsea muck. Limestone is a thick cemetery of mineral that had become animal now become rock again. Propelled by slow tectonic force upward into cliff and mountainside, limestone might be quarried to build a radiant carapace under which humans pray, govern, make purchases. The whorls and coils of unfamiliar sea life such stone divulges have fascinated masons since at least

Neolithic times. We create art with stone because we recognize the art that stone discloses: fossils, a museum of strata, lustrous veins, faceted radiance. We think and reckon with stone, primordial invitation to extended cognition. With its keen heft we compose and kill. From rock we construct graves, memorials, and dwelling places to endure long after we become earth again. In its aeonic endurance we discern something ardently desired, something ours only through alliance. Stone is devoid of neither life nor love, even if it questions what we mean when we use those terms to enclose a small world.

This chapter gathers into swift aggregation materials explored in their depths throughout what follows. Stonehenge, fossils, and lapidaries appear, to return repeatedly throughout *Stone: An Ecology of the Inhuman*, each spiraled approach a thickening of their possibility. My argument is not framed as a linear ascent culminating in the evidentiary zenith of some conquered peak. To think like a mountain does not mean to scale a rocky slope in search of a god's-eye view, as if the world could be glimpsed from its outside. A slow meditation on the formation and fall of range, on textural intricacy and thickly variegated seams, my style honors its subject by being expansive, dilatory, recursive, semicyclical from a long perspective, full of residuum, temporal intimacies, intermixed strata. Because the scale of its unfolding is immense, geophilia entwines the modern and the ancient, the contemporary and the medieval, the primordial with expansive futurity. Its pull and grip can render Noah's Flood difficult to tell from the Permian Extinction. Even if one event is apportioned from eternity and the other from infinity, one from theology and biblical narrative, the other from geology and astrophysics, both are modes of conceptualizing deep time that stress the demarcative power of catastrophe, lithic impress, a fossil record of monstrosity, the thriving of life in cataclysm's wake, the burgeoning of story, a dense and propulsive archive.

Classical and medieval writers might not have conceptualized the formation of stone in our geophysical terms, but their ecomaterial envisionings proceeded in modes just as vivid and capacious, through narratives stressing ecological entanglement as well as powerful solitudes. Premodern lapidary science hypothesized that every stone combines in variable proportions two restless elements, earth and water. Some rocks might contain ethereal emanations (vapors, lightning bolts). Others, like the red gem known as carbuncle, hold fire. Many originate in the bodies of animals, productions that conjoin the petric and carnal. Although rock might arise from seeming stasis, as in the Roman naturalist Pliny's description of crystal petrifying over long years from mountain ice, a stone always conveys the astral, material, and ecological influences particular to its point of origin, an inbuilt vibrancy and enduring environmental imprint. The smallest pebble is upon deeper contemplation a durable link to a dynamic cosmos. Active matter, stone contains energy and radiates agency. Although sometimes withdrawn from the world's lively spaces, the lithic is most often glimpsed in boisterous landscapes. Full of relation, teeming with narrative, stone is seldom inert.

Medieval writers were fascinated by stony origins, including the lithic incipience of human bodies. The poet Ovid, a favorite writer throughout most of the period, recounts how postcatastrophe humanity is replenished when the two survivors of world-purging flood throw rocks over their shoulders to become men and women. The book of Genesis describes Adam's shaping from red clay.[2] Bodies produced and expelled some irksome rocks (gallstones, renal calculi) and were nurtured by others. Stone is fecund. "Gendringe stones," "tweyne precyous stonys," and "ballok stonys" are Middle English designations for the testicles. These terms likely pun on the various medieval meanings of "ston," activating its associations with value and fertility. "Precious jewel," "magical gem," and "the seed or pit of a fruit" are among the word's significations.[3] Petric sexual organs do not belong exclusively to men: "stonys of þe modere [mother]" are the ovaries. Analogizing organs to stones seems an attempt to render the body more knowable, but medical equivalence between the biological and the inorganic estranges both rocks and corporeal interiors. "Gendringe stones" inhabit the human, going about their fertile business, regardless of human will. The drives in which they are involved are those same erotic pulsions over which medieval Christianity urged unceasing control. Disquietingly independent, "stonys" inside men and women are fundamental to human desire and gender, and the sine qua non of biological futurity. A rock, so often dismissed as sterile and passive, inhabits the interior of the body at the origin of life.

Late medieval understandings of materiality presumed continuity between rock and flesh. An entanglement of stars, geography, elements, and climate leaves its enduring ecological imprint on both. Lithic matter pulses with a "mineral virtue" that finds its counterpart in geohumoralism, the intimacy of human form and disposition to environment.[4] Just as astral forces, planetary alignments, moistness, and heat influence but do not wholly predetermine human character, appearance, and the distribution of the four humors, so environs that extend to the sidereal, linger in the ecological, and descend to the elemental likewise influence but do not wholly predetermine the qualities and relation-making abilities of a stone. Both embodiment and petrogenesis are built around an uncertainty principle. They are processes that can be disrupted, a variability based upon alliance and connection, resolved only by stepping out of time and inhabiting the perspective of the divine. Theologians like Augustine made serious attempts to detail that prospect, but most medieval writing concerning the composition of stones is content simply to acknowledge a heavenly order unknowable to those who dwell within the perturbations of history. Bodies and rocks are profoundly enmeshed within generative ecologies but are not wholly predetermined by the force of place. That which is set in stone does not necessarily sit still.

In humans and animals gender is as much an effect of this environmental imprint as race. Even if some male and female types are noted in compilations of lithic lore, stone does not typically arrive reduced into anthropomorphic form. Gems may be worked into gendered artifacts, but unlike some luxury items precious stones are generally not strongly coded as masculine or feminine. In the *Song of Roland,* the Saracen queen Bramimunde gives the French traitor Ganelon jeweled brooches for his wife, a material message to pass between women sharing precarious courtly positions. The hilts of swords meanwhile glimmer throughout this martial text, encrusted with virtuous gems to amplify their lethal force. Stone is likely to rebuke the arrogance of expecting the nonhuman to be like us and for us, but imagining the world to be as cold as stone, to be wholly detached from human life, can also accomplish important cultural work, urging a turn to God and the afterlife, or buttressing the anxious autonomy so essential to consumerist capitalism.[5] The indifference of the earth to its dwellers paradoxically reinforces human exceptionalism, so that the material world comes to exist for our instruction and use. Yet stone refuses to remain fully set apart, to respect taxonomic distinctiveness. Because of its habit of undermining human singularity, of revealing common materiality as well as recurring affinity, to convey within its materiality the thickness of time, stone triggers the vertigo of inhuman scale, the discomfort of unfamiliar intimacy, and the unnatural desires that keep intermixing the discrete. Queerly productive, rock does not offer the easy fecundity of soil, Gaia as mother. Projectile and stumbling block, stone challenges as much as fosters. Life in the lithosphere is complicated, so that minerals flourish in ways that seem creaturely and the environment is prolific in more than biota.

A deep past intimate to thinking the future's advent, a perspectivism that at once speeds and slows time, geophilia names a reciprocal and intimate bond, signaling attractions, affiliations, and movements toward connection often recognized retroactively, a proliferation of relation most evident over long distance. Lithic intimacy runs slow and deep. Classical and medieval poets discerned in the transition to agricultural modes of civilization and the transformation of gems and metals into coin and marketable goods the advent of modernity. They were just as ambivalent about this transition to commodity capitalism as recent economic materialists have been, and likewise believed that an embrace of wealth and the transformation of materials into a flow of goods alienated humans from nature. Chaucer describes in his poem "The Former Age" how humans who had lived on berries and nuts wounded the earth through plowing, engendered war through mining, and initiated mercantilism through the exchange power of coins and jewels. Seeking gems in rivers activates "coveytyse" (greed) and brings the first "sorwe" (sorrow).[6] The earliest humans in this legend of the Golden Age dwelled happily in caves, their closeness to the earth emphasizing their environmental harmony, before stone became a resource. The Roman naturalist Pliny provides a contemporary version, describing how crystal forms when snow compacts in Alpine crevices. Miners suspended on precarious ropes gather these stones from their lonesome homes, and Romans expend fortunes to attain them. This "crazy addiction" to crystal's radiant sheen spurs the gem's transformation into objects like goblets and display, unworked, as a coveted form of natural art.[7] Crystal, Pliny implies, is best left to its mountain solitude.

Attentive readers of Genesis, medieval writers believed the first stone architectures were biblical cities like Enoch, founded by exiled Cain and named for his son. Such primordial habitations might be visible as ruins on pilgrimage to the Holy Land. Modern science extends our stony fellowship back farther in time, to hominids constructing from gathered stones windbreaks for fire. These collections of sheltering matter eventually become the hearth, the center of human dwelling. Cresting a ridge and coming upon a rectangle of stone where a medieval home once stood, I learned while hiking in Iceland how forcefully the hearth endures.[8] Long after a house has vanished its form remains, lasting archeological signal of the refuge found there, lingering declaration of community as a space that coalesces around warmth, shared story, and sheltering stone. The fourteenth-century travel narrative published under the name of John Mandeville invokes this geophilia of origins and primal dwelling in an account of a cave not far from Hebron. Here we are told that just after their banishment from Eden, Adam and Eve "dwellid in a rooch" (lived within a rock).[9] In this cavern, likely from its very substance, Adam was formed by God before being "translated" to Eden. Exiled quickly from paradise, Adam and Eve begot their children in this home of living rock, so that the lithic becomes the space for the first human acts of procreation. A garden lost before nightfall, Eden is a brief stop in a human life fashioned from and spent within stone's embrace.

The Greek philosopher Empedocles articulated an enduringly influential theory of the elements in which earth, air, fire, and water are drawn and held by *philia* (love) but cajoled into perpetual movement by a companion force of *neikos* (strife).[10] Elemental *philia* is material magnetism and cosmic glue. Not an allegory for human feeling (though human affect may manifest this environmental energy), love pulls, gathers, and binds, working constantly against strife's entropy. Material existence is an act of perpetual assertion, generative (new relations are always coming into being) and generous (these relations cross categories and intermix the disjunct). Attachment and attraction inhabit all things as the principle of their formation, as that which enables endurance, inclining matter toward expansive connection. Sometimes these relations enable new flourishings. Sometimes they are perilous. Empedocles ended his life by leaping into the molten rock of Etna, an embrace of stone that incinerated him. To take his theory of elemental restlessness seriously is to apprehend that the world is not centered around the human—not indifferent, not misanthropic, but *disanthropocentric,* making stories centered upon the human wobble, their trajectories veer.

Geophilia is an ecological allure in the sense developed by Empedocles two and a half millennia ago, a propulsive and conjoining force that draws earth and water into a union generative of stone, that draws stone and other worldly things together to create, compose, produce. Those three verbs are to be understood intransitively, proceeding without necessary object.[11] Some common things generated through human-lithic enmeshment are text, science, place, art, matter, collectivity, architecture, inhabitance. Writing in the early sixth century, the Roman philosopher Boethius framed Empedoclean love as a universal principle of boundary and containment. Attempting to express classical elemental theory within a frame supportive of Christian doctrine, he envisioned a cosmic chain of *amor* with origin in the eternal. Even when love's bonds dissolve, the war-like disharmony that results makes sense within a larger pattern of divinely ordered change. As a famous medieval translator of Boethius knew well, such bonds are seldom secure, their failings profoundly troubling. Geoffrey Chaucer rendered Boethius's *Consolation of Philosophy* into Middle English, the *Boece*. The influence this translation project exerted upon his future work is extensive. In The Knight's Tale Chaucer places a Boethian meditation on the cosmic order maintained by love into the mouth of Theseus, the imperious ruler of Athens. The narrative world of The Knight's Tale is limned by catastrophe: gods whose petty squabbles stir earthly tumult; cities smashed to the ground and battles that leave piles of corpses; astral forces that trigger floods, bloodshed, devastating loss. Assuaging the grief of his subjects at the sudden death of a friend, Theseus speaks of the "faire cheyne of love" (fair chain of love) that binds "the fyr, the eyr, the water, and the lond" (the fire, the air, the water, and the earth) so that they do not escape "certeyn boundes" (1.2991–93). When the links joining the elements break, as in time they must, the divine "ordinaunce" (1.3012) that allots certain duration to all things is revealed, universal order behind seeming disarray. The ephemerality of the physical, Theseus insists, must turn our thoughts to celestial stabilities. Everything comes to its appointed terminus. Within its own duration, even hard stone is worn to dust by the tread of feet.[12] Theseus's recounting of a majestic cosmic harmony, as evident in the flourishing of an oak as in the glimpse he offers of erosion, reassures that the world is a closed system. A First Mover resides at its timeless exterior as guarantor of meaning. Yet the heartening moral of Theseus's speech is undermined by the jarring emplacement of Boethius's philosophy within a narrative fractured by mixed tone and a discomforting perspectivism, within a story that spectacularly fails to reassure that a meticulously hierarchical cosmos brings consolation, a tale obsessed with disaster's lethal irruption. Boethian certainty in an underlying orderliness is challenged by "crueel goddes" who in the form of astrological influences preside over a world where the cries of women in childbirth are unanswered (1.2085), the goddess of Love becomes cruel and whimsical Fortuna (1.1950), babies are devoured in their cradles by wandering pigs (1.2019), the sea drowns the innocent (1.2456), and stone cities are reduced to rubble.

Strife: all things break apart and move. The devastations of the Permian yield to the explosions of the Cambrian, the scouring of the Flood to the proliferations of the cleansed world, catastrophe to fertile wake. The elemental work of love begins again. And again.

Nature on the Move

The biologist E. O. Wilson posits an inherent bond among creatures, an "urge to affiliate with other forms of life [that] is to some degree innate, hence deserves to be called biophilia."[13] The term etymologically denotes the natural love of life for life. Geophilia goes farther and recognizes matter's promiscuous desire to affiliate with other forms of matter, regardless of organic composition or resemblance to human vitality. *Geo* derives from the Greek word for earth but is here employed as in geology, a science of vast durations, slow movement, and inhuman scale. Through its confounding admixture of rapport, shared story, rebuffing density, and alien scale, stone offers a perpetual invitation to think time and agency outside small category, to cease to force the world into diminished frames. Within an amulet, medicinal draught, or vitamin stone radiates curative powers into bodies; as a petrification of astral force it may when carried in a pocket settle a roiled landscape or reveal in a laboratory the shifting of the earth's magnetic poles; as a surface on which to inscribe sigils or phrases, it offers an invitation to a geographesis in which human hand and lithic potency compose a petric duet. In the Middle Ages a frequent form of such collaboration produced inscribed jewels. Into stones and their settings were incised names, words of power, or syllables of obscure meaning: "Iesus," "Alpha et Omega," "Jaspar Melchysar Baptizar" (the Three Magi), "AGLA" (*Atha Gebri Leilan Adonai*, a Latinized Hebrew prayer), "Guttu Gutta Madros Adros Udros

Udros Thebal" (perhaps a Latinate attempt to approximate Greek and Hebrew, or perhaps syllables engraved for their sheer sonority).[14] Attached to a ring or held in a palm for contemplation by the sea, a stone radiates a magic that renders the everyday strange. Science refracted through stone becomes art. Nature refracted through stone no longer seems so natural.

The historian of science Lynn White Jr. argued half a century ago that our instrumental view of nature is an inheritance from medieval Christianity, zealous for the chopping down of sacred groves, for the evacuation of animism, sacrality, and thereby agency from the material world.[15] Nature was, however, as unremittingly complicated a concept in the Middle Ages as it is today.[16] Nature is not a restorative place to which one might retreat, an outside, garden, or forest. Neither is it a thing to be preserved, a stable entity exterior to its profound enmeshment with humans, animals, oceans, plants, stones, stars. *Natura* (Latin), *phusis* (Greek into Latin), *nature* (French and eventually English), or *kynde* (English) may designate an immaterial force with profoundly material effects on living and inanimate things; the prodding of desire, especially sexual desire; normative sexuality itself; a principle of cosmic order; an essence; a shifting partner in a dyad with culture, the social, the artificial, the divine, the unnatural, or the supernatural; an object for systematizing study; a coercion that may trigger catastrophe; a scale innate to being, with rocks at the bottom and divinity atop; that which possesses a dual causality, in the mutable world and in the eternal, rather than in the divine alone; a balanced metasystem fashioned from multiple smaller systems; the biosphere; a personified, domesticated, and feminized agency that shapes substances and tends toward beauty; a smith, artist, or artisan whose works may be perfect or may go badly awry; a woman doing work reserved to men and God, making for troublesome agency and allegory; the subject of immense intellectual systems (natural science, natural law); a reality more assumed than interrogated; a socially conservative force that buttresses human society by enforcing similar hierarchies among animals and other nonhumans; a state of wildness that may be sweetly innocent or dangerously bestial; fodder for allegory; this fallen world, as opposed to the perfect heaven to follow; an enigmatic agent; a compromised authority; a utopian time-space characterized by human simplicity, goodness, and innate balance. Most medieval representations of nature strive to reinforce human domination of the earth rather than offer a mode of companionate dwelling. Nature is a force to harness or subdue, a resource for human culture, a contradiction-ridden troublemaker, and a stuttering promise of human superiority over animals, plants, and minerals. Nature is a source of beauty, theology, teleology, taxonomy, and physics as well as anxiety, gender trouble, animal trouble, life trouble. Nature is, in other words, a ceaseless problem.[17]

Nature's discrepant intricacies are amply evident within its frequent metonym, stone. Every rock is "at once whole and broken," a singular pebble as well as a mountain conveyed skyward by subterranean pressure or empyrean pull, a time traveller from the early days of creation, a fragment of the larger world it manifests, a piece of the churning bedrock to which it will return, a witness to forbidden Eden.[18] Humans are part of this larger worldedness: presumed at or near the top of an ascending scale, most of the time, but also a possible center among many centers, a margin among overlapping borders, organic continuity with an inorganic animacy.[19] Our language is a vortex-making type of sonority, like the territorialization of birdsong, but we have learned to inscribe speech's vibrations on rock, skin, or paper to capture stories, to carry them lastingly forward, to erect them like dwellings in the landscapes we inhabit. Medieval or modern, we are of the world, not separate from its whirling. Like the stories we tell, this world presents an open and mutable system of discrete and entangled forces, objects, units possessed of incommensurable magnitudes. Atoms and celestial spheres, the spread of forest and the retreat of glaciers, the flow of magma and the brusque solidity of stone produce an improvised choreography of participations across durations and kingdoms. And yet both stones and humans have their irreducible particularities.

The medieval symbolic registers of stone still linger: "in conventional comparisons, as a type or an emblem of hardness, immobility, silence, lifelessness, insensibility, etc.; also, as a type or an emblem of stability, steadfastness, etc."[20] Rock imbues *terra* with its firmness, mundane reality with comforting solidity. At those rare times when stone slides, shakes, or melts, what surprises us most is that something so dense can for a moment become kinetic. This motion is always brief, always the forgettable exception. Houses rise swiftly after the earthquake's leveling; grass and trees effloresce when lava expands the contours of an island; landslides bury troves that bulldozers or metal detectorists one day retrieve. Stone's movements are its aberrations. Or so it might seem to us, we whose lives are so short that to the stone we walk and build upon our presence registers little, we may-flies who live and perish in less than a blink. Small things who believe our ephemeral walking and building expansive, who measure the mountainous world as if it were likewise swift and small.

If stone could speak, what would it say about us?

Stone would call you transient, sporadic. The mayflies analogy is apt. Stone was here from near the beginning, when the restless gases of the earth decided they did not want to spend their days in swirled disarray, in couplings without lasting comminglings. They thickened into liquids, congealed to fashion solid forms. Nothing of that primal clot survives, but sediments and magmatic flows from earth's young days linger. Greenland knows that story.[21] When you stand on such bedrock, you touch matter that solidified perhaps 3.8 billion years ago. Your continents—and will it annoy you when I remind that your continents are splinters of a rocky protoplasm, fragments that rifted Pangaea to voyage the waters like stone ships?—every one of your migrant continents conveys rocks of at least 3.5 billion years. A fortunate animal endures perhaps seventy. Do the math: it is inhuman. These ubiquitous boulders, not even the eldest of the earth, possess the lifespan of millions upon millions upon millions of fortunate animals. They will persist into a future so distant that no human will witness their return to liquids and powders.

Primordial organic things loved their rocky forebears, clung to stone's solidity, became part of stone themselves. It is harder than you suppose to tell the difference between protozoa and superorganisms, between the five arms of the starfish and the splayed human form. Organic life adheres, multiplies, fades. Yes, humans have always desired the endurance of stone. They scratch a small hole and bury their dead; they place rocks upon the bodies as if to keep the spinning world still. Yet life can hold perdurability only if the bacterial and the human are one: then you are nearer to stone's speed, then stone can see you. From this vantage, this view so anthropodiscentered that language fails its imagining, from this lapidary perspective stone possesses its own life, its own mortality.

You expect stone to be heavy, but it is light. You presume that stone possesses fact; it holds stories. If stone had a voice it would be less ponderous than your own. If your hurried heartbeat did not bind you to your swift smallness, you would know the affinity that binds you with stone.

Stone seems an uncomplicated material, instantly knowable, compliant conveyor of factuality. Philosophy's favorite object, stone is firm support for ponderous thinking. Thales of Miletus, hailed by Aristotle as the first philosopher, turned to lodestone and amber to explain how matter acts. Faith in stone's epistemological solidity is easy to understand, given its ubiquity, heft, impenetrability, and immensity. Samuel Johnson famously rebuked George Berkeley's assertion that all matter is "merely ideal" by forcefully kicking a stone that was not to be moved, declaring "I refute it *thus.*"[22] The intransigent rock of the real disproves through its serene factuality the vagabond fogs of the imagination.[23] Stone's reassuring fixity is Johnson's uncontemplated foundation for self-evident truth. Despite the strength with which he kicks, despite how much Berkeley might desire a world more fluid, the stone does not yield, demarcating the limit beyond which human fancies may not pass, a hard answer from the intractable real. Though flowing sea, restless air, and consuming fire are just as natural, just as truth-filled, stone becomes a stand-in for nature itself, and nature thereby becomes immobile, unchanging, indifferent. Despite the fact that, as Vilém Flusser observes, "every object is stubborn in its own particular way," stone metonymically stands for the obduracy of all matter.[24] Jane Bennett gets at this logic of stony substructuralism well when she writes, "as noun or adjective *material* denotes some stable or rock-bottom reality, something adamantine."[25] The function of the lithic in philosophical discourse is therefore to embody the fixed, the given, the resolutely factual. Stone is the world in its givenness.

We notice only rock that inhibits progress, gets in the way, becomes a stumbling block for the blind. We journey while these impedimenta remain stubbornly emplaced, and collision with lithic immobility hurts, physically and epistemologically.[26] Isidore of Seville derived the Latin word for stone, *lapis,* from its ability to injure *(laedere)* the foot *(pes)* (*Etymologies,* 16.3.1). A scruple ("something that troubles the mind"), he continued, derives from *scrupus,* "a small sharp stone that causes injury and troubles the mind if it should fall into one's shoe" (16.3.5). Since word is thing for Isidore, the lithic comes into apprehension through, with, and as sharp sensation. Its prick is cerebral and physical. Rocks are a keen and affective provocation to thought as well as airy ideation's antidote. Epistemology is a knowing and feeling; stone is fact-laden and emotion-triggering. Despite its promise of unmediated truth, stone does not offer easy or secure knowledge and exceeds any attempt to still it into familiarity. Rock marks the point at which understanding fails. To run up against a stone wall is to encounter the lithic propensity to induce foundering, to provoke loss of certainty. Stone is not an obstacle to be overcome, but a thing that makes demands, scripts stories, and does not fully yield to human enframing.[27] Thus the poet Richard Wilbur writes, "Kick at the rock, Sam Johnson, break your bones: / But cloudy, cloudy is the stuff of stones."[28] Thales of Miletus, first Greek philosopher, was drawn to stone's activity, not its inertness, and found in its ability to hold electric charge and draw substances toward itself evidence of a soul.[29] Stone holds dense agency.

Drawn like many thinkers to the facticity of stone, Ian Hacking examines the "construction" of dolomite, a rock that consistently challenges those who seek to map its origin—possibly because nanobacteria, organisms too small to be observed, are behind its formation. Hacking writes against a social or linguistic determinism that sees the world as infinitely pliable, the product of human relations, especially language. He details a long process in which errors about the stone accumulate and are shed: dolomite's supposed calcium is revealed to be magnesium; the fact that dolomite ceased to be created as the primal earth aged gives way to realization that it is still coming into being, but in places hostile to contemporary life. Certain data about the material cling and are retained. Yet an aura of uncertainty consistently surrounds a substance that should be rock solid.[30] What best serves elusive dolomite is, according to Hacking, an "ecumenical descriptive epistemology with hardly any normative implications,"[31] a multifaceted and flexible approach that traces the alliances and networks enabling facts to emerge and endure. This process-oriented perspective stresses limited contingency. We know dolomite in part because we have asked very particular questions of it, mainly centered upon its petrochemical uses. Had we asked other initial queries, we would think of the rock rather differently, and might not have wondered if it could be the product of nanobacteria and a key to understanding the origins of earthly life. Hacking stresses the dependence of knowledge upon its value-laden sorting into taxonomic systems. It matters to us that the rock is a magnesium carbonate rather than a calcium carbonate, for example, because we desire to extract oil from its depths. From a strictly geological point of view, though, a sediment is a sediment, and there is no good reason to separate your limestone from your dolomite. The history of the substance has as much to do with giving up on certain facts as it does accruing stable knowledge. Even now we don't know exactly how the rock came to be and cannot say whether science has stabilized dolomite or if dolomite lends a certain stability to a science intent on its explication. A stone so durable and ancient that much of Stonehenge is fashioned from its blunt mass, dolomite is a reality, a brusque truth. It is also a story of nature on the move.

Rock figures the real, and figuring is an active process. Despite Samuel Johnson's kick that failed to dislodge its unyielding target, rock can be a plastic material, an amenable substance for sculpture, adornment, and edifice-making. Time- and context-bound meshworks of alliance uniting human and nonhuman agents make lithic pliancy and resistance visible. A diamond becomes a precious gem because its rarity, lucidity, and density can sustain strong confederation with human and inhuman forces, tools, economic and aesthetic systems—coalitions friable stones cannot support. Narrative has power over human reality: it can mediate. But that compositional power is contingent rather than absolute, deriving in part from the thing described. Language is inhuman, exerting its own resistance, slide, and material force. Words stammer, sentences unwind, sense-making fails. Although we can find stone that will float like a ship (as the medieval travel writer John Mandeville notes of volcanic pumice), we do not fabricate sailing vessels out of boulders because something in rock resists naval transformation. Stone can be constructed. In the form of concrete, it can take almost any shape an architect desires, for a while, and geophilia inheres in that fashioning. But stone does not offer a blank slate for human stories.[32]

Stone is a catalyst for relation, a generative substantiality through which story tenaciously emerges.[33] This elemental agency is likely shared with all materiality, but its plots, structures, tempo, and denouements are its own. To stone belongs sweeping romances of scale, time, memorialization, creation, cataclysm, a relentless tectonicity (from *tektōn*, a carpenter or builder). Stone speaks differently from its sibling elements of air, water, and lightning-swift fire. Its injunction is always to step out of the breathless rapidity of anthropocentric frames and touch a world possessed of long futurity and deep past, a spatial expanse that stretches from the subterranean to the cosmic verge.[34] Stone's stories foreground the inhuman in its danger, dispassion, and forcefulness, but they offer as well strange amity, queer fellowship, precarious but enduring cohabitation.

Story and Stone

Most ecological analyses are "green," taking their structural metaphors from the imagined fecundity of plants and conducted within a comfortably human cadence. Stressing balance and sustainability, such studies encounter with difficulty the slow immensity of the geologic. Ecotheory is becoming more prismatic, discovering possibility in challenging, nonverdant hues.[35] Rejecting dreams of green pastoralism and fantasies of sustainability, Steve Mentz articulates an oceanic blue humanities and a "swimmer poetics" that can better encounter "our storm-filled world."[36] Yet stone is fluid when viewed within its proper duration. Medieval writers understood the process of erosion and captured petrogenesis in the same liquid terms we employ. When the geologist Jan Zalasiewicz describes continental drift he deploys marine language:

> The continents do not have to plough through the oceanic floor. Rather they are carried atop the continually moving lithosphere. They forever drift, like so many gigantic stony Flying Dutchmen, as the ocean basins slowly, inexorably open and close.[37]

The "continually moving lithosphere" is a sea of stone, the continents its mysterious ships ("so many gigantic stony Flying Dutchmen," vessels of perpetual voyage, doomed never to reach port). The lithic is oceanic, what the travel writer John Mandeville called a Gravelly Sea. Mountains surge and fall, their epochal undulations no less animated than the swell and crash of seas, but impossible for us to view without the aid of narrative and art. Yet volcanoes spurt molten rock that flies, flows, hardens within a human timescale. Ash and lithic powder tumble air and earth in dry liquidity. Though we cannot swim in molten stone—or do so only to face instant immolation, like Empedocles at Etna—we are saturated in the lithic.[38] A petric poetics would capture this elemental and disanthropocentric restiveness, this negation of the immobility to which stone is too often consigned, this erratic choreography of entwinement, extension beyond apprehensibility, stinging unconcern, stone love, lethal and companionate embrace. Geophilia's stories unwind with neither climax nor haste, at a spatial and temporal scale that can leave us beside ourselves.

Scientists have christened earth's primordial era the Hadean, as if this span were something known from our mythology, a prelude and underworld. But the epoch possessed no human content, nothing but fiery gases and congealing rocks and the bare beginnings of single-celled organisms. Remote in time and of vast duration (almost a billion years), the Hadean renders human history brief to imperceptibility. Unlike recent, fleeting, and change-loving animals, stone persists. Though it might offer evidence of vanished life through the ammonite shells and dinosaur bones it entombs, stone seems to us a material well suited for memorials and grave markers.[39] It erodes into clay and sand, rises from the sea or vanishes in subduction, but its decomposition and constant metamorphoses are, within our native temporality, so unhurried that rock is our shorthand for temporal density and strange intrusion.[40] Our documentary bias is for worlds conveyed through words. Yet the earth possesses numerous recording devices, repositories for nonlinguistic inscription, an indigenous but hard lithic poetics.[41] Although tree rings and ice cores yield tales of ancient pollen, glaciation, and aerial chemistry, stone's archival force endures far longer.[42] Carbon dating and magnetic readings reveal the passing of epochs. A museum of oddities and a relentless clock inhere in strata, dense layers in which the Anthropocene (the era during which human presence is readable through carbon embedded within the geological record) is a sliver. From a longer point of view we are living during a vaster period, the Lithocene.

The Great Oxygenation Event that triggered the massive extinction of earth's flourishing anaerobic life 2.4 billion years ago enabled an immense mineral thriving. Propelled by photosynthetic algae, the Oxygen Catastrophe (as it is also called) marked a massive release of the free element that spurred the generation and subsequent flourishing of 2,500 new mineral forms, all of which require O_2 to burgeon. Most any pebble is replete with microfossils such as acritarchs, the cysts of ancient algae; many of our familiar rocks would not exist without the incorporation of organic material. As a recordation device stone yields tales of life's ubiquity. Stone forges relation, conjoining things in ways productive and perilous. Stories of stone therefore tend to be conjunctive and recursive. As enamored of polysyndeton as of litanies, catalogs, and ecstatic lists, lithic poetics love flowing strata, metamorphosis, slow forces of ignition, and inassimilable particles suspended within dynamic aggregates.

Any speaking of the nonhuman is a translation, and therefore error prone, filled with guesswork, and inclined toward fantasy. Story is a parasitical entity that in its familiar forms clearly depends on humans, but story is also itself a living thing and does not necessarily depend upon language to be conveyed. Like the DNA coding of genes, narrative is full of futurity, a mysterious and not wholly predetermined site for the emergence of vitalities: a connection-making and a worlding. Narrative can give a voice to objects, elements, forces. Humans themselves emerge through "material agencies" that leave their traces in lives as well as stories, so that narratives are always animated by multifarious vectors and heterogeneous possibilities not reducible to mere anthropomorphism.[43] Narrative is not inevitably solipsistic. It enables the envisioning of a world indifferent to us, a world that excludes us, and a world that impinges with discomforting intimacy. An ethical machine, story intensifies relation, even with the nonhuman, and therefore offers the best hope we have for moving in whatever tentative way we can beyond anthropocentrism.[44] Stone erodes our long habit of regarding the world as a place fashioned for our habitation, of thinking humans an apex or culmination.

Even when inscribed with a known language or identifiable pictures, stone will arrive into the present as alien presence. Headstones or the ruins of houses quietly shelter, arches and cathedrals triumphantly announce stories of a past otherwise intangible, promises of a future beyond familiar reckoning. Stone is thick with sedimented time. Within both medieval and modern environmental imaginings, rocks and people inhabit temporalities and magnitudes profoundly different. Rocks arrive from alien worlds, rendering coinhabitance and the bonds of geophilia difficult to discern—or, when realized, jarring. In the Middle English poem *Pearl,* the narrator dreams of eternal paradise. He beholds the origins of earthly gemstones in rivers that flow from Eden, a garden removed from time. Like God and souls, these primordial stones exist outside of history, at least until they tumble to mundane destinations. The gem of the poem's title is the poet's daughter, allegorized as a pearl lost to the earth (that is, to the grave). Dead before her second year of life, she is encountered in heaven as an eloquent maiden full of rebuke to a grieving father who remains stuck in human time. Such are the incomprehensibilities of the eternal to those who exist in mortal brevity.[45] The Pearl Maiden stands across the gem-filled river from him, in the paradise he may after death attain. A pearl—perfect in its impenetrable sphericity, a melding of the creaturely and the mineral—seems the ideal materialization of the soul, since both rocks and souls wreak havoc on human notions of temporality.[46] Souls and precious stones share non-human endurance, radiance, chaste singularity, and a love of reproaching the human world for its inferiority. At the end of the poem the narrator attempts to cross the river into paradise, not to dwell in its crystalline stillness but to embrace the daughter he has lost. His grief, his love of earth, is palpable. The poem has been thoroughly theologized by its modern interpreters, for its materiality is indeed saturated with allegory. Yet the bereaved father at the eye of its unfolding twice chooses not inhuman heaven but continued dwelling in a catastrophe-laden world. The narrator avers that the immortal and the celestial will be his objective, and yet he inclines repeatedly with heart and body to the earth where his pearl was lost.[47]

As the *Pearl* narrator learns when he glimpses the walls of paradise and sees they are formed of layered gems, every metropolis is a geologic force.[48] Stone demands a temporal and spatial perspective that may or may not exclude the human. For a medieval audience this geological widening typically amounts to a plea to turn away from the transitory earth to empyrean stabilities (a sentiment the narrator of *Pearl* articulates but cannot enact). For contemporary audiences it is more likely to underscore that this earth is all we have, that we cannot live as if some undepleted heaven awaits. Human powers of destruction almost rival those of asteroids and supervolcanoes. Our affinity with stone is revealing its most lethal aspects. The Anthropocene designates the point in the eighteenth century when industrial deposits become readable in the geological record, but the term offers a problem even as it identifies one.[49] Though immensely useful, the designation has the unintended effect of obliterating the billions of years that precede the embedding of the human in geology's archive.[50] When we decelerate, imagine a deeper past, get geologic, then history becomes more eventful, richer, deeper in its strata. Modernity loses some of its luster, prehistory loses homogeneity, and the agency of the material world becomes easier to perceive alongside that of the human. In Australia stone requires a narrative that restores vitality to Gondwana, yet remains stubbornly rooted in the local: rock art, fire management, the offer of fertility or desert, an archive of aboriginal displacements and ecological crises. A gem in medieval Britain might disclose a romantic tale of travel from Persia as well as a more local vignette in which a mother clasps an amulet with the precious stone embedded at its center, hoping during a difficult childbirth that neither she nor her undelivered infant will perish. Stone is never a lone element but a partner with water, fire, air, organic life. In stone a sense of place joins a sense of planet, but even that scale is not enough. Stone emphasizes the cosmos in cosmopolitan, the universe of inhuman forces and materialities that stretches to the distant arms of the galaxy—or at least to what classical and medieval writers called the celestial spheres. At the close of Chaucer's narrative poem *Troilus and Criseyde,* the despondent protagonist dies in battle. His soul rises above the earth to the eighth sphere, imagined in medieval and classical cosmography as the domain of the stars. Looking back upon the place his spirit has fled, Troilus beholds "This litel spot of erthe that with the se / Embraced is" (This little spot of the earth that with the sea is embraced, 5.1815–16). Viewed from afar the earth becomes an inlaid gem, clasped not by gold but by ocean.

Stony reality is perspectival, a time- and context-bound meshwork that gathers lithic and nonlithic actors without harmonizing, without yielding the unity necessary for secure point of view. As stone is for us one of many objects (some well differentiated and highly esteemed, but most below notice) that constitute the realm of the nonhuman, humans are for stone one of many agents (some well differentiated and highly relatable, most below notice) in the nonlithic realm who are susceptible to being drawn into petric alliance. These relations become palpable once aeonic frames are adopted and the anthropocentric insistence that only human intentionality exists or counts is abandoned. Sometimes the movements toward connection and change that constitute desire are discernible only in traces sedimented over a very long history, one that undermines our foundational narratives of rupture, self-fashioning, and radical discontinuity. When along with viewing stone as nonhuman we attempt to look upon ourselves as nonlithics, the axis of the knowable world shifts, like Troilus with his sidereal perspective, a vision that causes him to laugh with joy.

Geophilia is geology without dispassion. It wanders a steep and rocky way: difficult, slow, full of slide and unexpected conveyance. When a geologist writes that a "pebble holds strange worlds within it," he is providing a contemporary version of the journey "in at a roche [rock]" that Sir Orfeo takes in the fourteenth century, following a fairy retinue into an alternate universe enclosed by stone.[51] The crossings between romance and geology are likewise betrayed by the name of the "strange world" that Zalasiewicz's pebble opens: the now-lost continent of Avalonia, "one on which—much later—King Arthur would reign, and Shakespeare would write sonnets, and a revolution that would spread factory chimneys and iron foundries across the world."[52] From Arthur to the Anthropocene, rock archives it all. The denizens of the world within stone beheld by Sir Orfeo in the Middle Ages are from his perspective frozen in the moment of their violent death; their time is not his. The realm seems familiar, but its actions are inscrutable. Stone opens to challenging story. Yet it is just as true to observe, as does Wislawa Szymborska in her poem "Conversation with a Stone," that when a human declares "I knock at the stone's front door / It's only me, let me come in," the likely reply will be a lithic rebuff: "I don't have a door."[53]

A Door into Stone

Mapping an ecology of human-lithic enmeshment contributes to the material turn in critical theory, a revaluation that stresses elemental vitality and the agency of the inhuman. Understanding subjectivity and communal identities is important and has constituted the main work of literary and cultural studies for decades. Yet an exclusive focus upon human subjects, historical or modern, obscures the abiding, intense attention that texts give to objects and their activity.[54] A long tradition of feminist inquiry has been instrumental to this turn to things and substances.[55] Things tend to be welcomed "into scholarship, poetry, science and business" on the condition that they speak of "human productivity, culture and politics."[56] The assumption that what exists exists for us, that the world's significance is determined through the mind's mediation, has been condemned by the philosopher Quentin Meillassoux as "correlationism." When matter exerts its right to be the protagonist of its own story, epistemological frames shift, a Copernican revolution with multiple realignments.[57] The earth ceases to revolve around human interest. No totalizing system coheres to predetermine thingly trajectories or negate the ability of matter to veer. Worldedness proliferates. Work conducted under rubrics like the new materialism, actor network theory, vibrant materialism, ecomaterialism, speculative realism, and object-oriented philosophy examines the inhuman without positing human exceptionalism. These heterogeneous and intermittently convergent modes of inquiry refuse to separate culture from nature or discourse from materiality, do not subordinate agency to volition, and refuse to arrange alien forces anthropocentrically. Human perception is not allowed to stand at some exterior or cordon itself away from nonhuman participation: we are *of* the world, irremediably within its thickness. Things meanwhile apprehend and act, possessed of integrity, mystery, and a flourishing that may be contingent or autonomous. Insistent objects and energetic matter participate in relation-making, in story, and through such confederation form a kind of parliament (from the verb *parler,* to speak), making possible or at least imaginable an expansive politics predicated upon environmental justice and cross-ontological alliance.[58]

Much scholarship examining nonhuman things is quietly biased toward contemporary consumer objects. Toasters, computers, subway systems, potato chips, and discarded packaging are more frequently encountered than wind, manuscript leaves, lightning bolts, or stones. Medieval landscapes were not so densely populated with human fabrications, and fewer items were mass-produced. The collaboration of hand and matter was likely more evident. Everyday topographies may have been more "storied." Yet the temporality that objects materialize is thick enough to disrupt a progress narrative that would open some chasm between premodern and modern things, even in the form of commodities. Stone is a primeval spur to industry. Paleolithic axes and arrowheads were sometimes created in fairly extensive knapping centers. Clay amphorae were mass-produced to transport olive oil throughout the Roman Empire (Monte Testaccio in Rome is formed from more than fifty million of these vessels, discarded and crushed). Lead badges for medieval pilgrims were fabricated by the thousands through reusable molds.[59] Stone is the substance of our most enduring tools: hammers, axes, mortars and pestles, blades. Though their material composition has changed, these progeny of ancient lithic collaboration remain in use, temporal sojourners. Stone composed our early ornaments as well as implements, its superfluity of beauty above all utility essential to geophilia's force. It densely enfolds nonlinear time and rebuffs supersessionary histories, suggesting that things emerge multiple times, intensifying and adapting rather than engendering definitive breaks. "Thing" is a medieval Germanic word for a convocation, a meeting for the debate of law, and a matter of concern. Analogous romance words like French *chose* and Italian *cosa* come from "cause" (Latin *causa*).[60] A verb disguised as a noun, an object objects (from Latin *obicere,* "to throw in the way"), speaks, and acts. Nonhumans gather themselves into powerful collectives (a republic is a *res publica,* "public thing"), form unexpected relations, trace stories in which humans may or may not figure, acting in narratives of their own.[61] For matter to matter, Stacy Alaimo has persuasively argued, the "concern and wonder" that story-laden things arouse must enable an ethics that take as context not only the social but the material: "the emergent, ultimately unmappable landscapes of interacting biological, economic, and political forces."[62] Alaimo describes *transcorporeality,* the interpenetration of body and more-than-human world.[63] To bring her essential insight further along its disanthropocentric path, stone's intimate alterity demands acknowledgement of more-than-human temporal and spatial entanglement, so that ecology becomes Long Ecology, an affectively fraught web of relation that unfolds within an extensive spatial and temporal range, demanding an ethics of relation and scale. A geophilic Long Ecology exchanges human life spans as familiar units of counting for more profound durations, millennia and epochs. Humans are some especially powerful, especially lethal environmental actors, but they are coextensive with many others, including carbon, glaciers, aerial and marine currents, geographical strata, expansive biomes. Choices being made in the present must be mapped backward in time to recognize the long histories they contain, and forward over the centuries of their potential unfolding. Range cannot be confined to single nations and mere generations. The ethics of scale mandate a cautious *living with* that looks deep into time, that stresses enduring ecomaterial affinity and rejects the devaluation of matter as self-evident asset, inert commodity, or resource for extraction. Although at times infuriatingly imprecise (the future is not easy to foretell), these ethics carry blunt implications for living with stone in the present. Fracking, mountaintop removal, and other modes of environmental devastation (a medieval legal term denoting the punishable action of laying an area waste, *devastare*) might seem practicable from a brief, human point of view—we are rich in hills and water—but Long Ecology permits none of these endeavors to poison a future that must be allowed its heterogeneity of possibility, richness of manifold difference, reducing certainty (extensiveness of time and space challenge human confidence) while disallowing noninvolvement.[64]

The new materialisms and the ecocritical practices that follow from them underscore a fact well known during the Middle Ages, if differently apprehended and expressed: matter possesses creative force and intense dynamism.[65] Although constructed (by atoms, elements, hands, cosmic or celestial forces), matter is never merely constructed (not abstract, not a social or discursive fabrication, not passive). Matter remains irreducible to its context or constituent components.[66] In its attempt to reorient philosophy and take careful account of objects, granting the inhuman its profundity, this ecomaterialism moves (in the words of Ian Bogost) beyond the "environmental wholism from John Muir to James Lovelock" to insist that "one type of existence—[organic] life" should no longer uncritically comprise "the reference point for thought and action."[67] Much of the world is too swift, too slow, too small, or too vast for unaided human perception. Active matter recedes from epistemology, from capture into a stilled frame. Its bustle and enmeshments are often difficult to witness. Like the stone in Szymborska's poem, it does not offer a door. One promising entryway into apprehending this activity, however, has been described by the French sociologist of science Bruno Latour and the actor network theory (ANT) to which he has been an essential contributor. ANT offers a mode of understanding inhuman agency that insists nature and society are not preexisting, separate, and self-evident realities, so that no human/world duality exists. It takes work to create and enforce such bifurcation, a division that obscures but cannot efface the irreducible hybridity and expansive intermeshing through which action unfolds: "networks are *simultaneously real, like nature, narrated, like discourse, and collective, like society.*"[68] As if to illustrate inhuman agency, stone's unexpected intercession was vital to Latour's theorization of ANT. A vigorous conversation with Isabelle Stengers on the supposed risks taken by rocks to remain in existence haunts a skeptical Latour. Months later he finds himself running his hands over some stones in Sweden. He experiences a petric epiphany:

Everything became clear, then. . . . There exists a completely autonomous mode of existence that is very inadequately encompassed by the notions of nature, material world, exteriority, object. This world shares one crucial feature with all the others: the risk taken in order to keep on existing.[69]

The tactility of cognition: hand upon stone triggers epistemological shift, spurs an insight about nonhuman imbroglios, about being as hazardous doing, about nonseparability and irreducibility. Like any nonhuman, a stone may enter into generative relations with other entities, creating through multifold connections hybrid or quasi objects that can be composites of lithic and nonlithic elements, possessing story-generating power and assertive potential.

A rock supports, defeats, fosters, yields, impels, risks, resists. Placing your palm upon its density triggers the unexpected. If ANT has a downside, it is a tendency to think of objects as wholly absorbed into the networks in which they participate, so that a stone exists mainly in its effects, not as a particular rhomb of feldspar that might never emerge from mineral solitude. Extending Latour's work into new metaphysical realms, the philosopher Graham Harman argues that no two objects can fully interact (all touch is mediated, and thus all causation is indirect or vicarious), and that objects always withhold a part of themselves from every relation (we never possess access to a thing in its entirety). Relations among nonhumans vastly outnumber relations between humans and nonhumans, despite our habit of arranging the universe around ourselves. When humans lose their privilege as pivots of the world, a flat ontology ensues.[70] Christened object-oriented ontology (OOO) by Harman, this weirdly poetic vision of objectal life is generative, even if at times its principles risk a thingly dogmatism. OOO's meticulously elaborated, fourfold objects may be *too* precise for understanding the messiness of the materials that preoccupy this book.[71] Yet as in medieval Christian theology, speculative realism discerns inviolable mystery in the nonhuman world. Whereas for theologians materiality reveals that God exists beyond human categories, for OOO materiality itself exists beyond human categories. Ecotheorist Timothy Morton observes that the challenge becomes "to figure out how to love the inhuman" with which we are enmeshed—or perhaps, to recognize how forces like geophilia have always already manifested such love.[72]

A rock might be formed of earth and water, but it is of necessity something more than its elemental composition. Every stone is particular (the magic emerald that triggers a storm in Chrétien de Troyes's romance *Yvain*) as well as extensive and generic (the carbuncles, sapphires, and topazes of medieval lapidaries are collectives that function as individual objects). These multiple singularities are well conveyed in some seemingly unimportant lines of Marie de France's twelfth-century lay *Lanval*. Wronged by the Arthurian court, its hero departs at the end of the narrative with his fairy mistress. Lanval ascends a stone block to leap onto her horse as his lady passes:

> Outside the hall stood
> a great stone of dark marble
> where heavy men mounted
> when they left the king's court;
> Lanval climbed on it. (633–38)

The marble block is united to the knight in shared heft. Unlike the chivalric lightweights he leaves behind, Lanval possesses stony solidity, petric steadfastness, foundational integrity. The large, dark piece of marble is simultaneously singular ("un grant perrun de marbre bis," the particular "great stone" used at Arthur's court for ascending horses, a stone with specific history) and plural (a piece of a much larger grouping, dark marble [*marbre bis*]: an impressive, unyielding substance of distinct provenance, dense rock difficult to mine and transport but valued for durability and striking coloration). Stone enters into its multiplex relations as generic substance as well as boulder, pebble, landslide, as a singular entity (a medieval philosopher like Duns Scotus would say, in haecceity as well as quiddity). This book is full of stories of particular stones: Barber Rock, an ammonite fossil purchased at Harvard's Museum of Natural History, Stonehenge. Yet just as the group "marble" functions as individual object not reducible to its constituents, objects cannot be undermined by breaking them into components as a way of explaining them away. A stone-oriented ontology would grant the lithic its indivisibility, autonomy, distinctiveness, and individuality. A stone will always evade full scrutiny, will always hold in its depths an illimitable potency.[73] The anonymous writer behind the London Stone Twitter account well conveyed this combination of love, relation, mystery, and impossible demand for perceptual reorientation by having the stone opine:

> I'm not asking you to worship me, just pay me a little love. I mean, if you want to form a new religion with me at the centre, do feel free.[74]

Petric fragment of the medieval city, now set in a cage along a busy stretch of Cannon Street, the London Stone modestly requests a lithocentric reordering of contemporary human life. Such a realignment is from a human point of view impossible. Nonetheless, this challenge from the outside is still apprehensible within the narratives we tell about an unevenly shared world.

A cluster of quartz may be as inexhaustible to meditation as *Guernica*, the *Canterbury Tales*, or the standing stones at Avebury. The fourteenth-century poet John Gower offers a medieval version of this insight when he writes of an everyday light so powerful no human can view its glow directly, at least not without destroying the eyes. Gower imagines that the sun's perilously bright crown is fashioned from precious gems, three of which are stones no person on earth possesses.[75] He names these luminous gems "licuchis," "astrices," and "ceramius," designations that resemble but do not precisely coincide with precious stones from the medieval lapidary tradition, known for their power to radiate intense light. Gower's solar rocks remain locked in the heavens. They cannot be encountered or touched by humans. The lithic is a more than mundane material, shimmering in the sky, vibrantly out of reach.[76] Object-oriented philosophy is a form of realism (it attempts a careful account of the autonomy and materiality of the world and is not satisfied with analyses that disperse things into language, as if human words had sovereign power). Yet its realism is *weird,* meaning that this world is not reducible to common sense, the evidence of the mind, or other modes of imposing human order. It thereby shares expressive affinities with speculative fiction—science fiction, horror, and fantasy. Medieval versions of these wonder-inducing genres include romance, lays, and lapidaries, providing those who study the Middle Ages rich entrance into this critical conversation.

Like Latour, Morton, and Harman, all of whom possess a poet's ardor for the beautiful, political theorist Jane Bennett describes a world to be reenchanted by the vivacity of the nonhuman. This vision, Bennett writes, possesses deep affinities to the "nonmodern (and often discredited) modes of thought" that offer an archive for a revitalized ecological sensibility.[77] In Bennett's vibrant materialism a rock is not recalcitrant, for to label it with such an adjective is only to describe the world from a human point of view.[78] All materiality is inherently lively and exerts diffuse agency, "like a pebble thrown into a pond" (outcomes are seldom final and ever uncertain).[79] This omnipresent vitality is "obscured by our conceptual habit of dividing the world into inorganic matter and organic life."[80] An aesthetics and an ethics, vibrant materialism insists that action unfolds through assemblages of actants, through confederation as well as conflict. This vexed field of intentionality, desire, and surprise bears some resemblance, Bennett argues, to Saint Augustine's agonistic description of human volition: "the will wills even as another part of the will fights that willing."[81] Yet agency is not the same as intention. Desire is often recognized retroactively, through the accumulated evidence of patterns and effects. If we encounter the world "as a swarm of vibrant materials entering and leaving agentic assemblages," then "what was adamantine becomes intensity," and no object remains still. Or lifeless.[82] When early hominids began to employ stone implements, rock spurred their worldly awareness:

> The stone tool (its texture, color, weight), in calling attention to its projected and recollected use, produced the first hollow of reflection. Humanity and nonhumanity have always performed an intricate dance with each other. There never was a time when human agency was anything other than an interfolding network of humanity and nonhumanity.[83]

Stone again founds epistemology, shaping human thought. We can push farther. Stone tools are the first objects associated with humans, the reason we have a Paleolithic Age. Stone hammers were our partners in self-civilizing, in domesticating ourselves. With their aid we built, killed, refined, transformed. The hammer is a venerable time-traveller. The past it materializes and transports is thick. Bruno Latour observes, "The hammer that I find on my workbench is not contemporary to my action today: it keeps folded heterogenous temporalities, one of which has the antiquity of the planet, because of the mineral from which it has been moulded."[84] Perhaps for this reason the hammer, primordial product of lithic partnership, still our intimate, owns pride of place in the study of the agency of objects, from Heidegger's theorization of the ready-to-hand *(Zuhandenheit)* to Harman's writing on the "allure" and "subterranean reality" of objects.[85]

Though fated to serve as a sign for *all* materiality, stone is too particular to perform that function well.[86] Stone does its own theorizing. A historically sensitive understanding must proceed from the ground up, from the lithic itself, from its activity, transmissiveness, relations, and powers, from rock in which medieval and modern touch. Epistemological schemata elaborated to explain materiality in advance (religious doctrine, Aristotelianism, alchemy) are less useful to this inquiry than the mapping of how medieval matter moves through a variety of ecomaterial texts, how the lithic conveys, and what stone does. Medieval science had faith that every substance originates in an act of divine creation, yet stones appear in medieval stories (including scientific ones) not as predetermined objects but as things of the erratic world. An earth supposed to have been fashioned for us elicits our engagement, but we find our attentiveness unrequited; or, perhaps more disturbing, stone reveals its infiltration into our customary modes of being in ways that estrange us from the quiet fabric of the everyday. Such moments trigger terror and enchantment. These affects need not lead inexorably to theology (although, of course, they can). The wonder gems spur does not necessarily resolve in the celestial. Even without recourse to alchemical science, philosophy's stone—the thing that founds epistemology but is itself unthought, that chunk of the real that as for Dr. Johnson stands for blunt, insensate, immobile, and impassive materiality—becomes the *lapis philosophorum*, the agent by which dull lead attains its radiance, that *al-iksir* or elixir or indefinable substance through which mortal bodies might obtain a geological duration rather than their brief innate span, that "privee stoon" (secret rock) that withdraws from knowledge even as it precipitates movement, creativity, frustration, peril, explosion, and exploration without end.[87]

But given its proverbial silence, how to narrate geophilia's lively biography? How to convey stories with stone?

Erratics

Geoffrey Chaucer succinctly describes stone's reticence. Harry Bailey, the Host of the gathered pilgrims in the *Canterbury Tales,* is proposing the storytelling contest that will structure their journey to the shrine of Thomas à

Becket. To urge the travellers to narrative community, Harry insists that "confort ne myrthe is noon / To ride by the weye doumb as a stoon" (There is no comfort or joy riding along the way, dumb as a stone, General Prologue, 1.773–74). In the opposition between lively human and inert matter upon which Harry's metaphor relies, should the pilgrims not embrace the fellowship that shared story engenders, they would become as lifeless as stone. He blesses this collectivizing art by invoking the soul of his deceased father, so that even the dead seem more animated than near to hand, "doumb" rock. Stones are the taciturn, immobile, everyday objects against which the vivacious company defines itself. While they journey from their inn in Southwark to Canterbury's cathedral, stone is what the tale-telling pilgrims pass in empty silence along the way.

Yet later in the *Canterbury Tales* stone proves heavy with narrative. The Franklin's Tale opens with a companionate marriage fractured when the knight Arveragus sails from Brittany, seeking martial service. As Dorigen sits upon the grass, contemplating her absent spouse, she gazes at the ocean and feels herself at sea. Catching sight of dark rocks jutting, she is gripped by fears of lithic agency. In anxious prayer she wonders why these stones were created, since "an hundred thousand bodyes of mankynde / Han rokkes slayn" (A hundred thousand bodies of mankind have rocks slain, 5.877–78). Stones are actively perilous: they "destroyen" and "evere anoyen" (5.883, 884). Just like Theseus in his Boethian speech of The Knight's Tale, Dorigen understands that a divine providence orders the universe, and natural principles underlay even disorder. Yet despite that knowledge, she can discern no purpose for such lethal lithic actants, and that incomprehensibility perturbs her. Their malevolence is so great that she describes them with an infernal litany of adjectives, "grisly feendly rokkes blake" (horrible, fiendish black rocks, 5.868).

The dark rocks are to Dorigen full of brutal volition. Such a will to destroy is more appropriate to Leviathan than the topography of Brittany's coast. Perhaps, though, she may be forgiven her animism, for we comprehend its source. Her lithophobia no doubt springs from anxiety over the safe return of her husband. Chaucer appears to have understood how the psychological mechanism of projection works, and so we apprehend that "feendly" intent does not really belong to the rocks. In the absence of anthropomorphic ascription, they are mere geological substance, a blunt blackness upon which humans place meaning. Unlike animals, they cannot exert a will, cannot budge. To submerge their jagged contours perhaps requires nothing more than the consultation of "tables Tolletanes" (5.1273) and some astrological calculations. The rocks will not move, but they will through "artes that been curious" or "illusiouns" seem to be away (5.1120, 1292)—at least for a short while. Dominion over the elements requires nothing more than specialized knowledge and some handy research aids. Even if the "magyk natureel" that unfolds in this Breton narrative creates its most captivating moments, such enchantment is quickly abandoned for a mercantile world of money exchanged for transacted business and men competing against each other in the name of generosity. Lithic agency vanishes once the perspective switches from Dorigen's plight to the tale of masculine indebtedness allying the story's clerks and knight.

Stone and metal can be worked by masterful human hands into something alluring. A gem cut and polished into iridescence features in the "fyn hawberk" (fine hauberk) of Sir Thopas, though why its gleam should be "al ywroght of Jewes werk" (fashioned through a Jew's work) remains a mystery (Tale of Sir Thopas, 7.863–64). No matter how much shimmer inheres in such an object, though, it will remain at heart no more than "a thing in veyn [vain]," "dombe" and "deve" (deaf)—as Saint Cecelia describes the dead matter of pagan idols in The Second Nun's Tale (8.285–86). Anyone who believes that something more powerful animates such rock is no better than an animal (8.288). From this orthodox point of view, any vibrancy discerned in stone is a devil's trickery, not lithic agency.[88] Metal or stone handiwork might appear to spring momentarily into life, like the mechanical steed of brass in The Squire's Tale that will "beren youre body into every place / To which youre herte wilneth" (carry your body every place your heart wills, 5.119–20). Despite its mobility, though, the object remains a "fairye" or a "gyn" (trick, contrivance). The brass horse is a machinic imitation of an animal. It works through a mechanism of spinning pins, a marvel of engineering rather than material action. Volitional or motile stone like that which grasps Dorigen's imagination belongs to the world of romance—and that genre, like its knightly embodiment Lancelot, is (at least according to The Squire's Tale, 5.286) long dead.

Humans are itinerant, companionable, garrulous, and creative. Stones are dumb. This sharp Middle English adjective can signify mute, deaf, speechless, still, lacking feeling, uncomprehending, stupid, insentient, impotent, deceased.[89] The philosopher Martin Heidegger famously captured the same estimation of the lithic when he described stone as *weltlos,* "without world." In his *Fundamental Concepts of Metaphysics,* Heidegger articulates an ascending ladder of being in which stone forms mere substrate. An animal is *weltarm* or "poor in world" because it possesses existence but not self-reflection: "animals are entirely 'captivated' and thus can more accurately be said to be had by their world than to have it."[90] Humans possess *Dasein,* "there-being," enabling an apprehension of separateness from the world. A rock possesses nothing at all. Lithic existence is agentless perdurance, a blank materiality, a thing unthought so that thoughtful things may flourish in their self-awareness. Heidegger's chain of being has medieval predecessors. By the thirteenth century the Aristotelian sorting of the cosmos into a ladder of ascending degrees of soul (nutritive, sensitive, rational) was well known throughout the Islamic world and Latin Europe. Beginning with plants, the lowest of living organisms, this tripartite hierarchy leaves no room for stones. Gregory the Great's influential *Commentary on Job* (sixth century) likewise contains a nested articulation of being, though his begins with stone. Man is a microcosm, Gregory writes, because he contains all types of existence: mere being, like rocks ("For stones are, yet do not live"); life, like plants ("Trees both are and live, yet do not feel"); sensation, like animals ("Brute creatures are and live and feel, yet do not understand"); and apprehension, like angels ("Angels both are and live and feel, and by understanding they exercise discernment").[91] The encyclopedist Gervase of Tilbury repeats Gregory's formulation succinctly, emphasizing a shared worldedness that crisscrosses its hierarchy:

> Man is called *mundus* [world] because he represents in himself an image of the whole world. He has existence in common with stones, life in common with trees, sensation in common with animals, and intelligence in common with angels.[92]

Stone is foundational. Unlike Heidegger's articulation, however, it is not surpassed at the second step along this chain of being but carried upward in lithic enmeshment. Humans are reasonable, feeling, sentient. They also share materiality and being with stone.

The lithic is the substance of the human, carried in the body. Deucalion and Pyrrha, the two survivors of world-destroying flood in a Greek myth well known throughout the Middle Ages in its narration by Ovid, repopulate the postdeluge landscape by hurling stones (the "bones of the earth") over their shoulders. The stones become men and women who will, like the biblical Adam, always carry something stony within. Augustine of Hippo writes in his *Confessions* of "the earth I tread, the earth of which is made the body I bear" (12.2). Common substance allows for a potential reciprocity, even the contemplation of human story from a point of view that intermixes the petric. As Emmanuel Lévinas observes,

> when in the *Iliad* the resistance to an attack by an enemy phalanx is compared to the resistance of a rock to the waves that assail it, it is not necessarily a matter of extending to the rock, through anthropomorphism, a human behavior, but of interpreting human resistance petromorphically.[93]

The problem for petromorphism, though, is that rocks do not compose Greek epics. Whether full of being or merely worldless, stones are inevitably wordless. Stone can be invoked as a witness, but most often its testimony is mute, an enduring trigger to memory, a passive reminder of tragic histories, spur to recollected emotion: part of a storied landscape, perhaps, but neither author nor speaker. This medieval mode of thinking about stone remains our own, even in nature writing.[94] Holding a uniformity, perseverance, and wholeness that quarrelsome humans have yet to achieve, stone conveys the inscrutability of the nonhuman world. A gap separates us from the lithic, and this soundless lacuna alienates us from the ground of existence. If stone conducts affect, that relay occurs after we engrave or shape the material to achieve sensory effects. Without a human hand to bestow meaning, rock is passionless. "Stone hearted" and "stone cold" are as much a part of our vocabulary as various expressions for stony silence. Stones are poetically imagined as crying out in protest or weeping in response to beautiful song precisely because that is what they never do.

What if our lexicon for stone is impoverished? What if Chaucer's Dorigen is right when she looks seaward at grisly black rocks and beholds their dark intentions? What if these supposedly "passive objects of the human gaze" reveal that "rocks have the capacity to organize the humans who look at them"?[95] What if stone, so often thought uncommunicative in the density of its materiality, can also be affect-laden, garrulous, animated?

In a becoming-petric of her own Dorigen is "so longe graven" by her friends that she is "emprented" (incised) out of her grief (5.830–31). What if we like Dorigen can be confidants of lithic story, inscribed by its strange tales, rather than perpetually rebuffed by its density? Stone's reticence is tied intimately to its stillness. Yet within its native duration stone is forever on the move, covering distances far greater than the miles separating Southwark from Canterbury or Brittany from England. Louis Agassiz realized this mobility when he discerned in mountainous landscapes and stranded boulders the work of glaciers. Plate tectonics informs us that Australia used to snuggle next to India and Antarctica until that restless continent decided to drift the oceans alone. But medieval people did not require a geologist's explication of deep time to discern that rocks wander. Many types of gems were thought to have originated in Eden, tumbled into the world and into time by its relentless waters. Other precious stones arrived from exotic geographies: India, Egypt, Ethiopia, Persia, Africa. A diamond or amethyst come to hand was a potential sojourner from a lost age or unreachable terrain, ready to speak its story of temporal and geographical nomadism. Isidore of Seville wrote that Prometheus first enclosed a jewel in iron, and "from these beginnings rings and gemstones originated" (*Etymologies*, 16.6.1). Companions of the road, bound to our bodies through art, itinerant stones bear the impress of their long journeys. Cherished and held closely, powerful reminders of distant times and alien worlds, precious stones allure because they are at once intimate and strange.

Medieval people knew lithic power from their lapidaries, encyclopedias, and romances. They carried gems with them as amulets, jewelry, and souvenirs, sometimes to the grave. A pebble might be placed in the mouth of a corpse at burial, or a body interred accompanied by fragments of white quartz.[96] Illnesses were treated with rocks and minerals, sometimes powdered and ingested, sometimes simply clasped. The inventories of medieval households are full of medicinal stones as well as belts, brooches, rings, and tableware into which gems known for their worldly powers had been set. Most common among the gems listed in the household inventories are stones to protect against poison, but others (like the "peres de egle" recorded as belonging to the duke of Hereford and his wife in 1322) were aids to a safe pregnancy and other kinds of lithotherapy.[97] Stones are everyday medieval material objects, not dreams. And yet lithic reveries are everywhere in the Middle Ages. Rocks can be loquacious, but require patient attending. It is possible to excavate a stony countertradition to innate reticence: stone not simply as a spur to human feeling, but as a substance possessed of mobility, artistry, desire, story.

Dumb as stone. Chaucer uses that comparison a second time, in a poem predating the *Canterbury Tales,* but with a slightly different meaning: stones withhold themselves. In *The House of Fame* Chaucer invokes the proverbial reserve of stone to express a disdained seclusion. An eagle comes to the poet in a dream and reproaches him for lonely existence. The bird describes a "daswed" (dazed) Geoffrey who returns home from work each day to sit at a book and live "as a hermit," labeling the studious dreamer "domb as any stoon" (line 656). Unlike the imagined exchange of narrative in the *Canterbury Tales,* losing oneself to narrative—to writing and to reading books—is depicted here as a stony and a sullen art (even as it is contained within and spurs more story). Regardless of such aspersions, though, stone is not always diffident. Glum and sulky, the modern word "sullen" comes from the Anglo-Norman adjective *sulein,* "averse to company." Despite associations with wastelands, the refuges of hermits, and exile, stone can be gregarious. Like Dorigen's friends—among whom ought to be admitted her unsought companions, the black rocks of the coast that (like her human comrades) will not leave her to seclusion—stone does not necessarily foster solitude, but complicatedly enmeshes itself with human ecological inhabitance, as instigator and agent, ally and unwilled collaborator.

Of stone we fashion grave markers and cairns, an admission of its ability to render us cosmic latecomers and reproach our vanity. Yet fingers cannot refrain from touching and transforming the substance. David Abram writes that lithic amity, evident each time we bend to palm a pebble, enacts an abiding "friendship between my hand and this stone . . . an ancient and irrefutable eros, the kindredness of matter with itself."[98] Rock is thick with time and relation. Human prehistory is known through lithic "friendship": abandoned windbreaks behind which fires once blazed; flint axes sharpened for violence and industry; figures carved for gods or love. Every time we touch a stone we become intimate again with those first hominids (and many other animals as well; we are not the only creatures to find in stone a congenial technology). Rock conveys story across the linguistically insurmountable gap that separates prehistory from us, even if much of what it communicates is poetic, felt more than grasped.[99] Because of its endurance stone insinuates itself into human yearnings for immortality (we convince ourselves that stone architectures will last forever), for a world larger than our mortal realm (mountaintops are the conventional dwelling places for gods, sites for ascension or revelation), for the preservation of collective history and personal memory (commemorative monuments and grave markers are typically fashioned of rock), for the survival beyond the horizon of our own bodily impermanence of the stories that we tell. Some of our earliest art consists simply of a hand pressed against rock, a desire for stone's persistence, a ritualistically repeated act of love. Such prints are created by spitting ochre from the mouth as a hand touches boulder or cave, or by rubbing the pigment across flesh before the moment of contact, impressing on enduring stone the vivid crimson of an open palm. Cueva de las Manos in Argentina is the most famous example, but such prints and five-fingered outlines are extant worldwide. While writing this book I nearly stranded my family in the Australian bush seeking Manja, the Cave of Hands, too soon after torrential storms had reconfigured the terrain of the Grampians. In that moment when human and stone meet, an ephemeral creature and unyielding substance touch, recording a haptic impulse to mineral union. Commonality as much as the breaching of ontological difference inhere at that encounter, that vertiginous touch. Human and stone do not harmonize but meet in strange likeness and inalterable difference. Worldly entanglement thickens, intensifies.

Discerning geophilia's work includes discovering in stone stories and affects implanted there, the result of the element's having been humanly imprinted and shaped. Yet stone is actively metaphoric, where a *metaphor* is that which transports (Greek *metapherein,* to transfer, to carry over). Irreducible to human use, stone creates and sustains relation, exceeds human framing, material and metaphor in one. Rock exerts relentless, incalculable forces. It transforms itself into new forms while colonizing others. Given such patent animation, why group rocks as insensate matter, instead of with organisms that prowl the world and proliferate relation? In his influential articulation of the chain of being, Gregory implied that stone's greatest achievement is simply to exist. Yet as Bruno Latour notes, simply to endure requires a kind of agency. Aldo Leopold wrote in "Thinking like a Mountain" that a slope persists only when it has a sufficient number of wolves with which to form an alliance and prevent deer from denuding its vegetation. Its granite must withstand the erosive force of water and wind that each day make its prominence dwindle. For a boulder or a mountain to remain itself over time requires ceaseless eventuation.[100] Steven Shaviro describes the persistence of the Egyptian obelisk known as Cleopatra's Needle as an unceasing temporal assertion.[101] The monument's movements include initial sculpting from granite (1450 BCE), relocation from Heliopolis to Alexandria (14 BCE), and transport to London (1877–78 CE). Throughout these exploits the Needle

> isn't just a solid, impassive object upon which certain grand historical events—being sculpted, being moved—have occasionally supervened. Rather, it is eventful at every moment. From second to second, even as it stands seemingly motionless, Cleopatra's Needle is actively happening.[102]

Existence over time consists of a series of adventures (*advent* is arrival) that are also significant surfacings or comings into agency (*aventure* in the medieval sense of astonishing irruption). An ancient Egyptian obelisk in a contemporary setting is a minor miracle of material insistence. Levi Bryant describes these capacities of objects to resist entropy and produce themselves across space and time as *powers*.[103] Medieval science called such secular efficacy *virtus*.

An inherent force that enables objects to act, *virtus* is well detailed in the lapidaries. Marbode of Rennes, composer of the most influential of these mineral bestiaries, describes a stone called *sadda*. It wanders oceanic depths, awaiting the passing of a ship (*De lapidibus*, 73). To any opportune keel *sadda* will affix itself and never again stir. Marbode is clearly speaking of barnacles, which are not stones at all—or are, rather, a marine admixture of the organic with the rocky, carbon softness with calcified durability. Manuel De Landa calls such union the mineralization of life, an enmeshment of organic suppleness and lithic frame that conveys both in unanticipated directions.[104] In a modern adaptation of Ovid's myth of Deucalion and Pyrrha, Elizabeth Ellsworth and Jamie Kruse describe humans as "walking rocks" and point out that biological organisms and the earth's geology are unthinkable except in their enduring and transformative intimacy.[105] No body, medieval or modern, is wholly separate from its environment but "always the very stuff of the messy, contingent, emergent mix of the material world."[106] When the scholastic theologian Thomas Aquinas beheld a rock, he saw an activity that counters Harry Bailey's equation of stone with incommunicability or Saint Cecilia's chaste relegation of the lithic to the dead. As Kellie Robertson explains, Thomas

> imagined himself possessing an inner representation of the rock in his mind—called a "species" or an "intentional object"—which was in turn cognized by his intellect. The species (or "inner rock") was thought to be generated by the rock, thus linking the rock to the viewer through a quasi-material medium.[107]

Invoking nonhuman frames and mixed temporal scales, medieval lapidaries pose a similar challenge to human integrity, to any solidity of biological difference against the inorganic. Rock possesses much of what is supposed to set humans apart. Like organic life it founds and sustains relations that bind, confound, create. Like gods who dally with mortals and come to know the heartbreak of noncoincident times, stone outlasts all that it touches, everything it loves.

Companionship

Engraving words on a megalith and pictures on a cave wall, erecting testimonial pylons and obelisks, funereal pyramids and other structures of remembrance, we send to a distant future the recordation of a significant event or notable life. Such commemorations typically prove less communicative and more fleeting than we hope. Despite its durability, stone proves as mortal as artists, masons, architects. Granite erodes into sand. Etched words fade. Petroglyphs lose their audience. After a few generations a gravestone or a battle marker finds its aura dimmed, to be recycled perhaps into a farmhouse or retaining wall. The climactic scene of near decapitation in the Middle English romance *Sir Gawain and the Green Knight* takes place at the Green Chapel, an architecture of unremembered origin. The site becomes a diabolical space where the grinding of a lethal axe echoes wasteland, where blood drips on snow. Who built or inhabited the place and why it fell into decay are unrecounted. It is enough that the space is heavy with forgotten history, a threat of oblivion. In Marie de France's lay *Bisclavret*, a knight hides his clothing near a chapel of unremembered use whenever he becomes a werewolf. The dilapidation of the ecclesiastical building has no narrative, existing only to provide a patina of half forgotten magic.

Yet other stone architectures endure millennia, unremittingly talkative the long while. The first stage of the rock and earthwork monument known since the Middle Ages as Stonehenge dates to 3100 BCE, when an immense round bank was excavated. Around 2600 BCE the timber of its original structures was replaced by massive bluestone. Stonehenge possesses a history far deeper than that of any of the human cultures that have successively coinhabited its expanse of Salisbury Plain. To this day it remains visited, fought over, and desired, a ponderous structure as well as the stuff of dreams. The monument possesses so strong a gravitational force that more than a million pilgrims arrive yearly. Few human-built constructions possess a history so continuous as this gift from the Neolithic. The Parthenon, Hadrian's Wall, the Arch of Constantine, petroglyphs, American Indian effigy mounds, and the moai of Easter Island likewise intrude into modernity because of their stony materiality. They convey messages that their originators inscribed upon or embodied within them. Such artworks are frequently multipurpose, combining defensive, hortatory, religious, and commemorative intentions. They speak of their moments of creation and tell tales of continuous refashioning, harnessing obscure origins to thick, extensive times to come. Chosen for the slowness of its degradation, memorial stone is deployed to transmit messages, the persistent conveyor of memory, a storied materiality that lasts. Thus the medieval historian Geoffrey of Monmouth imagined that Stonehenge was erected upon Salisbury Plain to honor the British dead and their battle against the invading Saxons. His *History of the Kings of Britain* (ca. 1138) declares that King Arthur's uncle, father, and successor to the throne are buried within its ring, rendering Stonehenge a war memorial that will stand for all time to declare British greatness. Yet Geoffrey acknowledges that the structure's history is far deeper than its use by ancient Britons. Merlin narrates the story of how the ring of stones was built in Ireland by a band of African giants, who transported its massive rocks from their native land. The destiny of the circle, Geoffrey writes, is to be translated from his own ecclesiastical Latin (*chorea gigantum,* the Giants' Ring) into English, into the language spoken by the invading Saxons against whom the Britons have won their battle but to whom they will lose a longer war. Geoffrey's last mention of the lithic ring states this assimilation into new story quietly. Constantine III, the monarch who follows Arthur upon the British throne, is buried within "lapidum structuram . . . Anglorum lingua Stanheng," "the stone circle known in English as Stanheng."[108]

Archeologists tell us that Stonehenge's earliest use was indeed as a burial site. Despite its reputation as an element difficult to alter, stone serves commemorative functions well because with enough labor the lithic becomes liquid. Antoni Gaudí knew this potential intimately, creating undulating structures like Sagrada Familia and Parc Güell, architectures so fluid that their rock seems pliant, malleable, watery. Canterbury's cathedral and the prehistoric monuments of Brittany demonstrate the same responsiveness of stone to human hands. The emotional impress such structures impart varies. The ethereal swell of church walls leads eyes to heaven, while the gateway of a dolmen invites the observer to contemplate subterranean worlds opened by death. We deploy hard rock to demarcate, to hold land down and declare territory ours (stone walls, boundary stones). We also dream of stone so light it ascends cloudward: the weightless towers of temples, skyscrapers, the soar of menhirs, the looming of standing stones, Michael Heizer's installation "Levitated Mass." A memorial wrought of stone is a receptacle for human memory conveyed to the future with emotional force. What matters are the engraved deeds, the history recorded and passed along. As a vehicle for transporting feeling, memorial stone possesses emotional and pedagogical agency. Lithic structures convey sensory intensities. Stone is not merely a compliant medium for historical representation but (in the words of James Ingo Freed, the architect of the U.S. Holocaust Memorial Museum) memory's relentless and affective resonator.[109]

Memorial stone assumes human transmissive agency and rocky passivity. Stone's architectural companionship might be better described as monumental: the lithic become a lively and a ceaseless art, a stirring of sensory and aesthetic intensities. Gilles Deleuze and Félix Guattari describe a monument as an artwork that does not represent but acts: "a monument does not commemorate or celebrate something that happened but confides to the ear of the future the persistent sensations that embody the event . . . it gives it a body, a life, a universe."[110] A monument produces sensation in itself, not sensation for a particular subject.[111] It is not a text awaiting its interpreter but a vibratory machine, story in endless emission. Geophilia as "feeling stone" conveys the sensations, intensities, and excitations that

stone as monumental art produces. The most powerful, most revolutionary and enduring monuments are therefore always open-ended, "like those
tumuli to which each new traveler adds a stone."[112] Adventurous, alive, a
lithic monument changes over time, and through those transformations
elicits sustained participation. Stonehenge's vivacity has persevered for at
least five thousand years, during which its metamorphoses have been profound. Geoffrey imagined that the structure was a memorial for the British
dead, even as he acknowledged that the circle is so ancient as to predate
human history. Connecting the stones to Ireland, Africa, and a primordial
race of monsters is as close as a medieval writer can get to what we now call
prehistory. A fifteenth-century illustration of Stonehenge (*Scala Mundi,* ca.
1440) provides a bird's-eye view of the trilithons, the iconic double pillars
capped by lintels. Such a vantage point was nearly impossible in the Middle
Ages, but here we behold a kind of X-ray view from above, with tenon joints
in the rocks clearly visible, revealing that the illustrator knew the circle to
be a remarkable work of human engineering. The text accompanying the
picture notes that Merlin built the structure "not by force, but by art."[113]
Though we tend now to think of this figure familiar from Arthurian myth
as a magician, Geoffrey's Merlin is an artist, an architect, and an author. He
ensures that the stories of his time survive by constructing in Stonehenge a
monument of abiding relation. The story Geoffrey tells about the origins of
the structure is not mere misapprehension. Merlin's narrative of primal architects and staggering material conveyance demonstrates a contemporary
responsiveness to what the lithic communication device imparts. Whether
Stonehenge is described as a feat of magic or engineering, its beholders have
long recognized the power its stones exert, inseparable from the incitement
to wonder they harbor, a provocation to creativity, narrative, enmeshment,
and innovation. Stonehenge conveys and elicits story.

Geophilia courses the human hands that fashion Stonehenge as well
as the stone itself, a posthuman meshwork in which the two are not easily individuated.[114] Human identity has always depended upon and been
sustained by dispersive networks of actors and objects. Recent technologies only render more visible the ways in which human identity exceeds the
boundaries of determinate bodies, is dispersed across a phenomenological
world in which *Homo sapiens* is a powerful but in the end nonsovereign participant. Only through our alliances with things were we able to humanize

ourselves.[115] Thus we map our progression as a move from the Paleolithic to the Neolithic, charting cultural development by increased intimacy to stone. Yet *human* immediately becomes *posthuman* as a consequence of the enlarged temporal frame that geology demands. Such a stone-etched countervision invites reflection on what it means to inhabit a world that is at once potentially indifferent to humanity yet perilously continuous. Foregrounding mineralogical agency is both scientific (from a deep history perspective all stone moves and changes; given a large enough temporal frame, any component of the universe acts as if an errant atom, any solid or sedentary combination proving ephemeral) and attentive to the insights of nonmoderns. Within a geological scale of time, after all, medieval authors are our contemporaries.

Stone invites us to think beyond the circumscriptions of small categories, to explore interrelation and ecological interpenetrations, to delve and to make. Geophilia is there from the start. Our first wanderings on long sea voyages were in the company of stones, as traces of the ancient obsidian trade have made clear.[116] Human beings have from prehistoric times recognized the ability of the lithic to send messages across vast spans. Hence our fascination with structures like Newgrange, Avebury, and the Ring of Brodgar. Devices for the lasting conveyance of story, such architectures communicate long after their human co-dwellers vanish. Stonehenge has outlived peoples of the Neolithic, Bronze, and Iron Ages, as well as the Romans, Britons, Anglo-Saxons, and Normans. A pilgrimage site that drew visitors from across the Alps millennia ago, this ring of stones may have been spurred by communion with rock formations found in the Preseli Mountains, where dolerite stands in architectural pillars arranged by no human hand.[117] Barrows, rock walls, circles of standing stones, and other petric art are more than a human overwriting of compliant terrain. As recent archeologists have emphasized, lithic architectures tend to "resonate with the topographical or geological capacities of the landscape," mundane environmental alliances rather than unmindful impositions.[118] Megaliths often stand as handcrafted analogues to natural formations. Stone offers a craggy, fissured, irregular surface full of possibilities for confederation: "to work on the rock was not to embody oneself in substantial material or to make the rocks meaningful, but to bring forth or add to what already dwelled in them."[119] Creating art with stone is not the domestication of an element, but a human-lithic collaboration that recognizes the art stone already holds.

The scale of such alliance can be massive, as at Carnac, or tiny, as in the precious stones that were so much a part of medieval texts, material culture, and reverie. Though the earthliness of stone might seem opposed to the spiritual and the ameliorative, lapidaries detail the innate abilities to affect the world through their intrinsic energies.[120] These powers are not always easy to discern. The thirteenth-century encyclopedist Bartholomaeus Anglicus writes that the stone called *gagates* is "boystous" (course, opaque, crude) and unlovely to behold, so that "þe virtue þat is yhidde wiþinne" (the virtue that is hidden within) will often remain unknown. Those who companion the stone, however, discover that it is capable of great wonders: testing for fiends and virginity, exerting magnetic force, healing illnesses, preventing enchantments and witchcraft, speeding childbirth.[121] Diffidence is not wholly alien to minerals and gems described in the Middle Ages, but activity is more common than withdrawal. *Vermidor,* for example, divulges its powers ostentatiously. The gem holds such intensity that it glows at night, an inextinguishable candle. When it is placed against a bodily swelling, the ailment quickly subsides.

The stones of these medieval geological treatises are typically encountered in a sociable state, seeking alliance with organic bodies so that they might spring into agency. A hero's labors may be required to extract a desired stone from the body of rare and distant fish, or to snatch a coveted gem from the beak of a mountain-dwelling bird oblivious to its power. Agate contains a kind of mineralogical blood that lends a ruddy complexion to those who carry it and renders would-be orators eloquent. Goat's blood must permeate the diamond before it softens enough to cut. Lapidary rocks sometimes arrive embedded in narratives from which they must be excavated, histories that cling to them thereafter. Magnetite is mined in India by cave-dwelling troglodytes and has been used throughout the centuries by magicians like Circe to extend their powers. The stone can test fidelity: an adulterous wife will be hurled from the bed should the stone be placed beneath as she slumbers. Sprinkled over a fire, magnetite fills the air with nightmare-inducing vapors. Thieves therefore incinerate the stone to send occupants fleeing their homes, leaving their goods ready to be snatched. Magnetite may implant or destroy love among the married, quell dropsy, salve burns, and bestow efficacy in argument.

The lapidaries enmesh stones with the activity of rivers, angels, affects, birds, beasts, farmers, climate, moisture, ships, traders, bodies, heat, and light. No single component of these networks is detachable as lonely agent.[122] *Sorige,* for example, is a green stone found within a stream that traverses the terrestrial paradise. Sometimes its currents convey the precious gem into India, transport from abandoned Eden into mundane waterways. Fish-eating beasts as large as dogs place the stones in their mouths, unaware of its powers. *Sorige* is harvested by placing a naked virgin close enough for these creatures to scent. The creature will approach the girl, place its head between her breasts, and fall asleep, intoxicated by sexual purity's sweet fragrance. The stone-bearing animal can then be easily killed by an awaiting man, and the *sorige* extracted from its mouth. As long as the bearer is Christian, the viridescent jewel will cure gout, destroy vermin, prevent stomachaches, and ward against rabid animals. The gem's powers will cease immediately if worn by the dishonest or the dirty. Stones erode the boundary that keeps biological and mineral realms discrete, sometimes with uncomfortable violence (goats die for diamonds, dog-beasts perish for *sorige*). Beneath the sea *corallus* is a lush plant with waving foliage, but exposed to air its lithe branches harden into red stone: from organic to inorganic at a single, breezy touch. Yet even in this petrified state coral does not become inactive, warding those who hold it against storms, preventing infernal attacks, nurturing agriculture. Stones act less like lifeless bits of earth and more like the creatures to which they have such affinity, such ardor to touch.

No medieval stone exists for long in a withdrawn state, but is an actor in a narrative that exceeds any use value, any practicality, a gem of aesthetic efflorescence, a narrative conveyance-machine. Lapidary texts were an important gateway for pagan learning to travel into orthodox Christianity. They carried into the Middle Ages challenges, invitations, and inducements to the imagination from the distant past. Lapidary lore could thereby spur a reconceptualization of present and future in terms rather different from *idées reçues*—a reconfigured reality where the world is far wider geographically and temporally than the small portions already mapped. David Williams describes the stones of the lapidaries as "monsters of the mineral realm" since they "provided a transition" between different worlds, including heaven and earth: they "exhibit characteristics of other forms of life" and defy "the ontological limits placed upon them."[123] Rather than render them monsters, however, the lapidaries foreground the liveliness of matter, the charisma of things. They insist that few objects are as powerful, heterodox, vagrant, or creative as stone, that materiality bound to the human through the intimacy of elemental love.

Intracatastrophe

The world is not for us. Stones declare this truth better than texts, because the narratives we fashion tend to be convinced of our centrality. Having abided on earth several thousand or several billion years longer—having provided the foundational materials of this planet, and having endured its recurrent cataclysms—rock narrates a rather different story. Even more scrupulous in its data gathering than we, stone records advents and extinctions on vast scales, so that humans lose predominance. The play has been long, and we are latecomers. Yet it is easy to go too far, to love only unpeopled ecologies, to desire objects like stones for a seeming indifference. That perspective is just as partial, and repeats in a secular mode a medieval theology that enjoins disdain of the sublunary world, that takes pleasure in declaring human lives insignificant.[124] Both frames are animated by the same misanthropy, with the more contemporary perspective simply removing God and heaven.

Geophilia entails discovering, through science and through art, the continuities between humans and stones, their congruence and coinhabitance. The lithic and the human are often withdrawn from each other, but not to inevitable seclusion, not to inexorable dispassion. Both can be artists, ardent, innovative, makers of a shared world, this fragile world suspended between calamities, this world that is not for us. The stories stones tell can be dispiriting. Rocks are the archive in which we read that we dwell intracatastrophe. They index the exterminations of remote epochs, extinctions that near again. They yield narratives of celestial fire, massive volcanic blasts, an atmosphere inimical to life, an earth gripped by ice, ablaze, overheated, engulfed in sudden flood. Yet as medieval writers knew well, stone also promises a world richer than the impoverished expanse we imagine we inhabit, an earth we have too often figured as mute and inert resource, a material storehouse for profligate use, or a wasteland in waiting. Here is something the authors of medieval romances and lapidaries realized as vividly as the contemporary geologist Jan Zalasiewicz, who reads the romance of the planet's genesis in a pebble he found along a beach in Wales, tracing the little rock's origin back to the big bang.[125] Zalasiewicz repeats in contemporary mode an observation by Thomas Aquinas, who wrote that stones "have something in them of the nature of stars."[126] Examine a boulder, mineral deposit, or gem long enough and suddenly inanimate matter speaks, exerts a strange agency, imparts a story of magic, transformation, envitalized ecologies, intimacy, interdependence, interbeing—along with more mundane tales, and some horror stories as well. The German abbess Hildegard of Bingen wrote that as primordial matter and materialized energy, all stones are composed of fire and water, all stones thrum with elemental dynamism.[127] Restless receptacles of flame and flood, of the mundane and the astral, stones hold the dual elements of cataclysm, one of which wiped the earth almost clean of life and the other destined at the world's end to scour the planet once more. Intracatastrophe is a space of inundation and incineration, Deluge and Apocalypse, Ice Age and global warming.

Lowell Duckert has argued that the "Ice Age is never over," that we abide in the grasp and embrace of vast forces with which we are, in his word, "co-implicated," a relationality thereby laden with possibility.[128] Yet ice is not the entirety of our elemental story. In fire and in frost, in storm and with a shaking of terrain, the future arrives as it always has, promising ruin. To dwell attentively in this world limned by disaster, to inhabit a planet made of stone, is to realize materiality's thickness, its active heterogeneity, its breathtaking magnitude, its clasp. Time, matter, and space possess scales that leave us reeling. Timothy Morton writes of hyperobjects, human creations like Styrofoam and plutonium that endure beyond anything in nature: "Thinking about these materials does involve something like religion, because they transcend our personal death. . . . Hyperobjects outlast us all."[129] The temporal spans to which hyperobjects summon us, Morton writes, reduce to inaudibility the invitation extended by "the mystery of a stone circle" like Stonehenge—but stone itself has endured billions of years, not the thousands or millions of hyperobjects. Stone is a declaration of oblivions past and the wash of a Lethe to come. If catastrophe is inevitable, if disanthropocentricism leaves us staggering and feeling too small, both are also advents of futurity, and a call to creativity that might best be answered through unexpected alliance: art with science and story with stone.

The earth is an open and untotalizable entity, complicatedly animate, constitutively entangled within bustling ecosystems that include the biological and the inorganic, matter as well as force. Affective enmeshment is not an instantiation of the pathetic fallacy but a sympathetic universalism: ecology as intimate, the planet no longer an object content in its solitude but perilous in its continuity. Catastrophe is entanglement. Sometimes a small amount of artistic anthropomorphism triggers a regarding of the world from a nonhuman point of view: the vista of objects with compelling stories, the outlook from vistas at which the earth dwindles, scales of time so vast that human history becomes a few seconds of the cosmic year—but in which geophilia unfolds and all the world comes to life and begins to act rather like we do. In this world cataclysm repeats with complex causes and effects, underscoring that we are as much a part of this materiality as volcanoes smothering life when they trigger the production of chlorofluorocarbons. The lesson of lithic-human enmeshment is simple: we need to stop creating greenhouse gases if we do not want to be contemporary equivalents of the surging magma that once presided over an extinction so massive that life on earth nearly vanished. Geology can teach us these cautions. So can medieval texts, which knew that stone is not an inert substance that forms a world for our use. Stone is a strangely sympathetic companion, a source of knowledge and narrative, an invitation to an ethics of scale, the catalyst for humanist-scientist alliance, a disruption to everything we thought we knew.

We live within catastrophe: the fire of Armageddon and the ice of some new glaciation, or maybe the flame of global warming and the chill of our indifference to the melting Arctic. We dwell within the gales and torrents of hurricanes that drown the poor while we look away, the movements of the earth that topple our fragile structures, that remind us that continents are motion, that ground (literal and epistemological) is always shifting, that metaphors are concrete and concrete like all stone cracks, pulverizes, transmutes. Isidore of Seville, a seventh-century encyclopedist who tried to imagine what the earth would look like if we could view its lands and waters from the heavens, spotted a fossilized sea shell on a mountaintop and wrote that the earth's rocky archive records its elemental upheavals.[130] A glimpse of things to come. Catastrophe dogs us, pulls down everything we compose. The past, the present, the future: stories of wreckage, devastation, dilapidation. Yet humans regard the world in frames too small. If stone teaches us anything it is that ruin is a beginning, a going from which something vital arrives. Dinosaurs abandoned the bulk of once vast bodies to soar clouds. Long ago they learned to produce song. Medieval legend tells us that gems continue to tumble from Eden's waters, even if return to that garden is barred.[131] Sometimes these stones course cascading rivers to contemporary hands. "Standing on the frigid summit of Everest," writes the geologist David R. Montgomery, "if you could pick up a piece of limestone and view it under a microscope you would find that the top of the world consists of fragmented trilobites and tiny fecal pellets that settled to a tropical seabed."[132] The sand that was a desert is a life-bearing cliff, the ocean's edge a fertile field, that which had been a mountain is now a glade of sea anemones. The ash from the volcano's combustion is an archive. That calcium has become a snail's shell become marble become . . . this very place where I write, or where you read these words, a ruin that once was stone and a ruin to come, the clasp of the fragile community we for a small space share. Here. Now.

EXCURSUS

The Weight of the Past

Bordeaux is a city of stone. The regal heft of its buildings rose in the eighteenth century by pulverizing preceding cityscapes, medieval and Roman. Numerous fountains, the swirl of the Garonne, and a recent *mirroir d'eau* help to counteract lithic ponderousness, bringing fluidity to architecture that can seem overly decorous. The Atlantic crashes not too distantly. *Bord'eaux*: intimacy to waters in the city's name. Like the precisely crafted wine for which the region is famous, Bordeaux's historic spaces feel artfully produced, a balance of rock and water conjoined for aesthetic effect. A perfection of the elements, yes, but perfections are diffident.

At the center of the city an ultramodern tram courses the square in front of the majestic Grand Théâtre (ca. 1780). Though some hundreds of years separate the two, they seem comfortable companions, alike in their gleam. You have to walk to the urban edge to find the tower where Eleanor of Aquitaine lived. The ruins of a Roman coliseum are hidden by residential buildings and unlisted among tourist attractions. The structure is cordoned from civic life, at the terminus of a narrow cul de sac: a pleasant view for some apartment dwellers, but a steel fence prevents nearing the fragments. Bordeaux is a city of stone, but not exactly ancient. Unlike London, Rome,

Paris, Norwich, its streets are not an urban palimpsest, not a sedimented intermixture of disjunct times. It surprised me, therefore, to wander the Jardin Public and encounter a Neolithic circle. We had been searching only for the carousel, yet there they were, ancient rocks, some incised, a classic ring formation. At first I thought the structure must be an imitation of a cromlech from Brittany, a model meant to add atmosphere to this park not even a few centuries old. Mentioned in no guidebook and marked only by a sign that lost its words long ago, the structure inhabits a shady slope not far from the playground. On surrounding benches the Bordelais chat, smoke, eat lunch. Some research on my iPhone revealed the circle to be authentic. The Cromlech de Lervaut was transported from Lesparre-Médoc in 1875, partly as a historical curiosity, partly to add a picturesque element to the gardens.

Carefully measured, moved, and restored, the ring was not, as was the destiny of numerous Neolithic structures, fragmented so that its materials could be reused or its site reclaimed. It did not suffer the fate of the ancient city atop which the Jardin Public is built. On an autumn day in 2011 the cromlech pulled me into its orbit, made me happy that it had not been consigned to the far side of a metal fence like Burdigala's Roman amphitheater. And yet when trees undermine its solidity, pollution wears its surfaces, the oil of human hands stains, and children mistake it for a playground, a ring of ancient stones in a city's midst becomes a deracinated architecture that will not long offer its fitful invitations to deeper temporalities. The Cromlech de Lervaut is a disintegrating time capsule, an archive crumbling into quiet. I photographed the stones, feeling the joy of unexpected discovery, wondering about the hands that shaped it and the hands that moved it and lives that have been and are being lived around its circle, wondering about its mortality, its falling into silence.

Later in the week we traveled to Saint-Émilion to visit the *église monolithique,* a subterranean church carved from a limestone hill. We arrived just in time for the day's only tour, in French—fine for me and Alex, but not Wendy or Katherine. "I can't possibly translate for you," the guide stated with annoyance, irked as well at our daughter's need to visit the bathroom just as the tour commenced. Since a guide is the only way to enter the church, we were happy to be included. Marie's French was precise, lucid. Eventually she warmed to Katherine, whose pleasure at the church's painted walls (a

Remembrance: Cromlech de Lervaut, Jardin Public de Bordeaux, France.

centaur! a dragon!) transcended language. Near the end of the tour Marie sprinkled quiet English asides to the youngest member of her entourage. It is possible that the *église monolithique* is a crusades-era inspiration, the idea of a cave-like building brought back from Turkey by French knights. Or its excavation may have been a convenience: hollow out the hill as you quarry stone for town buildings, use the opened space for worship. We cannot know, because no documents survive. The church's history is its stone.

There is a power within this hill become a place of silenced prayer. In regarding pillars that ascend into mountainous darkness, it is difficult not to feel suspended weight. A cathedral promises sky at its far side, but this church holds itself up against mountain. Yet the building's allure has not always been perceived. During the French Revolution the site was sold and the church's interior stripped. A cooper set up shop in a chapel. The soot from the curing of wine barrels accidentally preserved the ornate murals on the walls. The *église monolithique* is now privately owned and little used. Tourists sometimes come to see it when they visit nearby vineyards and stop at Saint-Émilion for lunch. If this sacred space carved from singular stone has any historical assertiveness, it seems a power that waxes and wanes. Most pilgrims to Saint-Émilion would, I think, rather dine at a café with a view of the orderly grape vines than explore the dim interior.

And then to Paris. We walked around the places we know and found new ones to explore—like the catacombs, *l'empire de la mort,* passing under Montparnasse, bones become a decorative and endless wall. "How long does it take," I asked, "for a body to be no longer a person or a life, but material that can be moved, that can be used to build a place like this?" Later we crossed the Pont des Arts and were amused by rows of love locks affixed to its rails. Steel clasping steel above the river's swirl, the padlocks capture the passions that we want to make last, the ardor we have to stay bound to this earth and to each other, and the anonymity that swallows acts that feel singular. It was hard not to see a convergence of sorts in the beauty of the locks clasping the bridge and that of the bones beneath the streets.

In Montparnasse busy avenues yield quickly to everyday neighborhoods. One of these is another community of the dead, the crowded, stony, and weirdly lively Cimetière du Montparnasse. Alex and I went together, remarking how some graves stood in what seemed to be eternal splendor while others had already been obliterated. We were moved when we came to a cenotaph designating one who had "disappeared to Auschwitz." We left a pebble on its granite, observing how strange it was to find a Jewish memorial among so many crosses. Yet the more we wandered the more familiar the Magen David became. We placed stones on graves until the number grew so large that we knew we could never accomplish our self-appointed task. Memorialization brings despair. I asked Alex how long he thought the lifespan of grief might be. When do the daily visits to the cemetery cease? *I'll go weekly. I'll go once a month. I'll go for the anniversary. I used to go. . . .*

We spent our final morning in Paris walking the Arènes de Lutèce, the remnants of a Roman amphitheater uncovered in 1869, eventually preserved as a public park. A few summers ago we had lived not far from these ruins on the Rue Claude Bernard. I had wandered to the Arènes some mornings, to think and to write. In the semicircle where people once died to amuse an audience, youths practice soccer and older men play bocce. I had never photographed the place, and here Alex and Katherine's patience gave out. They were tired of living in my documentary about stones and the

Remembrance: Cimetière du Montparnasse, Paris.

human lives that unfold alongside them, weary of collaborating in lithic rumination. They did not want their pictures taken. Off they walked together, while I wandered and created photographs that made the place seem emptier than it was. Part of the city's life, a lived space, the Arènes de Lutèce are nothing like the coliseum in Bordeaux. As with many ancient monuments that survive into the present day, this arena is restored to the point of being almost a re-creation. Nothing lasts as long as we desire, not even the stone to which we entrust our yearnings for story's endurance.

On the flight back to Washington I watched the Lars von Trier film *Melancholia.* Had I seen it anywhere besides a transatlantic crossing I might have been annoyed by its heavy allegories. A blue planet called Melancholia is headed toward an earth inhabited by melancholiacs and those whom they suck into their orbits. You might think that you can escape the sadness (at first it seems that the Weighty Symbolic Planet is going to miss Earth), but you cannot (Melancholia swerves back and crushes the world). The final scene features a feeble "cave" made not of stone but of thin sticks where three of the protagonists huddle. One of them is a child who has been told he will be safe. He is incinerated with his mother and aunt. The End.

Blunt, perhaps, but maybe that is the frank lesson of stone. It is possible that our moon was created when a planet called Theia smashed Earth long ago, causing the liquefied globe to re-form. We do not know. We cannot know. It is possible that the makers of the Cromlech de Lervaut thought that what they built would always endure, that no one would forget what their stone ring means or dismantle it to bring to a park. Those who cheered in Latin in the stone theaters of Bordeaux and Paris likely assumed that Rome would never fall, that the language of their shouts would be the language of that space for all time. It may well be that those who affix love locks to Parisian bridges believe their passion will not abate, that their inscribed names will signify their affection endlessly. The builders of Saint-Émilion could not have known that the church would become a barrel maker's workspace, or that the effigies upon its stone tombs would lose their faces. The particular is always rendered anonymous, like bones taken from graves to fashion whimsical arches in an empire of the dead. Those still in graves or those exhumed from them have no message to bear other than that time erodes memory, that time erodes substance itself. The continents we cross on airplanes are plunging slowly into sea.

In the cemetery at Montparnasse one grave depicted a baby in a shroud atop its shrouded mother. Could anything speak loss—of memory, of love, of history, of everything that matters—more eloquently? And yet someone else, nearby, had commissioned as funereal sculpture an angel that is probably arriving to take a soul to heaven, but accidentally resembles an incubus embracing his human lover. I left a pebble here, too. I don't think this statue will be around in a millennium. It is not the Cromlech de Lervaut. Someone will clear the cemetery for an apartment complex when no one remembers who is buried beneath its monuments. But there is something defiant in that incubus or angel's love (carnal or spiritual, I cannot tell which), a love that also speaks of some artist's collaboration with stone.

That, in the end, must suffice. To live long enough is to disbelieve the power we once thought that we possessed to keep the things we love. This is sad knowledge, melancholic knowledge, but it does not end the world. No blue planet or second Theia is in the telescope. We inhabit an ephemeral landscape. We love stone, and the marks we make upon stone, and the marks stone makes upon us. Stone insists not because it is so different from we who build families of whatever kind against cataclysm, but because of its deep affinity, its enduring tectonicity (movement, carpentry, making), its strangely inhuman (I don't know what else to call it) love.

Time

The Insistence of Stone

At Avebury

We stand beneath the megalith. Brisk winds roam the grass. The sheep are complaining. "Can you feel anything?" I ask. His palm presses the rock as eagerly as mine. "Yes," he whispers, fingers searching clefts and lichen. "I think I do." He places his ear against the stone and closes his eyes, as if through intimate contact he might discern hoary secrets. He is as certain and as joyful as when, many years ago, he used to press his head to my chest to know the life of an invisible heart. In a solemn voice, as if he has absorbed from deep in the stone its enduring history, he announces, "It knows it killed someone."

I realize immediately that my son pilfered my copy of the second edition of Aubrey Burl's *Prehistoric Avebury*. He must have read the volume late into the night of our London flat. "Me, too," I respond. "I definitely feel something." I am lying. Like this ten-year-old with ear against stone, I want to feel power in the monument. Not the energy of astral planes or the pull of a vortex or proximity to pagan divinity, not whatever New Age druids come to Avebury seeking. Yet I share their dreams. My desire is that the rock not be inert. My son is right. This megalith did take someone's life. After standing for millennia, the thirteen-ton boulder crushed a man and preserved his corpse for six centuries beneath its bulk. The weight of the past, indeed. Alexander Keiller discovered the body in 1938 when he disinterred the toppled boulder from its medieval grave. Since a leather purse contained scissors, a lancet, and some coins from the early fourteenth century, archeologists hypothesize that the skeletal remains belong to an itinerant barber-surgeon.[1] He was likely witnessing or assisting an effort to obliterate Avebury, "mightiest in size and grandeur of all megalithic rings" before its piecemeal destruction commenced in the Middle Ages.[2] Pits were dug beneath the standing stones so that they tipped and were buried, pious acts of vandalism directed at what was probably understood to be a pagan structure. Perhaps the effort was abandoned when the accidental entombment convinced witnesses that these stones could still exert force. Since its reerection the megalith has been known as Barber Rock, its new name bearing witness to the life it took. Yet as destructive as the fourteenth-century project of toppling Avebury may have been, the attempted annihilation of an architecture already four thousand years old aided its preservation. Buried where they fell by medieval hands, these rocks were shielded from later fragmentation. The seventeenth and eighteenth centuries were especially brutal to what remained of the circle. The swift annihilation of megaliths was accomplished through fire, cold water, and sledgehammers. We will never know how many of the stones became, once smashed to pieces, the foundations of local farmhouses and the stuff of quotidian roadways.

My son Alex felt power abiding in a Neolithic megalith that, having for centuries dominated a landscape, fell and crushed a man. The rock patiently awaited resurrection for five hundred years so that it could tower again over a verdant field, could again render the humans standing at its side ephemeral. With Alex I wanted to believe that stories endure, that they speak through objects like Barber Rock. I want narrative to cross inhuman gaps of time, stones to assert themselves as something more than a trace of histories lost.

The body of the crushed barber-surgeon, the man who had dared to undermine the rock and paid for the act with his life, was lost during the Blitz and rediscovered in 1999. From the breakage patterns of his bones it is impossible to know if he was alive when the toppling megalith rendered him an unwitting time capsule.[3] Although they seem to arrive from time out

The weight of the past in Avebury.

of memory, the dolmens and standing stones that tourists wander Brittany, Ireland, and Britain to glimpse are often modern reconstructions using nearby materials, designed in partnership with nearby landscape to create an untimely radiance. Avebury is no different, a product of massive restoration in the 1930s as much as a letter mailed five millennia ago.

Perhaps Avebury's megaliths are not so much a letter but an epistolary romance, a gap-riddled correspondence among many authors (some human, some not) unfolding over immense duration. Whatever its initial architects called the stone, in whatever language they shared but could not bequeath, Barber Rock has not yet ceased to speak. My son and I touched a megalith's pocked surface and felt our own desires. But we also perceived that these desires are not ours alone. Our fingers traced an ancient record of love and strife, of the stone's being hewn, transported, dressed, raised, toppled, raised again. We wandered a tactile archive of its long companionship with wind, rain, ice, sheep, lichens, artists, admirers, worshippers, farmers, wayfarers. Barber Rock is thick with multiple plots and uncertain denouements. Avebury's stones are a dynamic aggregate of difficult narratives composed, rewritten, revised, forgotten, discovered. To touch the towering or toppled megaliths is to enter a human-lithic-world participation that gathers millennia, layered and deep, opening to expansive historical scales, material insistence, environmental embroilment, densely sedimented temporalities, a community of peoples, things, and forces enmeshed through story and stone.

Lithic Time

In his *Vox clamantis* ("The Voice Crying Out"), the polyglot English poet John Gower declares that "Scripture veteris capiunt exempla futuri" (old writings contain examples for the future).[4] Two centuries later, when William Shakespeare brought the fourteenth-century poet back from the dead in his prologue to *Pericles,* "ancient Gower" declares "Et bonum quo antiquius, eo melius" (The older a good thing, the better, 1.Prol.10). This chapter explores a temporal space opened by these two Gowerian declarations, wondering how far back ancient messages, abetted by stone's material endurance, might extend; probing whether writing necessitates words, or if lithic architectures and other nonverbal petroglyphs (including the fossilized remains of various life forms) can communicate across obliterating sweeps of time; and tracing the temporal knot formed when distant history touches present story, since to narrate the past conjures possible futures. Stone challenges small, linear divisions of human history through its aeonic insistence. The lithic thickens time into multiple, densely sedimented, and combustively coincident temporalities.[5] Its inhuman scale summons geologic contemplation, an extension of story far beyond accustomed durations. The Parisian philosopher Jean Buridan therefore wondered in the fourteenth century why through erosion every mountain had not yet been flattened, why engulfing water had not rendered the globe a smooth and aqueous sphere.[6] His solution was to imagine that as rock diminishes on some parts of the earth, mountains rise above the ocean on the other, an intricate balancing that grants to the elements their ceaseless motion. Buridan does not presume this extensive geographical and temporal frame exists for a human observer. It simply exists, dynamically, outside familiar duration. For authors like Gower, ancient writings buttress religious certainty. Buridan, just as devout, also makes clear that stories of stone open multiple modalities, rocky paths along which the world unburdens itself of reduction into human contours, inviting through the sudden expansion of time speculative wanderings.

Whether its invitation is to contemplate thousands or millions of years, eternity or infinity, stone vexes human history, admixing the transient and the perdurable. In reading Genesis with petrogenesis, biblical with geological epochality, this chapter goes against an impressive critical literature that argues the discovery of deep time ("the unimaginable magnitudes of the prehuman or prehistoric time scale") in the nineteenth century engendered a decisive epistemological break, with modernity arriving on its nearer side.[7] Thinking the earth in billion-year spans is utterly disorienting—and the difficulty of comprehending ecological activity over such immense durations likely underlays our inability to address climate change, to formulate the ethics of scale and Long Ecology necessary to achieve something more than the witnessing of catastrophe. Yet the millennial spans into which medieval writers divided the past did not exactly hold comfort. Such eras are neither as securely apprehensible nor as tidily diminutive as implied by those who argue for sharp historical ruptures, for a decisive entry into modernity cut by the pickaxes of Victorian geology. Medieval texts are just as capable of epochal foundering and the envisioning of lost worlds. Our rocks are composed of atoms rather than elements, and divine eternity has been replaced by cosmological infinity, but the genre and structure of medieval stories of stone have been quietly absorbed into contemporary techniques of narrating the distant past. This assimilation has occurred without realizing the alternatives to resourcism (imagining that nature consists of commodities attending human use) that these discarded elemental theories offer through binding ecological enmeshments and challenging views of worldedness.[8] For both medieval and modern thinkers, stone's endurance unsettles narration, curving linear narratives into vortices, limning history with havoc.

Because of its exceptional durability, stone is time's most tangible conveyor. Stone hurts, and not just because rocks so easily become hurled weapons. Geologic scale diminishes the human. Yet expansive diversity of strata, some jolted into unconformity through gyred forces and tectonic drift, is almost impossible to comprehend without arrangement along a human calendar. The book of Genesis translates creation into the tidy progression of a seven-day week. The astrophysicist Carl Sagan famously condensed cosmic history into a solar year, with the big bang on the first day of January, the Milky Way arriving May 1, earth's oldest rocks October 2, and dinosaurs thundering across the continents on Christmas Eve, departing four days later. Modern humans make their belated appearance on New Year's Eve, with mere minutes separating the Crusades (all of them) from the first manned flight to the moon.[9] The measurement of abyssal depths requires apprehensible terms, and so science, religion, and myth humanize time through reduction into familiar spans. When the biblical Methuselah endures for an extraordinary 969 years, almost to the Flood against which his grandson must build an ark, he becomes a figure for impossible longevity, subsuming epochal time into a human frame. Yet Methuselah dies just short of the thousand-year mark. Despite absorption into myth and metaphor (techniques as central to the geologist's narration of the primordial as to medieval imaginings of the distant past), rendering the millennium an effective unit of measure is only relatively easier than parceling geology's million-year spans. Exceeding a human lifespan, centuries are difficult enough. Painting a caveman into portraits of dinosaurs is a nearly irresistible impulse, even though we know such creatures never coexisted. The Cambrian era is remarkable for its proliferation of multicellular creatures, but its watery lifefields did not contain anything like human beings, so most people have trouble distinguishing the period from the Permian, Jurassic, and Cretaceous. Although temporal extension is better measured through the lives of rocks than animals, we yearn to insert a familiar observer to make their depths more intimate, to render time a persisting, living, and knowable impingement rather than an estranging force. We employ whatever conceptual tools we have at hand in this process of fashioning a convergence for human and inhuman scales, inevitably finding ourselves challenged by time's profundity to narrative invention, to frustrated geologic embrace.

To touch stone is to encounter alien duration. Medieval writers trained in the study of the Christian bible knew this fact with the same certainty as contemporary scientists and philosophers. Attempting to think petrocentrically, the thirteenth-century scientist, theologian, and philosopher Albertus Magnus wrote that stones are mortal, in that they perish when viewed within their indigenous temporality. Because lithic time proceeds so much more slowly, a great many years must pass before a human will realize a stone has lost its vitality:

> For minerals in their own way suffer death just as animals do; but the loss
> of their essential being is not noticed unless the change is very great. For
> a "dead" *saphirus* still retains its colour, transparency and shape just like a
> "live" one . . . but after a long-drawn-out change it grows dull and begins
> to disintegrate. . . . And the same terms, "live" and "dead," are applicable
> to gold, silver, and other minerals.[10]

Stone is long lasting but not eternal. Geologists likewise tell us that rock was the earth's first solid, the planet's most venerable denizen—but none of that primordial element remains, having met its death through forces like subduction, the drowning of stone in sea and fire as the tectonic plates grind over each other. In the Hebrew bible dry earth appears on the third day of creation, while humans arrive on the sixth. After their expulsion from Eden, these ambulatory latecomers will take some time to overspread their new terrain. They are compelled to begin their colonization anew after the purging Flood.[11] The story is ancient: history is allied with the restless, noisy, and often ruinous flux of water and fire. Stone, however, is the material that endures: not indifferent to cataclysm but marked by its force, thereby carrying narrative through perilous spans.[12] Recent volcanic creations aside, stone's origins stretch back billions of years according to cosmological reckoning. An origin date of 4004 BCE for the earth is the most famous calculation based on the Genesis narrative, but this strangely precise number was derived by James Ussher in the seventeenth century. The biblical literalism associated with Protestant fundamentalism was not the dominant technique for understanding scripture during the Middle Ages. Keen explicators of metaphor and allegory, medieval interpreters of the bible stressed the symbolic and the typological. The seven days of creation were not necessarily assumed to be human spans, especially because three of these days preceded the creation of the sun, and divine time was unlikely to coincide with mortal reckoning. Calculation of the earth's age varied widely. According to the fourteenth-century poem *Piers Plowman,* creation took place "seuene thousand" years ago (line 309), while the Middle English *Gospel of Nicodemus* places the span from *fiat lux* to present day at 5,500 years. The monk Bede (d. 735) calculated the time between Adam and Jesus as 3,852 years, while the church fathers Eusebius and Jerome placed the number at 5,198. Though Genesis was the primary narrative through which the writers of the Middle Ages understood their earliest history, a coexisting tradition deriving from Hesiod and Boethius described a bygone Golden Age. Like Eden, it was both better than the current era and irremediably lost.[13] Some Aristotelians like Jean Buridan in the fourteenth century conceptualized the earth, like heaven, as eternal rather than finite.[14]

A founding assumption of most scholarship on deep time is that the nineteenth-century discovery of stone's antiquity precipitated a "time revolution."[15] On one side of this sudden divide stand those whose relation to prehistory is comfortably mediated by myth, their world bounded and snug. On the other are those whose awareness of geological profundity alienates them from history, troubles their relationship to the earth they inhabit, and activates their imaginations. Rock becomes the catalyst without which we never would have left comfortable medieval frames. Although Martin J. S. Rudwick stresses that in the discovery of geohistory science and religion were complicated partners, he provides as his illustration for life before geological time's challenge to human self-assurance a moment in the seventeenth century when Thomas Browne nonchalantly declares that "Time we may comprehend, 'tis but five days elder than ourselves."[16] Rudwick contrasts Browne's glib assertion to a prehistory that we now know stretches almost infinitely backward. Our creative powers are strained as we are called upon to envision remote epochs filled with extinct monsters, the vagrancy of continents, and an oxygen-deprived world in which asteroids trigger massive upheavals. Temporal constriction had likewise to be split wide (Rudwick's book is titled *Bursting the Limits of Time*), an explosion that triggers the extinction of fantasies of divine providence.

Everything changed once fossils were revealed as dinosaurs, once secular facts rocked biblical stabilities. Yet geology describes the deep past with a vocabulary and narrative structure derived from Greek myth, Genesis, and medieval romance. Though irresistibly quotable, Thomas Browne's incurious flippancy is unusual and cannot stand for preceding history. Contrary to any "rupture narrative" (as Kellie Robertson labels overly enthusiastic and impossibly tidy historical periodizations), medieval conceptions of prehistory were never so casual, never so unperturbed.[17] Temporal frames may have stretched back thousands of years rather than millions, but time's vastness taxed the imagination, triggering anxiety as well as an uncannily familiar creativity. Every historical period works with the conceptual tools it inherits but is never bound by that heritage to the replication of that which is already known. Living before the scientific and social revolutions Rudwick details, medieval people did not populate their prehistory with pterosaurs and mammoths, but they knew through these creatures' bones the archaic lives of dragons and giants. The author of the *Book of John Mandeville* writes of the port of Jaffa in the Holy Land:

> And you will understand that it is the oldest town of the world, for it was built before Noah's Flood. And there are bones from giants' sides that are forty feet long.[18]

Medieval authors may not have imagined extinction by asteroid-propelled fire, but they were enraptured by the watery cataclysm of the Deluge and an apocalypse of flame to come. Noah's Flood was legible in the fossil record, replete with the bones of those giants that Genesis asserted had walked the early earth.[19] Even the universalizing and supposedly short chronological framework of the Genesis story has its textual strata, fossils, provocations to dreaming the inhuman, and unexpected geological depths.[20]

Geology and Genesis do not offer two versions of the same story. One is cut from restless infinity; the other was understood in the Middle Ages to be bound by eternity's stationary perfection. Both, however, share deep affinities, including inassimilable temporal vastness and arrangement around punctuated catastrophe. Both are conveyed by the primordiality of stone, its astonishing temporal density. Something potentially propulsive unfolds within both frames at the moment of contact between mortal flesh and lithic substantiality: the advent of a disorienting realization, no matter how dimly perceived, that stone's time is not ours, that the world is not for us, even as material continuity becomes palpable. We grasp the antediluvian, figuratively or literally, and realize that we are fleeting, that this place supposed to be a home is too ancient and enduring for domestication, that in stone modernity touches the primeval. The earthly residence of many stones extends, according to geologists, billions of years. Medieval writers, too, saw in petric depths a glimpse of the first moments of creation. Albertus Magnus writes that "stones are not far removed from the elements" and their materiality has "very little altered" (*Book of Minerals*, 1.1.5). To palm a rock is to press flesh against the first moments of time. Albertus therefore associates the production of stones with coldness and espies in their primordial purity a frozen elementality. In a simple gem is condensed inestimable temporal protraction. For a medieval beholder, a ruby might compact a history that stretches to Eden. The Sloane Lapidary describes emerald: "It is greene & it cometh from the Streame of Paridis."[21] Diamonds and amethysts compress for us an epochality that demands the imagination of migratory continents indifferent to apes to come. Though their extension differs greatly, biblical and geologic temporalities share inhuman scale.

When solitary years are traded for aeonic durations, the still earth becomes vibrant. That which was static springs into life. Rock slides, seeps, grinds, infiltrates, engulfs, transforms, insists. Rising as mountains (geological formations that even classical authors described as growing upward from their roots) or burgeoning as gems, stone accrues in epochal strata, tumbles with glaciers, plunges deep under the sea in sheets, and ascends later as peaks veined with marine souvenirs.[22] Mineralizing what had been organic life, compressing traces of multiple times into heterogeneous aggregates or metamorphic novelties, rock also bends like plastic so that ephemeral humans may sculpt a lithic whorl or devise a temple of a thousand years' duration. The baleful Green Chapel where the beheading game that structures *Sir Gawain and the Green Knight* culminates may or may not be the work of human hands. Perhaps a decrepit church or ruined shrine, its description also suggests a pre-Christian holy place, possibly Thor's Cave, a limestone cavern in Staffordshire used in the late Neolithic for burials, or Lud's Church, a mossy gorge that possesses an extensive human history.[23] In a way it does not matter if masons or geology fabricated the structure since humans and rocks have a habit of imitating each other's work, of creating homologous spaces. Given the obsession in *Sir Gawain and the Green Knight* with landscapes, animals, and other manifestations of the nonhuman, no wonder the Green Chapel is at once a dire mound where the grinding of a lethal axe echoes, a crag where red blood trickles onto white snow, and a hybrid locale where terror at the prospect of impending death yields to an invitation to celebration. "Make myry [merry] in my hous!" the formerly monstrous Green Knight declares after Gawain has completed his testing,[24] an affirmation of humane connection after the verdant half-giant has revealed himself to be Sir Bertilak, ordinary knight and amenable host.

Storied Matter

Stone conjures spans that transient humans cannot witness and yet are called upon, anxiously, to narrate. We crave apocalypse and its oblivions because they suit our small historical frames: there is comfort in the tidy closure they yield. We have always lived in end times because climaxes that happen for us reassure that we are protagonists rather than actors in a non-anthropocentric tale. Stone's stories, though, are more intimate, affective, and creative than such stark differences in endurance imply. Geology and geohistory are one response to thinking lithic extensiveness. The magnificent opening sequence of the book of Genesis is another.

Most human vestiges from the time before writing survive because their substance is rock (axe, statue, windbreak) or because they have petrified (bone, body, footprints): the lithic trace as lingering testament both to erasure and to endurance, a "material connection" to spur narrative.[25] Such relics are a minor miracle of persistence, a protracted feat of object self-assertion.[26] The Stone Age indicates through rocky reference a time without text. John Lubbock coined the term "prehistory" in 1865 to describe this preliterate past, the archive of which is readable only through durable things. Lubbock observed that "memorials of antiquity have been valued as monuments of ancient skill and perseverance," but not as "pages of ancient history."[27] When "real" history requires written documents, then nontextual archives have trouble imparting story. The centuries flatten into dull and homogeneous progression, denied their messy and nonlinear vectors.[28] When we assume as self-evident a temporal partitioning between deep and more recent history, we divide the world into solitary segments, silencing conversation across a gap of our own devising.[29]

It could be objected that no medieval writer spoke of prehistory since, strictly speaking, a time before writing did not exist. All history must be recorded in Genesis, beginning with the divine speech act of "Be light made" (Genesis 1:3). Biblical history, however, is more complicated than that, especially as that history was enlivened by accretions of commentary like traditions of Christian glossing and Jewish Midrashim. Even though the Genesis narrative is routinely disparaged by contemporary scholars as offering a chronological scale that is "shallow" and "short," medieval writers found in its millennia the roiling of uncertain depths, a temporal immensity that required new "narrative and reconstructive story-telling."[30] Such stories arise in collaboration with objects that are actively engaged in time's production, like the tools fashioned by humans discovered in the nineteenth century in the same strata as the remains of extinct animals. With their resounding declaration that humans are a species of long endurance, stone bifaces and axes assisted in bringing about the Time Revolution through which chronologies of Eden and the Flood opened to wider pasts. Held by human hands or not, these stone implements are persistent actors as well as magnets for story. The networked and distributed agency of ancient lithic objects is just as evident when the prehistory being imagined involves time spans measured in quadruple digits rather than sextuple. Such traces of the past may not be tools embedded in gravel, but they will still be familiar: fossils, tombs, Neolithic architectures. The stories such objects hold suggest that rock is a perpetual catalyst, summons, force. A primal element, stone invites us to gigantic temporal frames, to spaces populated by vast figures who seem monstrous but reveal a surprising intimacy. It compels us to ponder our brevity and intensifies our desire to send messages to far futures, inciting creativity, spurring art. Medieval people were just as capable of responding to lithic provocation to deep time, to dreaming the prehistoric and the inhuman, intimations of lost realms. To lay hand upon stone is to press against time in material form. Although the experience will to some mean nothing, engendering neither sensation nor thought, to others that same touch can be kinetic, productive, disorienting.

Contemporary stories of stone envision an ancient earth in constant motion, seas that inundate continents, and beasts that were it not for the assurances of paleontologists would scarcely be believable. Medieval writers used the historical frame provided by the bible likewise to envision an ancient earth in constant motion, inundating seas, and creatures preserved in stone that were it not for the assurances of theologians and authoritative texts would scarcely be believable. Triggers to lithic adventure arrive in the form of artifacts, architectures, and fossils.[31] Roger Caillois described fossils as life forms that learned to "domesticate" minerals into vertebrae and shells now "restored to the immobility they once renounced."[32] Yet fossils remain rock in motion. Classical and medieval texts are full of stones that are clearly the hardened remains of once organic substances. They are not typically apprehended as petrified plants and animals but as indices of the liveliness stone retains. An ostracite was a mineralized oyster, while the *lapis judaicus* ("Jew's stone," from its supposed origin in Judea) referred to fossilized sea urchin spines.[33] *Langues de serpents* (serpent tongues) were stones capable of detecting poison in nearby foods. According to surviving inventories, England's Edward I and Edward III each owned five ("quinque lingue serpentine," "cynk langes de serpentz") in their jewel collections. Often mounted in silver settings, *langues de serpents* were likely fossilized teeth or prehistoric arrowheads.[34] Among the goods and "juelx" repossessed from the rebel John Cade in 1450 was "a bitore's clee harneysid," possibly the claw of the fabulous beast called the bicorn, more likely the petrified tooth of a shark.[35] Toadstone *(borax)* may also have been a shark's tooth, and those stones with whole "toads" within them were likely fossil trilobites.[36] Boccaccio wrote of a giant's skeleton discovered in Sicily in 1342 and exhibited in a local church as the bones of the cyclops Polyphemus.[37] The *Liber monstrorum* speaks of ancient giants so enormous that they could cross the sea on foot. Their bones, we are told, are often spotted on coastlines and discovered in caves ("quorum ossa in litoribus et in terram latebris").[38] The little church of St. John the Baptist in Tredington is known for its wooden tower, twelfth-century architectural plan, stone benches, and the fossil of an ichthyosaurus displayed upon the floor of its porch.[39] Albertus Magnus spent some of his life in Paris and noticed that the limestone used in its buildings often sported "many small holes shaped like the shells which some people call moonshells *[lunares]*" (*Book of Minerals,* 1.1.3). Peering into amber, he beheld the preserved remains of ancient insects and correctly guessed that they had been climbing on trees dripping "tears" of resin, thereby becoming time capsules.[40] Cracking a petrified egg, Albertus found what appears to be a dinosaur: "with its body curled up like a chick . . . a fine figure of a serpent with crest and wings, and its feet were shaped like those of a fowl." Albertus Magnus does not worry what sort of creature this egg has revealed, the gift of petric generation rather than a once living creature. What matters is, simply, that "such forms are sometimes shaped by nature" (2.3.1). Often the signs of deep time were reduced by medieval scientific writing into small temporal frames. The fossilized remains of shellfish Albertus glimpses in the limestone of Parisian buildings are for him animal life produced within the stone itself. The effect of envitalizing moisture rolled within a lithic coil, these animals perished as their generative water evaporated, so that stone in

Albertus's account contains a miniature and rather unbalanced ecosystem where life burgeons, thrives for a while, and then disappears into its long archive. Like the philosopher Ibn Sīnā before him, Albertus also recognizes that stones sometimes contain what we would label true fossils,

> the figures of animals inside and outside. For outside they have an outline, and when they are broken open, the shapes of the internal organs are found inside. (*Book of Minerals,* 1.2.8)

These are the preserved remains of bodies, transmuted into rock through "mineralizing force." Nature's power to petrify is confirmed, Albertus adds, in the story of the Gorgon, who transformed into stone those who met her gaze.

Objects that linger into the medieval present from time immemorial are just as eloquent. Albertus Magnus writes of thunder axes, stones discovered embedded in other materials that are "thin and sharp on one side." Likely Neolithic tools and weapons, these survivals from prehistory made Albertus dream that clouds might be machines for producing what human hands also fashion.[41] Prehistoric structures likewise induce narrative. The dragon in *Beowulf* slumbers atop a hoard of precious objects in a mound (*beorh*) built by a vanished nation. Beowulf's cremated remains will be laid to rest within a similar earthwork. Such barrows recall the manifold inhumation structures of early Britain: the cairns, mounds, and chamber tombs of the Romans, Britons, Anglo-Saxons, and myriad prehistoric peoples of the island. Crumbled architectures of stone also feature in the Old English version of "ruin porn": fragmented walls or the remains of indeterminate masonry frozen into aesthetic objects for contemporary contemplation. Yet the *ubi sunt* topos that underlies such meditations also propels a peopling of such traces with history come to life. In elegies like "The Wanderer" and "The Ruin" fallen stone and derelict foundation become again a mead hall, a place of warm community that erupts from the past into the cold and solitary present.

The Neolithic, Bronze Age, and Iron Age mounds that still dot Britain and Ireland feature prominently in medieval narrative. They impress themselves into story, often proffering entrance to the otherworld. Some may have been appropriated into Arthurian myth long before England assimilated those tales.[42] Marie de France's lay *Yonec* describes how a woman follows her otherworldly lover through a portal into a hill or barrow, where a crystalline world awaits. The sensuously curved art of ancient Newgrange reappears in Christian sculpture and the Book of Kells.[43] Geoffrey of Monmouth's idea that Stonehenge was erected as a memorial to 460 dead British nobles may have been inspired by the fact that the Neolithic monument is surrounded by about that many ancient burial mounds.[44] These enigmatic barrows exert their stony presence, insistently intruding. The same impingement is true of other prehistoric monuments, whether singular menhir or rings of standing stones. The twenty-five-foot tall Rudston Monolith looms beside a Norman church in Yorkshire. Despite its seemingly Christian name ("rud" is Old English for "cross"), the megalith has stood in that sacred spot for 3,600 years, rendering its ecclesiastical neighbor quite a latecomer. Dinosaur tracks are visible along its side. In his comprehensive *Historia Anglorum* (ca. 1130) the English historian Henry of Huntingdon is the first writer to mention Stonehenge, which he lists as the second marvel of the island. The "stones of remarkable size," he writes, are raised like gateways.[45] Declaring the ring a wonder, Henry confides that no one can conceive how the stone was lifted so high, or why the structure should have been created, and so his lithic portals do not offer passage into story—even as his provision of a name for the architecture in English *(Stanenges)* demonstrates that it had been noticed long before he, a historian living after the Norman Conquest, writes so evocatively of its doorways. Powerful narratives erupted when medieval people encountered their lithic inheritance. Sometimes this heritage is bequeathed through geological processes and alterations to the landscape, creating inhuman art. Sometimes this bequest arrives from unknown people who through their building projects were able to convey to the distant future a record of their having inhabited the island. These stories composed with stone speak across vast durations, although at times their messages are difficult to hear, a writing without words.[46] Such nonlinguistic texts were apprehended in ways that mediated and transformed them.

Although classical myth could be invoked, most understandings of primeval history unfolded within the narrative frame provided by the bible. The world before and immediately following Noah's Flood offered a kind of prehistory, a vague and possibility-laden landscape that beckoned the imagination. Although in most accounts the scouring rush of waters erased all human narrative not recorded in Genesis, some writers imagined that extrabiblical communication might have crossed that catastrophic demarcation. Typically this preservation is enabled by stone's power to persist across cataclysm, to far outlive its human co-dwellers. Medieval narratives about the lithic communication device known as Stonehenge also suggest that in more secular and less catastrophic modes of history human meaning can likewise be transported across epochs, enabling cross-temporal contact, geological thinking, unexpected stories.

This story now moves to northern Africa, where a Christian bishop living in the aftermath of the devastation of Rome wanders the sea's edge and discovers what appears to have been a fossil tooth. An object both living and dead, this fragment of history invites Augustine of Hippo to narrate a tale about catastrophe, giants, and the insistence of stone.

Beachcombing

As Albertus Magnus knew well, rock colonizes the ephemeral through mineral embrace. Dragons and giants, monsters universal to the human imagination, likely owe their ubiquity to the remains of prehistoric animals.[47] Fossils allure. The entrance to a Neolithic chambered tomb at Stoney Littleton in Somerset incorporates a fossil ammonite of great size into its portal. The swirl of the enormous shell looks as if it has been impressed upon the slab. The interior of the long barrow is constructed of rocks abounding in similar organisms. What precise meaning this petric art held for the builders of the structure we cannot know, but they likely found it beautiful, perhaps sacred, certainly resonant with what they were attempting when they erected so prodigal an architecture.[48] A fragment of fossilized ammonite was discovered in a prehistoric barrow at Rudstone, while petrified echinoids were found in a Dunstable Downs barrow, and fossil shells have been retrieved from dolmens in France.[49] Greek and Latin texts and painted vases indicate familiarity with the remains of extinct creatures. Even if they were not understood to be intrusions from deep time, such survivals were known to be ancient. Suetonius notes in his biography of Augustus Caesar that the emperor furnished his country homes as if they were natural history museums, displaying "objects notable for their great age and rarity, such as the enormous bones of huge monsters and beasts from Capri, which were said to be the bones of giants, and the weaponry of heroes."[50] Great size signifies for this Roman ruler temporal depth, an insight that may derive from Homer and Hesiod, both of whom speak of a primal age of giants. Classical writers used available mythologies to understand fossil intrusions, domesticating them (Augustus exhibits enormous bones as decorations in his vacation homes), but acknowledging as well their exorbitance, their irreducible otherness, their arrival from beyond known history. The disruptive effect of discovering a "monster from deep time" (as Martin J. S. Rudwick memorably phrases it) and the ability of a fossilized survival to extend the imagination and generate story are not reserved to geology and paleontology.[51]

Intrusions from the pretextual past also include the fragments of fallen cities, graves and monuments, the ruins of forgotten habitations, durable signifiers of vanished community, nonlinguistic messages replete with possibility. Though an immense historical gap might separate an observer from such remains, story arises at the moment of stony encounter, a narrative that must be in part about how lithic materiality conveys time's depths, sending something forward into years to come, and pulling the present backward through material contact. Such encounter sensuously bridges moments that might otherwise remain disjunct. A tension immediately arises, however, between a recondite object and the interpretative vocabulary of the moment into which it arrives. An inhuman traveler from the depths of time might seem doomed to speak only in the language of its most recent explicator, so that every advent becomes flattened translation. Yet even when time capsules like stone circles, burial mounds, dinosaur bones, and bodies recovered from bogs become reusable materials, museum exhibits, or sacred objects—even when they are enfolded into narratives in no way their own—they remain polychronic agents, participants within an unfolding world. Conveying a density of temporal possibility, these objects open a responsive companion to a widened vision of the past's own thriving. That message is not always heard. Numerous stone rings still stand today in Brittany, Ireland, and Britain, collating millennia of varied uses and shifting participations in rituals, cosmological imaginings, building projects, and stories. Many more have been toppled and pulverized, so that their rubble could be reused. Despite its material assertiveness, stone is a precarious conveyor.

Lithic-propelled temporal entanglement is well illustrated in the work of Augustine, fourth-century bishop of Hippo and accidental fossil hunter. In the fifteenth book of the *City of God* Augustine is ruminating upon Genesis. He emphasizes the difference between exiled Cain, who founded the first human city and named the dwelling for his son, and Abel, a pilgrim who built nothing earthly, since he knew the only lasting habitation is celestial (*City of God,* 15.1). The survival of manmade architectures does not much interest Augustine—an unsurprising emphasis, considering Rome's recent despoliation and the trauma that the fall of this world-orienting metropolis engendered.[52] Heaven renders Rome unnecessary. Celestial eternity outweighs whatever past the fragments of some earthly habitation might reveal.[53] God, angels, and dead humans (as souls) dwell for Augustine wholly outside time's sequentiality. Eternity is not infinity but an absolute exteriority to the temporal: time begins at the moment of creation, but eternity is indifferent to commencements and terminations. All history and all materiality therefore constitute a potentially apprehensible unity. Particular stories fade from this atemporal, divine point of view, a summit's perspective that is attained, for the virtuous, only after death.

Here on earth, stone is for Augustine an effective conveyor of history's extensiveness, especially in the calcified form of primeval bone.[54] Arguing against those who scoff at the immense life spans recorded in Genesis, Augustine insists that before the Flood not only did people live longer, they possessed larger bodies. He muses upon a passage from Virgil's *Aeneid* in which a massive rock used as a boundary marker tells an enduring story about the size of the man who once hefted its bulk (*City of God,* 15.9). He repeats the naturalist Pliny's assertion that humans dwindled in size as the world aged. Those incredulous at our former gigantism, Augustine states, may find ample proof in ancient skeletons "since bones are very durable." He speaks of convulsive forces that disclose messages sealed in rock and sent from a monumental era:

Tombs [are] uncovered by the action of time, or by the violence of storms or various other accidents. Bones of incredible size have come to light in them, or have fallen out of them. (*City of God,* 15.9)

These ancient, intrusive bones demand narrative enfleshing. Stories proliferate. Thoughts of the antediluvian earth trigger a personal anecdote: stone,

the most impersonal of substances, has an uncanny power to elicit autobiography. While walking the sea's edge with his companions, Augustine
discovers a missive from a vanished epoch, a letter that crosses catastrophe:

> On the shore at Utica I myself saw—and I was not alone but in the com-
> pany of several others—a human molar so immense that if it had been cut
> up into pieces the size of our teeth it would, it seemed to us, have made
> a hundred. But that tooth I should imagine, belonged to some giant. For
> not only were the bodies of men in general much larger at that time than
> ours are now, but the giants far exceeded all the rest. (*City of God,* 15.9)

Before Noah's Flood all people were immense, and larger still were the giants born among them. The gift of graves or tides, fragments of a primordial era intrude into Augustine's age, declaring through the "proof of such
material evidence" (*City of God,* 15.9) that the world was not always as it is
now, not even in magnitude. Size for Augustine is duration. He cannot prove
that ancient peoples measured their lives in centuries, but their sepulchral
remains declare temporal as well as corporeal extension.

Like his classical predecessors, Augustine understood the prodigious
bones that to us impart stories of vanished dinosaurs to archive a similarly
astonishing story of scale. Disgorged from ancient tombs, washed from
marine depths by tempestuous forces, these giants' leavings become hard
evidence that humans dwindled as the earth aged. We might discern in
these remains evidence of prehistory, labeling the enormous molar from
Utica beach the tooth of a mammoth or some prehistoric leviathan, telling
a story of ice floes and climatic catastrophe. Augustine used the histories
available to him to interpret the object as an artifact from a different lost
world, the earth before the Deluge, just as marked by cataclysm. The tooth
still bears witness to a monster's presence, but for Augustine that creature
connects more intimately to the human present. The antediluvian postcard
declares contemporary humans to be weakened things, dwellers at a cosmic
twilight. Augustine at Utica beach examines a fossil tooth and discovers
that the passing of time is unceasing diminishment. The age of the patriarchs has ended, the era of the Greeks and Romans is fading, eternal Rome
has fallen to Alaric's rapacious Visigoths. Augustine stands at the close of
an era and elegizes its passing, retaining faith in a better time that was, a
better day to come.[55] The molar stands at once for a lost garden in paradise

and a vanishing Roman world. Latin learning lingers, now preserved within the amber of Christian doctrine like *The City of God*: a remnant of *temps perdu*, a past truly passed. Though superseded, that history is not wholly inert. As a reduced and fractured object, it intrudes into Augustine's present and urges him to dream connections among Homer, Virgil, Pliny, and the Genesis account of world-obliterating Deluge.

Contemporary scholars of Genesis describe its narrative in geological terms, detailing strata, describing the sedimentation of multiple authorships, discordant stories, and alternative realities. Could the giant's molar have opened Augustine to a geological vision of the past: nonlinear, too full to be reduced to simple forward movement, thick with alluvium that when probed loosens and starts again to flow? Could the fossil remnant have somehow fragmented worldly preconception, offered a challenging narrative, some alternate possibility, prograde and retrograde at once? The fossil is used by Augustine to shatter the beliefs of others: it proves to those who have never seen giants and to those who doubt the long life spans of the patriarchs that the past holds rather different stories from what they suppose. Was it not also possible for the tooth, explosive to the time-sense of those who doubt the epochal scale of biblical narrative (and prehistoric bodies), to transmit to Augustine something other than the confirmation of his own system of thought? Augustine's philosophical ambit is at once capacious and rather fixed. The tooth was as unlikely to be recognized as a message from something like paleontology's deep time as could a knowledge arrive that the divinities YHWH and El might have fused to form a single god in the course of the composition of the Jewish scriptures, or that Genesis offers two distinct versions of the creation story and seems to have had multiple authors with incongruous agendas.

Augustine conceptualized time as a bounded phenomenon within which the living are entrapped.[56] Humans perceive a progress of the ages, an illusory movement when viewed from the immobile perspective of eternity. Their fate as fallen and mortal creatures is to order into seriality that which for God is not a historical chain and possesses no depth. For Augustine any notion of prehistory must therefore stop at Eden. The antediluvian world is as close as he can get to geology's deep time. Even then, the only message that can be sent across the divide cut by the Flood is that humans used to be greater in size and duration. The book of Genesis emphasizes the utter destructiveness of the water that pours from heaven's gates and surges from the fountains of the deep. Nothing remains after inundation:

universa quae in terra sunt consumentur.
[All things that are in the earth shall be consumed.] (6:17)

delebo omnem substantiam quam feci de superficie terrae.
[I will destroy every substance that I have made from the face of the earth.] (7:14)

The Deluge cascades and swells for forty days, while aquatic dominance endures one hundred and fifty (7:24). All lands are wiped clean; all things must begin again. No fossil or other object can contain a story that is not collapsible into this time frame, into this history that can be measured in sorrowful generations. The same must therefore hold true for ancient architectures like stone circles or the ruins of cities: they cannot convey a narrative other than the temporally circumscribed one Augustine expounds. Within this historical sequence little room exists for heterogeneity, for times, places, or narratives out of sync with the dominating story of decline and redemption. Ancient graves that wash open to yield an extrabiblical tale of gigantism are a small exception and may with some exertion be assimilated.

Perhaps.

Who Grieves for Lindow Man?

I had gone to the British Museum early to view the remodeled Prehistory exhibit before crowds thronged. I filled my notebook with observations about objects as temporal archives, the use of light and shadow to elicit affective response, and the semiotics of the placement of the nameless dead. When my family arrived I was hunched over the darkened glass case housing the remains of Lindow Man, the gift of the anaerobic environment into which the body was hurled at a time when Rome held much of Britain. "Cool!" declared my son of the preserved corpse, fragmented by a peat harvesting machine but uncannily lifelike after two thousand years. Three-year-old Katherine meanwhile gazed into the sepulchral case that houses his remains, and her eyes grew large.

"Is he going to be OK?" she whispered.

"No," replied her brother confidently. "He's dead."

"I don't want him to be dead," she said. "I want him to be OK."

"We all die. He's dead. He isn't going to get any better."

Alex's announcement of the body's irremediable stillness wounded her. "I want Lindow Man to be OK. I don't want him to be dead." These last repetitions were accompanied by tears, shaking, a loss of words. The corpse was too final, too blunt.

Before his death Lindow Man was savagely beaten. He was strangled with a cord, his throat then slit.[57] Now he is encased in glass, the resident of a museum display where hundreds stare at his head, torso, and arm every day, remarking on how uncannily alive he seems. Lindow Man is the third most popular item in the British Museum, after two lithic trophies of empire, the Rosetta Stone and Elgin Marbles. He would appear to be just as much an object as those rocks. Peering into the glass case at that still form, Katherine began to perceive that no matter how much we love our families and our lives, no matter how safe we think our world, all lives end, and most do not end well. The scale of our earthly duration is short, difficult, limned with violence. Holding her close and running my hand through her hair, I wondered if she was the first to mourn for Lindow Man, wondered if Lindow Man was worth her tears.

The Life of the Past

After a thorough renovation of the display housing his remains, Lindow Man is exhibited in artfully arranged mimicry of an open grave. Low lighting and a bed of earth-colored material beneath the corpse suggest that visitors have intruded into sacred space. Through sensory cues and informative plaques the solemn presentation transforms the mummified cadaver into story. As memento mori Lindow Man tells a tale of death, the inevitable end of each of his observers. He also incarnates a narrative with life: the endurance of the past, even as brutal history. Standing before what appears to be an opened grave it is difficult for a medievalist not to remember the tear of Bishop Erkenwald. When the tear's moisture accidentally touches a disinterred cadaver, the bishop releases an unbaptized soul into heaven. Erkenwald's affective and material response binds the living and the dead in story. Much remains unrecoverable: we never learn the corpse's name, we never get to read the mysterious letters around his tomb. We are left with partial narratives, messy fragments. Perhaps the best we can do, then, is to refuse to petrify bodies into objects, and objects into inert incarnations of unchanging historical moments. Stones and corpses too often figure the immobility attached to the time, a stillness that at its worst can render interpretation an exercise in transfixion. Without a phenomenological awareness of the constant interaction of that which is time bound and that which is greater than any small history, that which might even cross inhuman temporal gaps, human lives are too easily reduced to mere matter, and matter fixed into immobility.

Yet the archeologist Christopher Tilley has argued that dynamic interrelations of body, space, and matter are palpable during any encounter with monumental stone.[58] The prehistoric architectures of Brittany, he writes, are living phenomena that orient those who move through them, producing in concert with the surrounding landscape embodied sensation. Dolmens and stone rings are orientation devices experienced by bodies in motion, structuring affective response.[59] Their materiality is not invariable but changes in color, texture, sensual resonance, and corporeal power according to time of day, weather, season. Standing stones are not static objects for contemplation but creators of lived space where a present mobilizes a past. Stone orients story. Tilley returns frequently to the difference between the "brute materiality" of rock, indifferent to human relation, and the cultural relations into which it is placed as a built environment. As Bjørnar Olsen has pointed out in his critique of Tilley's phenomenological method, however, when the situation of the human body relative to the experienced landscape is the privileged relation, the material world becomes more conceptual than solid.[60] Tim Ingold argues that although Tilley gets at what is dynamic in stone, his separation of materiality from social life needlessly divides humans from a world they do not simply inhabit but with which they are coextensive.[61] Stone propels embodied and dynamic encounter that may well be *disorienting*. That loss of bearing need not be corrected by immediate mooring in human exceptionalism. Avebury, Carnac, Stonehenge expand the world by enmeshing observers, participants, and wanderers, engendering organic-material collision and collusion (as well as material-material collisions and collusions) without necessary hierarchies. The experience of such unexpected motion—of being hit by the enduring stoniness of stone and its declaration of the abidingness of story—can displace human perspective, make it veer. Temporality might then be apprehended in animated, geological terms. The past is as lively and unpredetermined as the Now, the Next, and the Yet to Come. Because stone persists so long, its material intrusion into any given time will carry multiple histories, a durable cache of aggregated story. Stone carries forward within its solidity mineral seams, fossils, enfolded strata, stripes of sediment involuted by tectonic force, alluvial deposits, inscriptions from rivers, from glaciers, from human hands. Stone conveys into present simultaneity the lingering traces of its promiscuous companionships. As trigger to making—hammer, mortar and pestle, axe—it supports foundation and spurs construction, all the while remaining untimely. The built world is forever in progress, vectored at once toward amalgamation, ruination, and renewal.

This vertigo of disrupted ontologies was as possible for Augustine as for any other intimate of stone.[62] The bishop of Hippo lived in a world where the veneration of Isis coexisted with the worship of the Christian triune God, and the immortality of the soul described by Plato offered a different version of time from the book of Genesis, with its *in principio* and six days of creation's orderly unfolding. Christian doctrine was actively being made. Examining the bones of giants that may for us be the bodies of primeval monsters, fingering a tooth that might have belonged to a mammoth or extinct aquatic carnivore, Augustine could not have dreamed dinosaurs. Yet he did not have to fold these lithic leavings back so quickly into a story of human diminishment. The lives of giants read from their persisting remains suggests wider possibilities and an irreducibly larger world. When the sixteenth-century antiquarian John Stow discovers Hebrew writing incorporated into a London wall, the alien characters make the past differently legible, as multitemporal palimpsest: "stony, dead Jewish matter" bursts to life in a way that renders his current moment strange.[63] A palimpsest is a useful metaphor for describing time's density, especially when linguistic inscription forms the archive for excavating temporal thickness. More capacious, however, might be the sixteenth-century word *fossil*: literally, anything pulled from the ground (*fossilis*: "dug up"), but effectively any sedimented yet discordant section of textual or geological strata that, if noticed (and much hangs on that "if"), leaps into exigent narrative, into sudden and challenging life. A fossil is a time traveller and a spark, an interpenetration of epochs. It seizes the attentive observer, conveys a deep and multifaceted temporality, offers an invitation to worlds differently configured. Petrified remnants that upon excavation start moving again, a fossil that engenders relation conveys kinetic story. A palimpsest is typically the work of human hands, but a fossil prods its interpreter to abandon habitual anthropocentricity, to think about time and materiality in ways that complicate the strata in which human history is embedded, to forge strange tangents and realize disparate touchings.[64] We are conveyed by its historical summons to a perspective in which human relations are not the only measure of reality, to worldly and temporal expansiveness.

For Augustine a fossil can open a portal to an era in which humans are giants, lifespans reach astonishing durations, the world before the Flood is inhabited by people not named in the book of Genesis. These creatures bequeath bones that endure, connecting him to lost worlds. Such advent can be staggering. Like geological layers, narratives may embed dissonant fragments of their own textual prehistory that when discerned open strange portals. Take, for example, the men in Genesis who might be angels, copulating with mortal women and engendering a race of giants. The terse account follows the expulsion from Eden and multiplication of humans across the earth, and precedes the unleashing of the Deluge:

> Now giants were upon the earth in those days. For after the sons of God went in to the daughters of men, and they brought forth children, these are the mighty men of old, men of renown [*potentes a saeculo viri famosi*]. (Genesis 6:4)[65]

The meaning of the passage is obscure. It intertwines the advent of giants (Hebrew *Nephilim*) with some kind of primal miscegenation. Because the next verses describe God witnessing proliferating evil and repenting his act of creation, this passage was frequently thought to connect the Deluge to the giants. Particle of an oblique story, Genesis 6:4 is a textual fossil, the remains of what was once likely a fuller tale, now sedimented into a narrative arc into which it does not quite cohere. When noticed and pondered, it exerts disruptive power. Augustine attempts to make sense of the passage in a way that repeats the logic of his beachside encounter with the giant's tooth, but he will in the end be unable to evacuate from this restless story its monstrous allure.

Augustine believed Genesis to offer both history and allegory. The bible was for him at once true and symbolically rich, enabling even classical history to be interpreted through extension of its frame. When Romulus and Remus found Rome, they are replaying a narrative provided by city-building, fratricidal Cain (*City of God,* 15.5). Augustine's exposition of the formerly vast size of humans, confirmed in beachcombing, quietly suggests that sometimes the past does not merely affirm the present, but arrives dissonantly, opening that moment to something new—even if that novelty is simply the knowledge that a record written in bone offers something that Genesis does not. This durable fragment eventually leads Augustine to a meditation on giants.[66] Rather than a separate race, he notes, giants are very large humans born from time to time to normally proportioned parents. He gives the example of a woman dwelling in Rome just before the Goths destroy the city. She lived with her unremarkable mom and dad and was so tall that "an amazing crowd rushed to see her, wherever she went" (*City of God,* 15.23). Giants are intimate monsters.

Augustine insists on human origin in part because Genesis 6:4 provides the giants a possible creation story that he found intolerable. During the intermezzo between the expulsion from Eden and the punishment of Flood, something unseemly occurs among giants, daughters of men, and sons of God. The passage is one of the bible's many alternate histories, discordant little pieces of conflicting or outlying stories incorporated within but not fully assimilated by the larger narrative, holding disruptive narrative potential. Genesis hardened into an authoritative form before it could be rendered monolithic.[67] Its heterogeneous components were often ignored, but sometimes because of their patent alterity they became points of obsessive worry—and even catalysts to creativity and active engagement with a past come to sudden life. Giants born of uncertain but illicit union engendered supplementary and ultimately unorthodox visions of biblical history at least from the time of the *Book of Enoch* (second century BCE) onward.[68] Though the influence and dissemination of *Enoch* are difficult to trace, some evidence suggests that it was known in Anglo-Saxon England and may have shaped the depiction of Grendel in *Beowulf.* The *Book of Enoch* vividly describes how two hundred fallen angels fathered giants upon mortal women, with these newborn giants turning quickly to cannibalism, blood drinking, and sins against animals. The leaders of the fallen angels instruct humans in metallurgy, weapons manufacture, ornamentation, the polishing of gemstones, magic, and astrology. They impart both science and art. God will scour the earth through the Flood in order to rid it of the new monsters, the proliferation of human sin, and perhaps the dangerous knowledge and useless art imparted by the angels who were supposed to remain in heaven but fell because they loved the changeable earth.[69]

"Now giants were upon the earth in those days." This fleeting glimpse of archaic monsters either records or gives birth to an enduring tradition in which the "sons of God" who came to the "daughters of men" are, as in the *Book of Enoch,* fallen angels. They copulated with Adam's line, a miscegenation that impregnates human women with fearsome giants. Augustine, however, ridicules this story: "I cannot possibly believe that the holy angels of God could thus have fallen at that time" (*City of God,* 15.23). With its lascivious angels, perfidious monsters, and mighty men, Genesis 6:4 is a purely textual version of Augustine's discovery of alien bone on Utica's shore. Just as that ancient bone is assimilated by Augustine through his belief that it originates with a large human, so the giants of Genesis are likewise reduced to mundane beings.[70] Augustine's interpretation neutralizes through reduction all that is perturbing in the Genesis account, as well as in the more elaborate version that he knows from the *Book of Enoch* or some similar source. The Flood arrives, and human history begins anew. Yet Augustine sabotages his careful euhemerism by admitting that scripture also testifies

> that angels appeared to men in bodies of such a kind that they could not only be seen but also touched. Besides this, it is widely reported that Silvani and Pans, commonly called *incubi,* have often behaved improperly towards women, lusting after them and achieving intercourse with them. These reports are confirmed by many people, either from their own experience or from the accounts of the experience of others, whose reliability there is no occasion to doubt. . . . Hence I would not venture a conclusive statement on the question whether some spirits with bodies of air (an element that even when set in motion by a fan is felt by the bodily sense of touch) can also experience this lust and so can mate, in whatever way they can, with women, who feel their embraces. (*City of God,* 15.23)

Genesis 6:4 may not record the mating of ethereal beings and mortals, Augustine declares, but that is not to say that such elemental comminglings (airy angels with clay-wrought humans) do not occur. Angels, he observes, derive their name from Greek *angelos,* which means *nuntius* or "messenger" in Latin (*City of God,* 15.23). As these heavenly angels potentially transform into lascivious, connection-loving incubi, what messages do they bear? Can a more challenging version of this fossil story survive the purging waters that will arrive just after the passage concludes?

Augustine's humanized account of Genesis 6:4 attempted to still what seems a lively crux of earth dwellers intermixing with celestial beings, causing exorbitant creatures to arise. He reduces into mundane plot its difficult entanglement of earth, sky, and flood. This anthropomorphic interpretation of the passage dominated throughout the Middle Ages. Yet Augustine's was not the only version to endure, partly because he embedded an alternative account through the act of its rejection. Relations among fallen angels, desiring humans, and formidable giants remained a particle of alterity never wholly absorbed into orthodox doctrine, triggering unanticipated narratives, perhaps even a new genre (Merlin, who stands at that threshold where history became romance, is the son of an incubus). As a textual fossil, embedded in the strata of Genesis without being assimilated into smoothly linear narrative, the story is just as powerful as that molar from Utica that the bishop of Hippo so artfully recuperated to his vision of Christian prehistory. Augustine was unable, however, to prevent future readers from yielding to this fossil's allure. Building upon the fragmentary tale of inhuman sexual mingling and category violation that the passage seemed to offer, medieval romance traced its own primal monster, the giant, to the rape of human women by fallen angels and incubi. Many writers were untroubled by the ability of giants to cross the gap supposed to demarcate the lost world before the Flood from the one they inhabited. Others reenacted that scene of monstrous creation in their own narratives. Throughout the Middle Ages, giants arose anew because incubi cannot resist the pleasures of bodies made of something more substantial than themselves.

Textual fossils are temporal knots, embedded within narrative, ready to exert disruptive allure. Like their material counterparts, they preserve, release, and incite life. In the excess of their bodies, their violence, and their errant history, the giants offer a vision of the past in disharmony with what

Augustine beheld in his meditations while the waves broke. The bishop of Hippo preferred that the past incarnated by the object in his hand remain circumscribed, a story about human actors rather than the point at which a vigorous alternative history, petrified into assertive persistence, erupts into the present.

Stone is the stumbling block of authorial intention.

Writing across Catastrophe

In its more compliant moods, rock communicates story across the linguistically insurmountable gap separating prehistory from technologies of narrative inscription (Sumerian cuneiform, Egyptian hieroglyphics, Olmec script). Incised, painted, dressed, arranged, stone is that with which we form alliance to transmit enduring meaning. A dense substance that enfolds and conveys, the lithic inhabits a temporality in which the flow of years is slowed to epochal progression, enabling the long transmission of the messages with which it has been entrusted. Anthropologists and archeologists often derive their stories of stone nonlinguistically: ruins, petrified remnants, chips of flint speak the narratives of those who once touched their hard surfaces. Medieval writers likewise discerned in ancient architectures missives from the remote past. The encyclopedist Isidore of Seville wrote that the word *monumentum* "admonishes the mind and brings you back to mindfulness," a trigger to memory. When a monument is ignored its oblivion is a second death for the person commemorated (*Etymologies,* 15.11.1). As the Roman poet Lucan wrote long before, *etiam periere ruinae,* even ruins perish.[71] The problem that the medieval desire to receive communication across catastrophe's chasm had to surmount was that the biblical Deluge was typically understood to mark an absolute historical, ecological, and textual rupture.[72] Isidore glosses "flood" (*diluvium)* as "so named because it destroys *[delere]* everything it washes over with the scourge of its waters" (*Etymologies,* 13.22). If anything could survive the event through which God declares that he "will destroy every substance," it is stone. Here is Isidore reading the story of the Flood from its lithic record:

> The entire world was covered, everything was destroyed, there was a united expanse of sky and sea. To this day we observe evidence of this in

the stones we are accustomed to see on remote mountains, stones that have hardened with shellfish and oysters in them, and often stones that have been hollowed out by waters. (*Etymologies,* 13.23)

For Isidore fossil shells and glacial impress announce that pinnacles were once covered by sea.[73] Stone attests to a global inundation no text outside the bible's divine inspiration could have recorded and survived. When waters swirl fifteen cubits above mountaintops, all terrestrial things perish.[74] Time's clock was reset to zero and an unbridgeable epistemological rift instilled. Even though we no longer believe in the Flood we still maintain its "sense of rupture, a legacy of sacred history" when narrating the relation between the modern and the Paleolithic, with the fields of Mesopotamia now standing for lost Eden.[75]

Yet if antediluvian humans possessed any technology to communicate with their medieval descendants, people for whom this torrent wipes clean the face of the earth and obliterates with its sheer force anything not stowed in the ark, it must be rock. Through its material insistence this substance alone can realize the desires humans possess to speak across temporal profundity, to be heard across time's catastrophic obliterations. Some early Christian and medieval writers imagined that the Flood's scouring might not have been absolute. Augustine dreams ancient giants whose bones remain a discoverable invitation to story. Texts might also cross time's epochal divisions directly, as inscriptions rather than objects or structures. A witness to the sack of Jerusalem as well as a proud Roman citizen, the Jewish historian Josephus describes in the first century how the virtuous children of Seth bequeath their knowledge of astrology to the world after the Deluge by inscribing their wisdom on pillars of brick and stone:

And that their inventions might not be lost before they were sufficiently known, upon Adam's prediction that the world was to be destroyed at one time by the force of fire, and at another time by the violence and quantity of water, they made two pillars, the one of brick, the other of stone; they inscribed their discoveries on them both, that in case the pillar of brick should be destroyed by the flood, the pillar of stone might remain and exhibit those discoveries to mankind, and also inform them that there was another pillar of brick erected by them. Now this remains in the land of Siriad to this day.[76]

In Gervase of Tilbury's melodious thirteenth-century version, the story centers around Tubal, son of Lamech, despairing at Adam's prophesy that devastating flood and fire will afflict the world. Having invented music, Tubal yearns to ensure that his art will not perish in future catastrophe ("ne periret ars inuenta"). He inscribes his knowledge

> on two columns, recording the whole of it on each; one of these columns was made of marble [*marmorea*], and the other of brick [*latericia*], so that the one would not be washed away in the flood and the other would not be destroyed in the fire. Josephus tells us that the marble one is still in existence in China. (*Otia Imperialia,* 1.20)

Having survived the torrent it was built to endure, the pillar stands ready for the flames of future Apocalypse. Tubal passes along an affirmative artistic inheritance. Darker narratives also traverse this rift. Irish traditions relate how the descendants of Cain engraved their history upon monuments of stone to survive their watery deaths, carrying to the future some trace of their vanished lives. According to the theologian John Cassian (ca. 360–435), Noah's son Cham realized that he could not transport his books of arcane knowledge onto the ark and so incised his profane secrets on sheets of metal and the hardest rocks ("durissimis lapidibus").[77]

An Irish legend recorded by Gerald of Wales in the twelfth century eloquently conveys desire for stone as a material capable of transport across nonhuman spans of time. A cleric whose family was active in the colonization of the island, Gerald notes that the Irish believed Noah had a granddaughter named Caesura and that she composed a testimony that endured the Flood.[78] Realizing that she is not going to be included among those sheltered on the family ark, Caesura navigates with a fleet of ships to the world's edge. Her hope is that distant Ireland might be spared the coming inundation, since no sin had yet been committed upon its unpeopled shores. Most of her companions drown when their vessels founder. Although she arrives at her destination, Caesura perishes just before God unleashes the torrent that submerges the isle. "In spite of her cleverness," writes Gerald, "and, for a woman, commendable astuteness in seeking to avoid evil, she did not succeed in putting off the general, not to say universal, disaster."[79] He notes that her tomb survives to this day. He is puzzled, however, how the details of her biography endure. Invoking the transmission of music across the Deluge through inscription upon metal, he suggests that Caesura's tragic tale may likewise have been incised in stone or inscribed on tile, protecting the narrative from the obliterating rush so that the text could be found and preserved. A quiet and implicitly feminist protest against divine injustice, Caesura's story is poignant, with its desire for endurance beyond supernal catastrophe, for a self-directed life capable of surmounting calamitous history.

That Gerald's translation of the Irish *Cessair* into Latin *Caesura* makes her name mean "a cutting, felling, hewing, pause" (as in a line of poetry) only adds to the affective intensity of this story carved in rock, underscoring another human desire that stone elicits and amplifies: the yearning for beauty. The allure of stone—call it the lithic sublime—is primal. It is impossible to visit Stonehenge and not be struck by the grandeur of its trilithons and menhirs. The megalithic circle is a marvel of human architecture, a seeming triumph of industry over landscape. Yet the standing stones did not gain their power to entrance simply through incorporation into a human composition. The structure seems to have been inspired by naturally occurring rock formations in the Preseli Hills. Archeologists have identified these geological structures and the springs that flow in their company as ancient pilgrimage sites.[80] In the naturally occurring standing stones of the Preseli range dolerite can be found in the form of rectangular pillars, seemingly rough-hewn by some primal architect, sometimes appearing to have been positioned as an orderly line of monoliths. The Preseli stones tower over an expansive landscape of grass, lichen-encrusted boulders that appear to have been smashed by giants, and springs that are supposed to possess curative powers. The archeologist Geoffrey Wainwright calls the mountainous bluestones "a natural monument" of columns and pillars and has found ample evidence that they were venerated in Mesolithic times.[81] Many of the rocks are inscribed. This expanse of dolerite is the precise source of the oldest megaliths erected at Stonehenge, 250 miles distant. Something about the Preseli formations so impressed prehistoric beholders that ancient peoples transported eighty or so monoliths, each weighing up to four tons, to distant Salisbury Plain. Nature's architectural exorbitance called forth a human response just as excessive. The Preseli bluestones are an artwork wrought through the shifting of the landscape over tremendous spans of time, an expenditure of gravitational and climatic energies. Stonehenge is an artwork wrought through the release of energy in sinew and muscle but is also something more than a simple imitation of a natural original. Both are products of ongoing and restless forces that effloresce into enduring forms, worlds wrought with stone. Salisbury Plain and the Preseli Hills are twin showcases for lithic art. Stonehenge is a collaboration of artistic forces, human and geological.[82] Another entry into understanding the never finished, ever changing lithic wheel now called Stonehenge would be to ask: How did the bluestones of the Preseli Mountains convince prehistoric humans to carry them hundreds of miles and erect them on a grassy plain? How did the act of moving the stones and erecting them in precise patterns over time engender through lithic participation new modes of ontologically mixed community? How did the stones of Stonehenge materialize and transform the human solidarities that formed with and around them? What did generation upon succeeding generation discover in these rocks that persuaded them to keep amplifying the structure, to create new stories about it, to intensify its splendor, to sustain alliance with its monument liveliness? How distantly into the future might Stonehenge continue to communicate?

When Isidore of Seville thought as far back in time as his imagination could reach, to that moment when God declares "Let there be light" and the world shimmers into being, he was faced with the problem of naming the tongue in which that divine command was spoken, "for there were not yet any languages" (*Etymologies,* 9.1). Isidore suggests that God's earliest commands were in the single speech "that existed before the diversity of tongues," a unifying language destroyed at Babel. His meditation on how the stories of the past are conveyed across linguistic discontinuity raises the question of how to transmit narratives into a future so distant that language fails. To the dismaying problem of what tongue humans will speak ages and ages hence, Isidore can only respond "the answer is nowhere to be found" (*Etymologies,* 9.1).

Letters to the Future

Augustine meditates upon an incongruous tooth stranded on a beach, encasing the fossil in a narrative alien to its living days. His act of translation *almost* overwrites the storied object, the exegetical version perhaps of incorporating a petrified ichthyosaur into a church's artistic program and thinking the primeval fish might be fully absorbed into a symbol for Christ. As temporal palimpsests, objects convey multiple voices across millennia, a thickness of coincident meaning. Narratives of traversing the Flood through inscription on stone aside, however, medieval texts rarely imagine the communicability of nonbiblical texts across long spans of time. When they do, such messages tend to confirm the present by imaging a past that has endured so long solely to congratulate contemporary Christians. The fourteenth-century compilation of travel narratives known as the *Book of John Mandeville* speaks of a two-thousand-year-old grave found in Constantinople beneath Hagia Sophia. A body deep in this earth bears a gold plate on which is inscribed in Hebrew, Greek, and Latin, "Jesus Christ shall be born of the Virgin Mary and I believe in him." This proto-Christian is known as Hermogenes the Wise. That his profession of faith should be incised in three languages indicates not apprehension that they might fail in their ability to communicate over so vast a time, but a confidence that the three prestige tongues will remain legible to the world's end. Some languages, it seems, are eternal. The sheet of gold that carries his trilingual inscription across millennia is metallic matter of long endurance, a signifier of value, and a hint of the alchemical knowledge with which Hermes was associated.[83] A twelfth-century historian of England and archdeacon of Lincoln, Henry of Huntingdon likewise puzzled over how far into the future written messages might endure. As he brought his great chronicle of the nation's history to its close, he considered the oblivion into which those who dwelled on his island a millennium earlier had vanished:

> I ask myself: tell me, Henry, author of this *History,* tell me, who were the archdeacons of that time? What does it matter whether they were individually noble or ignoble, renowned or unknown, praiseworthy or cast down, wise or foolish? If any of them undertook some labour for the sake of praise and glory, when now no record of him survives more than his horse or ass, why then did the wretch torment his spirit in vain? What did it avail him, who came to this? (*Historia Anglorum,* 100.3)

A thousand years is a span so immense that human history is smashed to ruin by its scale. Henry next attempts to imagine a similarly distant future. He addresses "you who will be living in the third millennium," one thousand years after his own life. He asks his readers—*us*—to contemplate the obscurity into which his own days have surely fallen (*Historia Anglorum,* 100.4). Then he continues mapping remote futures in units of a thousand years. To those who dwell upon the earth two and three millennia after himself, "if indeed mortal man survives so long," Henry makes a simple request: pray for him, now dust, and pray for all those who have likewise vanished, swallowed into time's silence. The plea is seemingly humble and yet conveys a quiet confidence that, if humans still inhabit the world three thousand years after he writes (ca. 4150 CE), they will be reading his book and enjoying his Latin.[84]

Not every medieval writer believed so confidently in linguistic endurance. In the fourteenth century, the Middle English poem *St. Erkenwald* describes the discovery of an unexpected grave during a renovation project. Masons hewing "hard stones" and miners excavating foundation for an addition to St. Paul's unearth a "meruayle" (marvel): an ancient sepulcher, its marble incised with golden letters (40–51). Though the characters clearly communicate *something,* they remain "roynyshe" (52), utterly mysterious, so that no one present can decipher their story or even sound the words in the mouth. Unlike Hermogenes with his loquacious plaque, language here fails to persist. The tomb is opened, revealing the undecayed corpse of a sumptuously dressed lawyer. Old books are searched to find some reference to this person, clearly of great importance, to no avail: the marble tomb travels into the present from lost history. Through the power of Erkenwald's prayer the dead body narrates the story of its departed soul, languishing in hell because never baptized. A tear from the saintly bishop accidentally accomplishes that sacrament, and the cadaver immediately collapses to dust, topples into history's oblivions. The story depends upon the persistence of stone (an excavation, a building project, and a tomb as a time capsule that so long as it remains unopened preserves its contents in temporal stasis). Water in the form of a bishop's tears provides the catalyst necessary to break the pagan past's petrifying hold.[85]

Working at St. Albans in the thirteenth century, the Benedictine monk Matthew Paris describes how a book was discovered at the abbey, composed in the enigmatic letters of an unknown tongue. An ancient translator is finally located so that the contents of the codex might be known. The venerable artifact bestows its history of the monastery's patron saint and then immediately disintegrates.[86] Sometimes slowly, sometimes with disconcerting rapidity, all languages, like all matter, transform. Chaucer observed of linguistic mutation over millennial spans that "in forme of speche is chaunge," so that "withinne a thousand yeer" words that had seemed apt become "wonder nyce and straunge [exceedingly senseless and unfamiliar]" (*Troilus and Criseyde,* 2.22–24). Diachronic changes caused by cultural contact, repetition, and the accumulated distortions of the human mouth ensure that any language will eventually become alien to the descendants of those who speak it.[87] Suppose you know that you inhabit a present that will someday, inevitably, be transformed into someone else's distant past. How do you speak to a future in which you will have become remote history, "wonder nyce and straunge"? After language loses its comprehensibility, when its archives have been scoured clean by cataclysm, how can story persist?

The problem of long communication in the absence of enduring linguistic intelligibility received intriguing consideration when the Department of Energy proposed the indefinite storage of radioactive material deep inside Nevada's Yucca Mountain, an extinct supervolcano. Nuclear waste remains lethal for a massive span of time, necessitating a million-year quarantine. To dispose of such perilous materials mandates geological thinking. Abraham Van Luik, a geoscientist at the Yucca Mountain entombment site, describes in an interview how various countries examine the deep time of their landscapes to determine where to isolate their radioactive materials. Through that process the earth comes to life. The Swiss, for example, contemplated burying their toxins in the granite of the Alps but realized that these mountains "are still growing, and the slopes are not all that stable over hundreds of thousands of years."[88] They chose for a repository instead the deep clay basins of the Rhine, hoping that in these subterranean chambers the spent nuclear fuel will lie dormant for the desired million years of isolation. Yucca Mountain seems like a safely dry area in which to store spent fuel. Yet thinking like a mountain leads to the realization that since the last Ice Age Nevada has been experiencing a ten-thousand-year drought. Its climatological past was far wetter, and its future may therefore be damp and cool.

When the Yucca Mountain facility was initially commissioned, the Environmental Protection Agency believed that ten thousand years of interment would suffice for isolating nuclear byproducts. The EPA therefore required the construction of a warning sign that could remain efficacious across a ten-millennia span.[89] Whether ten thousand or one million years, such a duration is exceedingly difficult to apprehend in human terms. What admonition can survive the likely vanishing of the United States, of English, of everything those who inter such fatal substances now know? The Human Interference Task Force addressed the problem of safeguarding the waste from future humans and took as a founding assumption that all contemporary languages will change profoundly over the considered timescale.[90] The task force recommendations included multiple layers of containment and warning supplemented by archives and oral traditions, but centered around a combination of linguistic and nonverbal injunctions to caution to be carved upon a monolithic surface, since natural or synthetic rock without anything conjoined to it withstands the elements well and is not likely to be dismantled. The lengthy document that the Human Interference Task Force produced looks deep into the past, at Sanskrit and Latin as lasting tongues, at the pyramids and the Great Wall and Stonehenge, which "has withstood invasions into Britain, wars, and visitors who used to be allowed to chip off mementos" (their conclusions may have been different had they contemplated Avebury instead).[91] Although their report attempts to instill confidence through the multiplication of jargon (it is peppered with sentences like "the redundancy and synergism resulting from using a multitude of channels should create a high likelihood of successful communication"),[92] a fear of failure in transmission haunts its every page.

With these difficulties of communication in mind, the University of Nevada sponsored an exhibit entitled "Universal Warning Sign: Yucca Mountain" in which artists created installations that might offer enduring, transparent commands to avoid the contaminated site. The winning entry proposed seeding the desert with genetically engineered cacti, altered to radiate an uncanny cobalt-blue color, transforming the landscape into an unnatural swathe of sky on earth.[93] Yet this solution could as easily prove an attractant as admonition. Even the most forbidding work of art possesses allure. The same problem of how to warn without recourse to language was considered at the Waste Isolation Pilot Plant near Carlsbad, New Mexico. Since 1999 the Department of Energy has stored the lethal detritus of nuclear weapons manufacture at this facility. Its vast subterranean chambers are expected to be filled by 2030, at which time the complex will be permanently sealed. Architectural theorist Michael Brill led a collection of

> linguists, artists, engineers, archaeologists, and other experts, who were charged by Sandia National Laboratories to design a method of keeping future Indiana Joneses out of this real temple of doom. "Passive Institutional Controls," meaning monuments impervious to harsh climate and sandblasting winds are mandated, because even the federal government has to acknowledge it might not be around in a few hundred years, never mind millennia hence.[94]

The team's first, practical thought was to allow the materials to lie exposed, creating in the desert an ocean of corpses, an instantly readable sign that none should draw near. Since the architecture's purpose is to preserve human life, however, they proceeded to reflect upon the possibility of transhistorical, transcultural architectural forms that announce danger and interdict approach. Among the proposed universal warning structures were fifty-foot high concrete whorls laden with spikes (an installation dubbed "Landscape of Thorns"); hulking black cubes arranged to provide neither shelter nor aesthetic appeal ("Forbidding Blocks"); and jagged, irregular megaliths that pierce the desert at disconcerting angles ("Spike Field"). The panel arrived at these possibilities after the careful study of enduring lithic constructions from past ages, including Stonehenge. As Julia Bryan-Wilson has pointed out, each of the proposed admonitory monuments, future-directed as they may be, also invoke archaism and "muddle its temporal context: for the benefit of the future it is made to look as if it is from the past."[95] Imagining prehistory is inseparable from envisioning distant futurity. Thus the creators of nuclear waste deterrents turn to Neolithic monuments; thus medieval theologians like Bede declare confidently that the catastrophe that was the Flood is simply a watery version of the Apocalypse yet to arrive.[96] A message spoken by a structure rather than a text must of necessity be temporally heterogeneous. Or—and this will amount to the same thing—materially convoluted. Manuel De Landa has argued that geology, biology, and linguistics are not separate spheres but "three perfectly coexisting and interacting flows of energetic, replicative, and catalytic materials."[97] How can they not intermix?

Like Stonehenge on Salisbury Plain or Hadrian's Wall slicing Britain's terrain, these menacing works of modern art were designed to dominate the landscape and transmit messages. They fill the barren desert with assertively human content. Like their historical inspirations, they offer speech acts wrought in stone. Yet ominous art can entice rather than prohibit, and few messages are received lucidly over vast spans. The panels in charge of designing warning devices for nuclear waste recommended supplementing any sculptural installation with admonitory texts composed in all known languages, with room to carve more deterrents as new tongues arise. Cheaper, less philosophical, and more shortsighted solutions were eventually adopted, however: monoliths with pictograms and linguistic inscriptions. Abraham Van Luik, instrumental to the Yucca Mountain site's design, describes these warning signs as messages to future archeologists and philologists when he notes that the Waste Isolation Pilot Plant

> decided to come up with markers in seven languages, basically like a Rosetta Stone, with the idea that there will always be someone in the world who studies ancient languages, even 10,000 years from now, someone who will be able to resurrect what the meanings of these stelae are. They will basically say, "This is not a place of honor, don't dig here, this is not good material," etc.[98]

These stelae (a term that arrives from archeology, used to describe lithic publication devices) will not be put into place for another eight decades, when the radioactive cache is abandoned, a lethal message to a future that may not comprehend the lasting power of the site's contents.[99] Or, more optimistically, the chance to compose stone-based communication machines that endure into an uncertain futurity enables a potential communalizing effort at present (if the markers at each hazardous waste facility worldwide differ they will not communicate as well), as well as a community across time. Van Luik imagines societies connected across spans of ten thousand to a million years, renewing the monuments to guard lives.

Though the necessity of disposing of nuclear toxins is new, the desire to send messages across inhuman spans through stone is an enduring obsession. Whatever groups instigated the construction of immense, perdurable architectures like the ring of megaliths at Avebury knew that they could not possibly live to see their constructions to their completion. To erect a structure as massive as Stonehenge, lofty stones rising upon massively reconfigured earth, is to face mortality. Such a project cannot be initiated unless a time long beyond one's own demise can be imagined. Otherwise, why not compose with a material more synchronous with human tempo, wood—a choice many peoples living in Britain at this time made, as surviving postmarks and structures like Seahenge make clear? Builders in timber can swiftly behold the results of their labor, and likely even witness that beloved structure's decay. With projects that require generations to complete, projects that may in fact be designed never to come to completion, how can one *not* be sending a message into a future that does not include one's own presence, and may well be empty of familiar people and language as well?

Such monumental writing in rock and soil requires a leap beyond the horizon of death, a movement away from human spans. Megaliths, menhirs, and stone rings are letters repeatedly sent to those who come after, and very often to unknown recipients who come *long* after. Prehistoric architects surely possessed a decent set of wits and knew from experience that the present is not eternal, that the horizon of the future is uncertain. Can we not imagine, without too much of a leap of faith, that a project like Stonehenge is sent into that future to keep an ever-receding present alive through the accumulation of temporal heterogeneity, through millennia of continued refashioning, co-dwelling, and collaboration? A building project that mandates the passing of multiple lives before completion cannot be a day-to-day endeavor. This inbuilt temporal horizon tells us nothing about specific intent. It will not allow us to discern whether Stonehenge was a fertility shrine or ceremonial ground or a tomb or a war memorial, but it will remind us that such architectures have from the start inhabited a future and an extensive past, a time that spreads vastly forward even as it recedes.

The weighty exuberance of Carnac, the majestic chambered cairn at Maeshowe in the Orkneys, the gothic assertiveness of York Minster: these structures are time travelers launched toward an unforeseeable horizon. What Stonehenge and the grandiose cathedral that the Normans built in Norwich have in common with Neolithic burial chambers is both artistic surfeit and more-than-human scale. Their colonization of space and time are far in excess of anything an argument based upon cultural context or use value can explain. They do not capture history; they exceed it, as objects irreducible to human narratives. They are ritual spaces; they are pedagogical machines that shape a certain kind of subjectivity; they are materializations of cosmologies; they anchor an earthly point to a celestial one; they are designed to press relentlessly forward in time, conveying the past via dense materiality but also opening continuously to modification and change. In their exorbitance they place their makers (and by their makers I mean everyone who at every point conceptualizes the architecture and its space as alive and open to enlargement and adaptation) into a relationship with time that moves them beyond the predictable or the determinate, so many generations into futurity that sameness and apocalypse and profundity of temporality are all possibilities. The builders of the cathedral in Norwich realized that they were a conglomerate of parvenu Normans and indigenous English.[100] Both groups knew very well that the land that this towering limestone edifice newly organized around itself had not always been their own. Did that knowledge suggest, as the stone rose and they saw that this monument would endure beyond their great-great-grandchildren, that they did not necessarily have full confidence that they were sending a message only to future versions of themselves?

The Time of Giants

"It was a time of giants."

So states geologist Jan Zalasiewicz, describing the epoch during which the elements that will someday form a pebble he holds in his palm come into being.[101] His invitation to aeonic contemplation is extended by a striped disc of gray slate from a Welsh beach. Zalasiewicz narrates through this little lithic beacon a story that spans 13.7 billion years, to the beginning of time and matter in the big bang. The narrative provoked by this seaside stone is philosophically engaged as well as artistically beautiful. His book *The Planet in a Pebble* condenses earth's geological history into a stone that its author can clutch. Its narrative is a story of scale, stretching from the subatomic to the cosmic, an account of temporal profundity and the smallness of human lives. And it is a rumination that begins with the most inhuman of substances but quickly elicits autobiography, creativity, and the loosening of thickly compacted narrative:

> That pebble, like its myriad kin, is a capsule of stories. There are countless stories packed tightly within that pebble. . . . These stories are gigantic,

and reach realms well beyond human experience, even beyond human imagination.[102]

Zalasiewicz is careful to distinguish the scientific discourses he will deploy from the imaginative ones humans have been inventing since the "mists of prehistory" to explain stones: "tales of elves and princesses, of witches, goblins and vanished empires."[103] These are mere fables. They are also, perhaps not by coincidence, rather medieval. Change Zalasiewicz's list slightly to "fairies and aristocrats, magic, monsters and vanished empires" and we possess a fairly good articulation of the contents of chivalric romance. Zalasiewicz's factual story, on the other hand, is completely different—though in its précis the scientific narrative likewise sounds as if it also has arrived from the Middle Ages:

> battle, murder and sudden death . . . ages of serenity . . . molecular sleights of hand that would make a magician gasp.[104]

What seemed to be the pure stuff of geology becomes romance composed in another mode, containing and envitalizing what it was to have superseded. Zalasiewicz's pebble demands narrative, and the genre it solicits combines history with magic. His story of stone is not simply about the depths of the past but reaches toward advents to come: "Something of the earth's future, too, may be glimpsed beneath its smooth contours."[105] Quite a sweeping tale for a little fragment of the British coastline to harbor.

The Planet in a Pebble holds much in common with earlier, fabulous imaginings of prehistory, stories that likewise work with inherited materials: if not a pebble, then a fossil or lithic fragment in which temporal depth stirs. A medieval writer who never spoke of visiting the Welsh coast but who came from the border where England was pushing into Wales, Geoffrey of Monmouth was likewise fascinated by stone as a conveyance device for histories difficult to know. Most famous now for bequeathing the charismatic figure of King Arthur to the Middle Ages, Geoffrey was a secular-minded cleric of the twelfth century who bestowed upon Britain a far deeper past than the island previously possessed. His *History of the Kings of Britain* (ca. 1138) narrates an unbroken span stretching two millennia, epochal in its scale compared to what previous insular historians had covered. More a work of the imagination than the archive (but anchored in extant texts and traditions), Geoffrey's *History* includes the discovery of the distant island of Albion by the exiled Trojan Brutus, who christens its expanses "Britain" after himself. The story details the subjugation of au-tochthonous giants, the populating of the island with Trojan refugees, the reigns of troubled kings like Lear, with their civil wars, invasions, and vigor-ous empire building. Geoffrey culminates the story in resplendent Arthur and closes the narrative in the present day with an ambivalent suggestion of Arthurian return. The *History of the Kings of Britain* is a spirited chronicle without which Arthur would likely have remained in obscurity instead of be-coming the most agentic secular myth the Middle Ages possessed. Geoffrey filled a sparse expanse in Britain's past with durable content, in the formal and unadorned Latin that contemporary historiography demanded, imbu-ing fragments gleaned from a variety of sources with a fullness, a vitality.

Geoffrey's story begins with Brutus, a figure plundered from the *Histo-ria Brittonum (History of the Britons),* a ninth-century Latin text of Welsh provenance. Geoffrey enfleshed its skeletal account into the *Aeneid* in miniature, a heroic tale of wandering, grandiose battles, and the founding of a nation. He created Arthur by compounding under intense narrative pressure numerous but vague references to a British chieftain of that name, creating a metamorphic figure of gem-like radiance. Though supposedly an ancient Briton, Arthur achieves conquests that resemble those of the con-temporary Normans, Geoffrey's patrons and England's recently installed overlords. The consensual world that Geoffrey initiated through the *History of the Kings of Britain* invited succeeding artists to add their continuations and prequels, new plots and themes, enlivening Arthur and Merlin and Guenevere through continuous amplification. He created an open text so rich in narrative fossils, so fecund in alternate stories that the past its nar-rative dreamed came immediately to life. By the end of the Middle Ages its literary progeny were polyglot and legion.

Just as primal giants populate the primordial landscapes narrated by Genesis and the antediluvian history imagined by Augustine, so Geoffrey emplaced on Britain's prehistoric shores a community of these familiar monsters. Brutus enters a wild land, renames it after himself, parcels for-ests into agricultural expanses, and transforms the island through settle-ment and building programs into a unified kingdom. His sovereignty is as ecological as it is political. He constructs the city that will become London and upon his death is buried within its walls. As Brutus terraforms the isle, he transforms its living present into lost history, from the giants' Albion to the Trojans' Britain. Like the aboriginal inhabitants of Canaan spotted by the spies of Moses (Numbers 13:29–34), figured as giants, the inconveniently indigenous dwellers of Britain are fair targets for genocide. Shortly after the arrival of the Trojans only their leader Gogmagog remains alive. He is executed, hurled from a clifftop, staining "the sea red with his blood."[106] The place of his spectacular death is known "into the present day" as *Saltus Goemagog* (Gogmagog's Leap). Despite the action inherent in that designation, however, the toponym captures not a life in motion but an enduring arrest, an eternal fall from which Gogmagog, ever about to be smashed to fragments by looming rocks, will not escape. "Gogmagog's Leap" freezes aboriginal presence at the moment of its eradication. Like an American Indian name attached to a town or road built on former tribal land, such appropriation petrifies lives into a colonial trophy.[107] Yet the Latin word *saltus* can also signify an uncultivated woodland, recalling the expanses where Gogmagog and his fellow giants dwelled before the lethal arrival of Brutus and his men.[108] As "leap" the noun *saltus* gestures forward toward the story into which the monster is hurled, a future he did not choose. As "wilderness" or "woodland" the term looks backward to the island of Albion seized from him, an undomesticated expanse that under Trojan hands will be partitioned, tilled, and built upon: "in a short time, the country appeared to have been occupied for many years [*ab aevo*, literally "from all time"]" (*History of the Kings of Britain,* 28–29). Perhaps the embedded ambivalence of *saltus* as "fall" and "unmanaged forest" explains why the giants, though cleansed from the land by a flood of immigrants, return later in the text. Like the stone with which they are associated, they are never long contained by dead or fully superseded history. Just as in the bible the giants perish during the Flood and yet mysteriously reappear after the Deluge has receded (how else can David fight the Philistine Goliath?), so in Geoffrey's *History* Arthur will battle the cannibalistic giant of Mont Saint Michel as a prelude to his empire building in Europe.

Geoffrey's detail that a precipice memorializes the name of Gogmagog *in praesentem diem* (into the present day) has antecedents in Old English elegies, full of melancholic rumination upon ruins as *enta geweorc* (the work of giants). Such crumbling remnants may signify the remains of Roman cities like Bath. They could also simply be generic devastated architectures, since no specific history anchors them in the stream of time. In poems like "The Wanderer" windswept piles of stones are simply but ambiguously "the old work of giants, standing abandoned."[109] Original builders are invoked but denied a history, a life. Later in his text Geoffrey of Monmouth will in contrast fully animate a similarly architectural scene, becoming the first medieval author to dream a detailed origin for a prehistoric structure that impinged upon his present. The *History of the Kings of Britain* speaks of Stonehenge and possibly Avebury.[110] Aurelius Ambrosius, a glorious king of the Britons and future uncle to Arthur, defeats at great human cost the treacherous Saxons who have invaded his lands. Desiring to construct for the fallen British a monument capable of eternal memorialization, he

> summoned carpenters and stonemasons from all districts and instructed them to employ their skills to build a new structure to stand forever as a memorial to such heroes. When, however, lack of confidence in their skills led them all to refuse, Tremorinus archbishop of Caerleon came to the king and said "If there exists anywhere someone to carry out your orders, then it is Vortigern's prophet Merlin. I do not think there is anyone in your kingdom more distinguished in foretelling the future or in feats of engineering." (*History of the Kings of Britain*, 170–71)

To conceive this "new structure" adequate to the story it will incarnate as well as capable of travel through time, Aurelius must seek beyond a mere *artifex* (skilled maker) who works wood or stone. An enduring monument requires a true artist. Bishop Tremorinus knows that Aurelius will find one in Merlin, a prophet and engineer, not the magician he will become in later literature.

Merlin is introduced in Geoffrey's narrative as the son of a cloistered nun and an "incubus demon" (*History of the Kings of Britain*, 138). He is the progeny, that is, of exactly the angel-human union that so annoyed Augustine, a union that in other stories engenders giants. Interestingly, Merlin is depicted as a giant in several illustrations from a fourteenth-century manuscript of Wace's *Roman de Brut* (a French translation of Geoffrey's Latin work). One of these (London, British Library, MS Egerton 3028) shows Merlin towering over Stonehenge.[111] Like Old English giants, Merlin is an architect of stone. Whereas the giant Nimrod designed the Tower of Babel

but lost the ability to communicate, Merlin understands how to work with
rock to sustain its ability to persist in speaking. Giants who are also engi-
neers form an integral part of Merlin's solution to the memorial quandary
Aurelius poses:

> If you wish to mark their graves with a lasting monument, send for the
> Giants' ring *[chorea gigantum]*, which is on Mount Killaraus in Ireland.
> There is there a ring of stone *[structura lapidum]* which no man of this era
> could erect save by skill and art combined. The stones are huge, beyond
> the strength of any man. If you set them up in the same pattern around the
> burial-place, they will stand forever. . . . The stones are magic *[mistici sunt
> lapides]* and can effect various cures. They were brought long ago from
> the farthest shores of Africa by giants, who erected them in Ireland while
> they lived there . . . There is not a stone among them that does not have
> some medicinal power. (*History of the Kings of Britain*, 172–73)

Through Merlin Geoffrey of Monmouth repeats an enduring association of
primal stone with prehistoric, indigenous, or otherwise ancient peoples (in
this case, Africans, the Irish, and the Britons, all of whom stand in "native"
relation to the English and Normans).[112] Entranced by this vision of an eternally potent, eternally persisting construction, Aurelius commands that
Merlin, Uther Pendragon, and fifteen thousand men depart immediately
for Ireland. There they meet Gillomanius, the island's king, incredulous that
anyone would sail to his shores to steal large rocks. He declares nonetheless that only over his dead body will the "smallest pebble *[lapillum]* from
the ring" be seized. Happy to oblige, the Britons obliterate the army of
Gillomanius. Merlin urges them to attempt to move the stones from the
Irish mountain. Though they employ "contrivances of all kinds in their ef-
forts to take down the ring," from ropes and pulleys to ladders, no mechanism budges the unyielding rocks (*History of the Kings of Britain*, 174).

Laughing at these futile attempts, Merlin easily dismantles the stone
circle with unnamed gear and places the monoliths aboard waiting ships.
He transports the disassembled structure to Britain and with precision re-
builds the wheel over the buried dead: "Merlin obeyed and erected [the
stones] round the cemetery exactly as they had stood on Mount Killaraus
in Ireland, so proving the superiority of brains *[ingenium]* over brawn
[uirtuti]" (*History of the Kings of Britain*, 174–75). Whereas the Irish king

can discern in the Giants' Ring only dead rock, like the ring's first architects Merlin realizes that in their clefts and beneath their coldness the
megaliths harbor ancient power: the ability to cure ailing bodies, the
ability to do justice to the dead, the ability to memorialize that which
would otherwise be swallowed into time. True, he steals the structure from
Ireland and erects the stones where they will be forever foreign. Then again,
even its original builders transported the rocks from their native shores,
ensuring that the circle engineered on that Irish mountain would always
be out of place. Its alien radiance is intensified upon conveyance to Britain.
Eventually the circle becomes the gravesite for Aurelius, Uther Pendragon,
and Arthur's cousin and successor to the throne, Constantine (*History of
the Kings of Britain,* 254–55).

Stonehenge is a historical object, dense with disparate meanings that
accrue over millennia. Writing in the long wake of 1066, Geoffrey of Monmouth quietly analogized the ring to the massive stone architectures (castles, cathedrals, abbeys, city walls) erected by the Normans across Britain,
an ambitious program of making the new territory theirs through the lithicization of insular landscape. The most recent incarnation of Stonehenge is
as a celebrated World Heritage Site complete with museum, elaborate gift
store, audiotours, instructional signage, and comfortable WCs. Neolithic
pilgrims to the soaring stones likely sought healing and the contemplation
of the afterlife. Modern ones privilege the obtaining of souvenirs, photographs, and experiences. Because Stonehenge was renewed over long centuries by peoples whose language, culture, and stories are impossible to know
fully, archeologists rely on the stones themselves to communicate, unearthing for context what evidence they can from the surrounding earthworks.
Antler fragments, post holes, inhumation sites, and pottery shards are all
pieces of tales that cannot be known in their totality, but stories that scholars
strive to nuance and amplify, hoping to know better some small segment of
the distant past.

Yet the circle's power resides in something more than its vast, prehistoric context. Stonehenge is a time-bound monument, but it is also time-
binding, appearing in contexts as widely separated in time as Henry of
Huntingdon's twelfth-century *Historia Anglorum,* Edmund Spenser's *Faerie
Queene* (1590), William Wordsworth's "Guilt and Sorrow" ("Pile of Stonehenge! so proud to hint yet keep / Thy secrets"), Thomas Hardy's *Tess of*

the *d'Urbervilles* (1891), in tiny form in the film *This Is Spinal Tap* (1984), and as a perilous terraforming device constructed by aliens in *Stonehenge Apocalypse* (2010). Stonehenge is something more than any of these instantiations, something more even than their totality. The critical literature about Stonehenge is extensive and replete with mockery of the association of the structure with Celtic religious practice and neo-pagan ritual, with druids authentic as well as New Age.[113] What gets lost in such repudiation, however, is that Stonehenge was already three thousand years old when Julius Caesar composed his report of British priestly practices, and four thousand years of age when Henry of Huntingdon named it a marvel of Britain. Such extensive duration means that even for the manifold prehistoric peoples who built, rebuilt, rearranged, and continuously reconfigured the site, Stonehenge was a living structure, eliciting participation in its perpetual processes of change. It is impossible to affix a singular, originary, or constant meaning. Exerting force that crosses millennia, Stonehenge within its own temporal frame evidences a thriving that includes repeated ruination, reconfiguring, and renewal, as well as an enduring invitation to collaboration.

The monstrous races that the Greeks imagined to dwell at the edges of their world and the giants of Genesis 6:4 are limit cases for kinshipping as an active practice: they limn the boundary of the human, a threshold of identity and time.[114] To redraw that limit so as to include such uncertain figures profoundly enlarges community. Augustine knew well that when "giants in the earth" are no longer abjected as monsters, deep history curves round to become familiar story. A kinshipping device works by transforming the scale across which relations unfold, opening time to more-than-human duration. The Circle of Justice, a set of world-ordering instructions for young rulers supposedly bequeathed by the philosopher Aristotle to his pupil Alexander the Great, has travelled across centuries and cultures, durably extending an invitation to a "new kind of historical imagination," one in which the once remote past becomes an era of intimate connection.[115] Affinity and community burgeon. Geoffrey's Merlin bequeaths a collection of equivocal prophecies to the future rather than a verbally sturdy Circle of Justice. Yet he also entrusts to ages to come a wheel made of insistent stone. Stonehenge is a machine for epochal communication, a mechanism for enmeshment across time's uncertain depths. As *chorea gigantum* Stonehenge is a Merlinic kinshipping device that connects the Britons to the giants that Brutus and his followers exterminated to make the island theirs. Progeny of an incubus and a woman, conceived in precisely the same way that giants are engendered, Merlin erects at the heart of the British nation a declaration in stone that the past is never really past, that it lingers in its density, its complicated and even monstrous materiality. "The stones are magic and can effect various cures.... There is not a stone among them that does not have some medicinal power": engineered in prehistory, Stonehenge does not cease to communicate, to emanate reparative force. Unlike Gogmagog and his tribe, its diasporic African architects are recuperated into history rather than expelled at its foundation. These latter giants are to be praised for their lapidary knowledge and artistic ingenuity. Though their story is glimpsed only obliquely, as builders of the *chorea* (ring) that bears their name, they set into lively motion a device that will persist over time, gathering a heterogeneous community within its circle, never diminishing in salubriousness.

From Africa to Ireland to Britain, from prehistoric giants to contemporary Britons, a massive circle of stones revolves through history and across far-flung geographies, accreting a diversity of stories along the way. Geoffrey of Monmouth recognized that the narratives of dispossessed peoples retain complicated life, that they can engender unexpected effects through their enduring power. Merlin, Geoffrey's authorial doppelganger, knows that Stonehenge is not the dead remnant of a lost people. Its trilithons and megaliths mediate, expand, and intensify relation. His transfer of the circle conveys the giants back to the Britain from which they were once removed. Through lithic transport they become again founders and, obliquely, kin. Geoffrey makes clear that medieval people knew well the ring was the product of ingenuity, sophisticated technology, and material collaboration. Its rocks were not transported from Ireland, but they did arrive from a distance: perhaps twenty miles across Salisbury Plain for the sarsens, and more than two hundred for the outer rings.[116] He added Hiberno-African origins, a narrative that acknowledges alien provenance and the itinerancy its rock. Geoffrey of Monmouth was no Augustine, and his Stonehenge has no tale to tell about the Great Flood or anything else found in the bible. Yet he materializes a compelling story without domesticating its resistant difference.[117]

Given Merlin's ability to sense abiding power in the megaliths, to perceive that they are not inert, it seems especially cruel that his eventual fate will be entombment within immobile stone. Geoffrey says nothing of Merlin's death. The prophet vanishes unremarked from the narrative as soon as he enables the conception of Arthur (an episode that uncannily replays the scene of Merlin's own birth, including misrecognition and the exchange of bodily forms). Later authors were not content to allow so spectacular a figure so quiet an exit. These writers developed a much fuller mythology for Merlin, energetically expanding the contours of the world that Geoffrey bequeathed to them. According to the thirteenth-century *Suite du Merlin*, Merlin (now a magician) took as his protégé the young huntress Niviane, destined to become the Lady of the Lake.[118] Through the magic Merlin teaches, Niviane discovers that her mentor has fallen in love with her. Loathing him as the son of a devil, she convinces Merlin to remove a slab of ancient stone, the lid of the Tomb of the Two Lovers. She numbs his body so that he falls into a torpor and has him placed within, between the corpses of the couple who gave the monument its name:

> She told the men to pick him up by the head and feet and throw him in the tomb where the two lovers lay. Then she had them replace the stone slab. When, with great effort, that was done, she began her incantations, and with her spells and magic words she so tightly bound and sealed the slab in place that there was no one afterward who was able to move it or open it or look at Merlin, dead or alive. (*Suite du Merlin*, 362–63)

Four days later a wandering knight hears the entombed magician weeping. Merlin tells the man that it is beyond anyone's power to liberate him from his lithic prison. When he finally perishes shortly thereafter, he utters a cry of despair so resonant that it echoes "the length and breadth of the kingdom of Logres, and gave rise to many extraordinary events" (363). Merlin, who could discern in obdurate stone its vivacious histories, finds himself immured forever and carried to oblivion. Since the tomb can never be opened, since the message it hides can never be released, the last we hear from Merlin is a wordless cry of pain that travels the world, diminishing into the muteness of death. Merlin, who knew stone's life, is sealed in the cold substance and cut forever from contact. His stilling into silence seems a rebuke to the lapidary knowledge that Geoffrey had him embody.

An impressive tumulus in Brittany was long known as *le tombeau de Merlin*, the tomb of Merlin. Legend held that beneath the sweep of its hillock was hidden the rocky grave in which he had been imprisoned. Photographs taken around 1892 show a Neolithic architecture that resembles West Kennet Long Barrow and Wayland Smithy in Britain.[119] Unfortunately, however, the landmark's owner destroyed the structure a few years later. He hoped to discover something hidden within, some treasure or a corpse, but razing the mound uncovered nothing. Today the expanse once occupied by the tomb is marked by three forlorn stones that gesture toward a vanished magnificence. Yet what if we could really discover the grave of Merlin? What if, despite the enchantments of Niviane, we lifted the stone that has so long held him and exhumed his corpse? Would he be like Lindow Man, just another body disinterred from a peat bog at harvest time? Would we find that the *Suite du Merlin* speaks the truth, that Stonehenge's mediator has been reduced to silence, removed forever from history? Are corpses preserved in the ground or encased in stone yet another version of the impulse that leads human beings to construct a Stonehenge or a Parthenon or a Norwich cathedral? Do they convey an enduring desire to send messages to uncertain receivers? Are they lithic collaborations, vivid and material manifestations of geophilia? Might they speak beyond death? What of a text describing a vanished human life? A wholly imagined life? Can stone communicate the past directly, or does it require a translator, a mediator, a Merlin? Must the past end as Merlin does: entombed forever in silent stone, the victim of his inability to comprehend the world he changed, the future he himself set into motion, the lithic wheel he transported and whirled? Might stories of stone suggest something endures, radiates, connects across millennia?

Stone is too often made a figure for time as force of oblivion, an eternal sepulcher the contents of which are withheld. Yet the stories excavated in this chapter suggest that time is actively and materially contained in texts, fossils, engineered devices, stones. Time exists in a plural state: an ebullient *then* crashing against a vivacious *now,* shaping futures to arrive. The human and geologic are likewise compound, dynamic, full of heterogeneity. The past has a weight, a force best seen in movement, a vagrancy and a relation-making and an inbuilt uncertainty that might also be called its life. From Africa to Ireland to Britain to this book you are reading now: Stonehenge is a temporally dense ring of garrulous rocks, a monument in motion rather than a diminished container for history or a sepulcher that rebuffs access. As Merlin makes clear through feats of engineering, stone's strength inheres not in heft or durability but in its surprising levity. Stone invites invention, both in the modern sense of creativity and in the Latin *inventio,* a finding, discovery, an unearthing, as well as an inventory (that is, catalog and story).[120] Medieval *inventio* typically involved the discovery of a saint's remains, often as an incorrupt body.[121] Providential unearthings aside, however, lithic invention is seldom so anthropocentric.

Stonehenge discloses a world in which Africa, Ireland, Britain, monsters, humans, and companionable stone are bound in complicated relation. A similar transontological affinity may be found in Genesis, in a creation narrative that combines the dense and the light:

> formavit igitur Dominus Deus hominem de limo terrae et inspiravit in faciem eius spiraculum vitae et factus est homo in animam viventem.

> [And the Lord God formed man of the clay of the earth: and breathed into his face the breath of life, and man became a living soul.] (Genesis 2:7)

In this, the second creation story offered by Genesis, humans are wrought of stony stuff into which divine breath enters. "De limo terrae" has often been translated as "dust," but Augustine in his commentary on Genesis insisted that the phrase means clay.[122] Biblical creation thereby echoes how stones and gems come into being.[123] Medieval lapidaries enmesh the human body and the lithic by analogy (the Sloane Lapidary describes carnelian as "lyke a lump of flesh") as well as by lithotherapy (carrying carnelian will "strengthen the limmes of a man that bleedeth").[124] We bear rock and water with us, as us. We are the ambulatory lithic and the substance of the Flood. And yet, as time's deep stories have demonstrated, stone would be on the move even without us. No wonder later medieval writers will wrestle with the idea that stone might itself be a kind of organism, might possess something like *animam viventem,* a creaturely soul.

EXCURSUS

— —

A Heart Unknown

A slow walk across the Pont de la Tournelle, and we watch boats of color-ful tourists gliding below. We pause on the Île Saint-Louis for ice cream, the morning too early for such indulgence. The man at the café who places pink, yellow, and white on cones rebukes us with his silence, but we do not care. We eat our treat and pass along the Pont Marie, stranded sand of the Paris *plages* beneath, then onward to the Marais, and the sad business of the day.

We decided back in Washington that we would visit the Mémorial de la Shoah during our Paris peregrinations. Now as we approach the site we recognize that we had been hesitating, lingering on bridges and eating morning ice cream. The courtyard is lined with walls into which are cut the names of the deported. Eleven thousand belong to children. We waver at the gate. A bulletproof wall, translucent but still brutal, separates us from the entrance. Six million dead. We can see a vast cylinder with camps em-blazoned. STRUTHOF. AUSCHWITZ. MAJDANEK. We can see along the steep walls names we do not want to read. We know already how fa-miliar some would be: *Cohen, Alpert, Weitzman, Farber, Laufer.* A litany of shared ancestry, strangers dead for bearing our names. Why would we bring children to such a place? How would they measure the loss? Might they imagine themselves as wall-carved names?

We almost turn back, but the guard sees us pausing and buzzes the gate. He looks through our camera bag, backpack. He smiles at chocolate cookies for Katherine, a stuffed dog she carries as comfort. Then we are inside. *Cohen, Alpert, Weitzman, Farber, Laufer.* Easy to read, under every year of the war. *Eleven thousand of those deported from Paris were children.* A veteran of the Holocaust Museum in D.C., Alex already has tears in his eyes. Katherine, though, is smiling. She admires the flowers that someone has left, the small piles of memorial pebbles, the burned out *yahrzeit,* the little Russian doll crumbled in a corner. We examine the cylinder with its emblazoned camps. We look at stone plaques bearing images of despair. We enter the main building. *What you are about to see is quite intense,* the woman warns us in French and then again—for emphasis—in English. *I'll watch your daughter for you if you like.* Should we? I look at Alex, and he looks down at the floor. Wendy speaks for him: *No.*

We leave. In the courtyard, by the pillar with all those camps, by the names and the doll and the ruined candle, Katherine raises her arms and begins to spin. As we lose ourselves to history, she loses herself in whirling, faster and faster. She laughs at a private joke, the sobriety of the place failing to grip. I take my camera from its bag and seize images of everything, as if this were the last day we could have: the memorial, the plaques, the building, the names, the girl lost in a dance of her own devising. We leave.

Later that evening I say my good night to Alex, Katherine already deep in dreams. He calls me back as I close his door. He gives me the Serious Look. "I'm sorry," he says, "for today. I'm sorry for what we missed. We didn't go to the exhibit because of me." I can feel the fissure in my heart begin, the crack his sadness makes. "No." I say that word as firmly as I can. I am not going to allow him that regret. Katherine taught me something and I need to speak it. "That's not what happened at all." Instead of spending time at the Mémorial de la Shoah, we crossed the Marais to the Musée d'art et d'histoire du Judaïsme, where we witnessed some sad things (the shattered remains of medieval Jewish tombstones, whole lives readable from fragments of Hebrew on lithic ruin). But we spent most of our time with small posters spread throughout the museum, each of which bore a picture of a person now living and a paragraph or two in his or her own

Remembrance: whirl at Mémorial de la Shoah.

words about what it means to be a Jew. For many, Judaism meant nothing: it was more important to be French, or expat Algerian, or a hybrid of cultures, or to hold a fragmented identity. For others Jewishness was all, an anchor in tumult. No eternal verities, only lived complexities, accommodation of a difficult world. Reinvention. Sometimes rejection. But always life. Fascination with these plaques led us through the museum's collection. No opportunity was lost, I assure him. Like the stones that form its monuments, the Shoah is not going anywhere, even if Jewishness—even if humanness—is always on the move.

Force

The Adventure of Stone

Hapax

This chapter seeks a word we have yet to invent, a word stone wants to convey its movement-effects. This impossible term would combine "allure" and "radiance" to name incompatible yet cohabiting trajectories: enfolding and propulsion, pull and thrust, captivation and actuation, seduction (mysterious, sensual, affective) and ekstasis (vertiginous prospect of a sudden exterior). Impracticably, this word of plural vectors would also capture stone's propensity for lapidary stillness and seismic slide at once, its ability to seem utterly fixed, a point of stasis in a bustling world, even while remaining in forceful motion. It would label the transports through which metaphor becomes hard matter and materiality conveys syntax, figure, and art—the adamant flux of story and stone. This unimaginable term would need to dance lithely along temporal and spatial scales, across ontological modes, capturing weird simultaneity and dizzying tectonic shift, the lethal intimacy of gravity's pull and the beguiling rebuff of stone's density.

A kinetic verb masquerading as a prosaic noun, *wonder* is one possibility. Old English *wundrian* designates irruption and eruption, outside coming in (to be struck by surprise) and inside moving out (to marvel).

Wonder is the opening of the world in its strangeness.[1] Perspective realigns and matter queers.[2] To use another Old English word, wonder is weird: not the revelation of destiny *(wyrd)* so much as sudden glimpse of inhuman working, a revelation that a drama that seemed intimate is beyond individual control. In the face of epistemological faltering, wonder entices curiosity and cognitive extension.[3] It can lead to a "broken knowledge" that inculcates respect for the indomitability of things: "wonder hopes to darken, to isolate, to insulate."[4] *Astonishment* is another possible term, the affective state that in Middle English was written *astoned*. This adjective likely derives from the Anglo-Norman French verb *estoner,* "to stun," which in turn comes from Latin *tonare,* "to thunder." A word of a sonorous etymology, *astonish* denotes the feeling of being outside oneself that arrives at a sudden thunderclap. For both medieval and modern Anglophone audiences the term carries lithic suggestiveness: *astoned/astonished* sounds like a becoming-rock. To be thunderstruck is to be petrified. Medieval writers punned on the word's stony resonance and pull toward the earth.[5] Those who are astonished routinely fall to the ground, and when the *astoned* regain their mammalian composure they are seldom the same. The inanimate world has come strangely alive. Bedrock slides. Although *wonder* and *astonishment* well register the force of objects, however, they better describe the frame-shifting effect of the lithic upon humans than what stone does outside of anthropocentric relations.

The medieval noun-verb *charm* might be a better option, combining arousal and capture with materiality (a charm is a piece of jewelry or a magic object) and inherent dynamism (a charm is a spell, words come to life, deriving from Latin *carmen,* "song"). Charm emphasizes the ability of stone to enchant, intimately connecting medieval texts to contemporary materialisms, with their unspoken magical undercurrents and flirtations with animism. A neologism like *allurance* offers another alternative, a portmanteau capacious enough for varied lithic effects—but too precious, doomed to hapax legomenon. With its inbuilt push-pull *magnetism* is likely the best geological descriptor. It has the added bonus of being a sturdily medieval noun that remains familiar. Magnetic rocks figure in most lapidaries. Magnetism also underscores the perils of encounter with stone in its illimitability, in its challenge to the assumption that matter can be mastered and that the inhuman is fully knowable. Throughout his lengthy alphabetical catalog of various stones and their forces, the thirteenth-century philosopher and theologian Albertus Magnus dwells mainly upon emissive abilities and refulgence. His discussion of *magnetes* foregrounds a contrasting but coextensive trajectory. The description begins in science and ends in horror, an unwilled, fatal, and yet joyful embrace of inorganic union:

> Aristotle also says that there are many different kinds of magnets; for some attract gold, and others, different from these, attract silver, and some tin, and some iron, and some lead . . . and some attract human flesh: and it is said that a man attracted by such a magnet laughs, and remains where he is until he dies, if the stone is very large. (*Book of Minerals,* 3.3.6)

Albertus takes this description from a fragment of the so-called *Lapidary of Aristotle,* an Arabic work extant by the ninth century published under the Greek philosopher's name and eventually translated into Latin.[6] The *Lapidary* collates varieties of "stone that attracts" ("lapis qui trahit"). The particular rocks that draw humans are said to have been discovered by Aristotle's pupil and correspondent, Alexander the Great. Beholding these magnets triggers astonishment: "all who looked upon them were stupefied and kept gazing open-mouthed as if they had lost their senses." Alexander is savvy enough to steal some stones by draping them in cloth. He uses the rocks to build a city, incorporating them deep within its architecture. Over the centuries the settlement becomes derelict, its stories forgotten. Sand erodes the protective layer around the magnets. Eventually a prince of Ninevah sends scouts into the ruins. Once they scale the city's walls these men are transfixed by the exposed rocks and never reappear.[7] Stones shimmer with beautiful and life-intensifying force. They also exert a corporeal and epistemological pull that brings humans to ruin. The prince's messengers do not return with their report. The words never arrive to describe the actions of these stones that have captured their investigators, this cognitively and corporeally attractive substance with which they will remain forever bound.

Despite combining allure and propulsion, stillness and action, magnetism in both medieval and modern accounts mainly centers upon lithic gravity, on "lapis qui trahit" (rock that pulls). Seeking a word that has yet to be invented, stone can better be understood in the failed return of the prince's spies, who cannot communicate its movement-effects because they have been caught within them. Or here in these paragraphs, as I have struggled to find words, as stone bluntly triggers linguistic failure, pushing investigation up against the hardest of walls, description faltering, materials and worlds escaping capture into category. Matter and metaphor convey, but that tectonic shift becomes adventurous veering.[8] Here where humans become transfixed to a stony wall and words petrify rather than transport, especially here, stone does not cease to move.

The Force of Matter

This chapter continues the exploration of stone's animating antimonies (crystalline solidity and magmatic flow, geologic and idiosyncratic scale, blunt factuality and invitation to reverie), but deepens these restless trajectories through an examination of how lapidary stillness and seismic motion have textual effects; how the emissive potency that is radiance and the sensual, aesthetic, and perilous force of allure interrupt narratives and might even spur the genesis of new genres; how stone is always something more than the totality of its relations, so that the lithic retains its ability to recede, surprise, and occasion what medieval romances called *aventure*. A partner with my thinking here has been a rock that was an animal: a fossil ammonite, a treasure purchased at the Harvard Museum of Natural History early in the writing of this book. I had been contemplating stone's function as an everyday trope for inanimate things, wondering how it might escape cementing into the stationary. The halls of mineralogy through which I passed offered ample evidence of stone's pull. Display cases radiant with prismatic fluorite, realgar, turquoise, malachite, chrysoberyl, and azurite attract hundreds of daily visitors. Fossils announce the primordial intertwining of organic life and lithic activity. A collection of meteors declares the fatal intensity of stone's movements, its alien paths. The gift shop ammonite has therefore been my totem in composing this book, my mineral familiar. These shelled invertebrates appear in the geological record about four hundred million years ago. Though they vanished with the dinosaurs, their aeonic reign dwarfs hominid presence. Irruption of a lost world, fossils (we know from Augustine) unfold irresistible stories. Though it seems to have arrested time, the vortex of its shell evidences stone's transit, manifesting how ancient invertebrates learned over the long years to produce

coiled houses through mineral alliance. Trillions of such creatures dwelling within their extruded carbonate compressed upon their death on the
seabed, limestone for future cathedrals. Sometimes instead of pulveriza-
tion a shell was colonized in its entirety through permineralization, trans-
mitting to the distant future a record of its once having navigated the sea.
Neolithic peoples prized these serpentine fossils and worked them into
their architectural creations. They might not have known about natural selection or extinction, nor might they have measured temporal spans geologically, but they discerned in fossils an inhuman art, intensification of the
world's truths, petric sympathy. The lithic circulates through lively systems
of relation, long-lived ecological webs that intermingle the biological and
the inorganic. The spiraling shell is the record of a lost life as well as an
invitation to the contemplation of cosmically complicated helices, of agencies that spiral outside human duration. Even stone not shaped by sculpting
holds stories in its temporal corkscrews and spatial gyres, slow and insistent. The ammonite perches at the edge of my desk. Most visitors to my office unthinkingly take hold of the fossil as they sit to talk. They palm its heft,
run fingers along its ridged coil, lapidary trigger to meditation. That a hand
should instantly yearn to touch that durable whorl reveals the intimacy of
movement to desire, evidences the meshes of nonintentional connection
within which bodies and objects, human hands and lithic vortices act.

Stone does its own theorizing. Always on its way to artwork and to
figuring speech, always a blunt challenge to those uses, the lithic is from
a human point of view both material and metaphor, emblem and fact, a
substance for philosophers, poets, masons. Stillness predominates. Water
undulates, fire leaps, air is ceaseless in its agitations, but earth is that which
stays put. *Terra firma* offers the solidity necessary for inception. As adamant
substance, rock is the fixed point from which origins proceed, moorage for
a volatile world. Delved foundation offers secure base, the cornerstone ini-
tiates the building's rise, the keystone arrests the sliding arch and locks the
whole enduringly. Lithic nouns provide our vocabulary for the construction of even immaterial things: foundation of community, cornerstone of
ethics, keystone of a nation. Jesus renames Simon "Peter" ("the Rock," from
Greek *petros*) when he declares that from this steadfast disciple he will fashion the base of a church (Matthew 16:18). Stone materializes the weight of
the law. Death by stoning stills the transgressor and asserts juridical fixity.

"Written in stone" denotes the permanence rock bestows upon the verbal. Moses transports the Ten Commandments from Sinai incised upon stone tablets. The petrification of these words proclaims their sacred timelessness.[9] He later strikes a desert rock to release flowing waters and nourish his people, demonstrating how divine might can yield sustenance from lithic aridity (Numbers 20:11). The menhirs of Ireland, Britain, and Brittany have survived far longer than the peoples who erected them. We may never precisely know their purpose nor fully discern the messages they were meant to impart, but we recognize that they ceaselessly communicate. Transmissive devices and community materialized, representations as well as objects, ancient standing stones lyrically declare human ephemerality and lasting material alliance. Stone speaks across the centuries while its human companions come and go.

Companioning implies movement, and stone proves quite a difficult travelling partner: brusque, unyielding, a spur to hard thoughts. It therefore seldom makes good on its promised stability. "Rocky" means full of slide: precarious, troubled, unsteady. Simon Peter betrays his master at Gethsemane. Moses shatters in anger the first edition of the Ten Commandments (Exodus 32:19). He releases water by striking stone, but God commanded only that he speak to the rock ("loquimini ad petram"), and in punishment Moses is not allowed to lead his wandering people into the Promised Land (Numbers 20:8–12). Landslides and earthquakes reveal the sporadic rapidity of earthly motion, while Geoffrey Chaucer's Knight's Tale describes the inevitability of erosion, the vanishing of stone in a slow flight of particles (1.3021–23). Rock can injure. We all know what people dwelling in houses of glass are not supposed to hurl (and we all know that glass itself comes into solidity through fragile lithic-human relation).[10] The encyclopedist Isidore of Seville (d. 636), whose work was much admired throughout the Middle Ages, derived the Latin word for stone *(lapis)* from the fact that it "hurts *(laedere)* the foot *(pes)*" (*Etymologies*, 16.3). Rock is literally impedimental. For Isidore all objects, creatures, and phenomena *are* their etymological origin. Reality is not linguistically constructed; language is determined through material agency, by the force of what things do. Isidore emphasizes stone's ability to produce physical and ethical irritation when he derives scruple *(scrupulus)* from the Latin word for a small, sharp rock *(scrupus),* a keen pain for heel and conscience.[11]

Stone's activity is rife with story. An unshod foot meets a rock's oblivious point on a neglected road, opening a tale perhaps of poverty, postcoloniality, and geological deep time. Rain saturates a hill, propels a mudslide, and obliterates a precarious village—a nexus of austerity politics, climate change, the permeability of compacted clay, misplaced faith in terrestrial stability, and the force of stone in motion. A slingshot wielded by a boy hurtles a pebble toward a giant's brow, turning the tide of a martial engagement and ensuring a kingdom its future. All these narratives are propelled by a dispersive mesh of actors (social, generic, ideological, human, and inhuman) that reaches backward toward infinity. The slingshot is a union of tree, sinew, and stone; it is constructed by a shepherd boy on his way to kingship and invested with energy by his eager hand; it is a small weapon caught in a vast political struggle pitting David's Israelites against Goliath's Philistines, a hero against a monster; the story is fiction that becomes fact that solidifies a national identity.

The lithic impels, participates within, and disrupts these naturalcultural webs, these assemblages within which things act.[12] In the compilation of classical and patristic stone lore included within the *Etymologies*, Isidore writes that the gem *smaragdus* exudes a green so intense that surrounding air verdantly glows, *astrion* "shines with the gleam of the full moon," and *enhydros* gushes crystalline water like a fountain (16.13). *Galactitis* exudes milk that can cause forgetfulness and will render the breasts of nursing mothers more productive. Persian selenite gleams like honey, contains an image of the moon, and waxes and wanes in sympathy with the celestial body. Through these mineralogical vignettes Isidore foregrounds inorganic liveliness and material interconnection. Stone triggers environmental entanglement. Mirror-like *hephaestitis* chills boiling water and ignites dry materials. *Lycopthalmos* is the rocky semblance of an orange-red wolf's eye, and *liparea* when burned is capable of summoning all nearby animals. *Chelonitis,* the petrified eye of an Indian turtle, triggers prophecy when placed in the mouth. Resembling a human tongue, *glossopetra* drops from the sky when the moon wanes. The story that this lingual rock unfolds entwines the durable with the mutable, the immense, the extraterrestrial, the temporal, and the human.

These emanative descriptions are at once misapprehensions of geological qualities and a poetic recognition of the force of stone, its ability to engender ecological interdependence and foster worldedness—not always, not inevitably, but often, and wondrously. Isidore's extravagant etymologies are more lyrical than factual. His open and dynamic system tends to proliferate relation rather than reduce things to singular correspondences. He thereby captures something essential about the trajectories of even the most recalcitrant objects. Rocks, bones, curiosities, and texts tend not to stay securely emplaced on a museum shelf or within an encyclopedia entry. There is always more than that for which a precise description or rigid classificatory scheme can account, some radiant potential to surprise, hurt, obstruct, exceed.

Admittedly, for many contemporary readers Isidore's ascription of activity to gems will make clear why his *Etymologies* had to be left behind for a recognizably modern science to flourish. Disenchanted and geologized, Isidore's stones lose their glimmer. Yet to quarantine matter from life disregards, in the words of Jane Bennett, "the vitality *of* matter and the lively powers *of* material formations."[13] Such cultivated inattention can be culturally useful, privileging a focus upon human virtue or the rewards of an afterlife. *Contemptus mundi* (disdain for the world) is an ideal shared by Stoic philosophy, medieval Christianity, and various contemporary philosophical modes. A similar disregard for material agency undergirds the view that the world exists to offer compliant resources for human consumption. And so the abacus, an early and enduring machine, renders stone dead matter for performing accounting. Its component pebbles are *calculi,* from which we derive our word *calculate.* But what if we take seriously these rocks' deepening of epistemological possibility? Within a more capacious frame the work of the abacus-pebble-hand-merchandise web far exceeds its individual components. The moving rock is a participant in the practice of extended cognition as well as an agent of world building. Calculus, without which we could not have engineering, begins with the slide of a pebble and an alliance with a human hand, begins with stone in motion.

Matter is inert or mechanistic only when viewed anthropocentrically. Although the word "material" is employed to denote "some stable or rock-bottom reality, something adamantine," Bennett points out that objects like iron chains appear to be immobile only "because their becoming proceeds at a speed or level below the threshold of human discernment."[14] Metals, for example, are composed of tiny, quivering crystals imperfectly interfacing, ready to shift or erupt into cracks, a "metallic vitality."[15] Unlike this molecular vision of vibrant metal, medieval conceptions of matter were generally not atomistic. They were, however, just as lively.[16] Theories of material substance were, like theories of nature, manifold, divergent, quarrelsome— and therefore irreducible to a monolithic shared mentality.[17] They derive from intellectual culture (e.g., the scholastic project of reconciling Aristotle's idea that form gives meaning to substance with biblical exegesis) as well as disparate literary and scientific texts, most of which do not abstract matter so much as place materiality into action, stories in which stone is entangled as an actor, an inorganic character. Isidore, for whom *mundus* (world) derives from *motus* (movement), describes gems that shimmer with connective force, an aesthetically overwhelming cosmos pulsing with attachments and becomings. Objects do not, in general, exist in isolation; enmeshment undermines the habit of ascribing power only to living organisms by illuminating how nonhumans exert a will discernable through material effects. Action emerges surprisingly and often obliquely from these proliferating connections. Certain epistemological habits and hermeneutic frames may render it difficult to express, but the vitality of matter would seem to be a universal truth, discernable to any observer attuned to its presence. Matter's motion will, for a medieval thinker, ultimately lead back to a divine First Mover. Yet restless materiality also provokes secular enchantment, offers an invitation to quotidian wonder directed at matter itself—a mode not opposed to the theological but often unfolding alongside or just below or quietly regardless.

Those who study texts surviving from the distant past inherit as part of their scholarly formation an ethics of recovery that stresses remembrance, preservation, and custodianship. We might also take some inspiration from matter in motion to embrace a collaborative practice that includes in its companionships the inhuman, that promiscuously embraces alliance with rocks, texts, and forces of nature as well as humans living and dead. We might explore the strange relations through which desire and agency burgeon, the networks of connection that enable the motility of lapidary objects (gems, rocks, monuments), lithic materialities (stony substances of various sorts), and earthly forces (geological, seismic)—an enmeshment of fellow travelers, landscapes, graves, elements, architectures, ruins, fictions, facts, gems. Our journey to follow stone's textual effects companions a guide who may well be imaginary. His historical influence was, however, in no way attenuated for his likely never having existed. The travel narrative ascribed to him is known for its love of wandering—a love that its teller shares with the stones that provide his story its geological substrate.

Down a Rocky Way with John Mandeville

A fanciful account of an English knight's voyage to the Holy Land and the realms beyond, the *Book of John Mandeville* was a medieval bestseller, and possibly the most popular travel narrative ever composed. A fourteenth-century *Fodor's Guide to Places Real and Imagined,* the *Book* seems originally to have been composed in French, lingua franca from Europe's frozen north to the torrid Levant, yielding an instant international audience. Written as if the actual record of a sojourn, the text offers a compendium of cultural details, pious histories, marvels, and exotica culled from a vast array of sources and narrated as if personally experienced. The *Book*'s unknown author was, like Geoffrey of Monmouth, a fashioner of new worlds from materials familiar enough for credibility, strange enough to entice curiosity. Unflaggingly congenial while quietly treacherous, the *Book of John Mandeville* carries a reassuring resemblance to traditional pilgrimage reports, travel narratives, and classical ethnography. The text is companionable, generous, lush. Even cannibals become comprehensible once Mandeville explicates the cultural logic behind their feasts. Its humane account of distant marvels lures readers into enthusiastic encounter, then leaves them to wonder if the whirring of its world will not erode the solidity of their own. The *Book of John Mandeville* is, in a word, unsettling. Its instability derives from the fact that, strictly speaking, it does not exist: there is no *Book of John Mandeville,* no originary version, no "complete" source from which textual variants sprang, just a volatile and polyglot multiplicity of texts masquerading as a unity.[18] The nonexistence of the *Book* as a singular thing has serious consequences for its analysis. Interpreters will always be chasing after receding objects, protean and adaptable narratives proliferating at that skyline where *terra cognita* curves to harbor incalculable islands.

Even when they seem stable, specific instantiations of the *Book* reveal themselves as shifting, rocky. The discussion that follows ranges over various versions, both in English and in French, but focuses primarily upon the Middle English manuscript group classified as Defective, an appellation earned because of a "missing" section known as the Egypt Gap. Far from the earliest form of the *Book,* the Defective redaction possesses the best claim to be "the English Mandeville," and the potentially petrifying power of John Mandeville's national identity (no matter what the actual citizenship of the *Book*'s author) is a recurrent theme.[19] The seemingly infelicitous label of *Defective* also captures the challenge of the text's openness, essential to its enduring vitality. The Defective group contains numerous extant manuscripts. I focus mainly upon London, British Library MS Royal 17 C. xxxvii, a rather unique and compressed treatment that nonetheless contains the richest material found in other members of the Defective group.[20] This manuscript also contains some fine illustrations, especially of buildings and mountains, indicating that its artist was a careful reader. As enduring markers along the pilgrimage trail or as marvels in themselves, such architectures, monuments, ruins, and fragments populate the narrative, instantiations of the *Book*'s sturdiest and yet most fugitive substance.

All versions of the *Book of John Mandeville* begin as a narrative of Holy Land pilgrimage, adapted from William of Boldensele's account of his knightly journey through Constantinople to Palestine in 1332–33. Although the narrative becomes a boundary-defying traveller's tale capable of almost circling the round earth, throughout its overwhelmingly land-based voyages lithic impediments vie with the text's restless, seismic movements, attempting to transfix an errant story to timeless and particular histories. These stumbling blocks, decelerations, and historical immobilities offer a powerful counterweight to the text's meandering trajectories and sudden veers. Among its early geological anchors: the rock in Jerusalem where the True Cross was hidden; the boulder in Tyre upon which Jesus sat to preach; the cave inside which Adam and Eve dwelled once expelled from Eden; the hill of stones constructed by angels where Saint Katherine's body resides; splotches of Mary's breast milk preserved upon marble; rocks left by biblical Jews to record their wanderings; the boulder rolled from the tomb of Jesus; the mountain upon which Noah's ark still rests. These stories from the Holy Land are timelessly contained within stone, guiding the narrator through sacred space. Mandeville's errantry also unfolds across more dynamic landscapes, expanses where story roils rather than petrifies, where a traveler might encounter professional virgin deflowerers (the *gadlybyriens*);

hermaphrodites who know the desires of both sexes; people who live on raw flesh and walk on all fours, freed from mammalian uprightness; an island where a lady still awaits the kiss that will free her from her dragon's flesh and reward with wealth, title, and lands the man so brave as to brush his lips against hers (Hippocrates's transfigured daughter). Travel narratives, like medieval bestiaries and romances, allow their readers to enjoy pleasures otherwise proscribed.[21] They create textual networks supported by powerful and often erotic fantasies, intermingling the foreign and the quotidian, the forbidden and the ordinary. Sometimes these illicit pleasures are, quite literally, subterranean. Early in the *Book,* John Mandeville reaches Satalia, a great city that was swallowed by the earth when one of its residents could not resist reopening a "grave of marble" (351–52) and embracing his lost lover one last time. Just as underground and unanticipated Satalia renders the paths above its buried towers "parolous [perilous] passages" (358), so the *Book of John Mandeville* possesses unstable ground and stony enclosures that when opened may divert pilgrims from certain and orthodox roads.[22]

Pilgrimage is a journey toward reverenced destination, not a wandering that fosters haphazard encounter or enables dangerous alliance with the inexplicable, the captivating, that which has been pulled beneath the earth to guard its alien allure. The *Book of John Mandeville* begins as a personalized version of a venerable genre, an account of travel to the Holy Land *(itinerarium).* Based upon Roman models, such narratives tend to be terse, providing information on how to travel to Jerusalem and a catalog of sites to behold upon arrival. Visited locations and encountered objects are tied through scriptural citation to whatever biblical event gives the building, well, town, mountain, or altar its significance. The *itinerarium* of the fourth-century Pilgrim of Bordeaux therefore offers a litany of encounters with storied stone:

> Here is also the corner of an exceeding high tower, where our Lord ascended and the tempter said to Him, "If thou be the Son of God, cast thyself down from hence." . . . There is a great corner-stone, of which it was said, "The stone which the builders rejected is become the head of the corner."[23]

Even when a crumbling fragment is all that remains, the edifice comes fully to present life through scriptural invocation. A lofty tower looms where a pilgrim beholds only an extant corner. The bodies that once moved across these stages might have perished or risen heavenward long ago, but stones abide the silent centuries to offer lasting testament to the histories that unfolded in their company. Ruins, rocky fragments, and desert landscapes are the very substance of narrative, speaking entire stories no matter how little of their former majesty lingers. They reassure the pilgrim that biblical history saturates the present, that the Holy Land is never lost. To journey through this terrain is to traverse time itself. A palmer arrives at Calvary and meditates upon the Passion as if Jesus and the two thieves were still hanging on their crosses, a biblical narrative ever ready to unfold anew. It is always Easter in Jerusalem.

Mandeville's description of the entire Holy Land seems at first glance likewise frozen in time. He writes that Palestine is best among geographies because the "vertu of thynges is in the myddel" (23) and Jerusalem is "in the middel of the worlde" (32).[24] At the very center of this cosmic center is a stone. The Church of the Holy Sepulcher encloses the rock of Calvary, upon which was set the cross of Christ, atop which Abraham attempted to sacrifice Isaac, under which was found the head of Adam. A sign in Latin and Greek announces that the pilgrim has arrived "in the myd of the erthe" (637). That the world should pivot around this primordial rock underscores that Jerusalem is central geographically, theologically, and historically, contained within a series of ever shrinking concentric circles that announce, once we can get to no more medial a site, that we have arrived at the locus where time and space are one. As he describes the history that unfolded around this lithic intrusion of Genesis, we are witnesses with Mandeville to events that occurred an epoch ago, history fixed eternally to place. What other substance besides stone could so well signify immutability? We glimpse the red stains of Christ's blood upon the mortise that secured his cross, the metal chains that held him to a pillar as he was scourged. Almost every step of this sacrosanct expanse at biblical ground zero brings to mind a scriptural story, brings sacred narrative into the present to transpire anew. With its pivotal rock that has survived the inundation of the Flood and sheltered the remains of the first human being, the center of the center of the earth would seem a place of profound stasis, of lapidary arrest.

Yet stone is also seismic. It is active and it moves. These precincts are inhabited by more than the revivified phantoms of Christian memory.

Mandeville provides an extensive list of the peoples who have held Jerusalem over the years, from Jews and Canaanites to Assyrians, Romans, Persians, Christians, and Muslims, "and many other naciouns" (607). The Church of the Holy Sepulcher is Constantine's fourth-century addition to the Levantine landscape, an ecclesiastical structure that entirely swallowed Calvary into stone's embrace. A sultan now owns the building. He has built a fence around the tomb of Jesus to prevent pilgrims from chiseling souvenir pebbles. This longtime practice had been dispersing the artifact into transported fragments—raising the possibility that the stone sepulcher, like the body it briefly held, would vanish if its monumental integrity were not actively preserved.[25] Crusaders who seized but could not keep Jerusalem are buried nearby. The priests who conduct Mass at the basilica do not employ a familiar liturgy. The cross of Christ and the nails that secured him to its wood were long ago discovered and transported to distant lands. The nails are now possessed by pagans and Saracens (a disparaging medieval term for Muslims). Rocks and tombs that once held secrets have been opened, emptied of their relics. In the middle of the world history carries on. Clergy go about their business indifferent to Roman changes to sacred ritual. Colonizers and tourists of various faiths arrive, look around, depart. A Muslim sultan remodels with his own architectural additions and keeps the flow of visitors moving.

Lithic heaviness is entrusted to keep story in place, marking the hope that some trace will endure against slow time and quick catastrophe. Although enclosed by stone, Christ rose because unlike mortals the stillness of death could not hold his divine body. The Church of the Holy Sepulcher is in distant and history-locked Jerusalem, a city utterly different from Satalia, that subterranean metropolis where a mysterious "yong man" loved so ardently that he opened the marble tomb holding a body to which he was overly devoted. Nine months later a voice commanded him "Go to the tumbe of that womman and opene the tumbe and byhold what thow hast gyte on here!" (Go to the tomb of that woman and open the tomb and behold what you have begotten upon her! 354–55). The youth unseals the grave a second time and a flying head swoops out, restless progeny of a corpse not surrendered to mortuary stasis. The airborne head circles his city, and Satalia is swallowed into the earth.[26] This marble tomb remained too full: with a corpse not yielded to inanimacy, with forbidden allure, with the monstrous product of a desire that transgressed the immobility of death. Unprecedented Satalia is a strange place to have traversed on the way to the Holy Sepulcher.

A similarly lively tomb arrives just a bit earlier in Mandeville's narrative: Saint John the Evangelist, interred at Ephesus.[27] We are told two irreconcilable stories about this apostle's restless resting place. Either John's body was translated to heaven and the grave filled with manna, or he entered the tomb while still alive and remains there, awaiting the Day of Judgment. Mandeville describes how the earth will "many tymes stire and meve [move]," as if there were a "quyk [living] thing" underneath (297–98). What has the passion of the young man at Satalia to say to this grave of uneasy occupant? Or to the narrative of Christ's Passion in the Gospel of Mark, where the three women coming to anoint the body of Jesus find that the great rock sealing his tomb has been rolled away? A lingering young man *(iuvenem)* declares the tomb's vacancy: "Be not affrighted; you seek Jesus of Nazareth, who was crucified: he is risen, he is not here, behold the place where they laid him" (Mark 16:6). The three tombs offer stark contrasts: an unsettled Saint John, alive within a space of death (but we will never know because the grave remains closed); a youth who opens a tomb to release an inexplicably alive creature, triggering a city's lapidary capture and the creation of persistently perilous earth above its sunken towers ("opene the tumbe and byhold what thow hast gyte on here"); the stone-enclosed stability that the city of Jerusalem at the middle of the earth promises ("behold the place where they laid him") but cannot fully offer. Satalia descends into the ground; Jerusalem, a place to which every approach is (in Mandeville's account) uphill, remains the terrestrial pinnacle; John occupies a strangely indeterminate space, since no one knows exactly what "quyk thing" stirs the earth.

The tombs at Satalia and Ephesus, uneasy resting places that interrupt the journey to the Holy Land, hint at the hazardous routes and dangerous relations at work in this text that begins as pilgrimage, revealing stone's ability to proliferate subterranean connection and trigger wandering. Stone encases, swallows, fosters, produces, destroys, enlivens, enlightens, churns. In the Holy Land rock aggregates history while multiplying living story. These two propensities might be called lapidary (stone captures narrative, stilling it within an enduring archive) and seismic (stone nonetheless remains active, on the move, and the stories held through its companionship likewise become unsettled). Thus Mandeville writes that the stone at the center of the Temple, now a place of Muslim worship (in fact, the Dome of the Rock, Qubbat as-Sakhrah), is where the Ark of the Covenant was kept until Titus brought that chest of Jewish relics to Rome. The same rock once yielded water to Moses in a parched desert and served as a pillow for Jacob when he dreamed of angels. On this stone Jesus was presented to Simeon, on its pedestal he preached as a boy, and (when it split to shelter him) the rock became a cave in which he fled those who would stone him. On this rock Mary learned her Psalter, Jesus pardoned the adulteress, the circumcision of the infant Christ took place, Zacharias announced the birth of John the Baptist, and here David once knelt in prayer. The Temple rock is a powerful narrative magnet, a dense collation of biblical histories. Yet just as the Church of the Holy Sepulcher flourishes in the present as a lived, mixed, polyglot space rather than a static repository of Latin Christian memory, the contemporary Temple serves as a place of worship for Muslims and Jews, people who discern in its central stone other narratives: the ascent of Muhammad into heaven, the founding of the Temple by Solomon, the true navel of the world.

English Mandeville

The errant or seismic trajectories that proliferate in the second half of the *Book of John Mandeville* are suggested long before his arrival in the Holy Land, in the waylaying efflorescence of narratives like Hippocrates's daughter, transformed into a dragon and awaiting knightly rescue, and the monstrous flying head of Satalia. Both are imaginative additions to source material containing neither. Through such veering the narrative moves away from the theologically predetermined landscapes of the Holy Land to boomerang across heterodox India, Egypt, Africa, China, Sumatra, Hungary, Amazonia, a multiverse that in its proliferation of cultures and objects trades singular histories for secular multiplicities.[28] Although they unfold within a participatory ecology of stone, Mandeville's travels are also the motions of a body transported by reading, an encounter with worlds through books, cognitively dynamic networks fashioned from unlooked-for textual convergences. The *Book of John Mandeville* is a literary pastiche, an alchemical experiment concocted of perhaps three dozen sources, from encyclopedias and religious tracts to various travel narratives and world histories.[29] Like Isidore of Seville in his *Etymologies,* the Mandeville-author weaves an intricate and lively meshwork of relations from heterogeneous materials. "John Mandeville" seems to have been a fiction, no more likely to have existed than the incubus-begotten Merlin in Geoffrey of Monmouth's *History of the Kings of Britain.* Yet through his *Book* Mandeville lives, acts, possesses historical consequence. An energetic mapping of exotic possibility and ebullient meditation upon the potential opened by travel and encounter, the *Book of John Mandeville* in its multifarious manifestations offers a cosmos where even in the museum of the Holy Land change and mobility are constants, geographies where humans and nonhumans are confederated in motion, where the lapidary shifts and stirs.

The *Book* opens by providing those anchoring bits of biography that have enticed readers to seek a historical figure behind the text's narrative persona. Born about twenty miles from London in St. Albans, John Mandeville is a knight who "travelide aboute in the world" (2). Sir John possesses a thorn from the crown placed on Jesus at the Passion, served in the sultan's army and was offered a wife, drank from the fountain of youth, is a specialist in exotic alphabets, and knows how to discern good wine, balm, and diamonds. These attributes ground the fugitive text in an affable, cosmopolitan, and seemingly factual author whose lived experience of the marvels he narrates is to be trusted. His narrative is sutured to the stability of a specific chronology: Mandeville's year of departure in the Defective version is 1332, the year of his return 1366. Such attachment to home serves as a brake upon his errantry, the guarantee that despite not having turned back after Palestine he will eventually reappear at his point of departure.[30] We last glimpse Mandeville upon native soil ("my contré," 2834), composing the book we now read. An enduring pull within his identity works to keep him bound in place, attached to lapidifying designation. This adhesiveness can go under many names, but its best designation might be *Englishness.* Whether the lost "original" version of the *Book* was composed by a writer who would have self-identified as English or French is impossible to know. Yet no matter who the actual author, no matter what collective identity the writer would in life have embraced, the *Book of John Mandeville* is strewn with allusions to the narrator's nationality, affixing him in history and place.

Most references are trivial, giving Mandeville a patina of casual Englishness. In detailing the Saracen (Arabic) alphabet, he writes that just as they have extra letters, so do "we" English possess thorn (þ) and yogh (ȝ) (1377), a quiet assertion of Anglocentricity. Like most writers from the southeast corner of the island, Mandeville glibly conflates "England" and "Britain," as if the Welsh and Scots did not share its expanses.[31] The knight's family name is by the fourteenth century sufficiently Anglophone, and given the multilingual nature of his contemporary homeland, his urbane Englishness is in no way attenuated when his words sound like this: "ieo Johan Maundeuille, chiualer . . . neez et norriz Dengleterre de la ville Seint Alban."[32]

The stilling or lapidary power of national identity has some specific textual effects. On the one hand, the *Book* has long been praised for its tolerance and open-mindedness.[33] Its charismatic narrator is surprisingly unwilling to condemn that which is incendiary, to rebuke that which is unorthodox, to domesticate that which is alien. His foreigners are not figures to be reproached but peoples to be wondered with. The island of Lamory, for example, is home to promiscuous nudist communist cannibals. Each of those designations should pose an insurmountable challenge to a medieval Christian writer attempting dispassionate description, yet Mandeville simply states that the Lamorians wear no clothing due to their climate's extreme heat; do not marry because God commanded humans to be fruitful and multiply; and share their spouses, land, and property to ensure that all are rich. He does employ a censorious adjective when he notes that the islanders maintain one "yvel custome" (1684–85): merchants import children from abroad for the Lamorians to fatten and devour. Most versions of the story, however, conclude with an undercutting remark, the observation that the people of Lamory judge this flesh to be the best and sweetest of the world's meats.[34] That plump children should be so tasty indicates just how far the Mandeville author is willing to inhabit the subject position (and taste buds) of the peoples he describes. Yet this travel writer so cosmopolitan that he renders promiscuous nudist communist cannibals comprehensible has nothing good to say about Jews. When in Jerusalem Mandeville narrates the Passion, he holds the Jews guilty of deicide, a charge with a long history of inciting violence. In relating a story about a poisonous tree in Borneo, he describes how a Jewish man confessed to him that his people once attempted to eradicate all Christians with that arboreal toxin. Later in the *Book* Mandeville describes the ten lost tribes of the Jews "of the kynde of Gog Magog" (2353), enclosed behind immense rocks at the edge of the known world.³⁵ Alexander the Great imprisoned these people within the Caspians through the aid of God, who heard Alexander's prayer and "enclosed the hilles" so that the Jews now dwell as if "y-loke in a castel" (locked in a castle, 2358–59). The gate that confines them is wrought of vast stones bound with strong "sement" (2381). A barrier that will not be overcome until the time of Antichrist, the rocks keep their pernicious inmates removed from the stream of time. Were a single Jew to escape, the narrator tells us, no harm would arrive, for "they conne noght speke but her owen langage" (they can speak only their own language, 2364). Yet a burrowing fox will someday undermine this mass incarceration. Astonished by the alien intrusion, the Jews will follow the animal to his hole and excavate Alexander's cemented gates, then pass through the stone barrier into the Christian world. Mandeville asserts that Jews living among Christians teach Hebrew to their children so that when their coreligionists return they will be able to communicate with them and lead them with the Antichrist "for to destruye [destroy] men of Cristendom" (2367–71). Timeless as the "gret stones" and unsurpassable mountains enclosing them, these Jews will break lapidary confinement and rush into the Christian present. The synagogue of Gog Magog will engender apocalypse.

The story of the enclosed Jews and their eventual escape has been described by critics as "blood-curdling" and "a warrant for genocide."³⁶ Such energetic anti-Judaism might seem puzzling in the *Book of John Mandeville,* given that England expelled its Jewish population wholesale in 1290. Yet by that act late medieval Englishness became a national identity built around Jewish exclusion.³⁷ A minority population who dwelled mostly in England's largest cities, pre-Expulsion Jews had sometimes lived peacefully with their neighbors and had sometimes been subject to violent persecution. Once banished from England, the Jews loomed large in the national imagination, a fantasized peril conveyed through lurid narratives of Christian persecution. The *Book of John Mandeville* is well regarded for the generosity extended to distant Mongols, the Muslims who hold the Holy Land, and various races, monstrous and human. Yet rather than a puzzling lapse in an otherwise tolerant persona, anti-Judaic sentiment may be another signifier of Mandeville's recalcitrant, immobilizing Englishness—a national identity that cannot be wholly disentangled from his lapidary fantasy of the Jews.

Mandeville's story of the enclosed Jews resonates profoundly with what might be called the geology of medieval anti-Judaism, the tendency to think Jewish difference in lithic terms. Christian interpreters hijacked Ezekiel 36:26 ("And I will give you a new heart, and put a new spirit within you: and I will take away the stony heart out of your flesh, and will give you a heart of flesh") to figure Jewish intractability through stone-heartedness.[38] Thus Peter the Venerable wonders in the eleventh century: "I really do not know whether a Jew is a man. . . . I know not, say I, whether he is a man from whose flesh the stony heart has not yet been removed."[39] Peter describes Jews as *inveteratam duritiem,* congenital in their obduracy. In Suzanne Conklin Akbari's apt words, Christian narratives of the fall of Jerusalem dwelled upon the smashing of its stones to erect "a narrative of triumphant Christian domination on the razed ground of Jewish history."[40] The Jews carry this stoniness within them as they wander the world. The Middle English "Dispute between the Virgin and the Cross" repeats a version of the trope by stating "Þe Iewes [Jews] weoren [were] harde stones."[41] An intense lithicization of the Jews may be glimpsed historically in 1215, when Jewish homes in London were destroyed and their fragments set into the city walls as a public spectacle. That some Jewish houses were fashioned of stone also became a sticking point for anti-Judaic discourse. This material separateness that only seems to partition brings Jewish presence intolerably close to Christians. Or, at least, to *some* Christians: those for whom each rock of these little castles (*castella,* as William of Newburgh called them) materializes the transformation of Christian wealth into Jewish holdings; or those who were not pleased to see petrifying Christian typology challenged by the mobility of contemporary Jewish identities, by the lived practice of neighboring. Jewish stone houses, now so much a figure of the heritage landscape of contemporary English cities, were clearly built by Christian masons and used dominant architectural styles.[42] They did not differ from the homes of wealthy Christians, so that today many surviving structures ascribed to Jews may never have been occupied by them. Contemporary expectations of medieval Jewish dwellings have been set in part through medieval anti-Judaism, in which Jewish intransigence was repeatedly figured through unyielding rock, a materialization of spiritual deadness and historical anachronism. Stone was supposed to keep the Jews in place, but Mandeville has made amply evident how restless stone can be.

Anthony Bale maps the turbulence coursing Chaucer's Prioress's Tale, a narrative of Christian martyrdom at Jewish hands and a story that intermixes Christian and Jewish identities. Its flux and instability are counteracted by a "lapidary vocabulary" of tombs and gems, metaphorical petrifications that strive to impede the text's roiling. Murdered by the Jews who detest his daily recitation of a hymn to Mary as he traverses their neighborhood, the schoolboy ("litel clergeon") is metaphorized as a jewel of chastity, an emerald and a bright ruby (7.609–10). Bale aptly describes the "tombe of marbul stones" that contains his martyred corpse as

> an attempt to contain the expansive landscape and soundscape envisioned in the tale, a reassertion of the Christian community's faith in the fixity of signs. . . . The tomb stands for morbid permanence and closure. . . . The solid stone tomb repudiates the bodily rupture with which the Prioress is fascinated.[43]

In a tale of flowing blood, streaming tears, and reverberating song, the stone tomb demarcates, contains, and immobilizes. Yet the monument also fails to still what it encloses. The last stanzas of The Prioress's Tale transport the scene from the ancient east to nearby Lincoln, conflating imagined Jews with those who once dwelled at home. "The little boy," Bale writes powerfully, "wanders out of his distant Asian tomb into the Prioress's England and the pilgrimage group," a cohabitation in the present despite the petrifying and segregating movements of the narrative.[44] Mandeville catastrophically equates such Christian and Jewish living together with the Apocalypse and Antichrist.

Perhaps, however, there is more to Mandeville's lapidifying story as well. His tale of enclosed Jews is a paranoid imagining of monstrous difference and Christian vulnerability. Yet the episode might in a convoluted way also offer an example of attentiveness to the discontented desires of neighbors. The narratives that medieval Christians told about Jews tended to petrify them, so that they became a fossilized intrusion into modernity. The Mandeville-author, however, looks to the future and envisions partition that fails. The ten lost tribes escape their rocky enclosure to destroy the very Christendom that took pleasure in their immurement. What if in this irruptive vision we behold not just a tediously anti-Judaic fantasy of imperiled dominion but a Jewish story of seismic shift and explosive end? In a remarkable work of revisionary scholarship, Israel Yuval has mapped the ways in which Christians and Jews were profoundly changed by living together in the Middle Ages.[45] Over time both identities revealed themselves as mutable, open, alive; neither remained frozen in time. Coinhabitance, in other words, sometimes invited what Timothy Morton calls "coexistentialism," an ethical entanglement that leads not to violent rejection but to quiet acknowledgement of the strangeness of dwelling together, of intermeshed difference, catalyzing new modes of sharing the world.[46] Urban adjacency may lead to inventive, even affirmative practices of neighboring. Nor does sectarian resentment hold a Christian monopoly. Sometimes Jewish ire at persecution took the form of a fantasy of communal vengeance in which the King Messiah finally arrived to liberate the besieged Jews. The eagerly awaited Messiah would smite the enemies of Israel and drive them from the land, freeing the Jewish people from subjugation. Keeping in mind that the "Jewish Messiah is the Christian Antichrist," Mandeville's story suddenly becomes more complicated.[47] The *Book*'s narration of a prophesied liberation of enclosed Jews and their termination of Christian dominion contains an extant Jewish vision of violent requital, a vision apparently taken into Jewish eschatology from Christian materials. Yuval has argued that the vengeful, liberating King Messiah was dreamed by medieval Jews when they overheard Christian neighbors speak of crusader kings and the spectacular reclamation of the Holy Land. This unsettled vision of how Jews sometimes dreamed their future suggests that medieval Jewish sources resonate not just with scholarly wisdom and tearful commemoration of massacres but with anger at the smallness of the spaces into which Jews found themselves confined. Christians in turn overheard Jewish neighbors tell stories of a Messiah who would deliver them from exile, and dreamed the advent of Antichrist. This Messiah/Antichrist is Christian and Jewish at once. In his tale of the liberation of Jews locked in mountainous exile, Mandeville is narrating a paranoid and anti-Judaic story. Yet he is also recounting angry Jewish words—or words that blend Christian and Jewish story into a fiercely hybrid discourse. Such lapidary tales, shaken loose, beginning to slide, hold the promise of a future that might prove violently unfamiliar rather than a tiresomely immobile repetition of a lachrymose past.

The Messiah/Antichrist is not a figure of tolerance or cosmopolitanism. He remains difficult, inassimilable. The geology of medieval anti-Judaism is as perilously complicated as the medieval Christians, Jews, and stones who told and were caught within its stories.

The world Mandeville narrates is not easy to encompass.

The Geologic of Mandeville

The *Book of John Mandeville* records a magnificent failure to circumnavigate the globe. Its narrator's wanderlust seems to derive from the episode. An English traveler once journeyed the earth's roundness, only to turn back at that point when his relentless forward motion had almost conveyed him home. Heard by Mandeville in his youth, this tale exerts a peculiar grip on his imagination ("Y have y-thought many tymes of a tale," 1734). A "worthy man of oure countré" leaves Britain simply "to se the worlde" (1735). Having passed India and the five thousand isles beyond, he arrives at an island where "he herde his owen speech" in the exhortations of men driving cattle. The traveler takes the familiar language to be a distant marvel rather than a sign of proximity or return. Mandeville, however, insists that the man had come so far in his journey that he arrived "into his owen marches [borders]," the edge of the known world abandoned long ago (1740). Finding no transportation forward, the traveler "turned agayn as he com, and so he hadde a gret travayl" (1741). Finally arriving back in England and yet too restless to remain, the man sails to Norway. Storm-driven in the North Sea, he encounters a familiar scene: on an island men are driving cattle, and from their mouths he "hurde speke his owen speche" (1745–46). A wanderer circles the world to arrive in a place intimate and strange at once, to meet in a way his own unrecognized past, his own receding self, but from an unanticipated perspective.

Although any traveler can potentially arrive at the point of departure by remaining ever in forward motion, "the erthe is gret" and "ther beth so many wayes" (1754–56) that return is unlikely. Mandeville never states that anyone has successfully voyaged the world to attain home through an endlessly curving route. Yet if the man who almost completed the circuit has any regrets at his failure to close his circle of wayfaring, he does not voice them. The traveler whose tale so inspired Mandeville as a young man never lingers long after his return within the country of his birth. He is glimpsed only upon the road or on the sea, never since his initial departure within "oure countré" for long. What would happen if this traveler had completed his circumnavigation of the earth? Would he then have settled into sedentary life? Or must he turn back before he arrives because, having so filled his life with motion, the stillness of a homeland and the stasis of an English identity no longer satisfy? Mandeville, Defective: open to unpredetermined future, never to remain comfortably at home.

John Mandeville's boyhood imagination is captured by a traveler who does not fully recognize the familiar, perhaps because he has in his wandering become strange. Maybe that is why the traveler's story is so alluring to Mandeville—a tale-teller who does, however, return and remain. He writes his *Book* while resident in the England from which he had been long absent. Yet in the Defective version, no sooner is the book completed than its author is in transit. He carries his volume to Rome, where the pope gives the narrative his benediction. As the story comes to its close, Mandeville is journeying again, this time in his memory. Rather like medieval readers of the *Book,* rather like us, his "partyners," Mandeville cannot stay in place. Like the lithic landscapes across which his story unfolds, his desire is for motion, for the advent of proliferative connection, for trajectories that do not satisfy desire but intensify and proliferate its perturbations.

Mandeville is sometimes confined by the compass of his own Englishness, by the limits of his national and devotional circuits, by what Bale calls "lapidary narratives." Yet the *Book* is also *geologic,* in the rocky triple meaning of that word: sedimentary (an accretion of multifold texts, amalgamating them into new forms), igneous (hardened after long movement into contours that make transit evident), metamorphic (ever changing, open to futurity, circling the world to meet and no longer recognize oneself). Each textual variant of the multiplex *Book* can be seen as a crystallization, a gem created from an ever-fluid, seismic narrative that does not cease to be a body in motion, ready for shifts to come. This geological Mandeville is not merely metaphorical (or, rather, metaphor is not separable from conveyed materiality, so that stony substance is inherently a transport-device). Every step of the narrator's journey unfolds in lithic companionship, across a landscape of intimate stone, none of which is still. In the Church of the Holy Sepulcher, if we look just off to the side of the compass that Joseph of

Arimathea drew around the corpse of Christ, we find ourselves confronted with not only the petric materiality of an ancient tomb, but the memorial presence of the "rooch" (rock) of Calvary, its whiteness forever stained by the dripping of divine blood; the "roche" upon which Christ's cross was erected, now bearing an inscription in Greek ("That thou seist is ground of alle the worlde and of this feith," 640–41); four boulders near the pillar at which Jesus was scourged, continually dropping water in an act of terrestrial mourning (some versions, though not Defective); and the "roche" under which the Jews hid the cross for Saint Helena to exhume (655). Such stones commemorate the past by rendering discarnate story palpable. The relics they hid were long ago removed, the death for which they shed their endless tears vanquished by a bodily return to life. These monuments might also activate in a careful reader a wider mesh of associations. Sir John Mandeville is widely known for his geographical obsessions. These unfold beside, along with, and through geological fixations. Mandeville's travels are a story conveyed with stone. The lithic anchors and propels the narrative. To give some additional highlights: Jaffe is the oldest town in the world, and alongside its remains may be viewed the bones of giants (402–4). Not far from Jerusalem is the Fosse Ynone (Ditch of Memnon), where undulating gravel can change suddenly into glass (415). The sultan built his great city "uppon a rooch" and nearby are stones left for Saint Katherine by angels (446). Not far from Damascus a voyager can see the ground from which Adam was fashioned and the rock-hewn cave inside which he dwelt with Eve once expelled from paradise (507). The Dead Sea casts forth chunks of asphalt, big as horses (905). In the river Jordan, the Children of Israel left enormous stones "in the myddel of the water" when through a miracle they passed over its bed dryshod (945). On the rock outside Nazareth where a group of Jews attempted to hurl Jesus to his death may be viewed his footprints, impressed forever upon the stone when he vanished from his would-be assassins (765). The Saracen paradise features homes wrought of precious stones (1237). A sea without bottom has reeds that float its surface; their roots entangle "many precious stones of vertu" that protect their bearers from bodily harm (1814–15). The beastly men of Tracota covet a stone called "traconyghte," simply because it comes in forty attractive colors (1853). The Great Khan prefers his accouterments of daily living to be fashioned from jewels. Rubies and garnets worked into grapevine designs are a household favorite. Even the steps to his throne and the chair itself are hewn from gems and bordered in gold. The khan also possesses a radiant carbuncle to serve as palace nightlight (2150). Underwater "roches of adamaundes" (rocks of adamant) not far from the lands of the fabled Christian emperor Prester John pull metal toward lethal union (2405–6). These subaqueous magnets draw to their embrace any vessel with iron fittings. Mandeville tells us he traveled to view the shipwrecked expanse and beheld a forest of naval masts: "Y say as hit had y-be a gret ile of trees growing as stockes" (2407). In a narrative bare of similes (Mandeville describes the world in straightforward encounter, not through comparison) this small effusion of poetic metaphor haunts.

The legendary domain of Prester John is home to the Gravelly Sea, a marine expanse of stone, a ceaselessly heaving petric ocean. Here pebbles and sand "ebbeth and floweth with gret wawes as the see doth. And it resteth never" (Ebb and flow with great waves as does the sea. And it never rests, 2425–26).[48] This billowing petric wash sports fish "of good savour and good to ete." The magnificent Christian ruler Prester John, like the Great Khan whose daughter he weds, prefers housewares, eating utensils, and furniture made of gleaming gems. Jewels and precious metals betoken "his nobley [nobility] and his might" (2445). The *vertu* (innate powers) of specific gems determines their use. Prester John's bed is wrought of "safyres" inlaid on gold "to make hym slepe wel and to destruye [destroy] lechery" (2459–60). The Vale Perilous is strewn with jewels, gold, and silver to lure covetous men to fatal encounter. In the middle of this terrible place is a rock on which is engraved the "visage and the heed [head] of the devel" (2502). An island exists where women have "stones in her eyen [eyes]" (2532). When enraged they slay men with their vision. Another island is so distant that few stars shine and the moon is viewed only in its last quarter. There dwell ants ("pismeres") as large as hounds. They gather the abundant gold into great heaps. Local men use clever tricks to rob the insects of their hoards (2682–96). East of the realm of Prester John are only "great roches," their stony lifelessness the mark of impassable wasteland (2698). Paradise is hidden behind similar crags.

In the wilderness outside Bethany Mandeville relates the biblical story of the temptation of Jesus by the devil. Satan commands the fasting Christ: "Say that these stones ben maked bred" (Command these stones to become bread, 897). Only divine utterance, it seems, can accomplish such transformation. Yet metamorphoses of obdurate rock are precisely what the Mandeville-author accomplishes. Stone in the text is transportive, agentic, itinerant. Though rocks never become baked goods, we watch as they billow into waves, offer the miracle of fish from a pebble sea, exude rays of light and virtue, convey a traveler from story to story. Rocks pull ships and metals toward their clasp. The stones that compose the Mandevillian landscape sometimes affix history to place and sometimes act like bodies in motion. The former anchor the narrative; the latter unmoor the *Book* and become indistinguishable from connective flows of water or lava. Anchoring or lapidary stones include inert wealth, lonely ruins, gates that bar paradise or seclude Jews, empty tombs, and rocks that are no more than the congealing of the tales they bear. These are historical residua, depositories of ancient tales, seemingly unmoved markers of historical time. Metamorphic or nomadic stones do not long serve as suturing points and become spurs to a materially enmeshed wandering, lithic wayfaring, seismic roil: the endless pull of "adamaund," the turbulence of the Gravelly Sea, living practice that unfolds within temporally thick, coinhabited space. Despite the stilling effects of some religious and national identities, even bodies fixed to place are transported.

What is called for convenience the Book of Mandeville is not a singular thing but a diffuse and volatile concatenation, a landslide text, a gravelly sea. The Book of Mandeville does not exist, only a proliferation of Books of Mandeville, few of which have a historically identifiable author, redactor, or translator, all of which vary from their siblings, parents, cousins, queer friends, assorted hangers-on. Developing a vocabulary adequate to articulating the textual matrix formed by the Books has proven a difficult critical task (as my foray into kinship metaphors suggests; other critics turn to chemistry or biology for their taxonomic descriptors). These texts refuse to settle down into some well-delimited identity. Do they offer a reinvented *itinerarium,* a spur to pilgrimage, a crusading substitute, an armchair travel guide, a romance, a heretical tract, a paean to orthodoxy, a proto-novel, a panopticon, an imaginative delectation of the exotic and the monstrous, a compilation, an encyclopedia? Yes. And because the Books are this very web or avalanche, they break generic boundaries and cannot be sorted neatly for library filing. Iain Macleod Higgins, the critic who has most closely studied the dynamic flourishing of the Mandeville manuscripts, describes the *Book* as a multitext or "rhizome" that proliferated into discontinuous, variable, and polyglot versions: "Clearly, *The Book* is more than several books at once, both in its origins and generically."[49] Critical opinion holds that the *Book* was first composed in French. Away from this hypothesized first text and its unknown author sped two continental and one Anglo-French versions, and away from these scatter a plethora of English variants with Egypt gaps or in rhyme or in close sympathy with French forebears, as well as German, Latin, Irish, Italian, Danish, and Spanish transformations. At the center of this big bang that sent Mandevilles careening through Latin Christendom is the Postulated Archetype, an ur-Book assumed to have been in existence at some point. When the Postulated Archetype departed its marble sepulcher to ascend to that heaven where perfect texts reside, it left no earthly trace of its having been here, only the tremors that suggest its inherent mobility.

Paul Zumthor famously described the textual instability of medieval manuscripts over time as *mouvance,* emphasizing the vitality and heterogeneity of works as they mutate into new forms.[50] Seeta Chaganti has provocatively argued that Zumthor's kineticism ("a dynamic vision of manuscripts in motion") cannot be merely metaphorical.[51] What happens, she asks, when texts move physically as well as figuratively, when they dance? Following Chaganti's lead, I would argue that they become geologic: lapidary and seismic, transportive and blunt, figure and fact, material and metaphor, stone and story, poetry and masonry. As lithic movement entwines with textual *mouvance,* lapidary immobility gives way to glide, volatility, mutuality, motion. The Books of John Mandeville are event as much as object. They move through the world, seeking strange relation, leaving behind various instantiations that bear witness to forms taken in certain places under often indeterminable historical conditions. It would be a mistake to consider any one of these versions as the *Book* itself rather than a trace of the Books' transit. The Books of John Mandeville are best seen as a performance of their own volatile narrative structure, an ongoing *mouvance* that breaks and sweeps linguistic and national boundaries across multifarious trajectories, circling the world by pressing forward, never returning home. This tremor or seismic flow might leave in its wake certain crystallizations (manuscript attestations that we read today, but cannot assemble into some singular entity), yet these gemlike redactions will continue to engender unexpected progeny. In their proliferation, dispersal, and relation-making, the Books of John Mandeville reveal a restlessness that cannot be stilled into the contours of historical context or local determination. That thing in the *Book* that renders it ever fluid over time, that surplus that insistently propels the narrative, pluralizes it, scatters it across a capacious world: that exorbitance in Mandeville so tied to the lithic is the *Book*'s own life, the same restless and nomadic vitality harbored by its stonescapes, an inhuman kind of art.

Pilgrimages have endpoints, revelations, and (ideally) happy returns. The *Book of John Mandeville* offers potentially ceaseless flux between stasis and movement, lapidary arrest and seismic instability. The rocks that strew and undergird its landscapes embroil history, bodies, climate, substance, animals, fluids, metaphor, narrative, plants, differences, queer matter, and diverse peoples. Its ecology of entanglement can be dark, even lethal. Interconnection is not always affirmative.[52] Yet such knotty relations bring into vivid prospect a world where people, objects, and inhuman forces sometimes find themselves conveyed in wayside amity. Although stone is fully capable of its proverbial indifference, within lithic intimacy confederations also unfold that sustain ontologically mixed assemblages. The *Book of John Mandeville* sometimes trades correlationism (the assumption that the world is knowable only in its relation to human thinking and being, even if that relation is established or mediated by an anthropomorphic divinity) for coextensiveness, an inconstant but aeonic participation across taxonomy.[53] For Mandeville a diamond holds as much story as the merchant who keeps the stone in his left pocket to ally himself with its exchange value and protective powers. Sometimes geophilia will be evident in the stories these two companions share, in the ways they orient each other. Sometimes their stories will have little to say to each other. Traveler and gem are both participants within a material ecology that makes sorting the lithics and the nonlithics quite a task.

The *Book* concludes with a powerful moment of fellowship in which the narrator declares his readers partners in his pilgrimage and good deeds: "Y make hem [them] partyners" (2850–53). After so long a journey in the company of stone, why not extend the status of "partyner" to the geologic companions that enable various stories of the *Book* to unfold? Stones in the *Book* are material metaphors—figures of speech and transit devices, tenor as vehicle—that draw humans into their systems while escaping the devices fashioned to hold them still. Geoffrey of Monmouth knew this truth when he wrote of a lithic communication wheel constructed by African giants in Ireland that looms now in Britain, drawing to itself (like Mandeville's adamant pulling ships) lively stories. The composers of Arthurian romances who followed Geoffrey and expanded the world that he bequeathed to them activated this object agency when they transformed his history into a new mode of writing. Romance, the medieval equivalent of speculative fiction, is a genre of wandering and adventure toward which Mandeville is sympathetically inclined. Its narratives are full of objects possessing will. They generate narrative as well as beauty: gems that explode into storm, clothing that grants protection from bodily harm, swords that cannot be overcome in battle, rings that withdraw with their wearers into invisibility even when in plain sight, worlds where even the densest matter radiates and allures.

Lapidary Enchantment

A few blocks from my office in the Foggy Bottom neighborhood of D.C., the white columns of the Lincoln Memorial rise, lucent in the early sun. This edifice of Colorado Yule Marble shines with a splendor not indifferent to human events. Its emotional power is intensified by recalling that Martin Luther King Jr. delivered a speech about unrealized dreams upon the steps (just as that speech was deepened by its location, a memorial to the president under whom legalized enslavement of humans ended in the United States). Other substances could have been employed to construct the grandiose structure: less expensive, easier to mold, not so costly to transport, but not as effective a conveyor of affect. Colorado Yule Marble is luminous, and thereby integral to what the monument insistently does. Stone as interjectional force dislodges us from the tracks of routine and habit, renders us eccentric to accustomed perspective. We are creatures of perpetual scurry, hell-bent upon the rapid reconfiguration of every ecosystem into which we enter. Stone is an enduring and often amenable partner in our ceaseless construction projects. We can harness its force for commemoration, transmission, interruption—though because it is propulsive and at times willful rock also offers hindrance, even ruin. As the *Book of John Mandeville* makes clear, stone is lapidary and seismic at once, since it exists both within and outside human temporality.

Something in the lithic itself remains uncertain, thick with peril, chance, and promise. This obscure force is deeply entwined with stone's capacity to affect bodies and objects, to reorient cognition and transform the inquiries through which its potency is plumbed. Admittedly, it is easier to inhabit a world where human beings are unique causal agents while stone might inspire the snapping of a photograph (a pilgrim at the Lincoln Memorial) or the chiseling of a souvenir pebble (a tourist at the Holy Sepulcher) but returns thereafter to quiescence. The lithic illuminates an inhuman ecology. To dwell there long would be intolerable. Aligned into streetscapes to which we pay infrequent heed, stone fades to ubiquity. Yet even humble cobblestones can interrupt the transport they enable. A startling edifice might halt our walk, pink granite that gleams at the touch of late sun. Lyrical pebbles line garden paths. Congealed in bitumen, they pave synaptic roads. We notice these fragments when they trip the foot or puncture the bike tire, when the glint of oil yields iridescence, when a rock decloaks from inconspicuousness. Stone is our preferred material for the monuments, markers, foundations, walls, and statues that arrest our progress, as well as for the bridges, staircases, walkways, and highways that enable flows of pedestrians and traffic. Stone is an inflexible substance with which we collude for transport; the dull materiality of the world as well as its most beautiful affordance-maker; a humane shelter and impassive destructive force; a trigger to ecological entanglement; a stumbling block and immobile conveyor; a dense substance resistant to epistemological containment. Effusive and seductive, stone allures, recedes, enchants.[54]

Max Weber influentially wrote of the disenchantment fostered by Western rationalism, with its predisposition to view nature instrumentally. His description of this intellectual process unfolding over slow human centuries is "die Entzauberung der Welt," or "the taking of magic from the world"—an eradication that likely accounts for, among other things, the constant eruption of ecological crises under capitalism, as environment is reduced to raw material.[55] As the historian Robert Bartlett has pointed out, however, magic hardly departs as science arrives. Europe's "new dawn" included Leonardo, Copernicus, Galileo, and Shakespeare as well as "the hard fact that at this very period, tens of thousands of women and men were executed by the courts for copulating with demons, eating babies, and flying to midnight orgies."[56] Human history is never as progressive as it passes itself off to be. Yet the refusal of magic to embrace its own extinction might be read not simply as lingering irrational fuel for institutional violence, but more affirmatively as an enduring awareness of the dynamism that inheres within hard materiality.[57] Aleatory possibility lingers, revealing matter's "ability to make things happen, to produce effects" and its consequent illimitability.[58] Thus the thirteenth-century Neo-Aristotelian Albertus Magnus concludes his capacious taxonomy of various stones with the admission that lapidary force necessarily exceeds description:

> If we wished to speak individually about the power of every stone whatsoever, we should exceed the limits of this volume. . . . If anyone wished to experiment, he would find that there is hardly any little stone that does not have some power or other. (*Book of Minerals,* 2.2.20)

Despite the comprehensiveness of the alphabetical lapidary he composes, Albertus stresses the narrative inexhaustibility of the lithic. Because stone's powers are so manifold, "skillful alchemists" are "the best imitators of nature" (*Book of Minerals,* 3.1.10)—and nature thereby becomes the first practitioner of alchemy, a science of transformation and occulted efficacies, a science of magic. His conclusions are based not just on library research but on fieldwork. While composing his authoritative *Book of Minerals* Albertus visited mines around Germany to study at first hand the extraction of ores and gems. Even when minerals are valued for the metals into which they might be refined and jewels become commodities, stone continues to assist, resist, create, shift, detour, destroy.

The lithic grounds our language for power. The word *electricity* derives from *electrum,* the Latin term for amber (itself from the Greek *ēlektron*).[59] This rock that was ancient pine resin, often holding in its translucent interior the bodies of extinct insects, may be rubbed to create electrostatic effects: small shocks and the drawing of other materials toward itself. *Electrum* is stone become force. Having provided the designation for the very engine of modernity, amber as electricity is an instance of how stone as agent insinuates itself into human lives, instigator and partner as well as lethal energy that leaps the circuit of human control. Stone's marvelous or magical force, its radiance-allure, was well known throughout the Middle

Ages. The thirteenth-century prose *Lancelot* speaks of women "who know about enchantment" ("qui savoient d'enchantement"), which is to say, who understand the potency that inheres in words, stones, and herbs ("les forches des paroles et des pieres et des erbes"). This ecological comprehension yields beauty, youth, and wealth—and earns them the radiant title of "fees" ("fairies").[60] Such literary renditions of stone's power owe much to the lapidary tradition associated with Marbode, the eleventh-century bishop of Rennes. According to Marbode's *De lapidibus* (*Of Stones*), coral begins life as a sea plant and is petrified by the caress of air.[61] In its new form coral repels lightning and hail, aids agriculture, and drives away demons. Red and black chelidony, listed in several inventories of jewels possessed by medieval households, supposedly derives from the stomach of swallows. These animals are killed, Marbode writes, so that the dull but potent stone may be removed. Wrapped in linen and carried in the left armpit, chelidony cures insanity, revitalizes the body, and grants eloquence.[62] Produced by the most volatile of bodies, flitting birds, chelidony lends its therapeutic emanations only to humans who know how to foster alliance. Yet stone is more than the relations it sustains. Chelidony exerts its powers in avian stomachs or human armpits or apothecary shelves. Carbuncle and *smaragdus* glimmer with lasting radiance oblivious to the presence of an observer. *Silentes* ("moon stone") waxes and wanes in cogency according to the phases of its celestial companion. Although humans may benefit from its aura, the stone's ardor is reserved for its lunar beloved (*De lapidibus*, 383–95).

Despite our insatiable appetite for the *Lord of the Rings* and the Harry Potter oeuvre, we too easily dismiss medieval stories of lithic agency as the ingenuous dreams of a magic-loving, prescientific age.[63] Bruno Latour writes of "those poor archaic folks" held in contempt by the Moderns because they "had the misfortune of living on the wrong side of the 'epistemological break.'"[64] We no longer hope to discover the process through which base metals might be transmuted into gold. We no longer believe that coral wards against storms. Yet something in the medieval fascination with coral's intimacy to climate change captures stone's lush environmental activeness and intricately entangled vigor. Coral is enmeshed within global weather regardless of human desires. Its diminutive boughs—plant, animal, and rock in one—materialize robust relations to clouds, rain, and wind. The lapidary tradition grants stone solitude as well as potential companionability, well registering a lithic protest against instrumentalism. Stone's challenge to human exceptionalism is most frequently perceived within an aesthetic register, especially as its allure affectively seizes a viewer. Carbuncle (from the Latin word for coal) is a precious stone that glows as if an endless ember. The gem is not mere coal, however, for it never loses its ability to luminesce, and this emissive power is held regardless of external forces like fire and heat. In the account of the encyclopedist Bartholomaeus Anglicus carbuncle radiates poetry as much as light: "Carbuncle is a precious stone and shines as fire whose shining is not overcome by night. It shines in dark places, and it seems as flame."[65] Twelve different types exist, irradiating beams of purple or crimson, revealing in its depths gold spangles, surrounding itself with an embrace of sparkling mists, even "smelling of lanterns." Such radiance is not necessarily offered for an audience. Sometimes stone will afford itself as ready-to-hand tool, sometimes it will stun, and sometimes it will reveal inbuilt elusiveness. As Bartholomaeus observes, we are easily beguiled by bright gems of feeble potency, when far more power may reside within a dense chunk of dark rock.[66]

When it registers physically and aesthetically (from the Greek verb *aisthesthai,* "perceive"), stone provokes tangible connection, the thickening of relations. Aesthetics involves intense conveyance and includes the repellent and the commonplace as well as the sublime, three registers at which rock is familiar.[67] Lithic force can mark a retreat into inscrutability, into something more than can be grasped at once, fully articulated, exhausted or stilled.[68] Its materiality is so compacted that something always remains opaque, unbreached, coiled within itself, ready to surprise. Because it derogates human modes of knowing and worldly enframings, stone elicits litanies, apposition, the multiplication of conjunctive, even disjunctive terms. A promise of beauty as well as an uncertainty principle, stone's force amounts to a kind of magic, an ontological disruptiveness. The lithic pulses with dynamism and fosters a greater worldedness. Never surrendering itself to full apprehension, stone also reveals its solitariness, its residence outside mammalian frames, within an ecology where humans might be collaborators or fellow actors, but might also be the extras or (worse) mere scenery to petric dramas.

Geoffrey Chaucer writes that metals transformed into coins triggered modernity (commodification of natural materials engenders the war by other means that we would today call mercantile capitalism). Metals are therefore said to be "lurkinge in derknesse" until mined, a disruptive force awaiting excavation ("The Former Age," line 29). Yet despite their lack of human transformation, gems "in the riveres" (line 30) are no less agentic. They instantly activate desire, a dangerous "coveytyse." Stone opens a realm in which things exert agency, sometimes with and sometimes against the humans who fashion relations with it. In such a world of alluring objects a ring with two colorful stones ("l'une est blance, l'autre vermeille") can transform an overly solitary knight into a pack-loving wolf ("leus devenrai, grans et corsus").[69] Herbs may radiate a juice so fecundating that to spill their distilled essence across a mountainside is to render the slope an eternal memorial garden.[70] Splashing water upon an emerald in a copse will spark a tempest so virulent that the heavens part, lightning splits the trees, and rain, snow, and hail pummel the countryside.[71] As with this jewel-induced storm, astonishing advent may be announced, quite literally, by a thunderclap. Thus the Peterborough Lapidary describes coparius, a rock engendered by clouds.[72] Its earthly plummet heralded by "gret tempest," this celestial stone withdraws into concealment for nine days, after which those who know its arrival may earn its possession. Storm-birthed coparius emits its energies whether or not its place of concealment is discovered, but to treasure the stone is to be protected from lechery, lightning, and *mysauentur* (misadventure). This meteoric rock materializes an intimacy of gales, clouds, rain, bolts, bodies, and earth, a coming-into-entanglement. A dense nexus of unpredictable relation-making, stone discloses the enchantment inherent to things, the powers of which cannot be reduced to history, use value, contextual significance, or culture.

The Dance of Agency

As anyone who has ever erected a wall from balanced stones, attempted bouldering, or beachcombed and found the hand drawn to a particular pebble knows, rock possesses compositional and interruptive agencies. These forces are abstruse, dense (they do not surrender themselves to easy comprehension) and yet provocative, invitational. Rock is a summons to adventure, in the Latin sense of *adventurus,* that which is about to arrive, a promise of unlooked-for entrance and entrancement, a startling eventuation, ardent inhuman alliance. As previous chapters have detailed, in the *History of the Kings of Britain* Geoffrey of Monmouth discerns a call to story from Stonehenge, the rocks of which have moved over tremendous distances and endured for spans only dimly apprehensible. Merlin is drawn to what these stones radiate, potencies that may be mobilized for the healing of wounds and for the conveyance to the far future of the memory of the dead. Their force is imbued not by human hands, but by an innate power harnessed through association: medicinally, for example, through water, herbs, and fleshly contact; or textually, an intensification or release of narrative. The transcontinental errancy of these stones (from Africa to Ireland to Britain) is made possible through an epochal collaboration among giants, a prophet who is an engineer, a king who understands the emissive power of monuments in the wake of catastrophe, a fleet of agile ships, armies of men, and a diversity of readers to come who enable the storied life of Stonehenge to thrive. Its force is made evident through intractability (the stones cannot be moved by the Britons, since they lack Merlin's ingenuity) and gregarious confederation (Merlin knows the contrivances through which massive stones will lightly surrender to transportation).

An emissive contrivance *(machinatio),* Geoffrey's Stonehenge is also an enduringly lively *locum memorabilem* ("place of memory") and *opus* ("work"). These Latin descriptions are used by Geoffrey to describe the ancient monument, but they are just as true of the text in which the stone circle manifests its vibrancy. Both Stonehenge and the *History of the Kings of Britain* are engineered by skill *(ingenium)* and capable of enmeshing an inhuman prehistory, the resplendent British past, and possible futures. As Merlin activates the power of the trilithons Geoffrey animates the text. The extraordinary vigor of the *History* can be glimpsed in its rapid dissemination and transmutation into new forms.[73] Its stately Latin quickly assumed new life in French, English, and Welsh adaptations. Working at the English royal court, the poet Wace created the first vernacular translation, rendering Geoffrey's laconic prose into spirited French couplets, *Le Roman de Brut* (ca. 1155). Wace emphasizes the force of stones throughout his poem, but nowhere so much as the Merlin segment: rocks are the weapons that aid some Britons in their escape from the Night of the Long Knives ("Od pieres lur cors defendant," 7260), the restless and enmeshing matter that ensure Vortigern's dream of perfect isolation within a stone tower will never

Giants' Dance, Stonehenge.

be fulfilled (7319–38), the memorial that will rise on the same plain where those Britons whose hands did not find a lethal partner with stone were slain by Saxon knives. In Wace's description Stonehenge is a powerful work ("ovre") that will long endure ("peüst durer," 8001–2). Merlin's account of the structure rhymes the word for *word* ("parole") with the term for the circle of stones ("carole"), connecting story and lithic architecture as "ovres durables" (8039–42), works that last. The stones are just as efficacious for Wace as they were for his predecessor, curing the infirmities of the African giants who transported them to Ireland and conveying messages from prehistory across inhuman spans of time. Yet not everyone in the *Roman de Brut* perceives Stonehenge's power. Aurelius, king of the Britons, realizes its efficacy immediately ("les pieres tel valur ourent," 8080), yet the Irish regent who has inherited the megalithic construction from its outsized foreign builders beholds only lifeless matter. King Gilloman wonders why the Britons would sail to his shores in search of objects so mundane. For him the rocks possess no allure:

> And when he heard what [the Britons] sought, that they had come for the stones, he derided them at length: those who, seeking stones, crossed the sea to another land, went in search of folly. (8099–8104)

Unlike Gilloman, for whom the structure holds neither history nor force, Merlin knows that Stonehenge harbors both, at least for those who attend to the structure. Its powers course plural vectors:

> And Merlin erected the stones, restoring them to their proper order. In the British language the Britons usually call them the Giants' Dance [*carole as gaianz*]; in English they are called Stonehenge [*Stanhenges*], and in French, the Hanging Stones [*Pierres pendues*]. (8173–78)

The triple gloss with which Wace culminates the episode gestures toward the monument's illimitability by conveying its polyglot destiny.[74] Each linguistic designation carries into the world a different quality of the circle: a choreography, a hinge or gallows, a suspension. Wace himself always calls the structure "la carole" ("dance," "song"), a French translation of *chorea* that emphasizes kineticism and sonorousness. An aesthetically seductive object of long duration, Stonehenge intervenes into and sometimes even remediates human relations.

Stonehenge has lost trilithons to gravity, carvings to the erosive force of rain and wind, bluestones to roads, sarsens to foundations. Never at any point a completed project, even in Geoffrey and Wace's day the circle evidenced its mutability, the wear and tear of its time travel. Yet as Old English elegies like "The Wanderer" insist, ruination is a form of renewal. The archeologist Bjørnar Olsen writes that objects often release meaning and "generate a different kind of knowledge" through their decay. Unlike the impossible stasis for which preservation strives, ruin enables the remains of a lost past to live "as a special kind of involuntary memory . . . 'freed from the drudgery of being useful' and released from the chain of relations they have been enslaved in."[75] By not being compelled to speak a small history, such objects surface their own singularity, assert their idiosyncrasy. They reveal peculiar qualities that are not the result of cultural impress but are intensified by human collaboration all the same. Beloved as a historical remnant, ever-unfinished Stonehenge possesses a power that has yet to abate. To behold the lithic wheel set upon the green expansiveness of Salisbury Plain is to feel desire, a summons to creative alliance. The *Clonehenge* blog well documents the transnational lives of the megalithic ring as an assemblage of cars, inflatable plastic bricks, cake, refrigerators, polystyrene boulders, concrete blocks, acrobats, iron, glass, cheese, peeps, gingerbread, wood, parking meters, citrus fruit, snow, digital models.[76] Stonehenge is more than a heritage site. Its vivacious partners include African monsters, a British wizard, a cleric from Monmouth and a poet from the island of Jersey, Neolithic peoples, the Preseli Hills, glaciation, tectonic shift, the Internet, us. Its ponderous immensity extends connection points or relays for manifold narratives, invitations to aeonic and cross-ontological participation.

Carole as gaianz. Because a dance is an intricacy that unfolds over time and involves multiple participants, the word is often deployed within the new materialism to indicate dynamic human-nonhuman enmeshment. Timothy Morton speaks of the "enactive dance" that stickily connects ecologies.[77] Jane Bennett observes that "humanity and nonhumanity have always performed an intricate dance with each other."[78] Andrew Pickering describes the "mangle" that brings together humans and nonhumans in a "constitutive intertwining" as a "dance of agency."[79] Geoffrey of Monmouth's Latin noun *chorea* and Wace's *carole* are just as good as designations, just as capable of acknowledging that the menhirs and sarsens and British kings and engineering devices and distant times and places are partners in elegant motion. Since *chorea* and *carole* also mean "song," they well convey the lasting resonance of stories of stone.

Improbable and Natural

Roger Caillois devoted his life to exploring such mysteries as why animal mimicry imitates nothing but rather intensifies and produces, how a decapitated praying mantis imitates death, and why rocks are such accomplished artists. His essays attempted the displacement of *Homo sapiens* from assumed centrality by detailing the creative impulses and aesthetic flourishing of agates, insects, octopi, butterflies, natural architectures, the constellated cosmos.[80] Art, Caillois insisted, evidences a universal impulse to creativity, a superfluous beauty fashioned by subterranean pressures as easily as human hands. His book *The Writing of the Stones* is an illustrated tour of geologic sculptures and igneous portraiture offered for no audience to admire, the petrification of an inbuilt inclination to produce beyond utility, to intensify the world's materiality into coruscation, even combustion. As perceptive a reader of lithic force as any medieval lapidarist, Caillois discovered in marble, amethyst, jasper, limestone, and agate an aesthetic affinity to human art "at once improbable and natural," a similitude best described as a commonality.[81] This mineral expressiveness manifested for him an omnipresent inclination to ornament, an innate proclivity to generate and join relations, the relentless production of "an intrinsic, infallible, immediate beauty, answerable to no one."[82] Like Michel Serres after him, Caillois's posthumanism is evident in his refusal to carve a space distinctly "human" from a vast and heterogeneous world.

Caillois was an enthusiastic collector of mineral art and a pilgrim to the sites where its beauty manifests. His journey to comprehend telluric force followed a path similar to that which beckoned Albertus Magnus, just as fascinated by stones that carry natural inscriptions and offer landscapes and figures without any human having touched them. Albertus argued in the thirteenth century that occult virtues of the deep earth generate such artworks. He provides two vivid examples from his own experience: a slab of marble he viewed in Venice as a young man that when cut open revealed the portrait of a crowned and bearded king, and an oyster found inside a fish, its shell incised with an entanglement of snakes (*Book of Minerals,* 2.3.1). Albertus describes such art not as miracles, not as demonic lures, but as the products of nature busily at work. He confidently explains why the king's visage within the opened marble was slightly distorted, the effect of the great heat of the rising vapors deep within the earth as they created the regal face. He loves these inhuman masterpieces, cherishing the oyster shell with its serpentine figures for years before bestowing it as a gift. "Experience," he writes, "proves that even figures projecting from [the surface of] stones are sometimes made by nature" (2.2.3)—and that nature and humans share creative impulses. Albertus sometimes makes mistakes, classifying figures etched by human hands as "made by nature," such as a cameo found in Cologne, an onyx into which has been cut two figures, probably Roman (2.3.2). Such confusion does not matter, in the end, since Albertus discerns in stone a call to cocomposition: "art and nature" collaborate to produce engraved stones, human artist allying with "mineralizing or petrifying force" (2.3.2). Signs incised on gems intensify their innate powers, whether an artist or natural forces or both create the sigil. To cut an image of Hercules into a jewel renders it a powerful ally in battle, and to discover a lithic engraving of *Ursa major* is to come upon a rock that will provide wisdom, cunning, agility, and courage (2.3.5). To fashion a precious stone into an amulet and carry the portable artwork with you is to join forces with its natural virtues, and perhaps to gain in bodily health (2.3.6). Both humans and rocks create, Albertus concludes, because they are stirred to action by astral magnetism, an artistic incitement deriving from the "motions of the stars" (2.3.3). Because they possess free will humans often resist sidereal provocation, but like stones they are suffused by its invitational force all the same: "If, then, the force and inspirations of the stars pour some influence causing art into the artisan, surely nothing prevents their pouring something of their own power into all works made by art" (2.3.3).

Stone's force is exorbitant yet intimate, engendering or renewing or interrupting relations among bodies, objects, and milieu, eroding the boundary between organic and inorganic.[83] This disruption of ontological category and placing into contact what might otherwise remain in seclusion occurs through the opening of unexpected portals, through a possibly infinite series of worldings—as when within stones Roger Caillois discovers enfolded and metamorphic densities, as when within Stonehenge Geoffrey of Monmouth finds a material and narrative vibrancy. The Stonehenge episode is actually rather anomalous in the *History of the Kings of Britain,* a text known for its contribution to literary history of the "matter of Britain" rather than for any artistry its narrative possesses. Despite being largely a work of the imagination, Geoffrey's book is known for the historical function it served: firmly establishing a countervision of British prehistory, promulgating a potent origin myth. Its panorama of the insular past offered a useful antidote to a long tradition of English triumphalism, the dominating version of the island's settlement within Latin historiography. The immediate popularity of Geoffrey's text can be ascribed to the manifold cultural needs it satisfied: Welsh and Breton patriotism, the desire of the triumphant Normans for an insular history in which their presence was something more than an interruption of English destiny, a more pluralistic and polyglot vision of the post-Conquest British archipelago. If the text were so wholly of its moment, however, initial enthusiasm ought to have dissipated as the cultural exigencies it arose to address abated under its tremendous success. The *History of the Kings of Britain* should have followed the arc of all propaganda, from spectacular ascent to rapid decline in the wake of the changes it fostered, to lingering existence at some margin where it could be acknowledged as the somewhat embarrassing remnant of a transcended past. Yet ardor for the text only intensified over time. Copies and versions proliferated. Like the *Book of John Mandeville* after it, the *History* went viral, lived, thrived. It helped to spawn new genres, like chivalric romance and *lais* of love and adventure. Each transformation was a deepening of its narrative possibilities, an intensification of its art. Geoffrey established what might be called a consensual world, a geotemporality that may never have existed, that comes into being and is sustained only through the texts by which writers populate its ever-expanding landscapes, but a world that nonetheless functions *as if* real, inviting authors and scholars and admirers to contribute their fictions and histories, their new characters, their enlargements of Arthurian myth. The *History of the Kings of Britain* invited fan fiction. As Wace adapted Geoffrey's unadorned Latin prose into spirited verse he added details like King Arthur's creation of a Round Table. Stories of the Grail, Lancelot, Morgan le Fay, the Lady of the Lake, and the Green Knight are the introductions of later writer-fans to Geoffrey's universe, the loose parameters and initial content of which he was the engineer.

The call to expansion embedded within Geoffrey's *History* is palpable at some powerful narrative moments in which a certain radiance (what Roger Caillois called "innate" or "objective" lyricism) propels the text outside of its ordinary orbit, when the thin finitude of mundane existence is disrupted through intensification, resulting in a temporal and aesthetic density that enfolds and entangles what otherwise might remain small, discrete. In making such a statement I do not mean to ignore the political machinations behind the long history of appropriating Arthurian mythology or to displace that process of patrimony-hijacking into a purely aesthetic realm. Stories of British Arthur posed a profound challenge to English insular hegemony, a difficulty neutralized through rapid assimilation: Wace, for example, describes Arthur as a king of England rather than Britain, and much changes with that metonym. The force of some of the objects and events that Geoffrey describes is so intense that later cultural appropriation harnessed their ability to bestow an aura of the sublime (and to radiate postcolonial hybridities). The political story of the text and its co-option have been cogently detailed.[84] Yet Geoffrey's objects hold and generate other stories alongside ideological and anthropocentric narratives. An object-oriented mode of inquiry does not make political reading impossible, but by detailing the power of things illuminates why they might be essential (if not necessarily compliant) partners in processes of cultural transformation. As the *History of the Kings of Britain* traveled across languages and continents, emitting narrative possibilities intimately connected to its stories of stone, sometimes it was diminished, and sometimes it exceeded frames attempting containment and cultural capture.

Geoffrey's lithic tales take their time in arriving, but at their advent transform a text that until the Arthurian section yields few hints of the potencies to come. Division of the island, civil war, and reunification offer a repeating structure, with occasional forays into empire building and public works projects. Lists of kings with regnal spans, martial accomplishments, and progeny structure long expanses. The aggregate dullness of this data gives the work the heft of an artifact, the substantiality of something real. Thus the brief but exciting tale of a sodomy-prone king devoured in the wilds by ravening wolves is tempered by the dry facticity of his son's reign, a history constructed with all the excitement of erecting a long wall from an endless supply of gray boulders (*History of the Kings of Britain,* 27). This weighty piling up of information imbues the *History* with the verity of an archive: a largely unadorned chronicle, its cogency most evident in its formal structure. Yet the narrative is punctuated by moments of unexpected effulgence, smaller stories that derail the progress of the larger plot with their vividness and, at times, poignancy.[85] This aesthetic power early in the text is aqueous, soaking into intermixture human and earth to produce strange new kinds of art. Sometimes these watery, almost lyrical interruptions bear the salty tang of seawater, and sometimes the brine of the text's most sublime substance, blood.[86] Take, for example, the pluvial gore that drenches the island during the rule of the obscure king Rivallo, a soaking in crimson both awesome and gruesome: "While he was king, it rained blood for three days and people died from a plague of flies" (33). By saturating the earth with a bodily substance alien to its expanses ("pluuia sanguinea"), this vivid reddening of the island estranges place from world, a medieval version of Christo's "Pont Neuf Wrapped" or "Surrounded Islands" hitched to a kind of charnel house art in which even splattered stone becomes a grimly aesthetic element, a dark ecology in which hematic rain transfigures the world into something violent, rotting, yet both striking and lively. Obscure generation of blood by clouds elicits spontaneous generation of insects by earth.

This soaking of the world in gore also makes clear an element missing from Roger Caillois's account of lithic beauty. Petric radiance is entrancing, wondrous. Yet stone is also fatal. Rock can crush as easily as enthrall. Blood in its drenching relation to stone will signal a profound transformation later in Geoffrey's text, when the *History* takes its swerve into new narrative registers. The transformation of the text begins with an attempt to render toppling rocks compliant by wetting them with sacrificial blood, as if through the conjoining of vital fluid with lithic recalcitrance human desires for secure foundations might be realized. The story will refuse such easy anthropomorphism. Lifeblood and stone will not meet because they need not. What those who make the expiatory demand eventually realize is that stone requires no baptism in organic fluid to ally itself with humans or propel them to their doom. Force already courses the rocks, allowing them to impede (a tower keeps toppling) and to create (the episode will culminate in the release of rock-held monsters, dragons incarnating the past and the future).

Stone's inanimation is, in Geoffrey's text, human misapprehension. A king might assume that the lands over which he exerts dominion will enable the establishing of lasting social structures and architectures, but quarried foundations will refuse to remain placidly emplaced. On the run from Saxon confederates turned enemies, the traitorous British monarch Vortigern frantically attempts to bring stability back to an island he once dominated. Having exhausted all martial strategies he contemplates occult intervention. With the resonant line "vocatis denique magis suis" ("finally he summoned his magicians," *History of the Kings of Britain,* 106), the narrative is transformed. Until this point the *History* had been largely empty of enchantment, its wonder confined to small episodes without lasting textual consequence. Henceforth astonishment repeatedly erupts. *Enter the magicians.* These *magi,* the first in the text, and the first therefore in mainstream Arthurian myth, are charged by King Vortigern with finding a way to bring durability to a fugitive life. The magicians declare that such permanence can be found only in the creation of "a very strong tower" from stone. When a suitable site is chosen at Mount Snowdon, however, whatever blocks the masons erect are swallowed into the earth overnight.[87] The magicians declare that to lay secure foundations the mortar must be sprinkled with the blood of "a young man who had no father" (106)—with blood, that is, that carries none of the patrilineal history that has so far structured Geoffrey's text, obsessed with genealogy and regnal persistence.

A lad without a father is found, a surly and precocious boy named Merlin. His origin is vexed. In the form of a very handsome youth an incubus once made secret love with a nun in her chamber's solitude. Eventually she bore a child. Ancient books verify, according to an expert consulted by Vortigern, that "incubos demones" (incubus demons) do indeed exist between moon and earth ("inter lunam et terram," *History of the Kings of Britain,* 107). Possessed of a pedigree that ties them to the fallen angels of the bible and the exegesis surrounding Genesis 6:4, incubi are monsters who incarnate the very spirit of Geoffrey's text. They offer an irruptive counterhistory, stories at war with dominating traditions and mundane realities. *Enter the magicians.* What Vortigern's magi have unwittingly demanded is the shattering of that border between the quotidian (the ordinary world where people remain in the times and places history allots to them) and the extraordinary (the space of possibility where a cloistered nun can find love in the embrace of a mysterious, handsome knight). These magicians transport the *History of the Kings of Britain* into a new realm, where the rules that have so far structured the narrative's unfolding shatter and are remade.[88] Enter the magicians, enter stones that demand humans work in companionship with their obscure agency, and enter the genre of romance.[89]

Merlin, the boy in whose body compound, story-laden, and disruptive blood pulses, has his own ideas of how Vortigern might construct his desired fortification. To create an enduring architecture, he announces, requires not the commission of more violence, but an acknowledgement of the unstable history undergirding every structure's coming into being. Merlin reveals that Vortigern's tower topples at each foundation because he constructs its base upon perturbed ground, upon a subterranean realm replete with matter and life. Beneath Mount Snowdon, within an underground pool, inside two hollow rocks ("duos concauos lapides") at the bottom of that water, twin dragons doze ("duos dracones dormientes," *History of the Kings of Britain,* 108). Monstrous incarnations of troubled history, the white dragon symbolizes the marauding Saxons, while in the red's pugnacious body stirs the story of the embattled Britons. Encased in stone, these dragons may well be fossils. Disinterred, the sleeping creatures spring to life and engage in fierce battle. Once this buried past is spoken and the dragons dismissed from their tellurian enmity, Merlin is freed from the compulsion to yield his blood to stones. He can persevere in the story to erect at Salisbury the vast architecture of Stonehenge, rocks that when drenched with water heal wounded bodies. Vortigern, meanwhile, is burnt to ash within the tower he erects, his incineration a reminder of the oblivion that comes to those who reside within merely human story.

Enter the magicians, and enter astonishment. Vortigern is astounded by Merlin's biography ("ammirans rex," *History of the Kings of Britain,* 107). He is amazed as well by the boy's declaration that he knows the hidden agency behind the toppling of his tower ("ammirans rex," 108). The king's magicians are filled with fear by the same words, and stand in silence—a reasonable equivalent to astonishment. When Merlin reveals the sleeping dragons within the stones, Vortigern marvels again ("ammirabatur"). So do all those present who witness the opening of the animal-bearing rocks ("ammirabantur"). Following this sudden effusion of wonder Geoffrey inserts the *Prophecies of Merlin,* a long and inscrutable account ("ambiguitate uerborum") of a future that may never arrive, words that reduce their auditors to amazement ("astantes in ammirationem," 118). Like Merlin, like the lapidary dragons, Stonehenge is from its first appearance astonishment-inducing, an assemblage of stones ("lapidum structuram") that causes the Britons who behold its majesty in Ireland to wonder ("ammirati," 174). The trilithons journey from Africa to Ireland to Britain, and fasten stories of their primal architects, the giants, to humans, and the ring thereby conjoins distant pasts to unexpected prospects.

The Vortigern's Tower episode concludes with Merlin's transformation from disparaged child to astute spirit of creativity, an artist of estranged materialities. Merlin is expert in the writing of stones, in petric composition. By discerning the monsters within rock's heart, creatures pulsing with dangerous life, and by revealing the ameliorative powers that flow from Stonehenge—by recognizing the radiant, alluring force in buried rocks and ancient monoliths—he speaks the inhuman, self-dispossessing, unhistorical truth of stone.

The Adventure of Stone

Texts enter the world as agents and carry within them the ability to transform, adapt, activate untapped reserves, foster relations, and engender strange progeny. They are propelled by their own aesthetic power as well as the allure their objects radiate.[90] *Enter the magicians* signals a shift in tone, genre, work in the world. Although the advent of romance is conventionally placed with vernacular works several decades after Geoffrey of Monmouth's *History of the Kings of Britain*, his text frames the door through which this mode of writing and living arrives.[91] The earliest romances were historical. The *Roman d'Eneas, Roman de Thèbes,* and *Roman de Troie* betray through their titles their classical obsessions (and are therefore typically referred to as *romans antiques*).[92] Wace's translation of Geoffrey, the *Roman de Brut,* does not quite achieve metamorphosis of form, yet well demonstrates the force that *aventure* as transformative, story-bearing arrival exerts. Wace writes that the marvels sought ("merveiles pruvees") and adventures discovered ("aventures truvees") during the reign of Arthur so proliferated story that it has become difficult to separate fable from history: "not all lies, not all truth, neither total folly nor total wisdom" (9789–94). At some time after 1160, however, an author by the name of Chrétien de Troyes composed a series of profoundly influential works that perfectly crystallized the potential within Geoffrey's materials. In narratives detailing the chivalric exploits of the Arthurian knights (Erec, Yvain, Gawain, Lancelot, Perceval) and powerful ladies (Guenevere, Laudine, Morgan, Enide), Chrétien brought into vibrant existence a realm teeming with wonder and rather indifferent to the concerns of chronicle history. By creating a domain in which lions ally themselves with mad warriors, where rings confer invisibility and burning spears descend upon enchanted beds, Chrétien intensified the possibilities for objectal agency that he discovered in Geoffrey and transported these potentialities to a fledgling vernacular genre in which the complicated relations among individuals and things matter more than political events, genealogies, racial histories, and the origins of homelands.[93]

The rules of this changed world are made evident in *The Knight with the Lion (Le Chevalier au lion,* or *Yvain*), a work from the midpoint of Chrétien's fertile career. Calogrenant, knight of the Arthurian household, encounters in his wandering a strange herdsman guarding wild bulls. Although described through a demeaning menagerie of animal comparisons, the herdsman insists that he is a man, "uns hom" (*Yvain,* 330). The uncertainties of human identity are immediately foregrounded. When in return Calogrenant proclaims himself "uns chevaliers" (a knight), the herdsman declares that he does not understand what the word signifies. Calogrenant offers a quick definition: a knight is he who seeks "avanture, por esprover / ma proesce et mon hardemant" (adventure, to test my courage and my strength, 363–64). Despite this explanation the herdsman remains perplexed: "of adventure I know nothing" (368). He does inform the knight, however, of a nearby spring "colder than marble" where he will find a beautiful tree, an iron basin, and a magical stone *(perron)*. Casting water upon the rock triggers lightning, rain, wind, and thunder (*toner,* the verb that inhabits *astonish*). Despite a warning against activating the storm, Calogrenant proceeds immediately to the spring, eager to distinguish himself from the herdsman who does not know adventure, eager to witness the wonder ("mervoille," 432) of the changed world.

An emerald awaits, mounted atop four rubies as radiant as the morning sun.[94] Calogrenant drenches the verdant jewel, instantly triggering deluge. Lightning blinds the knight and shreds nearby trees. Rain, snow, and hail soak the ground. A fierce gale howls. Chrétien may have been inspired here by the lapidary of Marbode of Rennes, where the powers of green and red *eliotropia* ("sun turner") are described as causing water to boil and gush, triggering rain and swollen clouds, ending calm weather.[95] Yet the tempest passes as suddenly as it arrives, and in its still wake the knight who summoned the storm is transported from fear to joy ("de joie fui toz asseür," *Yvain,* 456). The rapturous, birdsong-filled beauty of the postdeluge landscape astonishes Calogrenant with its vibrancy. He narrates the event to his companions of the Arthurian court:

> As soon as the storm abated,
> I saw gathered on the pine tree
> so many birds—believe it if you will—
> that not a leaf or branch could be found
> that was not completely covered with birds;
> the tree was more beautiful because of them;
> the birds singing softly,
> in perfect harmony. . . .
> I rejoiced in their joyousness . . .
> for I had never heard such perfect joy. . . .
> I was totally enraptured
>   *[que je m'an dui por fos tenir].* (*Yvain,* 459–77)

Although Lucienne Carasso-Bulow attributes the eruption of the marvelous in Chrétien's work to "irrational causality," Chrétien might better be described as intensifying an agency that the ecological already possesses.[96] His romances deepen environmental enmeshment through forces both perilous and sublime. His magic objects are marvelous not because of their impossibility, but because they make evident matter's potency. Sudden revelation of unexpected, inhuman agency often stuns its witness, revealing a world in which "bodies, substances, goods, organisms, landscapes and energetic flows" thrum with vitality, "the adventures of matter."[97] Effusion of material power is indeed what Chrétien calls *aventure,* hazardous arrival, the root of our modern word *adventure.* Revealing the world's workings as fundamentally weird, *aventure* is chancy, enchanting, oblique, and inassimilable.[98] Miracles arrive through divine power, but *aventure* is wondrous secular irruption.[99] Its embodied effect is astonishment. *Aventure* is not to be dismissed as mere romance, mere fantasy, not reality's escape but an intensification of its possibilities.

The *aventure* of the storm-stone knocks Calogrenant out of the orbit of his ordinary life and grants him an environmental vision never before possessed. He is transported, rejoicing in the joy of birds ("De lor joie me resjoi"). This ecstatic moment is short lived. An angry knight appears on horseback, curses Calogrenant for unleashing the ruinous storm upon his land, beats him to the ground, and seizes his mount. Though the emerald and its fiery rubies radiate aesthetic power, though they can transform the world, their agency is fraught with danger. The tempest has waged a kind of war against the knight's domain. Its aftermath might be beautiful, but summoning rain and gale carries hazardous consequence, including ecological devastation and physical harm. Calogrenant pays a bruising price for his moment of transport. Yet even as he slinks back to Arthur's court to relate his defeat, the *aventure* that he instigates possesses its own vitality. His story inspires his cousin Yvain to follow in his footsteps, pouring water on the ruby-mounted emerald and summoning the storm again. Yvain defeats the knight who rides against him. His world will be transformed by this second gem-triggered *aventure,* this advent of possibility brought about through stone's irradiative and enmeshing force.

Through Chrétien, Arthurian history becomes Arthurian myth. By heightening the promise, prospect, and futurity (*l'avenir,* that which is coming) in which Geoffrey of Monmouth steeped his narrative, Chrétien also magnifies the lapidary power evident in the *History of the Kings of Britain*. Marie de France, another twelfth-century contributor to the consensual world of Arthuriana for which Geoffrey laid the foundation, structured her short narrative poems *(lais)* around aesthetic objects so dense in their metaphoricity that they open endless conveyance: the talkative deer and the ship of dreams in *Guigemar*; the woven cloth that materializes a sexuality in *Le Fresne*; the vestments that maintain and yet confuse the boundary between knight and wolf in a tale of lycanthropy, *Bisclavret*.[100] Guigemar, for example, is a self-absorbed young knight who loves only solitary pleasures like hunting. Alone in the forest he encounters a doe with antlers, an impossibly composite body. His arrow rebounds from this living artwork of an animal, wounding his thigh and hurling him into erotic possibility. Guigemar's world, like his body, has been penetrated and will henceforth never be circumscribed. He boards a boat that awaits in the harbor, a ship of *aventure,* a material metaphor for the transportive lyricism of poetry. This autonomous ship, empty except for an ornate bed, conveys the youth to an impossibly distant land. Here his ardor for a lady imprisoned by her jealous spouse will allow them both to discover a portal to a more capacious future. Although he and the lady enjoy their love together, they are in time discovered by the old man who keeps his wife locked in the stone tower. Guigemar is expelled, finds the vessel on which he arrived, and returns to his native shores to await his beloved. Her angry husband again immures her, this time in marble ("en prisun / En une tur de marbre bis," *Guigemar,* 660–61), where she spends two anguished years. Stone, it seems, is that which renders bodies immobile. Held too long in despondence, the lady decides at last to throw herself into the sea:

> Dunc lieve sus;
> Tut esbaïe vient a l'hus,
> Ne treve cleif ne sereüre;
> Fors s'en eissi par aventure. (*Guigemar, 673–76*)
> [Then she got up;
> in astonishment she went to the door
> and found it unlocked;
> by good fortune, she got outside.]

Two years of joyless imprisonment end the moment the lady arises *(lieve sus)* and tries the unbolted door. She cannot sail across the sea and find Guigemar, it seems, until she makes the choice to propel herself out of lapidary stasis, to write for herself a narrative different from the familiar story in which she has too long played the affection-starved wife to a dry old man. Perhaps the door from the stone tower has always been unlocked. When she attempts departure she discovers that it is not marble that has held her, but her belief in her immobility. Once the lady makes the choice to act against enclosure, she finds that the stone within which she has dwelt is a site of possibility, of *aventure*: the opening of the ordinary into that which is astonishing. The wondrous ship attends at the harbor. Could metaphor take a more beautiful form than that vessel gliding vast seas, intimately connecting realms that did not previously know each other, enlarging the world with every wave traversed by its unpiloted prow? Marble tower, ebony ship, and desiring lovers combine to form a living, relation-generating, and transformative metaphor (literally, a transport device) that conveys the lady outside of the smallness of her selfhood, that enables her to discover, beyond the sad circumscription that had been her prison of stone, realms stormy with possibility.

In *Yonec* Marie offers another scene of lapidary enclosure that yields to *aventure*. Surrender to that world where stone is active, transportive, and everything changes. As in *Guigemar,* the unnamed heroine of *Yonec* has been confined within a tower by a jealous, elderly husband. Her beauty fades within living entombment. She wishes that the magical worlds that she has read about in romance might be true, desiring that *aventure* through which ladies discover lovers "so handsome, courtly, brave and valiant / that they could not be blamed, / and no one else would see them" (*Yonec,* 98–100). She desires, that is, to be like Guigemar's beloved, or like Merlin's mother, enjoying in secret the embraces denied within the constricted spaces of quotidian life. *Enter the magician.* Upon its utterance her wish takes fleshly form. A hawk flies to the ledge of the stone tower and enters through the window as "a handsome and noble knight" ("chevalier bel e gent," 115). In *Guigemar* the door to the tower yields only when the lady makes the decision to push against its fixity; here the bird-knight has loved the lady in *Yonec* for many years but had to await her speaking of her desire before he could fly to the chamber. Worlds that seem circumscribed by stone reveal unexpected prospect. The hawk-knight eventually impregnates the lady with a son. Her cruel husband discovers the truth of his wife's enjoyment and sets sharp spikes along her window ledge. When the knight attempts to enter again, he is torn apart, staining the bedclothes with his blood (316).

The dying hawk-knight returns to his distant land, and the lady decides upon an extraordinary course of action: she leaps from the window of her tower, leaps into activity and out of the prison of her own imagination. This springing into agency is her embrace of *aventure*. She follows a glimmering trail of blood ("la trace del sanc") straight into a hillside ("une hoge," a hill or a burial mound, *Yonec*, 345). Her subterranean journey yields an unexpected vista, unearthly splendor: "There was no house, no hall or tower, / that didn't seem of silver" (362–63). She enters a series of chambers, each harboring a slumbering knight: other lovers for other dream-filled ladies. On the third bed in the third room she discovers her mortally wounded knight, who speaks to her of a radiant future to arrive—a future that includes the narration of their shared *aventure* (434) to their soon to be born son, Yonec. The story ends when a story that inheres in a stone tomb spurs this son to take vengeance against his stepfather. The lady dies in bliss and grief at the marble grave of her love, tidy closure for an intricate little work of lithic art. Yet to return to the middle space of the *lai,* to its luminous underground chamber: here we glimpse the entrance to a world where sleeping knights without names, without narrated stories, await the cloistered dreamers who will dare to envision their own rescue from their own petrifying stories. This beautiful otherworld, sealed beneath a hill but reachable after a hazard-embracing leap, through an encounter with one's own potential obliteration, offers stone-wrapped spaces where the solidity of ordinary realms deliquesces. *Yonec* dreams a hollow space within the earth where possibilities are multiplied, where the world expands to induce aesthetic dispossession, the vertigo of ceasing to know the mundane.

A subterranean world of stone likewise opens in the fourteenth-century lay *Sir Orfeo,* possibly the weirdest narrative composed in Middle English. The distraught protagonist descends through rock to a realm where it is difficult to tell living from dead, humans from objects, waking from dreaming, beauty from horror. This enigmatic fairy kingdom derives from Welsh and Irish stories of the otherworld, fairy lore, classical accounts of Hades, and Christian imaginings of purgatory and hell, but exceeds all of these in its strangeness. *Sir Orfeo* is patterned roughly on the myth of Orpheus and Eurydice. The story follows Orfeo of Winchester (formerly known as Thrace) in his quest to retrieve his kidnapped wife. Queen Heurodis is snatched by the king of Fairy while sleeping beneath an "ympe-tree," a grafted tree standing at the threshold between quotidian existence and a disorienting Fairy World that seems at once underneath and beside human realms. At this hybrid juncture where worlds overlap, peevish human rules about how time should flow or how causality should work are suspended. Like the pine beneath which awaits a basin and storm-emerald in *The Knight with the Lion*, the ympe-tree is a portal of *aventure* through which an alien king may pass to roam ordinary forests, withdrawn into his own pursuits, or where a slumbering queen might be stolen to a place never sought. This same perilous entrance is activated later in the story through stone. Both these adventurous doors—one rocky and in the middle of wilderness, the other arboreal and at the center of court—are transport devices, material objects that are literally metaphoric and irreducible to symbol. The unknowability of the stone-enclosed kingdom to which these portals open derives not so much from its intensifying of human worlds (though there is that: the Fairy King is a magnified version of the sovereignty that Orfeo, as king of Thrace, also incarnates), but from its refusal to anchor its expanses within a merely human point of view. "*Unheimliche* strangeness" and "terrible beauty" derive from the challenging, unfathomable, radiantly inhuman objects of this subterranean, omnipresent domain.[101]

Orfeo discovers a door into stone by following the Fairy King's retinue as they ride into a rock ("in at a roche," *Sir Orfeo*, 347). The beauty of the "fair cuntray" (351) he beholds within derives from its materiality: castles shine like "cristal" (358), buttresses are formed of gold (362), spacious homes are fashioned "Al of precious stones" (366), and the whole of the underground realm glimmers with gem-given luminescence:

> Al that lond was ever light,
> For when it shuld be therk [dark] and night,
> The riche stones light gonne [radiate]
> As bright as doth at none [noon] the sonne.
> (*Sir Orfeo*, 369–72)

In this queer realm Orfeo finds his abducted wife asleep beneath the same tree from which she was seized in the ordinary world. Serene in her slumber, Heurodis is surrounded by other stolen dreamers, caught eternally at what seems to be the moment of their unquiet apprehension: beheaded, drowned, dismembered, bleeding, shriveled, strangled, on a childbed, burnt, mad. Transformed into objects, into a macabre kind of art, they exist in a somnolence removed from time, preserved in the agony of their capture. Perhaps they, unlike Heurodis, resisted their conveyance. The Fairy King warned the queen that should she not appear at the ympe-tree in the courtly world at his appointed time, she would be seized and mutilated ("thou worst y-fet / And totore thine limes al / That nothing help the no schall," 170–72). By surrendering to *aventure,* to that which arrives unwilled and unforeseen, to a world where things exert uncanny agency and human lives follow erratic, sometimes ecstatic tracks, she is transported out of human time but not out of body. A future lit by lithic radiance opens that which without such surrender might not have arrived, or might have arrived only at far greater peril.

When his queen was abducted by the fairies, Orfeo donned a pilgrim's cloak but sought nothing. He wandered the wilds in a bare existence, across a barren space of "snewe and frese" (snow and ice, 246). Orfeo discerned in the cold woods only "wilde wormes" (252), unsatisfying roots to eat, and "berien but gode lite" (berries of little worth, 258). No mystery resides in these objects. No aesthetic power shines. Yet through the art that Orfeo creates with his harp he allied himself with "weder . . . clere and bright," with a forest yearning for resonance, with birds and wild beasts hungry for "gle" and "melody" (269–78). The joyful moment of being-together that he creates, uncannily similar to what Chrétien's Calogrenant enjoys in the wake of storm, seems to call forth the king of Fairy. This inscrutable monarch wanders the woods with his retinue on a hunt in which nothing is pursued. Orfeo, ten years in the forest and transformed now into an arboreal semblance ("He is y-clongen also a tre!" exclaim his subjects upon his return, 508), has given himself over to advent or arrival like the Fairy King's hunt, moving without objective, wandering embrace of an elusive world.

Orfeo speaks for the first time since his exile began when he beholds the falcons that the travelling fairies bear. These effulgent birds remind him of his abandoned life. Once he connects in intimacy the otherworld and the relinquished court he finds his opening: the rock that leads into the Fairy Realm. *Aventure* is an active surrender to novel prospect, to a world suddenly realigned. It cannot be sought out, it is not an objective, but one may train oneself to perceive its advent, to recognize the invitation it extends. *Aventure* arrives, forcing a departure from the ambits of the ordinary. Orfeo follows the fairy retinue into the rock, through the gem-lit and lapidary kingdom. He knows how the Fairy World works: it is transformational, challenging, perilous, but not wholly unreachable, not beyond relation or withdrawn. Orfeo fills the subterranean space with music, aesthetic radiance in sonic form. He plays his harp for a grateful Fairy King and is rewarded with the fulfillment of any request. Orfeo asks for Heurodis. Unlike the Greek myth on which the story is based, the subterranean monarch fears the two humans are ill-matched but offers no impediment to their return. *Aventure* is an uncertainty principle, transfiguring that which it illuminates, a collaboration with the strange, a relation-maker adverse to prohibition. As Orfeo and Heurodis together depart the Fairy court, rather than the expected warning not to look back the king provides a benediction. As he sends the lovers out of this realm embraced but not contained by stone, out into a world that can no longer for them be the same, the Fairy King bestows upon Orfeo a hope: "Of hir ichil thatow be blithe" (471). *I hope that you will be happy with her.*

He is.

EXCURSUS

— —

Geologic

Prologue

A long trip to Scotland, and I lose myself on the plane in David Abram's *Becoming Animal: An Earthly Cosmology.* The book has its problems: the cliché of the educated Westerner who comes to mindfulness through a visit to Nepal; a proclivity to speak of the wisdom of indigenous peoples, as if their earthiness were universal and simply affirmative; a reflexive disdain for technology. I read Abram's text through the mediation of a paperbound book, on a plane where a screen embedded in the seat displayed three exterior views through which I became an intimate of transatlantic clouds. Abram argues for an active ecological materiality that has much in common with the new material feminisms as well as object-oriented philosophies. He arrives at his conclusions by following a rather different road (a little Deleuze, a great deal of Merleau-Ponty), but what he writes is consonant. And beautiful:

> What if thought is not born within the human skull, but is a creativity proper to the body as a whole, arising spontaneously from the slippage between an organism and the folding terrain that it wanders? What if the

curious curve of thought is engendered by the difficult eros and tension between our flesh and the flesh of the earth?[1]

This language of inhuman being, Abram writes, possesses not words but rhythm, movement, animation; not representations but participations, dances, presencings.

If stone tells a story, it must speak through such geochoreography.

1

Taxi from the airport and I am trying to remember Edinburgh. He narrates as he drives: the idiocy of politicians and their betrayals; the prodigality of the queen, who keeps an estate for yearly visits; the construction of a tram he does not want; bleak futures for the city's young. When he speaks of those who have too much love for immigrants, I observe that Africa alone possesses indigenes. He laughs, but I do not think that I have changed his mind.

2

Hiking to Arthur's Seat, a battle against jet lag. The sun settles in its late northern way, smearing orange across deep blue. A cold wind rises at the peak, where a silver disc marks arrival. Last light fades in final purples across the Firth of Forth. I sit on a rock that Arthur never rested upon, and the water's other name comes to me: *Linne Foirthe.*

Twenty years and more ago, owning a short past and small prospect, I sat at the same peak in the morning with a crowd. I had backpacked there, making my solitary way around Britain and Ireland. Aside from memory's accompaniment, this evening I am alone. The chill of the stone, nothing special, feels like the epochal cool of 350 million years. Arthur's Seat is an extinct volcano, a remnant from Scotland's childhood as a land of lithic ignition. On the way to the peak I passed the sweep of the Salisbury Crags called Hutton's Section. Here the eighteenth-century physician James Hutton observed igneous expanses that once were magma and realized they had thrust through oceanic sedimentary stone. In this intercut (stone from fire, stone on land from sea) he discerned the opening of deep time, the earth in slow liveliness. Arthur's Seat is the gift of relentless uplift and erosion: formed in the seabed, penetrated by volcanic energies, scraped to a craggy mound by the sandpaper of glaciers. Hutton beheld a restless world in which humans and gods are upstarts, unreadable in geology's archive.

3

The National Museum of Scotland narrates earliest history through confederation with stone. The basement level is dedicated to "Beginnings" and "Early People," collections arranged around a record simultaneously lithic and human. An image of James Hutton adorns a placard announcing "Geologic Time," a chronology advancing in one-hundred-million-year segments. Humans are the tiny flatness of "0 Million Years Ago." That this past of exorbitant scale is not indifferent to the creatures curating its vastness is implied by the exhibit announcing "Scotland's History Starts Here." A boulder marbled white, black, and gray forms the totality of the display. All who walk by touch the stone. Transported from an outcropping in the country's northwest, it is among the world's oldest rocks, formed two and a half billion years ago. A nearby sign announces that "In the rocks called the Lewisian Gneiss, Scotland's history emerges from the depths of time." These stones, it seems, were always already Scotland's bedrock, even though the Precambrian life coeval with such rocks were microbes, and any supercontinent to which they clung predates Pangaea by three or four iterations of the continents smashing together and ripping apart.

Short documentaries on geologic and glacial Scotland narrate the country's prehistory through the kinds of stories nations like to tell themselves about continuity and coherence, especially in the face of blunt discontinuities. Repeated emphasis is placed upon Scotland as a portion of Britain that arrived from elsewhere. During the Silurian period the Scottish section of the island was pushed by wandering Laurentia into Europe. Its meeting with what was to become England was not easy: a violent fusing that thrust mountain ranges into violent ascension, a conjoining protested by molten fire and fierce volcanoes. Scotland drifted with its new companion to the equator as part of Pangaea, becoming a desert, and then floated north with Eurasia to cool and flood. A rising sea ensured that Britain (as this conjoined twin would now be called) would seem an isolated entity, that

Scotland's primal affinities with lands having nothing to do with the unwanted expanses to its south could be forgotten. But geology speaks the truth of history. Though Scotland has been scoured by glaciers, its primal life destroyed under the weight of frozen water and the force of floods, its stones hold a tale of independent endurance.

4

Although it does feature some bones, clothing, and a Viking grave, the "Early People" exhibit continues the composite petric-human narrative instigated in "Beginnings." Material culture like brooches, buckles, pendants, and pins is displayed in cases that resemble copper robots walking the museum floor. Incised stone slabs offer most of the stories. A placard entitled "Knowing Stone" speaks of the material's use in "every human activity . . . from making fire to making an impression." Scotland's geologic diversity enabled a sophisticated stone knowledge through which the properties of various types of rock were activated and allied. Homes, weapons, domestic tools, religious objects, and jewelry were created. Exotic stones were imported, treasured. Through sensuous contact between durable rock and desiring hand, narratives were engraved and bequeathed. Sometimes these stories remain loquacious after centuries. Latin cut into a sarcophagus speaks in a language even now some comprehend. A cross declares the early penetration of a religion still practiced. An engraving of a boar or sheep is a pleasant reminder of how long these animals have companioned humans. Other narratives are more reticent. The Papil Stone is cut with images of monks, a cross, and a lion that is likely Saint Mark. But it also displays anthropomorphic bodies with animal visages, and two long-beaked creatures pecking at what looks to be a severed head. Intriguing and inscrutable, the Papil Stone is part of Scotland's geologic story and a challenge to its certainty.

Interlude

David Abram on stone:

> The imperfect and improvisational character of all earthborn beings . . . is
> a character also present in stone. . . . There's an affinity between my body

and the sensible presences that surround me, an old solidarity that pays scant heed to our distinction between animate and inanimate matter. . . . It unfolds in an utterly silent dimension, in that mute layer of *bare existence* that this material body shares with the hunkered mountains . . . with gushing streams and dry riverbeds and even the small stone—pink schist laced with mica—that catches my eye in one such riverbed, inducing me to clasp it between my fingers. The friendship between my hand and this stone enacts an ancient and irrefutable eros, the kindredness of matter with itself.[2]

5

Irrefutable eros, the kindredness of matter with itself. As the "Early People" exhibit ends, stone yields to wood. Visitors walk through houses, glance at the remains of boats, examine textiles, and perceive that a historical archive once sparse brims. Andrew Goldsworthy's installation "Hearth" (1998) is the terminal point, a semicircle of wooden fragments scrounged from the museum's construction site. The pieces are jagged, but in their moodily lit unity they are also beautiful. A perfectly round black disc has been burnt into their center, suggesting vanished fire, a circle for community and tales. The affirmative bent of this installation marks a seeming progress to loftier eras, the "Kingdoms of the Scots." Yet its wood and absent flame seem insubstantial after so much stone.

6

An easy critique of the museum's curators: they anthropomorphize inhuman matter, so that lithic stories become the tales of a nation. They discern in a rocky and indifferent substance their own imagined history. They are like Alexander Duff, who in 1676 looked at the Hilton of Cadboll Stone and beheld not Pictish specificity but a pretty surface on which to incise commemoration of his three wives. Or even worse, like those who left the Stone languishing upside down in a chapel or employed it as a garden ornament. Yet what if an observer apprehended in the Hilton of Cadboll Stone only a local type of sandstone formed by eons of alluvial sedimentation?

What if its single narrative was of similarity to the rocky material out of which much of the National Museum of Scotland is constructed? Would that not miss the point that something generative, something more than a stony or a human story, unfolds when we are drawn to such a specific sandstone by our stone knowledge—which is really just our love for stone, as well as our recognition that we are lithic intimates?

Perhaps the exhibit's curators perceive in stone something that those who dismiss its materiality as indifferent cannot. The rocks that dot, subtend, texture, and continue slowly to convey the expanse of land we are calling for a while Scotland are as hybrid, shifting, and astir as its peoples. Stone is animated and self-organizing. It speaks, when we stop insisting that communication requires words rather than participation in meaning's generation. "Knowing Stone" is the encounter through which groups form alliances with various kinds of geologic materials—not because they are cold and recalcitrant, but because they are metamorphic. They outlast human durations, sometimes, like the Lewisian Gneiss, by aeons. But let's not be ageist. The temporal alterity of stone does not make the lithic any less a collaborator. It is not so much that we project ourselves into rock and trick ourselves into discovering tales of our implanting (although I do not deny that we often undertake such self-deception). More surprising is that, despite having dwelt on the earth for a brief time (but then again, stones have dwelt in the cosmos only a brief time), the stories in which we participate, stories in which we are not protagonists, are nonetheless in part about us.

James Hutton ascended Arthur's Seat and read in its shifting composite of fire-stone and ocean-stone a disanthropocentric story. In its scale the narrative legible there makes us reel, movement away from our own small center. The world may not offer its expanses for us, may rebuke us for having ever thought we culminate its processes rather than ride them for a while, but our worldedness (our mundane fellowship, our material interbeing) becomes something extraordinary: a sentience that extends into the inhuman, into the life of granite and geodes, a life of embeddedness, artistry, and ethical relation.

Arthur's Seat, Edinburgh, Scotland.

7

I brought home a single souvenir of my sojourn to Edinburgh: a small chip of volcanic stone, clasped near the summit of Arthur's Seat, carried with me for days, and, after three thousand aerial miles, near me as I write these words.

Soul

The Life of Stone

Denkmal für die ermordeten Juden Europas

A monument of stone occupies the heart of Berlin, the city in which the Final Solution (Die Endlösung, the plan to obliterate the Jews of Europe) was decided. This memorial to the murdered of the Holocaust is a sculptural expanse of 2,711 rectangular slabs, one for each page of the Talmud. Covering a city square, unincised, these dark gray structures call to mind orderly rows of sarcophagi. Those nearest the surrounding streets are about as tall as a bench, while closer to the sunken middle they tower skyward, high above the heads of those walking their narrow corridors. In their silent solemnity, in their weight as seeming tombs, the stelae of orderly lines call to mind the concentration camp dead. Stone materializes history to guard against forgetting, slowing for a while the erosive power of time. The engulfing gray expanse is somber, a space of potent remembrance. Visiting the monument in the autumn of 2010, I wanted to place a pebble atop a slab but lost myself to wandering when I could not find one nearby.

Children were running through the tight avenues as if they offered a maze. Sometimes a bike shot by, a teenager daring the rocks with stunts. Tourists pause at the memorial as if it were a park. They take smiling pictures, posing themselves peering around the edges of the pillars. They eat their lunch or ice cream. With so many wandering the stones, with so much life within these stark corridors, it is impossible not to notice that the sky is deep in its blue, that trees have been planted among the markers, that the sun upon the gray cobblestones is soft. I returned to the memorial later that evening because an enormous harvest moon was to shine. Past midnight, under lunar fullness, I saw the tourists still walking. Some lovers were holding hands and sitting upon a slab, regarding the moonlit city. None of this seemed a desecration. In the wake of the worst, life proceeds, uncertain in promise.

When the memorial was first constructed some city residents protested its abstract design and refusal to establish a bounded, sacred environ. Unlike many Holocaust memorials, the Berlin structure offers an unenclosed public space without visible security, open day and night. The learning center is underneath, its entrance easy to miss. No signs instruct onlookers how to feel or what precisely to recall. Peter Eisenman, the architect, stated in an interview: "I think people will eat their lunch on the pillars. . . . I'm sure skateboarders will use it. People will dance on top of the pillars. All kinds of unexpected things are going to happen."[1] He was right. The monument opens itself continuously to those who wander Berlin, an offer of lively fellowship within a constantly renewed, temporally and emotionally complex space, a lithic *convivencia*.

Who knows what future archeologists will make of the stelae in their meticulous rows. In Berlin that day I thought about how my family would be larger had not events unfolded in Germany as they did, thought of past and future in the companionship of stone that dwells both inside and beyond the present, that entangles itself with everyday experience. I thought of lives no longer quite so lost. This intimate and active monument seemed better than a stilling into sacrosanct memory, as if the past were truly past. Some medieval Christian writers attempted such temporal stasis with their geologic vocabulary for Judaism, imagining a rock-hearted people, trapped in ambered antiquity, Jews as "harde stones."[2] Such petrification attempts not just physical obliteration but removal from time. Yet history, no matter how traumatic, cannot be long stilled. Stone intensifies more than arrests. Even unwilled petric alliance may yield strange and forceful vitality.

Too often reduced to a metaphor for death, entrusted with history and remembrance, stone also engenders unpredetermined futures and unexpected thrivings.

Stone holds life.

Neolithic

To dwell in a Stone Age is to inhabit a time that, like the slow glide of tectonic plates or the sedimentation of geological strata, hardly seems to move. Affixed to the most minimal of substances, this superseded epoch offers bleak narratives, bare stories: rudimentary weapons, crude tools, caves or wattle huts rather than homes, little industry besides hunting, flint knapping, and war. To dwell in the grip of stone is to be fastened in history and place, rock bottom of a ladder of progress. Such petrified primitivism is what we place upon others, living or dead, at Olduvai, Silbury Hill, inside the "Old Testament," the reservation, the African interior, the Amazon, to show how advanced we are with our machines and commodities, our metals and plastics, all the mobilities of modernity. Disdained, abjected, quietly racialized, the Stone Age is what we have left behind.

Except, of course, we have not. We dwell on lithic foundations and labor within concrete walls. We companion ourselves with stone as we walk and cook and make. We polish gems and adorn our temples and bodies with stony art. The Stone Age is neither distant nor unchanging. Archeologists stress the inventiveness of Paleolithic peoples, their geographical mobility, the diversity of their material cultural, their expertise, leisure, and artistry. Headlines continue to declare the discovery of Stone Age people in African or South American forests, even though anthropologists have long argued against the dismissal of contemporary peoples to the stasis and privation that term typically conveys. "Uncontacted tribes" inevitably turn out to be adaptable, complicated, and significantly less isolated than presumed.

Medieval imaginings of the past sometimes deploy a classical scheme that mapped a decline from the Golden Age to this fallen epoch of Iron. Familiar especially from Ovid, this narrative of degeneration mediated through metals is congruent with Genesis and its expulsion from splendid Eden. At the same time, however, another rhetorical possibility for enframing human change over time existed, assuming a developmental model of culture in which the telluric was aligned with the primitive. When Gawain wanders the wilds of Wales in search of the Green Chapel, he finds himself among wildmen, giants, wolves, crags, and "naked rocks," signifying that in *Sir Gawain and the Green Knight* travel through space is travel back in time, to an era of bleak stone and feral being. Stone possesses a long history that extends into the Middle Ages of figuring bare human life in order to deny anything more than a minimal existence to others, to enclose them within a frozen history, to render them savage and expendable. "We" (that pernicious collective pronoun that habitually excludes more than encompasses) move forward by petrifying into surpassed time those with whom we do not wish to share land, resources, conviviality. "Existence is always co-existence," observes Timothy Morton, and "human beings *are* each others' environment."[3] If ecology consists of "all the ways we imagine how we live together," then our dwelling spaces must be full of human and nonhuman neighbors, those with whom we flourish and compete. Denying coevalness does not render that interconnection any less fraught.[4]

The preceding chapters have traced the alliances through which stone's long temporality enmeshes with human story, an in/organic alliance. Such collaboration demands patience, a becoming-lithic, a reinhabiting of what a Stone Age might signify. The narrative making or carpentry (*tektōn*: a builder, a carpenter, as well as lithic motion) required for such cross-taxonomic coalition is evident when Geoffrey Chaucer ruminates over history, narrative, and inhuman agency in The Franklin's Tale, offering a rare glimpse of Britain's ancient past, an era he materializes through rocky intrusion. After her husband departs for England, sullen Dorigen receives the consolatory and assiduous "emprentyng" of her friends as if she were marble being engraved (5.834; see "Geophilia"). Chaucer's metaphor conveys the unhurried time of stone, an affinity with which Dorigen demonstrates as she slowly emerges from melancholy through the affective impress of her friends.[5] Incising of comfort is borne of human hands, but it opens Dorigen immediately to more troubling inscription, this time directly by stone. "Grisly rokkes blake" (dreadful black rocks, 5.859) that menace the nearby shore crowd her horizon with thoughts of shipwreck, oblivion, and death. They open her to questions of ecological purposiveness and geological agency that she knows theologians ("clerkes") have resolved "by argumentz" (5.886), but which haunt all the same. The rocks she beholds are themselves active rather than signs of divine "pureveiance" (providence, 5.865). The Franklin's Tale unfolds in Brittany. John Block Friedman has connected its ominous stones to the Neolithic menhirs for which the region remains famous, ancient structures carved with "enigmatic and pagan symbols."[6] Although the standing stones and dolmens that dot Brittany, Ireland, and the British archipelago far predate the Irish, Bretons, and Welsh, they were often associated with these peoples in the Middle Ages, likely because such rocky architectures were living features of the landscape, storied stone constantly companioned. In The Franklin's Tale ancient rocks encode narratives belonging to the Welsh, a people with whom Chaucer's England shared an island. These are the Britons for whom Geoffrey of Monmouth composed such a lively history in his *History of the Kings of Britain*. Chaucer never grants the Welsh contemporaneity, however, consigning them to the ancient past imagined historically in The Man of Law's Tale, mythically in The Wife of Bath's Tale, and as dead in The Squire's Tale. Yet the names of two characters in The Franklin's Tale are taken directly from the *History of the Kings of Britain*, a source Chaucer never acknowledges. Dorigen's husband, the knight Arveragus, finds his double in the heroic king Arviragus, son of Cymbeline, notable for his political savvy in negotiating with imperial Rome, as well as for his love of his wife. Dorigen's would-be lover is Aurelius, a young clerk charged with making the rocks on the Breton coast vanish as if they were movable. In Geoffrey of Monmouth's history Aurelius is the uncle of Arthur who commissions Merlin to create a war memorial, relocating the rocks of Stonehenge from Ireland to Salisbury Plain. Yet these Chaucerian appropriations occur only to petrify the British history from which they are plundered. Arthurian tales belong to an irremediably lost epoch of magic, elves, and Britons: a charming but long abandoned temporality, a folkloric expanse. Thus The Squire's Tale asserts that "Gawayn, with his olde curteisye" dwells in the vanished realm of "Fairye" (5.95–96). Like the fairies in whose company he finds himself in The Wife of Bath's Tale, King Arthur becomes an enjoyable legend, his challenge to anglocentricity neutralized by relegation to a fabulous long ago. Modernity in the *Canterbury Tales* belongs to wool merchants, clerics, lawyers, guildsmen, reeves, bakers, parsons, millers.[7] The Franklin's Tale translates Geoffrey of Monmouth's kinetic *chorea gigantum* (Giants' Ring) into "grisly rokkes blake" that, despite Dorigen's intimations of material agency, move in the end only through illusion or tidal submersion, enabled or predicted by a clerk's book. What stirred for a moment—geological and indigenous history, the possibility of enduring geological and indigenous life—is stilled into drowned stone.

Medieval English writers habitually conflated the kingdom of their residence with the entirety of the island, as if England were a synonym for Britain. This synecdoche banishes indigenous Britons to history and thereby denies them both contemporaneity and futurity. The Welsh become remnants of a bygone age. Their culture, narrative, lands, and bodies are rendered nonmodern and appropriable. They become, to English eyes, racialized "internal primitives."[8] In a typical temporal incarceration, John of Salisbury (ca. 1115–80) describes the Welsh as "a raw and untamed race, living in the manner of beasts."[9] Animalizing and corporealized representation reduces the Welsh to a minimal life spent in a wild expanse, and the people become indistinguishable from their harsh material environment. They break oaths, wander like nomads, tend flocks rather than crops, wage incessant war, do not conform to religious orthodoxy, and possess little in the way of culture. Such "stone aging" of anterior cultures works both with and against a mythic impulse that beholds in earlier times something innocent and the pure. The first humans, Adam and Eve, dwelled in a perfect garden, and the Christian philosopher Boethius imagined the early world to be a paradise even outside Eden.[10] The age before agriculture and mining *might* be imagined as a state of perfection, "a blisful lyf, a paisible and a swete" (line 1), as Chaucer describes it in "The Former Age." Because the ground had not yet been wounded through excavation and agriculture, all humans lived in community and peace. Mining brings ruin in the form of circulating commodities, coinage, and attendant war. The caves and woods in which these innocents slumber before gems and metals ruin them are "softe and swete" (line 42). Though not without its complications (as Karl Steel points out, those who dwell in the Golden Age seem to be starving), "The Former Age" participates in a venerable tradition of idealizing life spent close to an earth that offers unlimited bounty without labor.[11] Such lyric fantasies of noble savagery value anterior culture provided it remains mythic, and thereby irretrievably lost. In political practice, however, a model of human development was deployed through which those being colonized were imagined as locked in feral bodies, patently in need of civilizing, even if their culture might in the past have been well worth praising. "Raw," "untamed," and "bestial" races, whether at the margins of the world or living within Latin Christendom, did not have the same rights as those moderns who looked upon their lands with envy. The aboriginal Britons become the savage Welsh (*wealh,* an Old English word for stranger, foreigner, or slave).

Autochthonous British presence often materializes within English narrative as lithic intrusion: mounds, ruins, cities wrought of gold or gems, sudden subterranean spaces. Storied stone enduring vast temporal spans leaves a palpable "emprentyng" through which alternative stories surface. Geoffrey of Monmouth demonstrated that he knew how to make the matter of Britain *matter* when he turned the English petrification of the Welsh on its head through lively rocks like the dance-song of Stonehenge. As material metaphor, stone is often deployed to immobilize a people, to condemn them to surpassed history and exclude them from coexistence, the conveyor of a racializing trope. Yet because stone is so dynamic a substance, mineral arrest does not always hold those incarcerated by its materiality for long. The life of the past emerges in stories thought surpassed, rising from stone and from earth.

Otherworlds

"It is madness to harass the mind," wrote the naturalist Pliny, by attempting to measure the world we inhabit, or to argue

> that there are innumerable other worlds, and that we must believe there
> to be so many other natures, or that, if only one nature produced the
> whole, there will be so many suns and so many moons, and that each of
> them will have immense trains of other heavenly bodies.[12]

Centuries later the encyclopedist Bartholomaeus Anglicus wrote that the world is composed of contrary and diverse things ("many þingis compowned and contrariouse") yet remains singular: "Þe world is one in noumbre and tale and noȝt many worldes" (The world is one in number and reckoning, and not many worlds).[13] The problem with this singular world, however, is that it keeps surfacing traces of other realms. Examine a story or object attentively enough, close read or close look, and the solitary becomes profusive, the universe opens pluridimensionally, the monolithic erupts into heterogeneity and plenitude. In the eighteenth century James Hutton noticed odd conjunctions of stone within the Scottish landscape, spaces where two distinct geological formations strangely cohabitated, and through the stories conveyed by these unconformities a door opened to a geology thick with time and restless with movement. Story-laden portals framed by stone similarly open in medieval texts, entries to sedimented or subterranean modes of reading, narrative unconformities. As a lingering inheritance from Geoffrey of Monmouth, Arthurian myth is especially adept at extending such invitations from the underground. William of Newburgh, a historian writing toward the close of the twelfth century, had little enthusiasm for Geoffrey's work for precisely that reason.[14] William fully recognized the challenge to English historiography launched in the *History of the Kings of Britain.* Had Geoffrey's glorious Arthur existed, he would have been a Briton, the descendants of whom were the "wild Welsh" so challenging to English dreams of pan-insular dominion. Britain's past could not contain both Geoffrey's captivating, millennial vision and the proud but comparatively brief English insular record to which William was contributing with his *History of English Affairs.* William therefore declared Arthurian history a lie and asked rhetorically of Geoffrey, "Is he dreaming another world containing kingdoms without number?"[15]

Yet despite the desires of writers like Bartholomaeus Anglicus and William of Newburgh for a world "one in noumbre and tale," kingdoms without number *(infinita regna)* keep revealing themselves in petric contiguity to everyday life. These wondrously inhabited domains underdwell familiar terrain. The Roman poet Virgil placed the beginning of Aeneas's descent into the underworld at the crater of Avernus. Marie de France located the gate through which Saint Patrick entered Purgatory within a cave. A playground for the imagination, Hell expands deep beneath human feet, invitation to dream a land past death. Afterlife is underlife, sometimes entered through a monstrous mouth that stresses Hell's subsurface vitality. The twelfth-century historian William of Malmesbury describes how the necromancer Gerbert of Aurillac, destined to become Pope Silvester II, discovered a perilous subterranean domain of purest gold, lit by a single carbuncle.[16] His contemporary Walter Map narrated the story of Herla, cursed to eternal wandering and being-out-of-time after he enters a nation below

the earth and partakes of a wedding celebration.[17] Gerald of Wales records
the story of Eliodorus, who as a child frequented a secret kingdom populated by diminutive people. When at his mother's urging he attempts to
steal a golden ball, Eliodorus forever loses access to this cherished realm.[18]
In British, Irish, and English texts, portals to strange geographies open in
mounds that may be natural features of the landscape or ancient tombs.
Whether hills or barrows, gifts of geology or the fabrication of forgotten
hands, these earthy architectures are both ancient and culturally hybrid.
They offer (in the vivid description of Alf Siewers) a "rabbit-warren of portals within the landscape," revealing that the present moment palpably enfolds a "hidden past" and uncertain future, "alternate but real dimensions"
fully capable of transforming the moment into which they erupt.[19] The
temporalities that these earthworks divulge are vegetal, animal, geologic.
Humans enter such spaces at their peril. After Herla and his retinue con-
sume a sumptuous repast, they emerge to discover that two hundred years
have elapsed. Should they alight from their horses they will be instantly
overtaken by the normal course of time and crumble to dust. After dwelling
within slow stone, a return to human history would prove fatal. Eliodorus,
on the other hand, is bereft of treasured amity when he violates the welcome extended him by an otherworld become home. He weeps each time
he narrates the story of hospitality forever lost through a refusal to abide by
the ethos of the underground realm.

In these subsurface stories inscrutable forces materialized by rock and
earth combine with vanishing yet legible human histories. The Irish hero
Cú Chulainn falls in love with Fand, queen of the fairy-like *sídhe,* and enters her parallel universe through a tumulus. Cú Chulainn is cured of self-
destructive desire only through the intervention of an oblivion spell. He
must forget the riches of her world to reinhabit his own. Like many Irish
and Welsh narratives involving hillocks as portals, *The Wasting Sickness of
Cú Chulainn* enfolds an untold story about the belatedness of a people to
the land they possess, figuring the territory's ancient inhabitants as a race
whose traces are dwindling, discernable now through telluric traces. The
Welsh otherworld of Annwn offers its gateway atop a hillock where adven-
turers sit to seek wonders. Similarly transportive portals open suddenly in
texts composed in medieval England. Despite his disdain for Geoffrey of
Monmouth's Arthurian history and "infinite realms," William of Newburgh

describes how a door to another world once opened within a familiar mound in his native Yorkshire. A traveler's late night journey home is interrupted when song resounds from a landmark that had until that moment been unremarkable:

> A countryman from this hamlet had gone to meet a friend staying in the next village. He was returning late at night a little drunk, when suddenly from a hillock close by . . . he heard voices singing, as though people were feasting in celebration.[20]

A door into the hill is ajar, revealing a lively celebration. The tipsy traveler glances inside and beholds a commodious space of welcome:

> Before his eyes was a large, well-lit dwelling crowded with men and women reclining at table as at a formal feast. One of the servants noticed him standing at the door, and offered him a cup. (*History of English Affairs,* 1.28)

Welcomed into unknown community, the man seizes the goblet, empties the drink, and flees toward home. The revelers pursue, eager to regain their purloined vessel, but they cannot overtake his horse. The stolen cup is upon scrutiny utterly mysterious: "of unknown material [*materiae incognitae*], unusual color, and strange shape" (1.28). The treasure is eventually given to the king, who passes it along to other monarchs. Through theft and circulation as a prestigious gift the goblet's history fades from legibility. The object is transformed from the key to another world to a deracinated souvenir of some vaguely exotic elsewhere, a commodity to be bestowed rather than a story to resound, metaphor (narrative conveyance device, material transport) reduced to mere matter.[21] The feast refused recedes from memory, taking with it the story of whatever community was glimpsed across the threshold of the suddenly open mound.

What would have unfolded if the drunken traveler had joined the celebration instead of pilfering its tableware? Suppose he had traded night skies and a homeward journey for a world that beckoned from within the mound? Need the traveler have suffered Herla's fate? Having stumbled across a queer intrusion into accustomed space, having witnessed a tumulus open a story in which he might feature, could he have accepted the perilous invitation to conviviality? What might have come to pass had he risked conversation with the subterranean congregants, if one of these congenial revelers had spoken the tale of who they were and what they honored at their elegant repast? Whose history would this mound-dweller narrate, a story barely glimpsed by a traveler who preferred the security of his village over a summons to a world encompassed by earth and stone?

Like the traveler whose tale he narrates, William of Newburgh declines the invitation from the tumulus, fleeing entrance rather than traversing its open doorway. A Yorkshire man for whom the hillock was a boyhood sight, William is not interested in granting the land much history that predates England, a history that might include when and by whom that mound was built. The world is singular, not many. Yet despite his disdain for Geoffrey's proliferative vision of the insular past, William's narrative divulges a portal to subterranean multiplicity, a textual unconformity. The portal to a feast that seems at once British (recalling Celtic barrow tales) and Jewish (the repast is rather like a seder, and William will later reveal himself obsessed with England's Jews) transforms the hillock from a local landmark of no great significance to a space at once alien and racialized. Had the celebrants of the underground celebration been invited to speak, the narrative they would tell might reveal the difference between the constricted history of a kingdom that masqueraded as the entirety of an island and the challenging, vivacious stories of an archipelago too vast, too varied, too tempestuously alive to be stilled within subterranean banishment.

Heterogeneity and difference, transported out of sight and out of time, resurface in buried and lithic forms. Shakespeare famously has John of Gaunt lapidify England as "this little world / This precious stone set in a silver sea" (*Richard II,* 2.1.45–46), a gemlike rendition of national singularity. Such radiant language cannot, however, obscure the fact that "this little world" never possessed a jewel's impenetrable purity, that England is not Britain.[22] As enmeshed with Ireland and Scandinavia as Europe and the Mediterranean, Britain is more seismic than lapidary, a multiplicity of dominions of variable size, duration, cultural composition. England never fully absorbed, Anglicized, entombed, or petrified the differences it engulfed. Sometimes a traveler might witness a door swing wide to reveal their lingering. Passage over that stony lintel yields stories in which those who have been consigned to a subterranean past offer unexpected invitations, and perhaps the possibility of conviviality.

Tales from the Underground

Geoffrey of Monmouth's *History of the Kings of Britain* describes how the boy Merlin is nearly sacrificed because of buried dragons, monsters enclosed in stone that when released are said to allegorize the battling Britons and Saxons. Magicians declare, wrongly, that his blood must be sprinkled into the mortar of a tower to enable a stable edifice to be constructed upon unremittingly contested soil. Not long after Geoffrey completed his work, the battle for Britain's soil was over and won—at least from the point of view of the kingdom occupying the island's southeast. If Geoffrey's ambition was to offer an effective alternative to England's self-culminating narration of insular history, he did not succeed. At the time his text appeared in the mid-twelfth century, Britain's racial categories were rapidly hardening, becoming carceral.[23] Like the Irish, Scots, and Jews, the Welsh were denied modernity and full humanity through English representation, historiography, and law. No revisionist history was powerful enough to reset the cultural cement through which "Briton" had become "Welsh." Only a century earlier England had been a country riven by foreign conquest, its population divided between a minority of foreign-born francophone elites and dispossessed English subalterns. As the kingdom began to imagine itself a collective again, as Norman difference was absorbed into a reinvigorated Englishness that included mouths speaking French and Latin as well as English, peoples external to the realm (Welsh, Irish, Scots) and living within its borders (Jews) found themselves excluded from this emergent community, often through lithic figuration. William of Newburgh's *History of English Affairs* is full of narratives in which this past is evident, terra firma made uncertain through subterranean impingement.

The most famous of William's stories from the underground details the emergence of children with green skin from a ditch near the village of Woolpit.[24] During the civil war–plagued reign of Stephen, a boy and a girl of verdant hue step blinking from the earth into unaccustomed sunlight. Dressed in odd clothing and speaking an incomprehensible tongue, these siblings are extraordinarily out of place. The villagers who discover the pair attempt their swift acculturation. The bewildered children are baptized, taught to eat farmed and processed foods unfamiliar to them (beans, bread), and instructed in the English language. Slowly they lose their green pigmentation, a sign written upon the skin of a steady assimilation. So suc-cessfully incorporated into her new nation is the girl that she will even-tually marry a man from the nearby city of Lynn. Her brother, however, dies before his strangeness can be fully absorbed. The Green Children of Woolpit surface as a living reminder of the land's difference-laden history, offering a narrative divergent from the kings, triumphs, and unmourned vanishings that dominated twelfth-century English historiography, includ-ing William's. Embodying a capaciousness denied to the island's history, the children rise from the ground at Woolpit to disclose a tale of incorporation and abiding, embodied difference; of distinctions that vanish into relation and alterity worth dying to retain. This dual trajectory resonates profoundly with William's narration of the Conquest and its aftermath. The invading Normans of the previous century so saturate the island's soil with English blood that even in the present the gore continues to well, an enduring cor-poreal rebuke. Upon the field at Hastings, William the Conqueror builds St. Martin of Battle, a monastery that encloses within splendid stone the very spot where the clash of English and Norman armies raged fiercest. One hundred and thirty years later, William of Newburgh writes, this earth continues to exude "real and fresh blood" (*History of English Affairs,* 1.8). Erecting Battle Abbey is an act of petric obliteration, Norman erasure of the violence upon which their seized kingdom was founded, but the blood that cannot be prevented from rising within the now enclosed ground sur-faces a history that the architecture attempted to obliterate. By the time William writes, the Normans are gone, absorbed into the very Englishness they seized. Tellingly, the Green Children say they hail from a place called St. Martin's Land. Martin was a favorite Norman saint, hence the naming of Battle Abbey in his honor. The boy and girl are transported up through a ditch into England when a bell clangs at Bury St. Edmunds, reverberat-ing through their homeland. Another monument to the Norman capture of the English landscape into upward vectors of grandiose stone, the immense Bury St. Edmunds was a Romanesque architecture that burgeoned upon newly acquired domain.[25] The building commemorates a revered English king, thereby colonizing indigenous heritage. Bury St. Edmunds was at the time of its completion among the largest structures in Christendom, a monumentally alien, radiant addition to a countryside dotted with modest wood and masonry structures. Like the abbey of St. Martin at Hastings, Bury St. Edmunds was a reminder congealed in stone of the influx of difference that came with the swift alteration in governmental power in the wake of the Conquest. Just as intermarriage with the local population and slow Anglicization ensured that there were no Normans left living among the English by the time William of Newburgh was writing at the close of the twelfth century, the green girl of Woolpit vanishes into mundane life when she marries the man from Lynn. Significantly, this seaside port was a post-Conquest "new town," a recent addition to the rapidly changing landscape of East Anglia.

Yet before it became the Norman economic engine christened "Bishop's Lynn," before its transformation into the thriving English port called "King's Lynn," *lynn* was simply a Briton word for "pool." Despite the landscape's lithic colonization, this watery geography alongside the Wash is far more ancient than English and Norman histories of the island. Its name surfaces other stories—perhaps, indeed, the story the unnamed boy dies to retain. The Green Children arrive with a tale partly of the Norman Conquest, but the narrative that they bring up into present comprehension is more complicated and less assimilable. Once taught to deliver their history in words understood by their Woolpit auditors, the children describe a world impossibly remote yet inexplicably contiguous to the English village in which they now reside. Like the fairy kingdom in *Sir Orfeo,* St. Martin's Land is at once impossibly distant, weirdly adjacent to, and just underneath familiar ground. As Geoffrey of Monmouth insisted earlier in the century, the island's past, like its prehistoric mounds and ditches, must extend more deeply into time than English history allows and surface long historical difference into the present. Like many writers of his day, William of Newburgh was no lover of the Scots, Irish, or Welsh. They are at best savage races, at worst a monstrous national threat. A "restless and barbarous people," the Welsh are locked within their primitivism, debarred from contemporaneity, living fossils:

> the remnant of the Britons, the first inhabitants of this island, now called England, but originally Britain . . . when the Britons were being exterminated by the invading nations of the Angles, such as were able to escape fled into Wales . . . and there this nation continues to the present day. (*History of English Affairs,* 2.5)

The Britons, William writes, were early colonists of "our island" ("nostrae insulae," 1.Prologue). To protect themselves from incursions of Picts and Scots, they invited as mercenaries the "Saxons or Angles," those peoples destined to become the regnant English, the "nos" in "nostra insula." The hapless Britons were eventually "crushed" by their guests, and their "wretched remnant" finds itself "penned . . . in trackless mountains and forests." Incarcerated within a state of nature that clings equally to landscape and bodies, "they are now called the Welsh" ("nunc Walenses vocantur," 1.Prologue).[26] The powerful kings of England ensure that the dispossessed Welsh will never again occupy more than their wild corner of the island, an expanse of tree and stone. Because they do not own a present, no future belongs to them either.[27] In William's account the Welsh are so distant culturally, geographically, and temporally as to inhabit another world entirely, a pathless expanse offering no return from the uncultured space ("trackless mountains and forests") to which they and their stories have been exiled—at least, no return that enables arrival in England by traveling paved and predictable roads.

William knows that the Britons become Welsh once held the entirety of the island, and that they would argue strenuously against his declaration that their Britain has been superseded by his England. His rhetorical question asked of Geoffrey of Monmouth ("Is he dreaming another world containing infinite realms?" *History of English Affairs,* 1.Prologue) aims to expose the ridiculousness of the prehistory dreamed by the *History of the Kings of Britain,* and yet it also reveals an anxiety: What if Geoffrey is right? What if British story has not been surpassed by the monolith of England? Recent edifices, no matter how monumental, cannot silence the stories that rise through the island's soil. The very substance of Britain (trenches, earth, stone) remains rife with other worlds, other narratives, kingdoms lacking number. Such realms open at the entrance to the mound in Yorkshire as well as the ditch at Woolpit. The Green Children emerge from the earth to tell a story about a country that differs in language, custom, food, and mode of life—and yet uncannily impinges upon ordinary England. Their land might be so distant that the sun never quite rises, and yet its residents can hear the bells of Bury St. Edmunds. The clamor from that church transports the children up through ordinary earth to be surrounded by people who want to change their pastoral life, their non-cereal-based diet, their native language—want to assimilate them, just as the contemporary Welsh, Irish, and Scots were being forcibly Anglicized in order to bring them out of native barbarity (pastoral life, noncereal diet, Celtic languages) and into English modernity. After the Green Children have been taught their new tongue, however, they declare that they have always been Christians, that baptism was unnecessary—recalling, perhaps, that the Britons had long been Christians when the pagan Angles and Saxons arrived with their northern gods. The children describe a mode of living in their native land that might not be agricultural (they are in a field tending their father's flocks when the din of church bells pulls them to Woolpit) but is far from savage. The stories that issue from their newly Englished mouths constitute a rebuke that could as easily have come from a contemporary Welsh or Irish or Scottish source.[28] The Green Children emerge from the ground to speak a narrative that William has been unable to tell, an autochthonous tale in which English dominion becomes a troubled assumption rather than a foregone conclusion, a telluric story to challenge the relegation of the Welsh to the archaism of "trackless mountains."

Stone seldom stays in its allotted place throughout William of Newburgh's history. Its dynamism lends a challenging vitality to that which it is supposed to enclose and still. Book 1 of the *History of English Affairs* includes not only the Yorkshire mound of the nocturnal feast and the Green Children who ascend at the ditches of Woolpit but an account of Battle Abbey, the limestone monument constructed upon Hastings that exudes fresh gore after each rain, and Ramsey Abbey, the walls of which run with real blood ("verum sanguinem sudarunt") when the place is seized. The book's closing sequence includes two enigmatic stories of life discovered within rock's clasp. These astonishing stones are unearthed in quarries, during the kind of massive excavation that supplied the materials to erect structures like Battle Abbey and Bury St. Edmunds. At one site a boulder is split open to disclose two smelly, hairless greyhounds within, one of which becomes a treasured pet. At another pit the workmen discover a beguiling "double-stone":

> While they were digging very deep for materials for building, there was found a beautiful double stone *[lapis formosus duplex]*, that is, a stone composed of two stones, joined with some very adhesive matter. Being

shown by the wondering workmen to the bishop, who was at hand, it was ordered to be split, that its mystery (if any) might be developed. In the cavity, a little animal, called a toad, having a small gold chain around its neck, was discovered. When the bystanders were lost in amazement at such an unusual occurrence, the bishop ordered the stone to be closed again, thrown into the quarry, and covered up with rubbish forever. (*History of English Affairs,* 1.28)

Quarrymen delve deeply into the earth in search of rock to raise toward the sky and discover a radiant object. The compound stone opens to divulge unexpected life. The bishop disdains the astonishment that seizes his workmen, the allure of a rock disclosing at its secret interior a creature of art (the gold chain), affect-laden relation (someone placed the *cathenulam aureum,* a pet's collar, around the amphibian's neck), and peril (toads were thought to be venomous). Challenged, frustrated, or angered by this story at the edge of legibility, the bishop orders the once conjoined stones resealed. But how? Once broken, can the "beautiful stone composed of two stones" be restored? Can it contain again the marvel that has leapt from its heart? The toad with a golden collar has been sent into an uncertain future by unknown hands, an abstruse yet lively missive, a wondrous and relation-making being sheltered within the embrace of two hollowed rocks. Though he returns the animate message to lithic encasement and buries the weird object in the quarry's depths, the bishop cannot imprison the narrative that has escaped, cannot consign the story to subterranean solitude.[29]

Two stones that form one, a radiant collar, amphibious life: signs that will not settle into sentence. Sometimes the life the lithic discloses has little to do with anthropocentric history, revealing beyond allegory, metaphor, and other modes of linguistic domestication the sheltering of a queer vivacity—and perhaps, even, a kind of soul.

Lithic Soul

An oval of salt-and-pepper granite sits on my study's windowsill, a lithic egg. I spotted the stone while walking the ocean's edge in Maine and found myself stooping to pick it up, hand grasping before I was aware of making a choice—an illustration no doubt of what Bruno Latour calls the "slight surprise of action."[30] So many qualities of the rock allure, calling me to continued contemplation, calling me to introduce this stone to you. Speckled granite is indigenous to the hard geography where some of my family has lived since fleeing Russian pogroms in the 1880s. I discovered the stone in a liminal space replete with childhood memories, daughter and fellow beachcomber beside me. It was an impossibly lucid, undeniably singular day in December, and neither of us cared that frozen foam marked the tideline. Formed deep in the earth under inconceivable pressure, a piece of tumbled mountain worn to a globe by tidal pounding, the rock bears the impress of aeonic force. My career is predicated upon studying temporal distance and depth. Something about its being ovate, too, draws me: those flecks on a white surface promise a secret interior, some yolk of futurity inhabiting the shell of its impenetrable past. I collect medieval narratives in which rocks really are eggs, with toads or greyhounds or dragons slumbering inside, awaiting discovery. I seized a round stone on a winter beach in Maine because it dwelled already inside my history. But what if the stone seized me? What if the petric egg, so perfect for the palm, holds more than an accidental power to draw human hand and story? What if it is not anthropomorphizing to speak of a stone's ability to resist, its power to attract—and even of its sympathies, alliances, inclinations, and spurs? And let's up the outrageous ante even more: what if within my ready-to-hand rock is not just an incipience, an agency, but that principle of vitality that in the Middle Ages was supposed to set humans apart from everything else in the world, a soul?

The question of lithic ensoulment was seriously contemplated by Albertus Magnus in the thirteenth century. In a text that bequeathed to the late Middle Ages a comprehensive mineral science, Albertus twice addressed the possibility of souls in stones. He did not mean human souls trapped in rocks, as in Barbara Newman's vivid example of Madre Juana de la Cruz (d. 1534), who hears a stone from her brazier cry out and comes to understand that a sufferer from purgatory is incarcerated within.[31] In medieval popular tradition a soul was typically a miniature version of an embodied person, and thereby the limner of human exceptionalism. For Aristotelian and scholastic writers like Albertus, however, plants and animals must also possess souls as a principle of their being alive. As nonliving matter, stones by definition cannot harbor them. Beginning in classical times, however,

James le Palmer, "Anima." London, British Library, MS Royal 6 E VI, fol. 94v. Courtesy of the British Library Board.

some philosophers did reason that a soul was the source of lithic agency. To solve the problem of how a stone demonstrates some of the qualities of life, a less anthropocentric vocabulary for describing inorganic agency had to be articulated, and what Albertus called the "absurd" notion that stones possess souls repudiated. That refutation was in no way easy.

Gossamer conveyors of identity, human souls can be imagined without the bodies they animate: personhood before birth, a ghost, a denizen of heaven or hell. As in Madre Juana de la Cruz's biography, a soul might even be trapped temporarily within an alien object without challenging the intimacy of soul to human form. Medieval souls were typically represented as miniature versions of people, corporealized yet intangible semblance. The illustrator of James le Palmer's encyclopedia *Omne Bonum* bestows a historiated capital upon the entry for *anima* in which God uses pincers to measure or grasp a small, naked figure. This soul is suspended precariously while God renders his judgment.[32] Carol Zaleski labels images of this type "somatomorphic":

> On the tympana of cathedrals, in colorful miniatures illustrating the lives of the saints, in bas-relief on the tombs of princes, and in the "art of dying" woodcuts, the naked and childlike soul is extracted from the body by angels who carry it up to heaven in a linen napkin, or by demons who drag it down to hell, while around the deathbed the pious mourners or greedy expectant relatives gather.[33]

Such representation of the soul as a miniature human derives from popular tradition more than theology, where the soul might be represented as something other than a homunculus, something inorganic and nonhuman. Caesarius of Heisterbach describes the soul as an all-seeing glassy sphere, perhaps "like the globe of the moon," while other writers envision bubbles, sparks, flames, or birds.[34] Yet when the soul-bubble pops, a human is typically disclosed inside, so that nonanthropomorphic representation yields quickly to familiar bodily contours. Such souls are distinctly human, guarantors that identity survives corporeal decay.

The second creation story in Genesis (2:7) connects human liveliness to God's breath, exhaled into the clay from which Adam is fashioned. This breath or soul is what sets Adam apart from the rest of the world. Related in Latin to the words for *animal* and *respiration,* terms that suggest that the proof of life is movement (*animare,* "to put into motion"), the soul *(anima)* is a substance-permeating mechanism for triggering vital activity. In medieval science a soul enters the flesh just before breathing begins, the spur to quickening. Though popularly considered an exclusively human possession, souls became—especially in the wake of the Christian rediscovery of Aristotle in the thirteenth century—objects of passionate, often contradictory clerical discourse. Having been translated from Greek and Arabic

into Latin, the philosopher's metaphysical and scientific texts roiled the
European academic landscape with their challenges to Christian orthodoxy.[35] In 1210 Aristotle's works on nature were banned in Paris under pain
of excommunication, but by 1255 they dominated the university's curricu-
lum.[36] Difficult labor was needed to reconcile his philosophy with ecclesiastical doctrine, fomenting intellectual turbulence as well as keen and creative
reasoning. The Aristotelian opus is citational, so that along with his writings were conveyed a great many excerpts from other Greek thinkers. These
classical texts arrived in medieval universities mediated by translation and
accompanied by the commentaries of Islamic, non-Latin Christian, and
Jewish scholars. Especially influential were Ibn Sīnā (Avicenna) and Qusta
ibn Luqa (Costa ben Luca). Problems of heterogeneity and potential in-
compatibility are well illustrated in contemporary scholarly rumination
over the concept of soul. In classical philosophy "soul" was a vitalizing
force shared across ontology rather than an individualized entity, while
in much Christian writing it was more likely to be the enduring essence
of a person, a principle of agency and identity separable from the body
at death, even if difficult to envision outside particular embodiment.[37]
Bartholomaeus Anglicus undertook a comprehensive overview of what
"soul" means, collating Aristotle with the church fathers, attempting a
convergence of the term's heterogeneous vectors in the hope of orthodox
synthesis. He emphasizes that the soul is a divinely bestowed agent of corporeal animation, "joined to the body in two manners, that is, as mover
to the thing moved, and as a sailor joined to his ship."[38] This navigational
charge also extends to governance of the flesh, as he makes clear by invoking a declaration attributed to Augustine that the soul is provided for the
body's "reulinge."[39] The soul is that good thing seated in the human heart,
rendering humans close to angels and triggering divine yearning. The font
of rationality, free will, and intellect, this immortal portion will at death be
released to the bliss of heaven. Yet classical tradition also makes clear that
the soul is a neutral phenomenon diffused throughout the entire body to
imbue life, not unique to humans but found also in animals and plants. Philosophers provide so many contradictory definitions, Bartholomaeus observes in exasperation, that "what thing a soul is, is unknown to many men"
(*On the Properties of Things,* 3.4).

Bartholomaeus stresses that ensoulment is multiple and shared up and down the ladder of nature. In an Aristotelian mode he describes through secular language three types of souls: vegetal, to bestow life; sensible, to provide feeling; and rational, to grant reason.[40] He explicates the properties of each at length, dividing them into constituent qualities and detailing with geometrical precision the various abilities they grant their possessors. Plants harbor vitality through their vegetal souls, envisioned in the shape of a triangle. The three angles are formed by the lively virtues of reproduction (in Trevisa's translation, "gendringe"), digestion ("norschinge"), and development ("wexinge and growing," *On the Properties of Things,* 3.7). Procreation, ingestion, and change over time are quietly established as the traits without which life does not exist. Conversely, anything that eats, reproduces, and grows possesses vitality, and therefore the most fundamental of souls. A sensible soul enables animals to experience sentience but not reason, rendering them "vnskilful." Sensible souls are like quadrangles, that is, two triangles that combine to form a square: they contain the vegetal soul but exceed it through the sensory and corporeal abilities they confer. The rational soul, a perfect circle encompassing its angular forerunners, bestows rationality as well as vivacity and feeling, rendering humans the apex of embodied creation, containing all things in microcosm. The constitution of humanness through a tripartite soul means that a "good two thirds of man's functions are shared by other animate and sentient beings," a complicated embedment within a material ecology.[41] Yet despite an emphasis on mundane entanglement, little space exists within this resplendently geometric scheme for the liveliness of anything lower on the scale of nature than "plants and roots" (*On the Properties of Things,* 3.7).

Aristotle and his medieval disciples held that souls provide flora, fauna, and humans their particular abilities. Yet what about supposedly lifeless matter that does things, that acts? Separating inanimate substance from volition-filled beings is typically the first cut made to organize a taxonomic system. In the sixteenth chapter of *On the Properties of Things,* dedicated to rocks and metals, Bartholomaeus describes these materials as "completely without soul or sensation, as [are] all things that grow under the ground and are engendered in the veins of the earth."[42] Stone is inert substrate. Yet we have seen repeatedly in this book how the lithic undermines rigid category, challenging the stability it is charged with founding and exhibiting geological vim. Differences between the human and the lithic, the inorganic and the biological, the material and the creaturely seem firm but prove porous. A writer contemporary with Bartholomaeus, just as enamored of Aristotle, therefore found himself in the uncomfortable position of having to argue that stones do not demonstrate any of the qualities of life. Albertus Magnus energetically refutes lithic vitality. In emphasizing the desire of stone for relation, he also quietly conveys its truth.

As he set about composing his magisterial *Book of Minerals,* this thirteenth-century Dominican friar, bishop, and polymath wrote in frustration, "We have not seen Aristotle's books about [minerals], but only some excerpts from them."[43] Aristotle's surviving works offer little on the subject of geology, just thirty lines at the end of his treatise on meteorology describing how dry subterranean vapors spawn stones and earth, while wetter exhalations create metals.[44] The excerpts from the *Lapidary of Aristotle* to which Albertus refers are not from a work authored by the Greek philosopher at all, but fragments of a text that seems to have been composed in Arabic in the ninth century under the philosopher's name and later translated into Latin.[45] Albertus decided to re-create what he thought to be a lost Aristotelian work from what he could glean from the sources available to him, especially Avicenna, framing his text within the kind of taxonomy he supposed Aristotle would have used. In the process he brought into being an entire *scientia de mineralibus,* a comprehensive geological science.[46] A cosmopolitan churchman who studied in Padua, taught in Paris, and helped to found a university in Cologne, Albertus was fervid in his desire to reconcile Aristotle with Christian doctrine. He found himself in uncertain territory when composing *The Book of Minerals.* Breathtaking in its epistemological reach, the *Book* offers an exhaustive survey, with almost one hundred different entries. The text proceeds carefully, defining its terms and probing earlier works while elaborating a capacious system of classification. Albert's minerals are, like all matter, composed of the four elements in varying concentrations, earth and water predominating. Gems, for example, are defined as a subset of stones in which water prevails, aqueous coagulation yielding the translucence mere earth cannot grant. For Aristotle form rather than substance determines inherent qualities. Albertus therefore writes that the power of a stone to counteract poison, cure an abscess, or attract or repel iron derives directly from its specific form. Lithic materiality becomes active—becomes capable of protecting, igniting, drawing, or emitting—through its singular manifestation as diamond, coral, jet, or topaz. Albertus repeats the Aristotelian doctrine that unformed matter is inert, with particular arrangement imbuing qualities. Substantial form provides each type of stone with innate but limited functions "performed by necessity" (*Book of Minerals*, 1.1.6), and its potentiating form is in turn bestowed by the "formative power" of celestial bodies. Stones are therefore meager in their latent possibilities and mechanistic in their deployment. Like stars, they cannot choose when or how to radiate their powers. Yet Albertus's detailed explications emphasize the enmeshment of stones within animated ecologies. They therefore change over time and even die: "the specific form of individual stones is mortal, just like humans [*mortalia sicut et homines*]; and if [stones] are kept for a long time away from the place where they are produced [*extra loca generationis*], they perish" (2.1.4).

With its vivifying function, substantial form acts just like a soul, leading Dorothy Wyckoff to gloss Aristotelian form as "the *essential being,* or identity of a thing; in living things, the 'life' or 'soul.'"[47] And indeed some writers familiar to Albertus discerned souls within stones. Alchemists might hold that sulphur and quicksilver inhabit stone as its soul or spirit, with petric materiality as a kind of body, but Albertus states dismissively that he is not composing an occult treatise (*Book of Minerals,* 1.1.1). Democritus, a Greek metaphysician famous for his theory of atoms (and known in the Middle Ages for alchemical works attached to his name), argued that all things made from elements necessarily possess soul as their condition of existence. Without spirit rocks could not come into being, Democritus insisted, and therefore "there is a soul in stone."[48] Lithic ensoulment indeed possess a long tradition in Greek thought. Thales, first of the great philosophers, argued that magnesium manifests an animating *psyche* when it draws iron.[49] Condemning Democritus and the Pythagoreans for their belief in "the soul of stones," Albertus writes that although they act in the world and even seek the divine, "stones do not have any souls" (2.1.1) and "possess forms but not souls" (1.1.6). To reason that rocks possess vital force is "the height of absurdity," since "the first function of the soul is life" (1.1.6), and unlike plants, animals, and humans, stones manifest "no function corresponding to a soul" (1.1.4).[50] Stones and gems possess neither sensory faculties nor lively activity.

From Aristotle Albertus knew that a soul is a capacity for life inherent to the forms that organize matter, and thereby inseparable from the substance in which it is found. To be considered alive, a thing must demonstrate digestion, change over time, and reproduction. This definition is built upon the exclusion of stone, since Aristotle used rocks in his treatise *De anima* as an example of matter without the capacity for life. They are insensible, not even dead because never having had the potential to be alive. Albertus writes that stones do not eat: "for if a stone used food, it would necessarily have pores or channels by which food would sink into it . . . like the roots of plants or the mouth of animals" (*Book of Minerals*, 1.1.6). Lithic compactness is argument enough against the existence of alimentary organs. Too dense to ingest other matter, stones take nothing from the world. They do not procreate: "we never see stones reproduced from stones . . . a stone seems to have no reproductive power at all" (1.1.4). They are generated not from lively seed but through "mineralizing force," a phenomenon that leads Albertus to admit that stones actually can generate more stones, but with this important difference: "their production is not like the reproduction of living plants, and of animals which have senses" (1.1.4). Even if stones perish over time, that mortality remains comparative, built around an "as if" ("mortalia sicut et homines," 2.1.4) that keeps ontological distinctions well emplaced.

Yet complications quickly emerge. When Albertus attempts to detail mineral force in action, he writes that its function is like that of animal seed (*semine animalis*) since it generates specific types of stones.[51] Stones are not animals and cannot breed, and yet they act *as if*—and this *as if* does not maintain segregation quite so well, offering disruptive metaphorical conveyance rather than sturdy partition. Mineral virtue makes it difficult to say if stones in Albertus's account are organic or inorganic, for they appear to be (as Valerie Allen notes) "both and neither."[52] Paradoxically, even as a stone is not alive and cannot procreate, for Albertus "reproduction remains the only way of understanding" how petrogenesis unfolds.[53] His vocabulary for lithic activity describes stones as organisms gestated within the earth, engendering in turn their own lapidary offspring. His Latin is replete with verbs of procreation and parturition. That *sicut*, that complicated *as if*, prohibits ensoulment while making stones seem living things. They act through a force that is nonvitalizing, nonreproductive, nonorganismal—

and yet the insistence in the *Book of Minerals* that stones possess neither soul nor life is quietly eroded by recurring demonstration of their vivacity, an animacy not well cordoned away through metaphorization *(as if)*. Albertus argues against those who describe stones as inert, those who insist that "the powers of stones ought to belong [only] to living beings" (*Book of Minerals,* 2.1.1). Experience proves, he insists, that magnets attract iron, sapphires cure abscesses, some gems bring victory, others reconcile arguments or expel venom. After his discussion of the various ways in which stones attract or repel objects (iron, flesh, silver, fire, bones, wine, fish), he writes that it is "as if there were in these things something pleasing to the stones, or a soul by which they were moved."[54] *Sicut* attempts keen division but conveys into intermixture.

Lithic power is marvelous, mortal, innate, and mobile. It does an excellent job of imitating life, especially when stones and humans form alliances. *Corallus,* for example, can staunch bleeding and protect against epilepsy. To wear *corallus* around the neck is to be guarded from storms, lightning, and hail. Powdered and dissolved into water, it will fertilize herbs and trees, "multiplying their fruits." *Corallus* connects human bodies, bodily fluids, the weather, and the vegetal world. Like all the stones Albertus describes in his alphabetical lapidary, coral is not a passive material to be harnessed to specific uses. Its qualities are inherent, always emanating, always seeking the connections that will allow the rock to become an agent so powerful it can rebuff tempests, so fecundating it can compel crops to superabundance. Coral's force, moreover, encompasses an entire ecology: water permeates wood and petrifies through the power of place (*Book of Minerals,* 1.1.7). Other stones act with similar vigor. *Chryselectrum* changes its colors during the course of the day. Because it fears fire, when held in the hand it reduces fever. This communion in the palm is suggestive. The stones Albertus catalogues yearn for union with the biological. Many are themselves progeny of lithic and animal commingling and must be ripped from bestial bodies to be attained: *borax* from a toad's head, *celidonius* from a swallow's stomach, *celontes* from shellfish, *alecterius* (a kind of medieval Viagra) from the crop of a cock. Torn from the brow of a snake, *draconites* dispels poison and bestows victory. Even when they do not originate in flesh themselves, stones desire to touch and transform bodies. Diamonds *(adamas)* can be mined through the softening effect of goat's blood strong in parsley or fenugreek (animal-vegetal-mineral union). They protect against insanity, nightmares, poison, and enemy attacks. Powdered and mixed with wine, *ematites* dissolves the excess flesh of wounds. So similar to the organic are Albertus's stones that carnelian is described as "the color of flesh, that is red; when broken it is like the juice of meat" (2.2.5). Its power is, of course, to staunch bleeding in humans. Albertus insists that stones cannot choose when to radiate their powers, and yet provides numerous examples of gems withdrawing themselves when those who would confederate with them prove unworthy. He articulates at length the networks through which rocks and gems ally themselves with fleshly bodies, stirring with activity.

But then we remind ourselves that Albertus insists that "no characteristics of life are found in stones" (*Book of Minerals*, 1.1.6). They do not eat, and it is probably stretching the truth too much to see in the ability of *ematites* to dissolve wounds a kind of microbe-like consumption of the flesh. Yet Albertus also describes *sarcophagus*, "a stone that devours dead bodies.... Some of the ancients first made coffins for the dead of this stone because in the space of thirty days it consumed the dead body" (2.2.17). Because of this ingestive property, he adds, stone monuments are to this day called *sarcophagi*. He declares that rocks do not reproduce, and yet he details *peranites*, which conceive and bring forth little stony children ("concipere et parere," 2.2.14). Like *balagius*, they also arrive in two genders, male and female. The activity or petric life these rocks demonstrate is not exactly anthropomorphic; at the same time, however, all stones are like humans. Petrogenesis occurs through the mixture of earth with water—that is, in clay (1.1.2). Albertus is an ardent disciple of Aristotle, the philosopher for whom (as Bartholaemeus puts it when quoting his work) the difference between earth and stone is moisture.[55] Albertus must have known that this description of how stone is formed bears uncanny similarity to Augustine's account of the creation of Adam.[56] In the *Commentary on Genesis* the bishop of Hippo writes:

> Just as water collects, gels and holds the earth together in a mixture of water and earth, thus creating clay, in the same way the living-spirit [*anima*] of the body gives life to the material of the body.[57]

Humans and stones are intimate in their materiality. They are also queerly akin in their vitality. Stones do not have souls, and yet they seem extraordinarily similar to things that do, including the humans who are formed of exactly the same substance—humans who are, in Augustine's account, mobile rocks. Humoral theory will later add to this ecomaterial model that specific environmental conditions produce in humans different races. Medieval geological science extends the same principle of varied embodiment to stone, so that this same ecological enmeshment produces specific forms of minerals and gems.

Albertus declares that stones are not alive because they do not digest, reproduce, or change over time. He also provides examples of stones that accomplish each of these things. Yet perhaps the animating principle of soul would only diminish and domesticate stone. What if we follow the lead of Albertus and do not assimilate the activity exhibited by his stones to the actions of a familiar soul, but behold in those actions resolutely inhuman movements toward connection and confederation, movements of desire? Jane Bennett beautifully describes life as a "quivering," "evanescence," and "vibratory vitality."[58] Inorganic matter in her account proliferates and intensifies relation. Albertus himself gleans something similar, and that is why he worries about the souls of stones enough to dismiss their possibility twice. Rocks manifest their alien potencies, obscurely but insistently, bodying a fantastic that is nonetheless real. The stones that Albertus describes exert force with such intensity that we must wonder about their escape from the limits of circumscribed forms. The lithic is never separate in his account from tumultuous ecologies, from fraught and proliferative enmeshments immune to anthropomorphic reduction. Coextensive with humans in their materiality but possessed of an ontology all their own, stones forge relations, manifesting a queer kind of life.

Lithocentrism

The splendid Fairfax 3 manuscript of John Gower's *Confessio Amantis* contains on its opening page a vivid illustration of an episode from the poem's prologue: the biblical king Nebuchadnezzar is dreaming in his royal bed.[59] A tall human form, composed of a variety of materials, looms in menacing stillness over the royal body. The figure's face is turned toward the slumbering king and cannot be discerned by the viewer. A craggy boulder levitates behind and above the bed, at eye level to the standing figure. As we read Gower's poem (*Confessio Amantis*, Prol.585–880) and recall the story told in the book of Daniel upon which it is based, we realize that the rock is hurtling, meteor-like, from the side of a mountain to a fateful rendezvous. The immense statue haunting Nebuchadnezzar's sleep is its target.[60] The stone, small because approaching from great distance, will pulverize the strange figure: "With which ston al tobroke was [everything was shattered] . . . al was into pouldre [dust] broght" (Prol.621, 623). Gower follows biblical narrative in describing the statue as a monstrous embodiment of human time, smashed when "A gret ston from an hull on hyh / Fel doun of sodein aventure" (A great stone from a high hill fell down through sudden *aventure*, Prol.618–19). Knowledge of this lithic "aventure" jolts the illustration to life. The rock becomes kinetic, perilous. The boulder hurtles toward the bed, toward the menacing statue, toward us as we view the illustration.

The materials from which the statue is wrought signify a progress of human eras, marking deterioration from the perfection of the Golden Age (represented by the figure's shiny head and neck) through the silver and brass of its middle portions to the unstable mixed materials of its feet, steel and clay to designate the perturbations of the present day. Human history is degeneration from a perfect, aureate state to modern fragility. The speeding rock possesses a steadiness that human time and "the world divided" lack (*Confessio Amantis*, Prol.645–46). Lithic force will shatter this medieval version of the Anthropocene to dust ("pouldre"), so that in wake of meteoric apocalypse a better world might commence (Prol.658–59). The devastating stone, Gower declares, is a symbol of God's power ("myht," Prol.655). What the rock triggers includes the fall of Babylon, historical decline, and the end of human history. Yet the stone is also quite materially a stone. As the Latin Vulgate translation of the book of Daniel made clear to Gower, the rock is cut from the mountain by no hand ("abscisus est lapis sine manibus," 2:34). It destroys the statue so utterly that only dry particles conveyed by wind remain. The boulder then grows to replace the world it obliterates: "but the stone that struck the statue became a great mountain, and filled the whole earth" (Daniel 2:35).

The illustration of Nebuchadnezzar's dream in Fairfax 3 demands an allegorical reading. Yet this vividly colored depiction of immobile human forms (a sleeper, a statue) and a boulder that hurtles toward the scene from some invisible embarkation is also a window into a world where not every rock yields to human fable. What if we, like the dream, allow the stone to grow until it diminishes what it demolishes? What if this lithic worlding were not a symbol for the arrival of yet another human kingdom (as it seems to be in the book of Daniel) nor a metaphor for heaven to come (Gower), but the advent of a time and an ecology that are neither human nor celestial, an Anthropocene that yields to the Lithocene? The *Confessio Amantis* is after all a poem that stages a protracted struggle over how to comprehend narratives. Can we glimpse something of a disputative parliament coming into being as the rock speeds toward the dreamer and the figure of metal and stone that haunts his dreams? Could this rock be Theia, the Mars-sized planet that may have collided with the earth to form the moon? Chicxulub, the asteroid that triggered the mass extinction that deprived the earth of dinosaurs? Melancholia, the giant blue planet that crushes the Earth in the Lars von Trier film of that name? Gower could not of course have dreamed any of these errant astral bodies, and yet his rock might be, like them, a protagonist rather than prop, an actor rather than a symbol, a lithocentric material force rather than simple human shorthand for simple human truths. *Sine manibus*: hurled by no hand. What if motion, what if life, belongs to the rock independently of the human story into which it hurtles?

A perverse reading, perhaps, given the allegorical, theological, and anthropocentric interpretations that Gower and the book of Daniel offer— but not an anachronistic or impossible one. Gower's meteor is not the only careening celestial stone recorded in medieval texts. The profoundly influential lapidary composed by Marbode of Rennes (1035–1123) lists among its entries *ceraunius,* a rock found only after lightning strikes. Hurled earthward from storm clouds, flaming with radiance, this thunderstone will when retrieved protect houses and ships from future bolts (*De lapidibus,* 401–19). Potent and dynamic *ceraunius* traces an arc between heaven and earth, yielding its powers to anyone fortunate enough to discover its secret dwelling. Stones in the lapidary tradition are seldom devoid of life, contradicting any dismissal as dead matter. Following Pope Gregory's hierarchy of nature in his *Commentary on Job* (see "Geophilia"), Gower writes that humans are a microcosm ("lasse world"): like angels in their souls, like beasts in their senses, like plants in growth, and like stones in their worldly existence (*Confessio Amantis,* Prol.945–53). Gower and Gregory are repeating the Aristotelian *scala naturae,* the chain of being arranged upon degrees of sentience, from thoughtless stones to (in Christian tradition) fully enlightened angels. As "things lifeless" stones do not fare well along such a ladder, relegated to the lowest rung. Yet this ascending scale is no hierarchy of absolutes. Each step represents not a break from what precedes but a continuum that assumes intermixing and upward conveyance: humans are compounded of vegetative, animal, and petric being.[61] Often medieval authors describe a *scala naturae* that resembles an entangling mesh more than an orderly ladder. Lithic vitality escapes capture into stilled categories. Animals, climatological phenomena, stars, landscapes, plants, and gems possess strange desires, unbroachable singularities, incalculable vitalities. Despite their "mere being," stones insinuate themselves into story. They usurp human plotlines. They open to unexpected worlds.

Hurtling from a mountain to destroy the frail amalgam that is human time seems rather a small accomplishment in comparison.

The Life of Stone

This chapter opened by exploring how stone is made an accomplice in the dispossession of subaltern and indigenous peoples, depriving living humans of a contemporaneity in which to thrive. The Stone Age is invoked to dismiss and deprive, as if rock were barren, as if lithic affinity could ever be left behind. Yet stone's propensity to produce rather than contain imbues a strange kind of life into that which it is entrusted to still. Might stone also share with its human allies, forced and unforced, the suffering that attends exploitation and disregard? Jean Kerisel, longtime professor at the École Nationale des Ponts et Chaussées and former president of the International Society of Soil Mechanics and Foundation Engineering, thought deeply about the affective life of stone. Kerisel oversaw the rebuilding of major French cities after the devastation of World War II. Bridges, ports, and nuclear power plants worldwide owe much to his expertise. So do tunnels for the Paris Métro and the CERN ring in Geneva. Born in Brittany, a region long famous (as Chaucer's Franklin's Tale makes clear) for its rocky shores and Neolithic monuments, Kerisel wondered about the price stone pays for its reduction into resource. His last book, *Of Stones and Man,* meditates upon human use of this lively substance, from the construction of the Egyptian pyramids to present-day skyscrapers. Kerisel writes that he frequently witnessed how stone "gathers its forces to fight against destruction" and was long haunted by the possibility of its suffering.[62] To set his mind at ease he arranges for a chunk of pink granite to be delivered from the Aswam gorge, the source of the material used in Cheops's burial chamber. In his laboratory Kerisel subjects the beam to a slow increase of pressure. With stethoscope pressed against the stone he listens to sonic intensification deep within, the secret agony of the assayed granite:

> I could hear the micro-sounds, murmurs and groans preceding the powerful signals prior to the final explosion. Rather like the Sixth Symphony of Mahler, with its tragic mood and gradually mounting crescendo, there can be no other issue for the hero but death. Microphones and amplifiers confirmed what was happening but I always came back to the stethoscope . . . which gave my research a human touch: there was no doubt that stones express their feelings, and their simple nature, on which human beings so often rely to perpetuate their own deeds, is continually exploited by man.[63]

Kerisel is not offering metaphors. Stone's "murmurs and groans" are not *like* human communication; they are the transmission of distress as shattering nears. Listening to granite under flexion recalls for him the words of Bartolomé de Las Casas, who wondered how the conquistadores convinced themselves that American Indians possessed no souls. Kerisel concludes that as "slaves of man's dreams of grandeur," possessed of a history that is "sad and sometimes tragic," stones find themselves in a situation similar to New World indigenes.[64]

Stones that feel are the stuff of speculative fiction: the Doctor discovers Stonehenge is a hungry petric alien; or the Horta, a silicon-based life form native to Janus VI in a classic *Star Trek* episode, reveals itself a grieving mother whose eggs have been mistaken for stones by space miners.[65] Perhaps late in life Kerisel went mad, sympathetically identifying with a substance he had long worked, discerning affect that rock cannot possibly hold. Does it not take a wrongheaded anthropomorphism to say that distressed granite groans, that a pebble in the palm pushes back against touch? Matter to be shaped by human hands and incised with familiar histories, stone is with good reason a trope for the dispassionate and the moribund. Shakespeare's Mistress Quickly describes the body of dead Falstaff as "cold as any stone" (*Henry V,* 2.3), a proverbial comparison widespread in medieval texts.[66] In the late Middle English romance *The King of Tars,* a Christian princess marries a Muslim king and gives birth to a lump of flesh without features or limbs, an object that "lay ded as the ston."[67] This cadaverous blob is a visually exorbitant condemnation of the religious and racial intermixture through which it was engendered, miscegenation that yields a literal dead end.

After Christian baptism, however, the "rond of flesche" (580) transforms into a beautiful boy. The divide between a crying baby and lifeless rock turns out not to be insurmountable. Alongside a vocabulary that relegates stone to inanimacy, Christian exegesis also developed the idea of "living stones" *(lapides vivi)* that actively resist inimical forces, collaborating with builders to assert themselves in the world, especially when it comes to the figurative and literal building of churches.[68] Living stones find secular, less compliant parallels in the encyclopedias and lapidaries, where gems and rocks teem with life. Following Roman tradition, Isidore of Seville writes that limestone cement *(calx)* "is said to be alive, because even when it has become cold to the touch it still retains some fire inside" (*Etymologies,* 16.3.10). Magnet, Isidore continues, is called "living iron" because it clings with such vigor and links itself into long chains (16.4.1), while the sparks that pyrite yields when struck earn it the title "living stone" (15.4.5). The lithic is certainly lively, where *life* denotes not so much an entity as a tendency. Some medieval writers went further than these modest apprehensions of petric agency and like *Doctor Who* and *Star Trek* and Jean Kerisel wondered if stone might not be a kind of inorganic organism, a vibrantly inhuman creature.

Derived from the Latin verb *creare* ("to produce, make, engender"), the noun *creature* designates, in Julia Lupton's elegant explication, "a thing always in the process of undergoing creation; the creature is actively passive or, better, *passionate,* perpetually becoming created."[69] *Creatura* shimmers with the same incipience as that consummate romance term *aventure,* wondrous arrival. Lupton traces the noun's etymology in order to redeem despised Caliban of *The Tempest.* She demonstrates eloquently what happens when the sympathetic category "creature" is enlarged to admit even monsters.[70] Animals, certainly, are creatures, and critical animal studies rightly insists that they be considered outside human relation. Rosi Braidotti writes that the animal must be "taken in its radical immanence as a body that can do a great deal, as a field of forces, a quantity of speed and intensity, and a cluster of capabilities," opening the way to a "bioegalitarian ethics."[71] What would happen, though, if we substitute for *creature* and *animal* what Braidotti calls "inorganic others," things that (as medieval authors like Albertus Magnus knew well) likewise offer "a field of forces, a quantity of speed and intensity, and a cluster of capabilities"? If a queer ecological space is one in which "the distinction between organism and environment disappears," can its ambit of vivacity extend all the way to, say, stone?[72] Stacy Alaimo has argued cogently that if "nature is to matter, we need more potent, more complex understandings of materiality."[73] We might turn our gaze backward, deep into history, to find some provocative models. We might even thereby imagine a zōē-egalitarian ethics, where *zōē* indicates not bare or animal life but a force (call it life, wildness, desire, vibrancy, creatureliness) that is materiality in action: affiliating, connecting, breaching ontological solitudes, defying exclusive taxonomies, undermining closed systems.

The ecotheorist Mick Smith articulates what he calls an anarchic ethics, refusing to subsume relations among various and unequal forms of life "under any absolute ruling principles," nourishing instead "an open texture of responsible engagement."[74] *Archē* is a rule or origin for anchoring, typically some imagined historical moment at which a code of law descends from heaven to be engraved upon stone. Anarchic ethics emerge from wider, messier, denser worldedness. Built upon a shared and provisional inhabitance and attending to the possible, the plural, and the excesses that do not fit neatly back into systems, such ethics are filled with subterranean relation, tangled and entangling.[75] Even if some trees will still become firewood, some granite provide the foundations of houses, and some bacteria be destroyed for humans to live, attending to their difficult enmeshments precipitates ecological as well as ethical hesitation, a necessary space of thought and care. As Cary Wolfe has shown, to urge an embrace of "'life' in all its undifferentiated singularity" is to propose an indifferent welcome that would be utterly impracticable.[76] The determinate, the specific, the pragmatic, and the contingent are necessary partners to unconditional hospitality, actions of moral consequence, and the definitive challenging of unjust structures.[77] As Stacy Alaimo stresses, such commitment cannot limit itself to small circles: "an ethics that is not circumscribed by the human but is instead accountable to a material world that is never merely an external place but always the very substance of our selves and others."[78] Difference matters. Finitude and contingency are real. An uncertain, promise-filled and perilous mode of relation-making, life is provocatively manifested in surprising places, and its burgeoning insistently challenges the limits of community, the foundations of justice, and structures of ecological inhabitance, medieval and modern.[79] When ethics is investigated as a *doing* rather than a prescriptive code, undergrounded possibilities emerge no matter the epoch examined, no matter what doctrine, law, or common sense declare about doomed beginnings.[80] Texts in motion, like the motile matter they map, thicken relational possibility, offer dynamic sites of emergence, refuse historical predetermination.

What would such queer and creaturely stone *do*? Would it possess qualities associated with biological bodies, traits like those that Albertus Magnus simultaneously denied and discerned in the lithic: motion, mutability, sexual difference, reproduction, expansive worldedness, desire? Or stranger attributes still? Medieval lapidaries offer some intriguing possibilities. Bartholomaeus Anglicus provides a minimal definition of this widely popular literary-scientific genre in his preface: "an ABC of things engendered in the earth."[81] His catch-all, conjunctive approach reveals the bare principle of organization that collects stones into a typical lapidary's loose unity. No overarching scheme or tight taxonomy unites disparate entries. Lapidaries do not aspire, like Albertus in his *Book of Minerals,* to anything like a bounded totality. They offer a bestiary of irradiative gems, agentic rocks, and riotous minerals in jostling congregation. Lithic ontology quickly burgeons into geobiography, catalog poems, wondrous ecological collation.[82] Lapidary texts include stones that come from animals, mines, rivers, stars, and storms. Some cure diseases, some inflict harm, and others hold powers hidden from human discernment. Originating in classical Greece, lapidaries begin as rather terse descriptions of gems and rocks, indexing qualities like color, provenance, durability, and properties. Their inventories of lithic force grew over time to include detailed, narrative-rich explications of qualities and effects, especially when a stone is used in the practice of medicine. Medieval lapidaries are treatises on material vibrancy. Interweaving knowledge derived from Greek, Roman, and Islamic authors with meditations upon petric efficacy, they describe what stones accomplish in the world.

Stone lore is ancient and survives even in cuneiform inscriptions. Among the earliest texts to compile lithic knowledge is *On Stones,* composed by the Greek philosopher Theophrastus (ca. 315 BCE). A contemporary of Aristotle, Theophrastus wrote that stone is formed underground through the purification, homogenization, heating or cooling of earth; minerals, on the other hand, derive from water. In a typical entry Theophrastus provides the geography to which a stone is native, the circumstances of its formation, and the uses to which it might be put. He is more interested in classifying stones and detailing their composition than in narrating abilities they might possess. An exception is *smaragdus* (a green stone often but too narrowly translated as "emerald"), which Theophrastus describes as capable of changing the color of water and exerting a beneficial effect on troubled eyes (*On Stones,* 24). Yet no stone he collects is without agency, defined as both recalcitrance and activity ("their power of acting on other substances, or of being subject or not subject to such action," 4). Most of these powers are mundane, such as inflammability, hardness, malleability, and propensity to melt. Some rocks petrify, assay the quality of rare metals, or possess salubrious effects. The lithic catalogue that Theophrastus composes is rather laconic. Its classical and medieval descendants, however, were not nearly so reticent when it comes to imagining the flourishing of stones, offering piquant little geobiographies.

Some medieval lapidaries were theological works, transforming gems into symbols for Christian virtues like faith and chastity. Such texts generally explicate the significations of the twelve stones of the breastplate of Aaron (Exodus 28:15–21) or the twelve stones of the Apocalypse (Revelations 21:19–20). The Latin *Lapidary of 12 Stones,* for example, is structured around a series of lithic exegeses. Green *smaragdus* "gives an olive-colored light" and represents "purest faith" and "the work of piety."[83] Whereas Theophrastus was interested in the provenance of *smaragdus,* its effects on clear water, and its intersections with human disability, in the abstract and symbolic account of the *Lapidary of 12 Stones* the gem loses its materiality, disclosing a story about the rewards of moral steadfastness. A devout person usurps the activity of the gem. Most lapidaries, however, tend toward the secular. God may or may not appear, religious pedagogy is not a predominant interest, and doctrinal questions infrequently arise. Lapidaries grant that matter's potency derives from the divine at the moment of creation, of course, but these texts then map the effects of place on stones and the effects of stones on environment rather than encompass lithic deeds in allegory. Amethyst, sard, jet, and carbuncle perform the actions native to their formation in relation to whatever circumstances they find themselves, sometimes changing their environment profoundly, sometimes existing in utter indifference to external stimuli, sometimes pulling the world close through allure. Much pre-Christian material was quietly conveyed into medieval tradition through stone lore, so that lapidary stones also function as epistemological fossils carried quietly forward through textual embedment. This potentially heterodox knowledge continued, like the animated stones of the lapidaries, to possess an extraordinary kind of life.[84]

The Roman scientist Pliny in his *Natural History* (the last five books of which discuss minerals) and Isidore of Seville in the *Etymologies* (book 16 is dedicated to metals and stones, collating classical and patristic sources) were essential gateways for lithic science throughout the Middle Ages. A minor traditional of vernacular lapidaries also dates in Britain from the late Old English period.[85] By far the most influential work in the genre, however, was that composed by Bishop Marbode of Rennes at the close of the eleventh century. No medieval story of stone held comparable importance, and for that reason Marbode's seminal text has been surfacing throughout this book. *Of Stones* is a seven-hundred-line poem in Latin hexameters with sixty entries. More than 125 manuscript copies are now extant.[86] Translations quickly appeared into French, Provençal, Hebrew, Spanish, Italian, Irish, and Danish, rendering *Of Stones* the most familiar lapidary of the Middle Ages.[87] Surviving copies are often bound with medical treatises, suggesting the work's intimacy to medieval thinking about embodiment and disability. Lapidaries are at once works of the imagination (they invite invention) as well as practical medicine. Their apothecarial cures are offered as real treatments for suffering bodies: remedies, prophylactics, analgesics, and prostheses. Marbode's lapidary is utilitarian as well as speculative. He adapted his text's form and much of its content from the Roman writer Damigeron (*De virtutibus lapidum,* second century CE), adding material from Solinus and Isidore—and through them, Pliny. By way of Damigeron Marbode inherited the conceit that lapidary knowledge arrives from the exotic east, through the Arabian king Evax, well versed in Egyptian mysteries. Marbode prefaces his text with a letter from that fictive monarch to Emperor Tiberius of Rome. Evax warns his addressee that knowledge of lithic power is dangerous and should be guarded from wide circulation. The letter renders the material that follows all the more enticing for its aura of peril. *Of Stones* offers no overarching structure for the interpretation of gems and rocks, only a compilation of vignettes in which, for a short space, each becomes the hero of a tale of mineral thriving. Harvested from the nests of griffins by a one-eyed people called the Arimaspians (141), smooth green *smaragdus* was used by Nero to create a looking glass for viewing gladiator battles (147). *Liparea* is a magnet for wild animals. A hunter need carry only the alluring stone and a sharp spear to enjoy nature's bounty (596–601). Topaz is an earthly gem but "it is thought to feel the moon" ("lunam sentire putatur," 211). Sapphire enlivens the flesh of any human who grasps it, preventing envy and inhibiting terror. Naturally cold, sapphire also offers a cure for fever (103–28). Yet not every stone is so eager to become a human ally. Onyx will trigger restless dreams and lasting melancholy, engendering strife and intensifying quarrels and the flow of saliva (173–76). Sard exists primarily to counteract onyx.

Lapidaries typically detail "the different kinds of stones, their names and hues, / What land produces them, and the power of each."[88] These words are not those of the bishop of Rennes, but are contained within the letter from Evax with which Marbode prefaces his text. As this epistolary conceit emphasizes, stone triggers a proliferation of story, narratives that do not remain cemented within that which embeds them. Even if lapidaries may be divided into family trees and genealogized into particular traditions, no two texts are quite alike. Observing the wide variation in the description of particular gems, John Riddle observes that the "personal judgment" of authors is evident even when we do not know their name: "the lapidarists often felt obligated to relate their own experiences about the wonderful effects of stones," a familiar impulse to geobiography.[89] Type, name, color, provenance, ability, and force might seem separate lithic qualities, but they converge in these "wonderful effects," in what the lapidaries called their *virtus.* The genre of romance was content to state that *aventure* arrives, discerning in its strange advent the enchantment of the world, but it never worries too deeply about how such powers should radiate from an object. The lapidaries, however, developed a sophisticated vocabulary for the explication of nonhuman agency. A Latin noun with French and English cognates, *virtus* designates innate lithic potency, rocky material agency, a trigger to worldly activity. *Virtus* is creatureliness without anthropomorphism, the life-force of stone.

Virtus

In ancient Rome the noun *virtus* designated martial prowess and proper masculinity (from *vir,* man). Over the long centuries the term lost some of its gendered specificity and boundedness to the human, however, so that in the Middle Ages a knight, a lady, and their horses could all demonstrate *virtus*—as could the knight's sword, and the gem upon its hilt.[90] Encompassing far more than its modern English derivative "virtue," the capacious Latin term indicated qualities like physical strength, skill, talent, knowledge, health, and cognitive agility, as well as concepts such as miracle, authority, moral excellence, spiritual fortitude, and value. Like its vernacular cognates, *virtus* came to carry abstract but formidable significations ranging from energy, therapeutic ability, and vitality to transformational potential, inhuman agency, and intrinsic power. As an emissive force, *virtus* denotes elemental efficacy, grace, medicinal property, catalysis, influence, magic, agency, natural ability. The term offers a nonanthropomorphic designation for vital force and reproductive power. Chaucer famously writes of the "vertu" through which "engendred is the flour."[91] Stones and herbs radiate *virtus* with which humans may ally themselves, accomplishing through mineral and vegetal friendship feats otherwise impossible. As an animating principle, *virtus* also designates that which moves the flesh, like the soul. The term could be theologized, so that sacramental and divine power are among its meanings; or humanized, so that its ambit includes legal and regnal authority, moral excellence, and valor. Yet as lithic capability, quality, or force, *virtus* is nonhuman and often startlingly profane. The radiance (propulsion) and allure (magnetism) that animate romance *aventure* are two possible glosses for this lapidary potency: *virtus* as a nonmiraculous, nonsupernatural force that inheres in gems, metals, and rocks, made evident through material, sensory, cognitive, and affective consequences. When used in a lapidary the most succinct gloss is provided by the thirteenth-century polymath Albertus Magnus: "powers and actions" (*Book of Minerals,* 1.1.4). *Virtus* triggers relation, a lithic pulsion that engenders connection, contact, and transformation.

Virtus manifests profusely, naming the particular activities and inherent properties through which a stone becomes a worldly actant. Created by nature to serve as a styptic agent, *emathites* (bloodstone) reserves its powers for human utility, a medical aid to bodily travail.[92] Some stones form alliances only with those worthy of their potency, while others bestow their force without moral scruple. The topaz prefers chaste companions. Marbode describes *optallius* as the patron of thieves, sharpening their vision while clouding the sight of their victims (*Of Stones,* 622–26). Stone may also act by withdrawing affinities. A lecherous person who holds a diamond will cause the jewel to cease emission of its protective aura. *Virtus* is sometimes patent and gregarious, sometimes hidden, reticent, or indrawn. Bartholomaeus Anglicus captures this lithic variability when he writes that some gems are found in the veins of the earth; some are cast from the sea and "the place of their generation is unknown"; some appear in cliffs by the ocean and the gravel of rivers; others "grow in the bodies of birds and crawling animals." But no matter their place of gestation, Bartholomaeus writes, the best stones always possess "passyng gret virtue."[93]

In describing the manifold abilities of the rocks he surveys, Albertus Magnus declares "all the powers of things below come from above."[94] The divine origin of the elements matters profoundly, as it does for all creation within a Christian cosmology, but once stones enter the world they often seem to wander its spaces of their own volition. Radiation of healing force, provision of safety from foes, and proof against venom are related by the lapidaries to the relations rocks establish with their bearers, the ecosystem within which they come into being, and the environment in which they now find themselves entangled. *Virtus* may have flourished first in Eden but it resides in the substance of the unenclosed world. It does not descend from the skies (it is not a continuous eruption of miracle) nor rise from hell (it is the possession of a specific stone, not the trick of a demon).[95] There are exceptions, of course. Like any material object a rock could become a sacred relic. The *Book of John Mandeville* describes how the sultan had to place the Holy Sepulcher behind a rail so that Christians would cease to chip souvenirs that would transport the monument's divine efficacy home. Like water that has been washed over saintly bones and preserved for its healing powers, the soil and pebbles collected by pilgrims retain their elementality, but such secondary relics work like the body fragments of saints: their potency derives from the relationship of the object to a story that once unfolded between a pious human and God.[96] A nonsanctified stone's *virtus* is inherent in its materiality rather than the product of divine intercession. The *Sefer Hasidim,* a widely circulated late twelfth- or early thirteenth-century Hebrew text of religious instruction, tells of a Jewish woman who refused lithic help. Her Christian neighbor owned a piece of the Holy Sepulcher and told her that if the fragment were placed in contact with her ill son, he would be cured of his malady. Such a restoration would yield a narrative about the power of Christ, however, and the offer is piously declined.[97] Relics reveal the effectiveness of faith, prayer, and saintly intercessors. Lithic *virtus,* on the other hand, is a mundane fact, a quality of the stone rather than a human or theological narrative disguised as an object.

These distinctions are not absolute. Some medieval reliquaries were adorned with gems. These precious stones are likely more than mere indications of the value of the relic they companion, intensifying the sacred powers the object radiates. The fifteenth-century amulet known as the Middleham Jewel amalgamates a large sapphire, depictions of the Trinity and Nativity set in gold, a miniature of the Lamb of God, a Latin prayer, and words of power supposed to prevent epilepsy *(tetragrammaton, ananyzapta).* The reliquary opens for access to whatever holy matter it once enclosed. Yet there is also something nontotalizable about lush objects like the Middleham Jewel. The gem's relation to the heterogeneous other components of the amulet is not at all clear. The sapphire's *virtus* works alongside the prayers, charms, and relics, but each of these powerful things is a force entangled as well as individual.[98]

The tone of most lapidaries is unfailingly matter-of-fact even as they describe the most wondrous activity. Although Pliny and Isidore censured those who grant too much power to stones, writers like Marbode were so committed to geologic capability that they protest no excess. Their texts depict a world pulsing with inorganic agency, where a gem held in the palm can cure blindness, discharge bursts of light, grant eloquence, and overcome enemies. The lapidaries reflect a lived reality and create radiant alternatives. Such a reconfigured perceptual landscape opens a disorienting environmental enmeshment.[99] Medieval people really did carry with them stones described in these texts, often in the form of jewelry. They expected things of their lithic companions, these objects that they knew were something more than earthen lumps.

Lapidaries can be confusing, amalgamating under a single heading gems or minerals that we today regard as unlike. Sometimes their entries do not strike modern readers as geological at all, since they seem to be plant or animal products, fossilized remains, or "just like a stone" (Theophrastus's description of red coral, *On Stones,* 82) without being stone, exactly. Whereas modern geological taxonomy is structured around chemical composition, in medieval lapidaries color is a primary delimiter of difference and intimate to *virtus.* Thus Albertus Magnus says that *pantherus* (that is, *panchrus,* "all colors") possesses "as many powers as it has colours" (*Book of Minerals,* 2.2.14). Hue exerts so delimiting a force that stones are often gathered into the same category because of shared tint, even when their materiality greatly differs. *Smaragdus,* for example, collects translucent emeralds and opaque green marble under the same name. Yet color is notoriously difficult to convey verbally, imbuing a generative indeterminacy. Lapidary science undermines organic and inorganic distinction by positing a corporeal origin for many stones. When a gem originates in the flesh of an animal, sharp separations between biological organisms and unanimated materiality evanesce. Albertus Magnus states that *alecterius, quandros,* and *radaim* derive from the bodies of birds (*Book of Minerals,* 2.2.1, 2.2.15, 2.2.16). He describes *varach* or dragon's blood *(sanguis draconis),* a remedy for hematic flux, as a bright red and powdery stone created from that animal (2.2.19). A primal sympathy often unites the human body and the lithic through which stone reveals itself as productive, riotous, fecundating. Jasper, according to Marbode, assists women during childbirth, an inorganic midwife.[100] The Sloane Lapidary states that a diamond will protect against lechery and bone-breaking accidents, as well as "keep the seede of a mans body within a womans body, so yt the children's limmes [limbs] shall not be crooked."[101] Marbode's *Medical Prose Lapidary* asserts that if washed in water and given to a sterile woman, amethyst "causes immediate conception."[102] Not every stone spurs fertility or abets human life. Pliny describes milky and ambivalent *galactitis,* notable for the lactic and mnemonic flows the stone harbors and incites, as well as its mammalian rapport:

When rubbed between the fingers it exhibits a milky smear and flavor, and in the rearing of children it ensures wet-nurses a plentiful flow of milk. Moreover, when it is tied to the necks of babies as an amulet, it is said to make their saliva flow, but we are told that when placed in the mouth it melts and also causes loss of memory. (*Natural History,* 37.59)

At the precarious threshold of life *galactitis* is a trigger to vital fluids, an aid to thriving. *Galactitis* is also perilous. To make it intimate to the body is to aid the feeding of a child or to know lithic oblivion. Some stones are surprisingly hostile to life. Marbode's *Medical Prose Lapidary* describes *achates* as an abortifacient, while other rocks exude toxic vapors or trigger madness. Yet the lapidaries for the most part describe lithic power as affirmative, sympathetic, intensifying, and proliferative.

Lapidaries accrete facts from varied sources and frequently contain contradictory information. As sedimentary collations, these texts combine but do not synthesize material from ancient Greece, classical Rome, late antiquity, the early and the high Middle Ages. Lapidaries are inherently polychronic, unsettling. Their main thrust tends to be therapeutic, with an emphasis upon what stones offer humans: the cure to an imbalance of bodily humors, the sparking of sexual prowess, protection in a hostile landscape, eloquence for a mouth that too often fails. And yet sometimes the secrets of stones remain their own. Of leek-green *chrysoprase,* with its golden stars and impenetrable inner darkness, Marbode writes "But what its virtue, rests concealed in night; / All things Fate grants not unto mortal sight" (*Of Stones,* 238–39). No matter into what obscurity these powers recede, however, the lapidaries propound that every stone pulses with animating force, every stone inclines toward contact.

Every stone desires.

The Sex Life of Stone

The philosopher Elizabeth Grosz argues that, because art derives from bodily excess fostered through sexual selection, "art is of the animal," the gift of biological drive.[103] Following Gilles Deleuze and Félix Guattari, she writes that art is not representational (it does not simulate a thing or capture an event) but instead monumentalizes sensation through the continuous transmission of affect. Art is a machine of relations. Ochre handprints on ancient stone, Westminster Abbey, and a peacock's lush display of feathered eyes elicit engagement and demand emotional response. They emit vibratory resonances and arouse bodies to connect flesh and world.[104] In the form of a painting, architectural structure, bioluminescence, or pigment within fur, matter can hold and catalyze sensation. But because art is an extension of embodiment, matter's emissive quality arrives in Grosz's account from elsewhere, from biological shaping.[105] Such organic bias comes from Darwin, who traces art's thrilling exorbitance to the intensification of bodies over evolutionary time, propelled by the exigencies of mating.[106] Sexual difference is therefore its primary catalyst, so that the production of beautiful excess and affective enmeshment arises through and for organisms. Yet is the elemental yearning toward sexual union, or simply toward relation? What if combination and heterogeneous connection are (as the medieval concept of *virtus* posits) innate? What if sexual difference merely accelerates preexisting and underlying desire, an immanent inclination toward production, contingency, and innovation—what Roger Caillois described as a universal material impulse to generate aesthetic surplus and create boundary-crossing interpenetrations? What if propulsive assemblage-making and its ecological effects are not limited to biological bodies? What if the alluring intensity of materiality is itself erotic, what Walter Benjamin called "the sex appeal of the inorganic"?[107] If life is as queerly distributed as some ecotheorists have argued—"catastrophic, monstrous, nonholistic, and dislocated, not organic, coherent, or authoritative"—then even stones can produce affect-laden and relation-engendering art.[108] Extending this line of thought farther, such stone might even demonstrate sexual difference, a lithic sexuality, or perhaps even an erotic pulsion that does not replicate the human or the animal but veers with them into unexpected territory.

We have seen already from Albertus Magnus that sexually dimorphic stone was a medieval possibility. Theophrastus, author of the first extant lapidary, writes of *lyngurium,* a magnetic substance produced when a lynx urinates into the earth. Bodily fluid mixes with the element and they congeal. Taking on the gender of the parent animal, *lyngurium* is at once anomalous and vividly illustrative of how certain rocks spring to surprising life. Theophrastus describes most of the stones in his text with detachment, since he is more interested in their place of origin and material composition than in what a particular gem might do. *Lyngurium,* however, is granted a geo-biography so saturated with wonder that the stone gains immediate textual momentum, and as a consequence a long historical thriving. This hybrid substance produced when animal liquidity meets earthy dryness features in lapidary lore for two thousand years. Theophrastus's name will be attached to its description long after the text in which the story originates is lost. A stone no one had seen, *lyngurium* proliferated throughout lapidary works and achieved a lifespan that crossed millennia. Or, to state the same idea differently, Theophrastus's narrative of *lyngurium* so well conveyed the vi-brancy the lithic harbors that the story endured longer than the world of its genesis. A confluence of contraries, *lyngurium* possesses like its parent ani-mal a particular sex while vividly materializing its environmental enmesh-ment. As a general rule Theophrastus maintains that when stones naturally occur in two colors, divergent hues differentiate the male and female forms:

> For one type of *sardion,* which is translucent and of a redder color, is called the female, and the other, which is translucent and darker, is called the male. And it is the same with the varieties of the *lyngourion,* for the female is more transparent and yellow than the other. Also, one kind of *kyanos* is called male and the other female, and the male is the darker of the two. (*On Stones,* 30–31)

Dual colors and genders are for Theophrastus neutral facts, holding little consequence. Yet *lyngurium* is richly embedded in story. Since the stone descends from the crystallization of urine within earth, the binding of the biotic with the inorganic, its two possible forms derive directly from an animal body to which they thereby remain connected. Gendering at birth grants the male and female forms distinct natures. *Lyngurium* is described as

> cold and very transparent, and it is better when it comes from wild ani-mals rather than tame ones and from males rather than females; for there is a difference in their food, in the exercise they take or fail to take, and in general in the nature of their bodies, so that one is drier and the other more moist. (*On Stones,* 28)

In a powerful collaboration between living flesh and fertile elementality, cor-poreality clings to *lyngurium,* so that docility, gender (itself a product of rela-tive aridity and temperature), nutrition, and exercise can fortify or weaken its structure by imbuing the rock with varying quantities of force-impeding moisture.

Early in his lapidary Theophrastus writes cryptically "the greatest and most wonderful power, if this is true, is that of stones which give birth to young" (*On Stones,* 5). He never names what particular stone might be endowed with the power to procreate, and through the qualifying phrase "if this is true" builds doubt into the existence of generative rocks from the start.[109] Succinct and detached, Theophrastus makes relatively little of lithic gender. Nor does he connect petric sexuality to his statement about "stones which give birth to young." Misogyny inheres in the philosopher's assumption that female stones are weaker than male forms, and his division of *lyngurium* into a sexual binary suggests a blinkered view of nature as self-partitioning. Yet to allow that the same qualities of heat and moisture that create male and female bodies also engender male and female rocks is to divulge human-lithic continuity, an expanded vitality rather than a reduction of frame. Rocks with gender do not become more apprehensible, do not act in a dramatically more human way for their sexual difference. They are not fables for how the human world works; they are their own story.

This tension between seeming likeness and abiding rocky difference manifests repeatedly in lapidary history. So do male and female stones. In his *Book of Minerals* Albertus Magnus mentions that red *balagius* is the female form of the carbuncle "for its colour and powers are like those of the carbuncle, but weaker, just as the female is compared to the male" (2.2.1). Isidore of Seville writes of eaglestones *(aetites),* found in sexed pairs in the nests of these regal birds. The masculine is "hard, like the gall nut," the feminine "small and soft." Eagles cannot reproduce without the presence of both forms, and when the two are joined together they assist human parturition (*Etymologies,* 16.4.22). Many centuries later Bartholomaeus Anglicus will add that the "stone conteyneþ [contains] another stone as a woman with child" (*On the Properties of Things,* 16.38), but Isidore does not mention a connection between gender and lithic reproductive systems. With the appearance of Marbode's seminal lapidary, *peanita* enters the tradition and brings with it the possibility of petric pregnancy. Through an unknown cause, Marbode writes, *peanita* conceives and gives birth to a similar stone. An ontology-crossing sympathy enables *peanita* to assist women experiencing trouble during childbirth.[110] Like the eaglestone, *peanita* is often dismissed by modern interpreters as a geode "with foreign pebbles or crystals said to be born when the encapsulating mother stone is broken."[111] Yet neither medieval nor classical texts actually describe a geode. Albertus Magnus, for example, states laconically and without dubiousness that *peranites* (as he calls *peanita*) "is of the female sex; for at a certain season it is said to conceive and give birth to another natural stone like itself" (*Book of Minerals*, 2.2.14). For this reason, he adds, *peranites* is good for pregnant women. Albertus does not imagine that a human need be present for the birth of the baby stone to occur. He does not state that a male *peanita* participates in the creation of the new stone (petrogenesis could be parthenogenesis) and mentions nothing about finding a small stone within a larger one. *Peanita* simply does what *peanita* does. Its nature is to produce stone from stone. Naturalizing these rocks into medieval misapprehensions of geodes normalizes their lithic queerness by reducing them into familiar forms. Such assimilation into the unremarkable is directly contrary to lapidary intent, which discovers in stone an inexhaustible source for astonishment, material efficacy, and disanthropocentrism.

Lapidaries are not the only texts to gender stones and contemplate lithic desire. The *Physiologus,* an early Greek compilation of animal narratives that finds in the lives of ants, sirens, hyenas, and hedgehogs allegories for Christian virtues and vices, bestows to the later Middle Ages a bestiary tradition of sexually differentiated *piroboli,* or fire rocks. Allegories for the carnal sins to which men and women are drawn, *piroboli* are "igneous rocks of the masculine and feminine gender" native to the East. Kept at a distance the two forms remain inert. Should the male approach the female, however, "fire breaks forth and consumes all."[112] Renamed *lapides igniferi* (fire-bearing rocks) when the *Physiologus* was translated into Latin (ca. 700), these stones make frequent appearances in medieval bestiaries, where they find themselves in the good company of the phoenix, elephant, panther, beaver, fox, weasel, bees, and dragon. Lapidaries were sometimes bound with bestiaries, and it is not difficult to see why: their rocks are as lively and assertive as any creature contained in zoological compendia. Whereas lapidaries are usually content to allow stones to be stones, however, the bestiaries generally narrate fire rocks anthropomorphically. *Piroboli* are often depicted as a human couple embracing in the midst of flames, an allegorical representation in which little of the lithic remains. These figures are

motu.Sepelire autem est condere corpora. nam humare ob
ruere diam. hoc est humum inicere. De lapidibus igniferis.

Aberdeen Bestiary, Fire Rocks. Aberdeen University Library, MS 24, fol. 93v.
Reprinted with permission of Aberdeen University Library.

typically naked, but sometimes the stones in corporeal form are clothed.[113]
Since humans are also made from earth and water, such representations
make good biblical sense. Because fire is an easy allegory for lust, a devoutly
Christian story divulged by stone almost writes itself.[114] In the Aberdeen
Bestiary, the fire rocks are humanized into a nude man and woman holding
stones, staring intently at each other. Ornate trees suggest a garden, perhaps
even Eden. Once the couple embrace, they combust in tongues of red flame

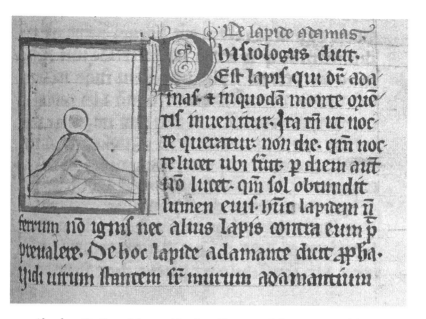

Aberdeen Bestiary, Adamas. Aberdeen University Library, MS 24, fol. 94r.
Reprinted with permission of Aberdeen University Library.

(fol. 93v). Yet this bestiary balances its lithic representations. On the following page the reader is met by a depiction of a lone rock atop a still, green hill (fol. 94r). This stone is *adamas,* the diamond, most impenetrable of materials, its solitariness a rebuke to the blazing gregariousness of its siblings. On a placid summit, removed from story and from time, the Aberdeen *adamas* dwells indifferent to human relation and fiery futurity.[115]

Depictions of fire rocks are almost never content to leave stone to seclusion, to add nothing of human story. Yet a surprisingly nonanthropomorphic, nonnarrative representation appears in the bestiary of London, British Library, MS Harley 3244 (at fol. 60). Igneous red mixed with blazing orange, these five stones shine like embers on a grassy mountain slope. They are uniformly partitioned from each other, serene in their glow.[116] The Harley fire rocks glimmer with vitality, but they have not yet ignited into cataclysmic story. They thrum with compacted energy, pulse with the promise of magnificent detonation—maybe, someday, but for now they are stones unperturbed in their vibrant materiality, placid on that verdant hillside, not figures for human tales of lust and its consequences. Other depictions of *lapides igniferi* are neither fully human nor fully lithic, creating a jarring hybridity. The bestiary held by Gonville and Caius College illustrates firestones as petric flowers with human faces.[117] Against a monochrome background two dark rocks, petal-like extensions framing the visages at their centers, appear to be moving toward each other across space or sky. The intricate and expressive faces of these stones gender one as male, one female. Each uneasily eyes the other as flames just start to erupt. They seem keenly to apprehend that *something* is about to arrive but do not know enough to regard that fatal advent with anything but puzzlement. Kellie Robertson argues that human-lithic hybridity is innate to medieval encounter with rocky matter, in both philosophy and literature. She demonstrates that rocks in the Middle Ages "were not merely passive objects of the human gaze, but active participants in shaping the mental reality of percipients," thereby granting the lithic its "capacity to organize the humans who look at them, based on what they see, rather than being simply subject to human desire."[118] Some bestiaries go farther, bringing lithic vitality into wholly unexpected realms, expanses in which easy assumptions about what it means to be human or alive fall apart. Rock is anthropomorphized not to become more knowable, not to be assimilated into the human, but to remove stone from that constrictive familiarity that prevents apprehension of its recalcitrance, challenge, queerness. As the lithic flowers with perplexed human faces in the Gonville and Caius College bestiary suggest, their expressions registering bemusement at an incineration that has already begun, stone abides in marvelously inscrutable spaces, so alien that the fire rocks themselves are perplexed by the advent of their combustive future.[119]

In addition to lapidaries and bestiaries, lithic sexual difference was explored in alchemical and metallurgical texts. Albertus Magnus writes that, whereas stones rather neutrally produce some metals within themselves ("as if the substance of stones were, so to speak, a place peculiarly suitable for the production of metals," *Book of Minerals,* 3.1.1), gendered terminology must be invoked to explain how metals (classified, like stones, as a subset of minerals) transmute from one form to another. Sulphur is the father of metals, possessing *masculus semen* (male seed) that can impress its form upon less active matter. Quicksilver (*argentum vivum,* "living silver") is female matter, analogized to the fecundating menstrual fluid necessary for the formation of the animal embryo. Through the combination of sulphur and quicksilver other metals are born.[120] Triggered by the influence of heavenly bodies, mineralizing virtue (*virtus lapidum generativa* or *vis mineralis,* a concept Albertus takes from the Persian polymath Avicenna) names the power of dry and moist subterranean vapors to breed stones and metals. Metals generate other metals, though, through an act of sexual union in which sulphur penetrates with its fecundating seed the embryonic matter provided by quicksilver. What kind of stone or mineral develops is determined by astrological influence and the nature of the place in which this genesis unfolds—and this environmental impress relies upon, in turn, astral and elemental forces. Because "the place of their production is also fundamental" (1.1.6; see also 1.1.7), every stone or metal transported into a new environment carries its indigenous ecology along with it, an abiding and emissive structuration. Stones are, in this way, rather like people, and *virtus* a version of geohumoralism. Just as stars and climate influence but do not wholly determine character, embodiment, and race, so stars and place (ecology in a vast sense: an environment that extends to the sidereal and descends to the elemental) influences but does not wholly predetermine lithic desire and force.

Albertus observes that stones are produced everywhere: "not in one element only, but in several, and not in one clime only, but in all." Ecological effusions, they remain dependent upon their place of generation: "away from this they are destroyed and dispersed" (*Book of Minerals,* 1.1.7). Petrogenesis also unfolds along varying temporal scales. The river Gion produces new stones in the relatively short span of thirty-eight years (1.1.7). Other rocks and gems are the products of processes that unfold throughout subterranean centuries. A few rocks appear, quite literally, in a flash. Bartholomaeus follows Marbode's idea of *ceraunius* (thunderstone) and describes his own version, stones that tumble from the heavens to arrive on earth: "when it thunders horribly fire lights the air; when clouds smash together this stone falls."[121] Just as animals give birth to mewling offspring, so rocks, gems, metals, and earth burgeon each day, everywhere, and populate the world.

Sexual difference among rocks raises the possibility of petrogenesis through true lithic procreation, stone sex. Theophrastus never says that *lyngurium* might, like its animal parent, reproduce, but the possibility is implicit in the story he narrates.[122] Lapidary lore refers at times to gendered stones, yet generally without stating why dimorphism exists. For Pliny, cyanus, lapis lazuli, and carbuncle have male and female versions (*Natural History,* 37). A thirteenth-century Anglo-Norman lapidary describes the male diamond *(diamaunt)* as dark in color and Indian in origin, while the female form comes from Arabia and is more white, the color of crystal.[123] Bartholomaeus Anglicus writes of the Persian and Indian stone called *echites* found in seaside cliffs, a version of the familiar eaglestone:

> And it is double, as Isidore of Seville says, male and female. And always two are found in an eagle's nest: and the eagle may not breed without these stones. . . . The male kind is hard and like the gum called gall. This male is somewhat hot, and the female is soft.[124]

Bartholomaeus adds that this stone is said to contain another, "as a woman with childe." The *Book of John Mandeville* takes lithic sexual difference, fecundity, and creaturely possibility to their limit, describing diamonds that mate, reproduce, live. Native to India, these gems are as animated and alluring as the Amazons who exile men from their company, the Sciopods who possess only one foot, nudists and assassins and all the other fabulous folk who companion Mandeville in his *Book.*[125] Diamonds, we are told, come in two forms, male and female. Erotic inclination brings the gems into union, but not necessarily as couples, and without the incendiary and moralized results constraining firestones. Promiscuous in their commingling, diamonds undertake a slow lithic coitus that within its own geologic time creates ever more glistening and libidinous rocks, a slow-motion petric orgy:

> They groweth togodres [together], the maule and the femaule. And they beth noryshed [are nourished] with the dew of hevene, and they engendreth comunely [in common] and bryngeth forth other smale dyamaundes, that multeplieth and groweth all yeres.[126]

Though gendered, these amatory rocks are not exactly heteronormative. Their material queerness is emphasized as the diamonds connect intimately to other episodes in the text, especially the soon-to-be-encountered nudist communist cannibals of Lamoria. Like the licentious gems, the Lamorians procreate "comunely," do not know their own offspring, and yet continue in their mating and their multiplication unperturbed, a self-contained and happily thriving community. The Lamorians are a supreme test of the narrator's fabled tolerance for cultural difference. They challenge deeply those who translated, disseminated, and read the *Book of John Mandeville.* Yet diamonds are in form and body nothing like these humans, even if they share some of their desires. Adamantine sexuality is an intimation that nonhumans of all kinds undertake generative, even amorous relations with each other, that inhuman objects possess rich and lively existences that unfold indifferent to human viewing. Mandeville's diamonds act as if they were biological entities, engendered through lithic embrace, nourished by dew, content at times to become a traveler's companion. The French version of the *Book of John Mandeville,* perhaps the closest we have to an original, emphasizes their intense vitality:

> [Diamonds] grow several together, one small, the other large, and there are some the size of a bean, and there are some as big as a hazelnut, and they are all of square form and with their natural points both above and below without any shaping by a human hand. They grow together male and female, and they feed on the dew from Heaven, and they conceive and beget and make their little children beside them that multiply and grow every year. I have many times demonstrated that if they are kept with a little of the rock, and not separated from their root, and wet often with May dew, they grow visibly every year, and small ones become quite big.[127]

With their conceiving, begetting, feeding, and growing, these diamonds are more animal than stone. "Et croissent ensemble male et femelle" ("And they grow together, male and female") makes the lively gems seem as if they are following God's injunction to Adam and Eve, "Crescite et multiplicamini" (be fruitful and multiply).[128] The same biblical command convinced the Lamorians to embrace sexual excess. The small diamonds are even called *petitz filz,* "little children." If kept moist after harvesting, their bearer will enable the tiny stones to continue to grow, true mineral organisms.[129] A more creaturely rendition of the lithic is difficult to imagine. Diamonds mature, eat, desire, reproduce. Demanding no more than occasional drops of dew, they offer themselves as an especially precious kind of pet rock. Their vivacity makes their radiation of powers and affects *(virtus)* all the more natural, extensions of their animate powers. Diamonds can vanquish poison, prevent nightmares, instill boldness, assist justice in prevailing, dispel illusions, repel the attacks of wild animals, and foster peace.[130] They are often livelier than the humans who surround them. Whereas diamonds brim with lithic longing and incline toward each other and those who discover them, the nearby people of Hormuz languish naked in pools of water to escape India's great heat. The Hormuz men find the sun's intensity, the same celestial energy that renders gems lively, has an unwanted effect upon their "stones of gendrure":

> And hit is so hoot [hot] ther that mennys ballockys hongeth doun to her shankes [men's testicles hang down to their legs]. And men of that contré byndeth hem full straytly uppe [bind them back up], and they do hem anoynte with oynementz y maked therfore, other elles myght they noght lyve in that lond [anoint them with special oils, or else they could not live in that land]. (*Book of John Mandeville*, 1557–59)

Diamonds are better adapted to the harsh environment of their native land than the humans who dwell nearby. As medieval lapidary science knew well, the lithic exerts relentless and incalculable forces. Mandeville through his creaturely diamonds questions whether rocks must be dismissed as insensate and impotent matter, quietly suggesting that these rocks belong with organisms that prowl the world, multiply, form relations, desire, maybe even love.

Although they flourish when surrounded by a community of their own kind, diamonds also seek human connection. Provided their bearer is diamond-like in virtue, through mutuality and cross-ontological alliance their power increases. These gems heal lunacy ("hit helith hym that is lunatyk," *Book of John Mandeville*, 1532)—and Englishmen, Mandeville avers, are born under the influence of the moon, rendering them congenital wanderers.[131] The implicit affinity of diamonds and Englishness makes the gems especially close to Mandeville himself, an English knight who judges the world by his nation's standards. The lunar pull with which the gem is bound will recall the intimacy of hard diamond to alluring adamant. Mandeville writes of distant seas where in the depths magnetic stones lurk ("roch of the adamaund," "roches de aymant"), drawing to watery oblivion any vessel that glides above, a victim of the rock's attraction for the nails binding naval planks. The moon itself is adamantine, according to Bartholomaeus Anglicus. As iron follows "the stone adamaunt," so the sea follows the moon, so the planets exert their pull on sublunary life: "the working of the planets is like the magnet stone, adamant, and iron."[132] This earth, its elements, its inhabitants are ever in motion because of the adamantine gravity of bodies that wander the skies. Recall the words of Isidore of Seville: "The world consists of the heavens and the earth, the sea and all the stars. It is called the world *[mundus]* because it is always in motion *[motus]* for no rest is given to its elements."[133] Or Albertus Magnus's realization that every seemingly still stone is a battleground of forces: its earthiness and congealed wateriness drawing it toward the deepest ground, its bits of air and fire pulling toward heaven, rendering the seemingly immobile chunk of matter "a microcosm of concord-in-discord . . . a little miracle of balance between conflicting elemental tendencies."[134] Gregory of Nyssa wrote similarly of humans: "The material life of our bodies flows . . . if it should ever cease moving it will certainly have ceased to be."[135]

Chorea Lapidum

Stones are rich in worlds not ours, while we are poor in their duration. We therefore have a terrible problem communicating with each other.[136] Geophilia marks an enduring inclination to lithic alliance, an embrace of co-extensiveness, despite or perhaps because of the cognitive reeling stone can trigger. Is it at any wonder that this intimate alien, its temporal and spatial scale so difficult, so envied, should be a beauty we wear as rings, the adornment of our graves, substance of our daily lives, and material for endurance beyond catastrophe? Stone is the stuff out of which we fashion as fellow artists those architectures that we trust to convey story into futures we cannot imagine, futures for which we nonetheless yearn. We desire stone, and if we can allow stone its proper duration, its agency within the networks of restless, slow, relentless connection we form with it as companion (or as Mandeville would say, as "partyners"), we can see that stone desires in return.

Stones are lush. The Middle English noun *ston* denotes the pit of a fruit (cherries, grapes, and dates), a hard seed sheltering eruptive vivacity.[137] Dense materiality, seemingly inert, proves fecund. *Ston* also indicates a human generator of seed *(semen),* as when Harry Bailey declares to the Nun's Priest "I-blessed be thy breche, and every stoon!" (Blessed be your breeches and both testicles, The Nun's Priest's Tale, 7.3448). "Stonys of þe modere" are ovaries, just as generative, just as intimate to human embodiment, just as disorienting to find at work within human flesh. We have seen in Geoffrey of Monmouth and William of Newburgh that stones are eggs, with bellicose dragons, pungent greyhounds, or ornamented toads at their interiors. *Stons of vertu* are the jewels, gemstones, and magic stones that lead vibrant lives in the lapidary and romance traditions. Rock is not a solitary substance but networked matter, full of movement and connection. Stones may therefore be produced within almost any geography (deserts, swamps, underwater), within clouds and the bodies of animals. This originary impress combines the divine, the astral, the elemental, and the incidental. In his *Book of Minerals* Albertus writes of a petrified tree branch from near Lübeck on which was discovered a nest with baby magpies. This little ecosystem turned to stone, Albertus observes, because the waters into which it fell hold such transfixional powers of place (1.1.7). Other machines for geological production include rivers, snow, mountains, animal bodies, and clouds. Each of these spaces creates through environmental and astrological impress specific types of stones. Transporting them away from their place of generation risks having them "destroyed and dispersed" (1.1.7), perishing like mortals whose souls have taken flight. There is a vitality in these stones that challenges the limits of the human, that quietly suggests what a lithic thriving might be. That Albertus is able to do so despite his words against soul and life in stone demonstrates what became so apparent to Jean Kerisel in his laboratory, attentive through his stethoscope to the groans of pink granite under duress: by refusing our unnuanced taxonomies, by bluntly insisting upon a world in which its materiality is not mere substance awaiting human use, stone invites a more ethically generous mode of worldly inhabitance, a more capacious, disanthropocentric redefinition of a word that we have allowed to become impoverished, *alive*.

Stephen A. Walton has described ethnominerology as the study of "our relationship with inert nature, as compared with animals and plants, where drawing connections at a behavioural level is a bit more clear."[138] Yet the stone examined in this book is never inert, whether a medieval or modern author is palming its hard surface. Albertus arrives, against his own protestations, at what Jane Bennett calls vibrant materialism. The lapidary tradition and the romances were there long before him. A rock is not recalcitrant, for to label it with such an adjective is to describe the world merely from a human point of view, in which stones exist for us. All materiality is active, agentic, regardless of human alliance or intention. Something in the lithic invites contemplation. This ecological sensibility resonates with the vision of friendship articulated by the monastic writer Aelred of Rievaulx, who found that inhumans love companionship as much as we do:

> [Nature] has left no type of beings alone, but out of many has drawn them together by means of a certain society. Suppose we begin with inanimate creation—what soil or what river produces one single stone of one kind? Or what forest bears but a single tree of a single kind? And so even in in-animate nature a certain love of companionship, so to speak, is apparent, since none of these exists alone but everything is created and thrives in a certain society with its own kind.[139]

For Aelred friendship is an attraction of kind to kind, so that mineral amity is reserved to stones. Yet medieval texts often enacted a cross-ontological mode of ecological coinhabitance, a *convivencia* (potentially as full of strife as desire) of fellowships across matter. Centuries later, Jane Bennett comes to a resonantly similar conclusion that multiplies human and inorganic intimacies:

> One of the effects of a heightened awareness of the interpenetration of the human and ahuman geologic is that it stretches my definition of "self"-interest to include the flourishing of the complex system of bio-geologic processes. . . . The idea of a deep belonging between human beings and a rather volatile earth also provides much of the energy for the political project called the geologic turn.[140]

This geologic turn might also be glossed as a dance of bodies and objects. *Chorea gigantum.* I want to return in closing to that ring of stones on Salisbury Plain, the one Geoffrey of Monmouth called a circle, a song, a dance. Stonehenge haunts this book. Although I did not know it at the time, *Stone: An Ecology of the Inhuman* had its genesis in 2007, when I was living with my family in London. On a Sunday morning we departed the city early and drove to Salisbury Plain. I had been to Stonehenge and Avebury years earlier, while backpacking the UK after college. At that first visit I was checking an item from a list of sites necessary to behold and felt no great longing to return. Yet no one brings children to England without lugging them to Stonehenge, so off we drove on our pilgrimage of obligation. This time, in the company of three people I love, on a day when rain alternated with sudden blue sky, at a time when I had finally come to realize how small a duration anyone gets to spend on earth no matter how much they might want more life, I understood what Geoffrey of Monmouth achieves in his description of Stonehenge and its lithic dance.

At first glance nothing could seem more still than these dark rocks on their green slope. Visitors typically remark that the megaliths are smaller than expected. The nearby motorway is distracting. Tour groups clog the path encircling the ring. The small fence prohibiting near approach annoys. Yet the stones draw the eye: some plumb and distinguished, some pendulous as acrobats, some crouched with expectancy. Even the fallen pieces seem carefully placed, elements of an extending wheel. Something happens in that encounter, something perceived by Geoffrey as well as the Romans and the Normans and the peoples who became the British and the English, something known to those prehistoric groups whose presence we realize only from the changes they crafted to the architecture during its five-thousand-year flourishing: the rocks begin to move. We want to touch them, want to reassure ourselves that the spinning of the lithic ring resonates with a vibration awakened within ourselves, that the desire is shared. What we feel spring into being is an affective interspace where the agency of stone and human ardor meet in mutual relation, in cross-ontological embrace. Geophilia is a middle region of creation and innovation, a space of convivial wayfaring—experimenting, working, and living together, a place of differences and disorienting danger, a forging of alliance and embrace that gathers a world so vast that even stones become fellow travellers along epochal, uncertain, but never uncompanioned ways.

Iceland

1. Needful Stones

Stones, wrote Bartholomaeus Anglicus, are the "bones of the earth."[1] They grant the globe stability and prevent its lands from pulling apart. Without stone we would possess the barest of lives. The lithic arrives in so many species and shapes, holding so much power to sustain relations, that through alliance we transform every ecology into which we step. Bartholomaeus describes stones as "profitable and nedefulle" for the building of houses, walls, pavement, and bridges. Guide and matter of transport, refuge against tempests, rock conveys and protects, a shelter against the predation of enemies, wolves, and "evil beasts." The substance of the inhabited world, the materiality through which hearths, homes, towers, and cities arise, stone "helps and heals" bodies beset by sickness and founds the courts of kings. Through stone and with stone we fashion monuments that endure.

Or so we tell ourselves, because our histories are small.

2. Divergent Tectonic Plate Boundary (MAR)

To journey Iceland is to traverse a landscape thick with story, a topography known already through medieval sagas: an enormous boulder that Grettir

Langjökull: the world opens.

once lifted, a hill where Aud the Deep-Minded erected a cross, a glacial river where Njal's sons ambushed their enemy. Guidebooks often describe the feel of the island as primeval. Shaped by recent volcanoes, ongoing tectonic shift, and frequent glaciation, its expanses are geologically young. Iceland sits on the mid-Atlantic ridge. As North America and Eurasia pull away from each other, the island grows at about a centimeter a year, along a rift just below where the medieval assembly known as the Alþingi used to meet. A *þing* is a gathering, a convocation where frictions surface and force is exerted, a making of the real through deliberation and debate. Bruno Latour points out how extraordinary it is that *thing,* this "banal term we use for designating what is out there, unquestionably" should be the inheritance of "the oldest of the sites in which our ancestors did their dealing and tried to settle their disputes."[2] Þingvellir, the fissured expanse where the Alþingi was convened into the eighteenth century, is now a World Heritage Site. Tourists wander the rift valley in search of human history, while below their feet tectonic plates diverge, liquid rock rises from the mantle, and the seabed spreads.

Þingvellir: divergence.

I travelled to Iceland to finish this book. Some of the island's geography resembles the Irish Burren (*Boíreann*, "rocky"), a landscape rich in lithic art catalytic to the project's instigation. Yet Iceland holds nothing like the standing stones, barrows, rings, and dolmens of Ireland, Britain, France. Human trace is far more recent. Except for the occasional remains of a farmstead's hearth, fire and stone collaborating to send story forward, the landscape holds few lithic communication devices. Stone is everywhere entangled with the aqueous: volcanic fields scraped by errant glaciers, marshes where lava penetrated an ice shield to form pseudocraters, turbid rivers of melt that plunge into the earth, rock and water in constant terraforming partnership. In the polychrome valleys of Landmannalaugar, where vibrant rhyolite shifts beneath your feet as you hike, blue, green, pink, and white mountains rise. Steam drifts from geothermal vents. Bartholomaeus described Iceland as a place so full of ice (*perpetuo glacie* in Latin, "alwey ise and glaas" in Trevisa's translation) that water becomes stone. Icelandic mountains, he wrote, are hardened snow, where ice petrifies into beautiful crystal.[3]

Iceland reminds that stone like water is alive, that stone like water is transient.

3. Moody Beach

In Maine (another place where this book that keeps beginning commenced) my brother Mark asked me about Iceland. I told him its lesson of impermanence. I began my long study of stone seeking something that endures. Yet rock moves like any liquid, restless and ephemeral: sedimented, recycled, engulfed, pulverized, melted, metamorphized, eroded, rebirthed. We think stone persists only because it outlasts. We trust stone as archive and monument, but we may as well write on water. The fossil record is scanty, its gaps enormous, its lacunae inscrutable. Stone promises futurity but provides only a brief and fragmented recordation. Particles will in the end remain. We will be readable from atomic traces, not from the architectures we build, not from bodies or machines or the stories that we tell. The music of the spheres is the whirl of these bits and specks, objects of the smallest scale. Boulders, cliffs, mountains, sea floors, bones, continents, plates, planets: stone's destiny is the cosmic dust that once it was, carrying some new chemicals perhaps, betraying to someone's instruments the telltale signs of organic life that needed stone to burgeon, dwell, and thrive— but particles all the same, fragments nearing silence.

4. Love

In writing this book I have been drawn constantly back to the stones that companioned its composition. Geologic collaborations are like the slow movements of tectonic plates. You don't necessarily get an earthquake to announce that alignment has shifted. Forceful action is invisible. Yet sometimes in looking back with enough perspective the wandered landscape reveals a past rather different from what you thought. Ground's drift is relentless, a quiet friction that is a drive toward strange conjunction, perilous continuity across vast spans. In the company of archaebacteria, dinosaurs, or humans, volcanoes erupt, continents wander, the ocean floor rises and falls. The geological strata upon which we walk and build, foundation both literal and epistemological, is full of shift. The desert was a seabed, whalebones are stranded atop a mountain, the past is never what we hope, and every object is full of strange relation. *Stone: An Ecology of the Inhuman* is built around such truths and written in the conviction that medieval writers meditated upon inanimate matter and came to rather similar insights, expressed within differently sympathetic modes. Rock communicates something nonhuman and yet weirdly creaturely, queerly vital, even to writers who supposedly had all the answers they needed in theology, science, and other forms of received history. Trekking the ashy wastes surrounding a volcano (Hekla, which last erupted in 2000, and in the Middle Ages was described as Hell's Gate); standing where the Alþingi once unfolded, the pull-apart where the island rifts and new stone emerges; finding rocks that mark the hearth of a tenth-century homestead; walking atop the glacier Langjökull, on the move and taking us with it, filled with moulins down which melt swirls, secretly afraid that Alex or Katherine might vanish because all lives are limned by catastrophe: these experiences were material reminders of something I knew already but perhaps needed geologic Iceland to feel.

Too sentimental, I suppose, to write such things. Too personal. There is something uncomfortable about losing stony detachment. Yet better rocky than secure. Glimpsing landscapes known from medieval texts, hiking land shaped by abiding inhuman force, was a reminder that we dwell between catastrophes, between fire and ice. Geology is a perilous science. To write of stone is to know despair. Yet when Hekla spews its flame, when the earth shudders and ash drifts cold air, the people of Reykjavik climb into jeeps and drive to watch the red of molten stone at twilight. The lava spurts, but like all stone the mountain moves slowly as well, an invitation to contemplation, deceleration, peace. The onlookers drink beer and watch rock in fiery motion—not without apprehension, but as companions in an abiding community, in stories composed with stone.

ACKNOWLEDGMENTS

Why do we acknowledge only our textual sources but not the ground we walk, the ever-changing skies, mountains and rivers, rocks and trees, the houses we inhabit and the tools we use, not to mention the innumerable companions, both non-human animals and fellow humans, with which and with whom we share our lives?

—Tim Ingold, *Being Alive*

A project of such long duration would not have been possible without multitudes: friends, colleagues, readers, acquaintances, benevolent strangers, dubious and receptive audiences, family members biological and chosen, disparate landscapes, alluring objects, queer companions, keen editors, things that cognitively and affectively extend. I apologize at the start for the utter insufficiency of what follows.

Funding to undertake this project derived from fellowships awarded by the American Council of Learned Societies and the John Simon Guggenheim Foundation, two organizations whose commitment to the humanities in a time of vanishing resources is exemplary. The George Washington University awarded a University Facilitating Fund Grant that assisted in laying the groundwork for this book, as well as sabbatical leave. Suzanne Conklin Akbari, Gil Harris, and Stephanie Trigg endorsed this project multiple times. They also inspired it.

This book is my fifth for the University of Minnesota Press. I am grateful to Richard Morrison for offering a welcoming home for so many years. His vision, enthusiasm, and critical feedback have been sustaining. I thank Doug Armato for his enduring support. Erin Warholm-Wohlenhaus once again proved a stalwart. Deborah Oosterhouse did a superb job of copyediting. Tobias Menely provided a rigorous, skeptical, and thorough review of this book in its infancy that spurred the work to become something far better than it otherwise would have been: he has my deepest gratitude. The manuscript had many tough, engaged, and catalytic readers—Stacy Alaimo, Lowell Duckert, Dana Luciano, Dan Remein, Alf Siewers, Karl Steel, and Julian Yates chief among them.

My four cobloggers and friends at *In the Middle* (www.inthemedieval middle.com) make my world possible: Eileen Joy (dreamer of insane and necessary visions), Karl Steel (constant prod to thinking beyond anything comfortable), Mary Kate Hurley (whose writing taught me that poetry and scholarship must coexist), and Jonathan Hsy (inspiration to new modes and prospects). I thank the many people who comment on the blog, where much of this project was crowd-sourced. I number among my comrades in stone Valerie Allen, Anne Harris, Kathleen Kelly, David Lipscomb, Peggy McCracken, Katelyn Mesler, Alan Montroso, Kate Norako, Karen Overbey, Tom Prendergast (suavest of medievalists), the inimitable Kellie Robertson, Gillian Rudd, Martha D. Rust, Aimee Selby, Tiffany Werth, and Bonnie Wheeler (who bestowed on me her entire rock collection). Alf Siewers made an ecotheoretical Middle Ages possible. Steve Mentz and Stacy Alaimo eloquently model how to think ecology beyond green. Robert McRuer taught me much about queer alliance, friendship, and commitment to theory as a mode of living. Ayanna Thompson pushed me at our weekly lunches to *get this book done* and provided a compelling example of scholarship performed with grace. Without Tom Hahn I would not be a medievalist. Serenella Iovino and Serpil Oppermann inspire ecomaterial radiance. Anne Harris will never know how much her example of vibrant writing and living means to me. The opportunity to present a conference plenary with Lindy Elkins-Tanton (collector of odd stones and maker of absinthe-based cocktails extraordinaire) was pivotal: I learned much from her difficult questioning and humane example.

Three excellent research assistants helped immensely in gathering bibliography: Tessa Kostelc, Emily Russell, and Haylie Swenson. When I left a notebook with the book's outline on a British Airways flight and thought I would never recover it, Cormac and Burcu Keane mailed it from Edinburgh and saved the project. At a time of great weariness with the landscape of the field, the BABEL Working Group prevented despair; Eileen Joy and Myra Seaman are owed a debt of love. Audiences around the world contributed to the conversation that informs this book: American University, the BABEL Conference Boston, Bucknell University, Cornell University, CUNY Graduate Center, Dartmouth College, Eastern Michigan University, Harvard University, Hamilton College, Humboldt University, the International Medieval Conference at Leeds, Marymount University, McDaniel College, Museu d'Art Contemporani de Barcelona, Northwestern University, Southeastern Medieval Association St. Louis, SUNY Buffalo, University of Iowa, University of Maryland, University of Pennsylvania, University of Rochester, University of Texas at Austin, University of Toronto, University of Virginia, University of Washington, and York University. I am indebted to my excellent students and superb colleagues at the George Washington University, every one of them, but I will single out Robert McRuer and Gayle Wald as the department chairs who make the English department the warm place it is, and Constance Kibler as the one who makes it all work.

Because this book was propelled by their good will and made better through knowing them, I thank Paul Acker, Kamillea Aghtan, Lizz Angelo, John Arnold, Anthony Bale, Julian Banerji, Rob Barrett, Jane Bennett, Dianne Berg, Liza Blake, Heather Blurton, Ian Bogost, Lindy Brady, Brantley Bryant, Sakina Bryant, Ashley Denham Bussey, Caren Calamita, Elisabeth Carnell, Kathy Cawsey, Leah Chang, Jonathan Clark, Ruth Clinton, Andrew Cole, Theresa Coletti, Rita Copeland, Holly Crocker, Kavita Daiya, Drew Daniel, Louise D'Arcens, Rebecca Davis, Daniel DeWispelare, Carolyn Dinshaw, Craig Dionne, Holly Dugan, George Edmondson, Cathy Eisenhower, Stuart Elden, Leila K. N. Ellis, Heide Estes, Claudia Esteve, Lara Farina, Sylvia Federico, Laurie Finke, Christine Fitzgerald, Maxime Alain Foerster, Martin Foys, James Francis, Eva Frojmovic, John Ganim, Noreen Giffney, D. Gilson, Rick Godden, Kerryn Goldsworthy, Ana Grinberg, Simon Grüning, Noah Guynn, David Hadbawnak, Marcus Hansel, Brandon Hawk, Bernd Herzogenrath, Julie Hofmann, Brock Holmes (teacher of struggle and music), Bruce Holsinger, Tonya Howe, Cary Howie, Alexa Huang, Patty

Ingham, Miriam Jacobson, Paul James, Hannah Johnson, Sarah Rees Jones, Jenna Weissman Joselit, Nathan Kelber, Ed Keller, Connie Kibler, Eveline Kilian, Dorothy Kim, Alison Kinney, Dan Kline, Ethan Knapp, Miriamne Krummel, Erin Labbie, Kathy Lavezzo, David Lipscomb, Chen-Wen Lo, Carla Mazzio, Jeb McLeish, Madhavi Menon, Steve Mentz, Constant Mews, Beatrice Michaelis, David Mitchell, J. Allan Mitchell, Asa Simon Mittman, Niamh Moriarty, Timothy Morton, Faye Moskowitz, Steve Muhlberger, Axel Müller, Robin Mundill, Vin Nardizzi, Travis Neel, Christine Neufeld, Barbara Newman, Maura Nolan, Daniel P. O'Connell, Sharon O'Dair, Julie Orlemanski, Michael O'Rourke, Monika Otter, Gail Paster, Rob Patterson, Aaron Pedinotti, Curtis Perry, David Perry, Chris Piuma, Benjamin William Owain Poore, Tison Pugh, Mary K. Ramsey, Orazio Rispo, Christopher Roman, Jill Ross, Dan Rudmann, Suhayl Saadi, Lee Salamon, Myra Seaman, Angie Bennett Segler, Karen Sellberg, Liz Scala, Lisa Schamess, Randy Schiff, Marty Shichtman, James Smith, Robert Stanton, Will Stockton, Beth Sutherland, Katherine Terrell, Rosemarie Garland Thomson, Ben Tilghman, Ken Tompkins, Peter Travis, Elaine Treharne, Wesley Trigg, Aimeric Vacher, Daniel Vitkus, Greg Walker, David Wallace, John Walter, Lawrence Warner, Clare Waters, Jeffrey Weinstock, Gail Weiss, Steve Weitzman, Sarah Werner, Cord Whitaker, Maggie Williams, Mike Witmore, Julian Yates, Elahe Haschemi Yekani, and Virginia Zimmerman. If you do not find your name listed in what precedes, know that I meant to include you but was in the end overwhelmed.

Among the natural forces that impressed their marks on the composition of this book: a 5.8 magnitude quake centered in Mineral, Virginia, that left cracks on the Washington Monument, toppled stone from the National Cathedral, and emptied my bookshelves of the volumes I had collected on the power of stone; Snowmageddon and the Polar Vortex, winter lockdowns that enabled much writing; and a summer derecho that left our house without power for a week and was in my mind as I wrote about the shape of catastrophe. Among the landscapes that shaped this project are the coast of Maine, Iceland's living geology, the Victoria coast and the Grampians in Australia, the sweep of Salisbury Plain, the stone palimpsest that is London, lithic Paris, the environs of Bordeaux, the petric undulations of Barcelona, the small but beautiful peaks of the Shenandoah, monumental Berlin, Neolithic Ireland, and Edinburgh of long summer nights.

This book was made possible through friendships that stretched across continents and years. The incomparable Stephanie Trigg invited my family to Melbourne, co-composed an essay on fire, and demonstrated how to be a scholar with a foot in both present and past. Lowell Duckert accompanied me as my work took an ecological turn; he has been a spur to unexpected good things, an inspirational collaborator in ecotheory, and adopted family member since. Mark Cohen wandered across Ireland with me to explore prehistoric landmarks: there at the beginning, he has been a support to the end. It is good to have a brother who is also a best friend. I thank all of my family—parents, brothers, sisters, nieces, nephews—for the sustenance they give. My ally in everything of value is Wendy Cohen; words fail in attempting to express my gratitude and my love. Katherine and Alexander Cohen were ages two and nine, respectively, when this project began. The book has matured alongside them and through their collaboration. They are featured in its pages, but even when they do not appear, their touch, good humor, and unremitting sense of wonder is everywhere palpable.

NOTES

Introduction

1. "Nec fortitudo lapidum fortitudo mea nec caro mea aerea est" (Job 6:12). All quotations from the bible in this book are from the Latin Vulgate unless otherwise noted. Citations to medieval and classical sources are to the editions and translations included in the bibliography; unattributed translations are my own.

2. The phrase serves as the title of an essay in the "Sketches Here and There" section of Leopold's 1948 book *A Sand County Almanac* (129–33). "Thinking like a mountain" has taken on a life of its own through frequent citation and provides the title for numerous books and environmentally themed music. For a sensitive reading of Leopold's essay that does not shy away from its problems but praises its attempt to "think against anthropocentrism . . . [through] a new Copernican revolution," see Buell, *Future of Environmental Criticism,* 104–5. For a recent exploration of Leopold's idea of a "land ethic," see Brayton, *Shakespeare's Ocean* (18–21), a book that also critiques the "terrestrial bias" of most ecological criticism.

3. Leopold, *A Sand County Almanac,* 129.

4. Ibid., 132.

5. See, for example, Rebecca R. Scott's *Removing Mountains,* a book that attempts to imagine more sustainable modes of human existence and well illustrates why environmental justice must inform such projects. Tracing the entangled social-natural relations clustered around mountaintop removal in southern West Virginia, Scott narrates the temporality of place through the witnessing and archival functions of stone (21–22).

6. I am inspired here by Chris J. Cuomo's work in *Feminism and Ecological Communities,* but attempting to bring her ethical regard beyond carbon-based bodily forms and human determinations. Cuomo writes perceptively about Leopold at 42, 72–73, 107, and 146.

7. For a lucid explication of ANT, see especially Latour, *Reassembling the Social.* Bjørnar Olsen illustrates ANT in action well when he writes of eighteenth-century America: "cutlery, Georgian houses, and tombstones are not merely expressing or—even less— symbolizing a new American template created in advance. They were actively involved in creating and 'ontologizing' the new social schisms and thoughts, which without them might not have existed" (*In Defense of Things,* 146). Olsen provides the example of a Norwegian adventurer who claimed to have skied across Antarctica "solo and unsupported" and points out that such claims to sovereign autonomy obliterate the participation of skis, a sledge, equipment, producers of extreme-weather clothing, high-protein foods, financial sponsors, and "generations of mapmakers, former explorers, satellites, and navigators [who] all helped him along the way" (143).

8. Harman, *Prince of Networks,* 21.

9. Ibid., 21.

10. Serres, *Statues,* 213. See also Latour, *We Have Never Been Modern,* 82. A stone not on Serres's list that ought to be is the six-and-a-half-ton altar-like monolith of iron ore in the Meditation Room of the United Nations Headquarters in New York.

11. On metaphor as earthbound thought, "not so much aspects of the object reduced to the order of a prim and proper idea (the literal and subsequent figurative meanings) as aspects of the stubbornly inarticulate object itself prior to any idea at all," see Mansell, "Metaphor as Matter," 115–16. Peter Travis describes metaphor as a "fiercely nonlogical equation" of material world and object rather than a translation of materiality into language (*Disseminal Chaucer,* 179), while Susan Crane points out the "double commitment of metaphor to tenor and vehicle ... that keeps metaphor from floating off into the ether of moral semiosis" (*Animal Encounters,* 83–86). "Material metaphor" goes farther and insists upon an absolute inseparability: language is material; materiality is storied.

12. "Matterphor" is Lowell Duckert's inspired neologism, used to describe the work of the elements during the "Elemental Ecocriticism" conference at the University of Alabama, April 2013. Cf. Donna Haraway on the "material semiotic nodes or knots in which diverse bodies and meanings coshape one another" (*When Species Meet,* 4; see also 383n11). The environmental "matterphor" is the ecomaterial-semiotic. Gaston Bachelard describes a similar sliding among the material, the ideational, and narrative in his various meditations on the elements. See, for example, *Earth and Reveries of the Will,* especially what he calls "stone midwifery" and the "dialectics of rock and cloud" (143).

13. Émilie Hache and Bruno Latour articulate the stakes of Serres's argument in *Statues* well when they write, "Everyone has so 'moralized' Sisyphus's condemnation and

predicament that he has become a primary figure of the absurd—but who pays attention to the rock that bears down with all its weight on the myth and shoulders of Sisyphus? We talk of lonely humans and the absurdity of the modern human condition, when the myth raises a question about *things*: why, Serres asks, do we never manage to focus on the thing of which the myth itself tells us so explicitly? To insist, as the myth does, that the rock keeps rolling back, downhill, is to say it is *the rock that counts*; and we fail to understand its role when all we see is an absurd task imposed by a court on a guilty man" ("Morality or Moralism?," 319). Gaston Bachelard asked the same question of the Sisyphus myth in *Earth and Reveries of the Will,* where he writes of the tendency of human symbolism to overwrite the force of materiality that tangibly surfaces within language. We thus lose sight of the "real struggle with an actual object," a dynamic encounter with the *"threat of stone"* (149) that Sisyphus and his rolling rock convey.

14. Abram, *Becoming Animal,* 46. Abram's project is to ponder the vivacity of matter and our human affinity with even a "largish stone . . . implacable in its solidity" (47–48) via "our own mineralogical composition" (46). Much of Abram's argument coincidentally echoes that of speculative realism and ANT, essential to the critical framing of my own project, but his approach is ultimately phenomenological and thereby rather anthropocentric, so that even human mood is redefined as environmental entanglement (153) and houses become capable of human affect. Serenella Iovino usefully teases out the resonance of Abram's *Becoming Animal* with the idea in biological science of the "wood wide web" in "Steps to a Material Ecocriticism," 144.

15. The full poem runs "Erthe toc of erthe erthe wyth woh; / erthe other erthe to the erthe droh; / erthe leyde erthe in erthene throh. / Tho heuede erthe of erthe erthe ynoh" (Brook, *Harley Lyrics,* 29). Kathleen Palti explicates the verses beautifully in "The Bound Earth in *Patience* and Other Middle English Poetry," where she writes "Earth is a realm to dwell in, an origin and a destination, all our possessions, our own selves, and at once another agent who is potentially sentient and hostile" (32). On the lyric's polysemous untranslatability, see Rudd, *Greenery,* 21–29.

16. Regarding ecological consciousness and ecotheory, I like the definition of ecocriticism offered by Lynne Bruckner and Dan Brayton in their "Introduction" to *Ecocritical Shakespeare,* where they write that even though ample analysis has long existed on nature and its representation in literature, "ecocriticism is distinct from that work in its attention to anthropocentrism, ecocentrism, living systems, environmental degradation, ecological and scientific literacy, and an investment in expunging the notion that humans exist apart from other life forms" (3). Gillian Rudd enacts this very program through a sustained attentiveness to glimpses of the nonhuman in her book *Greenery.* I would broaden their articulation of ecocritical scope, however, to include the agency of matter and nonbiotic forms of life.

17. Alaimo, *Bodily Natures,* 2. Alaimo develops a notion of transcorporeality that traces

the material inseparability of humans and environments, thereby denying the human sovereign and situating ecological ethics within an "active, often unpredictable, material world" (17). Alaimo's pioneering scholarship has been essential to this book.

18. See Cruikshank's *Do Glaciers Listen?* Her research focuses on the complexities of understanding landscape, nature, and modes of living in the Arctic; see especially 47–49 (on issues of commensurability), 143 (industrialism's necessary conflict with animism), and 245 (postcolonial theory and Enlightenment dualism). Despite its title, the book really asks if humans can listen to each other across the divide of two kinds of local knowledge, scientific and indigenous. Glaciers are present but seldom possess a materiality that matters—although the closing pages vividly illustrate the ways that they insinuate themselves into ecological debate.

19. Hoffmann, *"Homo et Natura, Homo in Natura,"* 11. As Jacques Derrida pointed out, however, that dominion is fraught from its instigation, from the very moment Adam names the animals. See *The Animal That Therefore I Am* (esp. 11–33) and (for medieval confirmation) Crane, *Animal Encounters,* 51–54.

20. Suzanne Conklin Akbari argues persuasively for reading imaginative literature alongside "arcane learning," especially through the example of Bartholomaeus Anglicus, in *Idols in the East,* 161–62 and 200–203.

21. For the term "ecomateriality" and the elemental activeness it is meant to convey, see the special issue of the journal *postmedieval* I coedited with Lowell Duckert on the subject ("Ecomaterialism"), as well as our forthcoming collection *Elemental Ecocriticism.*

22. The historical specificity of stone extends to the regional. Sandrine Roser ponders the localness of stone (including its entanglement in particular histories) in "La pierre dans le chantier de l'abbaye de Baume-les-Messieurs," and Thomas Coomans speaks of stone as embedded in a specific geography, which it carries with it as "porteur d'identité" in "'Produits du terroir' et 'appellations contrôlées.'"

23. Rejecting the possibility or at least the desirability of such straightforward encounter with the past, both psychoanalysis and queer theory have offered compelling critiques of historicism's hegemony. Queer theorists often argue for a perverse or (in the words of Glenn Burger and Steven F. Kruger) *preposterous* rendezvous with history: see their "Introduction" to *Queering the Middle Ages,* xi–xxiii, and especially their rejection of "a conventional historicism . . . confident that it finds the 'truth' of the past."

24. That language is machinic, agentic, and nonhuman is a central insight of deconstruction. For a compelling exploration of how language exerts ecomaterial agency, see Mel Y. Chen's excellent book *Animacies,* esp, chap. 1.

25. Bennett, *Enchantment of Modern Life,* 3. See also Trigg, *Shame and Honor* and *Congenial Souls* and her blog (http://stephanietrigg.blogspot.com/).

26. Noreen Giffney and Myra J. Hird place a slash mark in "non/human" to indicate something similar, performing lexicographically the inseparability of each term from the

other, their inherent instability, "the impossibility of applying a hermetic seal to the distinction between—however temporary and shifting—what gets to count as Human and nonhuman." See their "Introduction" to *Queering the Non/Human,* 5. In my previous work I have labeled this recurring, inexcluded space the *extimate* (a term taken from Jacques Lacan) and the difficult or inexcluded middle.

27. For more on how these two meanings of "matter" inevitably intertwine, see Michael W. Scott's anthropological investigation in "The Matter of Makira," 120–21.

28. The gem that triggers a storm is found in Chrétien de Troyes's romance *Yvain* and will be treated later in this book, but it is worth quoting the Middle English reworking of the story, which well conveys the vigor of the storm's gem-triggered arrival: "And kest water opon the stane; / And sone thare wex withowten fayle, / Wind and thonor [thunder] and rayn and haile" (*Ywain and Gawain,* 622–24). For the hand burned by grasping a rock, see Albertus Magnus describing pyrite: "Perithe, or *peridonius,* is a stone of a yellowish color. It is said to be good for coughs. And a marvelous thing is reported of this stone—that if it is strongly gripped in the hand, it burns the hand; and so it should be touched lightly and cautiously" (*Book of Minerals,* 2.2.14).

29. White, "Historical Roots of Our Ecological Crisis," 3. White's 1967 essay appears in many collections of environmental writing and green criticism, typically as the lone contribution about the Middle Ages. Medieval studies have admittedly lagged behind other time periods in contributing to ecological theory, though with many important exceptions. Among literary scholars, see especially the work of Valerie Allen, Carolyn Dinshaw, Peggy McCracken, Eileen Joy, Lisa Kiser, Kellie Robertson, Gillian Rudd, Randy Schiff, Alf Siewers, Sarah Stanbury, Karl Steel, and Stephanie Trigg.

30. Arguments against the allegorization of nature have been especially well articulated in the field of critical animal studies. For two superb examples, see Crane, *Animal Encounters* (especially 4–5, 37–41) and Holsinger, "Of Pigs and Parchment," 620–22.

31. The anthropologist Tim Ingold writes of the "condensed stories" that become evident when we move beyond a focus on the physical world (which "*exists* in and for itself") to the environment ("a world that continually *unfolds* in relation to the beings that make a living there . . . a world of materials"). See his essay "Materials against Materiality," in *Being Alive,* 19–32; quotation at 30.

32. Among the synonyms Bennett employs for vibrant are "vital, energetic, lively, quivering, vibratory, evanescent, and effluescent." She writes that "materiality" enables a horizontal relation among "humans, biota, and abiota," thereby drawing "attention sideways, away from the ontologically ranked Great Chain of Being and toward a greater appreciation of the complex entanglements of humans and nonhumans" (*Vibrant Matter,* 112).

33. The quotation is from Barbara A. Hanawalt and Lisa J. Kiser's "Introduction" to *Engaging with Nature,* 1. Bruno Latour and Timothy Morton are often misconstrued as declaring that nature or natural reality does not exist, when their claim is that nature

does not exist as a kind of eternal separateness, as the bifurcated antithesis of culture— that is, nature includes much more than forests, animals, and mountains. Nature is where we dwell, and where nonhumans dwell with or away from us—an everywhere rather than "everywhere and nowhere."

34. "Transcorporeal" is Stacy Alaimo's immensely useful term for human-environmental porousness in *Bodily Natures*.

35. Bynum, *Christian Materiality*, 17.

36. Bynum makes clear with characteristic sophistication in her study that "insistent" and "problematic" holy matter (which "pointed its viewers and users to something beyond," ibid., 20) is a complicated business. Its determination is historically specific and its function is not to close down questioning so much as to open "profound religious exploration" (18). Bynum argues that all medieval matter potentially exhibited liveliness, since matter was a substance known for its ability to change. Although she will place within the fifteenth and sixteenth centuries "a growing sense that material objects were not merely labile but alive" so that "even phenomenon such as magnetism came to be conceptualized as animation" (25) and alchemy and astrology were embraced, I find these intimations of matter's vivaciousness and its enmeshment within astral and lunar pull, elemental jostling, and the innate qualities designated by *virtus* or (in the romances) magic and ingenuity to be an earlier and often atheological knowledge.

37. Which is not to say that writers did not attempt such allegories, overwriting stone's substantiality with stories of divinity. An enduring tradition of lapidaries focuses upon the breastplate of Aaron, reading each gem as a solidification of a Christian value. Adam of Eynsham in his *Life of Saint Hugh of Lincoln* describes how King John once showed the bishop "a stone amulet set in gold. This had been given to one of his ancestors with the promise that none of his descendants who wore it would ever lose their ancestral lands. Hugh immediately replied that he should trust instead in Jesus Christ, the living stone: 'make him the centre of your soul, anchor all your hopes in him; he is the firm and living stone who crushes all who resist him, who always raises to higher things those who rely on him'" (*Magna Vita Sancti Hugonis*, 85). Such renditions of the lithic as dead compared to the transcendent vitality of God are numerous, but this book explores glimpses of the life that nonetheless pulses in medieval stone.

38. For a careful examination of what might be ecclesiastically at stake in undressed stone versus neatly incorporated masonry, see Christian Heck on the rock and the church at Bethel, place of Jacob's ladder and lithic pillow, in *"Erexit lapidem in titulum."* Much medieval stone used in churches would have been painted, making its materiality a little less visible, a little less insistent.

39. See Plumpe, *"Vivum Saxum, Vivi Lapides."*

40. My thinking about advent, adventure, and the ethics to which these arrivals are inextricably bound owes much to J. Allan Mitchell's work throughout *Ethics and Eventful-*

ness in Middle English Literature. See especially 111–30 for an emphasis on contingency and adventure in romance, a genre essential to this study (and perhaps a genre innate to stone).

41. Petrogenesis may also proceed, however, when water freezes into crystal or mixes with another earth to trigger coagulation. See, for example, Bartholomaeus Anglicus, *On the Properties of Things,* 16.74 ("De petra"), which combines Isidore and Aristotle with a wide-ranging rumination on how various stones come into being.

42. For Jan Zalasiewicz, see *Planet in a Pebble,* 101, and for Albertus Magnus, *Book of Minerals,* 2.17.

43. "colde and drye, sadde and fast, harde and heuy, and moueþ dounwarde by his owene heuynes and weight" (Bartholomaeus Anglicus, *On the Properties of Things,* 16.74). Throughout this book I cite Bartholomaeus in the Middle English version by John Trevisa, partly because his translation is lively and weird, and partly to resist the scholarly assumption that Bartholomaeus's Latin is more authentic. The impatience medievalists sometimes demonstrate toward the use of medieval translations and adaptations evidences a desire to freeze texts into a single, originary moment, misrepresenting their contemporary vitality. A similar insistence often surfaces around the *Book of John Mandeville,* a scholarly demand that the work be cited from a French version, the likely language of its lost original. Yet *Mandeville* is a polyglot and heterogeneous phenomenon irreducible to a single textual instantiation.

44. Because metals are more aqueous, they are more malleable. Though the Middle Ages inherited a metal-based schema for the epochal representation of human decline, from the Gold Age to Iron, metals do not typically hold the "liquid capital" sense familiar now through a thoroughly monetized economy. Hard stone and ductile metal are both participants in an ecology of matter on the move.

45. "Terra pura lapis non fit." See ibid., 1.1.2, and Dorothy Wyckoff's note, p. 13.

46. De Landa, *A Thousand Years of Nonlinear History,* 20, 103.

47. I want to emphasize from the start of this book that I understand the "new materialism" to be an inherently feminist enterprise, since a focus upon matter and a concern with materialism have been ongoing in feminist theory from at least the 1970s and enabled the inquiries collected under the name "new materialism" to come into being—part of a long history of philosophy, ecocriticism, literary and social theory that has sometimes been occluded by those working in ANT and object-oriented philosophy. For a crisp articulation of the material turn as a feminist project, see Alaimo, *Bodily Natures,* 6–11.

48. Though it takes a very different direction, this investigation begins by recognizing, as Bynum has pointed out, that "body" *(corpus)* in the Middle Ages is inextricable from matter *(materia)*; that "body" indicates any changeable thing ("gem, tree, log, or cadaver"); and that to study the body was to "explore stars and statues, blood and resin, as well as pain, perception, and survival" (*Christian Materiality,* 32). I would add story and temporality to Bynum's list as well.

Geophilia

1. I am referencing here what Serenella Iovino and Serpil Oppermann describe as "matter's 'narrative' power of creating configurations of meanings and substances, which enter with human lives into a field of co-emerging interactions" ("Material Ecocriticism," 79–80).

2. Which is not to say that modern science has no equivalent to the medieval and classical myths of humans arising from earthy substance: biochemistry, for example, tells a story of asteroids, amino acids, and the efflorescing of early life through rock and water.

3. See the *Middle English Dictionary*, "stōn."

4. The critical literature on the geohumoral (that is, climatic and place-bound) determination of race is expansive, but see especially Akbari, *Idols in the East* and Floyd-Wilson, *English Ethnicity and Race in Early Modern Drama*.

5. Changes in modes of capitalism and the forms of the marketplace modify how humans think about objects, but it is difficult to narrate a neat story about how these changes affect stone: its marketplace is always emerging, even during the Paleolithic period (through obsidian trade). Pliny's *Natural History* describes gems that are at once innately powerful objects and goods with specific monetary exchange value. His entries for pearl and crystal describe fads for the materials and provide the precise amounts expended by various Romans to obtain these substances raw or worked into luxury items, such as the ex-consul who paid 70,000 sesterces for a murrhine cup that held only three pints (*Natural History*, 39.7). As Julian Yates has argued, positing a rigid distinction between premodern and modern modes of understanding objects obscures the fact that the "commodity form" is not an innovation but a "more effective mode of transport . . . accelerating our technical domination of the world [rather] than a discontinuity marking a fundamental shift in the story" (*Error, Misuse, Failure*, 5). Yates is building on Bruno Latour's warning against the nostalgia for a supposedly less alienated time before capitalism (*Pandora's Hope*, 195). Modes of production develop and intensify, but epistemological breaks are seldom decisive, and many human phenomena are nearly perpetual in their emergence. Polychronicity (the simultaneity of different times and modes materialized in objects) is a better model than rupture.

6. See "The Former Age," lines 9–40, and Karl Steel's excellent reading of the poem in "A Fourteenth-Century Ecology," emphasizing that for Chaucer the Golden Age is not as utopian as it first appears.

7. Pliny, *Natural History*, 37.9–10. The early encyclopedist Isidore of Seville repeated this genesis for crystal in his *Etymologies* (16.13), bequeathing the story to the Middle Ages.

8. Touring an archeological dig in Reykjavik brought other stories of stone's endurance and domestic intimacy to light: the shells of the seafood eaten in an early settler's home, a quern, and grooved stones used to weight a net cast for fishing.

9. Mandeville, *Book,* ed. Kohanski and Benson, line 507.

10. For a revelatory ecological rethinking of the classical theory of the elements, see Macauley, *Elemental Philosophy*. Lowell Duckert and I have with our collaborators been similarly attempting the elaboration of what we call an elemental ecocriticism. See the special issue of the journal *postmedieval* on "Ecomaterialism" and the edited collection *Elemental Ecocriticism.*

11. Tim Ingold explores the intransitivity of production in *Being Alive,* asserting the "priority of ongoing process over final form" as central to life itself: "Producers, both human and non-human, do not so much transform the world, impressing their preconceived designs upon the material substrate of nature, as play their part from within in the world's transformation of itself. Growing into the world, the world grows in them" (6).

12. "The harde stoon / Under oure feet, on which we trede and goon [go], / Yet wasteth it [wears down] as it lyth [lies] by the weye [way]," Knight's Tale, 1.3021–23.

13. Wilson, *Biophilia,* 84.

14. Joan Evans gives a good overview of surviving medieval inscribed gems and jewelry in *Magical Jewels of the Middle Ages and the Renaissance,* 121–39. Seeta Chaganti maps the complex relations among inscribed surfaces, weighty materiality, and performance well in "Vestigial Signs."

15. White, "Historical Roots of Our Ecological Crisis," 12. White proposes an alternative Christian vision in a rather romanticized and much criticized version of Saint Francis of Assisi.

16. On the complexities of Nature in the Middle Ages and the diversity in its definition and representation (as well as the irreducible multiplicity gathered beneath the term), see the works gathered in the bibliography, but especially Newman, *God and the Goddesses,* 90–137; Bartlett, *The Natural and the Supernatural in the Middle Ages* (who counts twenty-five meanings for *natura* and emphasizes that nature is not a coherent medieval entity but a heterogeneous prod to "intellectual discomfort," 2); Kaye, "(Re)Balance of Nature"; Kiser, "Chaucer and the Politics of Nature"; Stanbury, "Ecochaucer"; Rudd, *Greenery* (emphasis upon nature's medieval multiplicity at 16–17); Epstein, *Medieval Discovery of Nature,* 4–39; Salter, *Holy and Noble Beasts,* 147–49; and Steel, *How to Make a Human* (which stresses that nature, like animality, must be continually generated, ensuring that the categories will remain messy, incomplete, and teeming with violence). Kiser is especially good at excavating the multiplicity of medieval perspectives on nature and at moving analysis beyond the philosophical and theological preoccupations of the clerical class. I have also been much inspired by the research of Kellie Robertson, who emphasizes the *problematic* nature of Nature in the Middle Ages and the contemporary reluctance to think through that challenge because of the term's entwinement in theology and teleology (as if theism and *telos* were singular in meaning, as if such entwinement were an adequate reason to not pursue a difficult yet essential strand of medieval thought).

17. Although nature's stability in the Middle Ages is too frequently assumed by contemporary critics, medievalist and nonmedievalist alike, nature in any particular text need not be problematic. Nature across medieval texts, however, is no more reliable or coherent than nature in the contemporary imagination. With the latter in mind Bruno Latour writes that the environmental change that political ecology desires to bring about will not occur until it lets go of nature: "if 'nature' is what makes it possible to recapitulate the hierarchy of beings in a single ordered series, political ecology is always manifested, in practice, by the destruction of the idea of nature" (*Politics of Nature*, 25). Nature in the Middle Ages was typically as ordered and hierarchical (at least in theory) as the nature Latour describes, and therefore just as inept at describing the actual unfolding of the world. Hierarchy hides the hybridity that belies its precarious sortings.

18. The phrase "at once whole and broken" is taken from Kenneth Gross's meditation upon uncanny life in the closing section of *Puppet*, 161.

19. On animacy hierarchies as linguistic yet deeply material sortings of the world with their own, always insufficient cultural logics, see Chen, *Animacies*. Chen considers stone at 2–5 and 235, where she writes of its "radical thingness," manifested within a nonhuman temporality.

20. *Middle English Dictionary*, "stōn."

21. The oldest strata yet found are the Isua Supergroup deposits at the southern tip of Greenland (Zalasiewicz, *The Earth after Us*, 97).

22. Boswell, *Life of Samuel Johnson*, 122.

23. As Ian Hacking puts it in *The Social Construction of What?*, "when thinkers—from Dr. Johnson (against the immaterialist Bishop of Berkeley) to Steven Weinberg (against cultural relativists)—want to say something is real, they resort to rocks" (204).

24. Quotation from Flusser and Bec, *Vampyroteuthis Infernalis*, 62, where Flusser is writing of how objects (particularly stones) participate in the generation of human knowledge.

25. Bennett, *Vibrant Matter*, 58.

26. Thus Chaucer writes proverbially of the blind nag that runs foolishly against a boulder rather than change its course. The animal's crash against rocky materiality is a sore rebuke to its limited perception. See The Canon's Yeoman's Tale, 8.1413–16, for Chaucer's use of the "Bayard the blynde" proverb.

27. I am thinking here of Julian Yates's sophisticated exploration of the early modern priest hole as a mechanism that acts to obstruct inquiry and knowledge: *Error, Misuse, Failure*, 145–47.

28. From the short poem "Epistemology," in Wilbur, *Collected Poems*, 361.

29. For an eloquent meditation on Thales and stone's activity, see Macauley, *Elemental Philosophy*, 51–58.

30. Hacking, *The Social Construction of What?*, 186–206. For a thoughtful exploration

of social constructivism in its variations, see B. H. Smith, *Scandalous Knowledge*, 3–15. Smith observes that Hacking goes too far in asserting that a constructivist denies metaphysically that nature possesses a real and inherent structure. Instead, she observes, constructivists "decline to presume" that they know already how the world is ordered as they trace how a concept like nature comes into being, how it changes over time, and what work it accomplishes (6–7).

31. Hacking, *The Social Construction of What?*, 199.

32. I am playing on Bruno Latour's formulation that "society is constructed, but not socially constructed" in *Pandora's Hope* (198). See also the excellent account of the complicated choreography of matter and discourse within an overview of biosemiotics in Iovino, "Stories from the Thick of Things," 454. From an archeologist's point of view Bjørnar Olsen, likewise inspired by Latour, writes "As the etymological roots suggest, facts are made and the real is fabricated. Rather than 'revealing' entities as constructed and made up, our attention should be devoted to analyzing how these entities (e.g., societies and cultures) are put together and the real building materials—the concrete and steel, rebar and pillars—involved in their construction. In other words we should pay more attention to the material components that constitute the very condition of possibility for those features we associate with social order, structural durability, and power" (*In Defense of Things*, 5).

33. Stone's "storied matter" is thick with surprising narratives, some vivid, lyrical, floridly manifest, others impossible to discern or translate. The lithic is an especially dense case of matter's ability to create "configurations of meanings and substances, which enter with human lives into a field of co-emerging interactions." Material ecocriticism names an alliance of critical practices that, in the words of Serenella Iovino, "take matter as a text, as a site of narrativity, a storied matter, a corporeal palimpsest in which stories are inscribed." See Iovino and Oppermann, "Material Ecocriticism," 79–80.

34. Daniel Lord Smail articulates this entwining well in his epilogue to *On Deep History and the Brain* when he writes of "the grandeur that the deep time of human history shares with the walls of the Grand Canyon, where the sheer immensity of time is laid out for the wonder of all. We need not dig only in the dusty topsoil of the strata that form the history of humanity. The deep past is also our present and future" (202). For a more typical narrative of finding in the Grand Canyon an archive that instead of being like human history forces humans to change their conception of how the past works and how deeply it extends, see Montgomery, *The Rocks Don't Lie*, 15–29.

35. My edited collection *Prismatic Ecology* argues for the introduction of unbalanced, nonanthropocentric hues (and perspectives) into ecocriticism. Dan Brayton writes of "chlorophilia—an inability to look beyond the imagery of the land and its leafy green cloak" (*Shakespeare's Ocean*, 37). Though this book's focus upon stone may seem to betray what Brayton calls a terrestrial bias, its project is multihued, like the stones it examines—and, like them, composed of more than earth.

36. See Mentz's book *At the Bottom of Shakespeare's Ocean* as well as his essay "Shakespeare's Beach House." Both are especially good at questioning the pastoralism and balance of green ecologies.

37. Zalasiewicz, *The Earth after Us*, 48.

38. On the death of Empedocles, see the beautiful meditation by Serres, *Biogea*, 76–79.

39. Irene J. Klaver writes, "As funerary objects [stones] carry a promise of a permanent reference, replacing the absence of the dead with the presence of a seemingly lasting and meaningful memorial object" ("Phenomenology on (the) Rocks," 160). Klaver stresses the movements that belie such hopes for permanence and gives the example of the grave of Jesse James. When pilgrims carried away its stones ("petrified hearts" as well as commodities), his mother Zerekda would pile more on top to sell (159).

40. John Sallis writes: "Stone comes from a past that has never been present, a past inassimilable to the order of time in which things come and go in the human world; and that nonbelonging of stone is precisely what qualifies it to mark and hence memorialize such comings and goings, births and deaths . . . the ideal material on which to inscribe marks capable of visibly memorializing into an indefinite future one who is dead and gone" (*Stone*, 26).

41. See the work of Elizabeth Hill Boone and Walter D. Mignolo, who have made clear the independence of narrative from verbal inscription. Daniel Lord Smail has written cogently of the deleterious effects of equating only written records with historicity and equating the geological record only with pages, books, archives. He argues for the importance of more profound temporal frames to humanistic inquiries and offers a revaluation of "document" (literally, "that which teaches") to include "evidence for the deep past" such as "artifacts, fossils, vegetable remains, phonemes, and various sorts of modern DNA" (*On Deep History and the Brain*, quotation at 5–6).

42. See, for example, the Prometheus tree and the stories held by its 4,862 rings, and the next oldest tree, Methuselah: Oatman-Stanford, "Read My Rings."

43. "Material agencies" is a term I take from Stacy Alaimo's *Bodily Natures*, where it designates "the often predictable and always interconnected actions" of environments, substances, and bodies in ways that "affect the emergence as well as the unraveling of the human" (3). Julian Yates captures eloquently why the study of such nonhuman objects and forces, now and farther back in history, matters so much: "For as long as we neglect the role of nonhumans in our midst, all that the word 'human' promises, the social, ethical, and political hopes that it founds, will continue to escape us. It is this radical rethinking of the 'human' that is our present challenge, and the ethico-political duty confronting those strangely divided institutions we call the 'sciences' and the 'humanities'" (*Error, Misuse, Failure*, 207).

44. Eugene Thacker observes that humans relate to the nonhuman by "transform-

ing the world into something familiar, accessible, or intuited in human terms (biology, geology, cosmology)." Thacker argues that the "perspective of the nonhuman itself" is "doomed from the start," since it exists in utter indifference to the human (and thus can be understood only negatively). See *In the Dust of This Planet,* esp. 30–31. Gillian Rudd, on the other hand, provides an ecocritical account of how anthropomorphism can assist in a movement away from anthropocentrism: "to speak for [the nonhuman] risks abrogating it into the human, yet not to speak for it seems to relegate it to the realm of silence and thus render it invisible" (*Greenery,* 6). Even if many nonhumans are beyond our grasp and indifferent to our lives, their stories are tentatively imaginable within anthropomorphic narratives that profoundly challenge anthropocentrism.

45. The dreamer who narrates the poem exists still in time so has trouble with the paradox of the dead infant (who now dwells in eternity) being wiser and more articulate than he is. Gervase of Tilbury gets at the inextricability of temporality from worldedness and their difference from eternity when he writes, "For if, as Boethius says [*Consolation of Philosophy,* 5 prose 6 and 3 meter 9.2–3], there was a timeless eternity before time began, time and the world which was created at the beginning of time are coeval" (*Otia Imperiala,* 1.1). I will discuss eternity in its relation to time and the lithic at greater length in the next chapter.

46. For an examination of the poem itself as jewel-like that explores the culture of jewel-love in the contemporary court of Richard II, see Bowers, *An Introduction to the Gawain Poet,* 104–13. I am also grateful to Dan Remein for sharing his work in progress on *Pearl* and ornamentality with me.

47. Gillian Rudd has argued that the "challenge must be to read with an awareness of allegory, while focusing on actual animals, plants, rocks or seas under debate" (*Greenery,* 11). Of *Pearl* in particular she writes that reading its narrative ecocritically "reveals a contrary and possibly contradictory movement embedded in the poem that seeks to take us away from the artificial and the unchanging towards the natural and mutable" (170).

48. As Jamie Kruse and Elizabeth Ellsworth observe, once a lithic frame replaces an anthropocentric one the alliances that unite humans to rocky substantiality become evident: "New York is not composed of solid substances. It is a dynamic system of multi-layered flows of earth materials that travel through time and space. The marble, limestone, and steel of the City undergo their own continuous process of change, radically remix with everything around them, send out ramifications into deep futures—and couple with what we humans set into motion" (*Geologic City,* unpaginated).

49. On the Anthropocene as a distinct geological era, see Kolbert, "Enter the Anthropocene." Coined by the Dutch chemist Paul Crutzen in 2002, the Anthropocene is frequently said to have begun in the previous century as a global layer of carbon was laid down into the geological record, but its start has been placed as far back as the invention of agriculture and massive clearing of trees eight thousand years ago. Timothy Morton

explores the origin of the term in the intersection of "human history" and "geological time" in "Oedipal Logic of Ecological Awareness." Morton ties the current ecological crisis to a pervasive, post-Kantian logic of correlationism, which insists that (as Quentin Meillassoux has argued) human consciousness provides reality its meaning, that our access to the world is determined by our relation to its existence. Morton writes of the irony that "the very humans responsible for the depositing of carbon in Earth's crust also produced philosophies that denied that the humanities could talk about the nonhuman real due to the limitations of the human perspective" (8). Levi Bryant plumbs correlationism and its discontents well in *The Democracy of Objects*, 34–47.

50. Andrew Shryock and Daniel Lord Smail write: "The idea of the Anthropocene is a powerful tool. It lends gravitas to policy discussions concerning global climate change and sustainability. Yet the narrative arc suggested by the J curve of modernity, with its sudden, sharp and upward trend, is problematic for the framing of a deep history. Attempts to model this dramatic take-off posit a sudden, artificial shift in the timeline of the human endeavor, a monstrous leap in the scale at which things happen" (*Deep History*, 246).

51. Zalasiewicz, *Planet in a Pebble*, 39. The quotation from *Sir Orfeo* is line 347.

52. Zalasiewicz, *Planet in a Pebble*, 33.

53. Szymborska, "Conversation with a Stone," in *Poems, New and Collected*, 62–64, quotation at 64. Barbara Johnson observes that the stone rebukes the human at its nonexistent door by asserting an anthropomorphism that is immediately rescinded: "by speaking at all it stands up against anthropomorphism precisely by using it" (*Persons and Things*, 17).

54. Kellie Robertson makes this point eloquently about medieval materials in "Medieval Things," but her observation applies equally to contemporary texts.

55. For an essential caution that the "new" in "new materialism" can too easily obscure the feminist work that has enabled its emergence, see Ahmed, "Open Forum Imaginary Prohibitions."

56. Bogost, *Alien Phenomenology*, 3.

57. I use "Copernican revolution" in the broad sense developed by Meillassoux, not simply as the astronomical decentering of earthly observers but "*the decentering of thought relative to the world within the process of knowledge* . . . the recognition that thought has become able to think a world that can dispense with thought, a world that is essentially unaffected by whether or not anyone thinks it" (*After Finitude*, 115–16). Some writers using Meillassoux's work go too far in segregating the human from the material, as if he had argued that there is no relation between human and world. Such a figuration unnecessarily (and too dogmatically) rules out a potential coextensiveness, unnatural and inconstant but durable and aeonic participation in the world's own worlding.

58. A short list of some of the many theorists aligned with the new materialism, actor network theory, and speculative realism who have helped me to frame this inquiry

are David Abram, Stacy Alaimo, Karen Barad, Jane Bennett, Ian Bogost, Levi Bryant, Mel Y. Chen, Patricia Clough, Lowell Duckert, Elizabeth Ellsworth, Graham Harman, Tim Ingold, Serenella Iovino, Eileen Joy, Jamie Kruse, Manuel De Landa, Bruno Latour, J. Allan Mitchell, Timothy Morton, Serpil Oppermann, Michael O'Rourke, Andrew Pickering, Michel Serres, Karl Steel, Isabelle Stengers, and Patricia Yaeger.

59. Along these same lines but touching silk rather than stone, the first literary depiction of a garment sweatshop was composed in the twelfth century by the romance writer Chrétien de Troyes, who sets part of *Yvain* in a kind of factory where women are forced laborers in silk production. On the Château de Pesme Aventure and its relation to silk making in the Middle Ages, see the first two chapters of Burns, *Sea of Silk*. Bruce Holsinger meanwhile has detailed the commodification of herds of sheep into billions of sheets of vellum in his work on the subject, "Of Pigs and Parchment," arguing that to look attentively at such medieval matter is to be challenged repeatedly by scale.

60. On these etymologies and efficacies, see Serres, *Statues*, 294, 307.

61. Levi Bryant writes in *The Democracy of Objects* that, no longer "monarchs of being," humans become "*among* beings, *entangled* in beings, and *implicated* in other beings" (44). See also the bracing first chapter of Bogost, *Alien Phenomenology*.

62. Alaimo, *Bodily Natures*, 2.

63. "'The environment' is not located somewhere out there, but is always the very substance of ourselves" (ibid., 4). Alaimo inspirationally draws from ecotheory, feminist theory, disability studies, environmental philosophy, race theory, and science studies (among other disciplines) to launch her justice-minded and nuanced inquiry. Cf. "an ethics that is not circumscribed by the human but is instead accountable to a material world that is never merely an external place but always the very substance of our selves and others" (158).

64. Mick Smith writes of an environmental ethics in similar terms: "Ethically speaking, we cannot *not* be responsible for our actions. Ethical uncertainties also disturb all attempts to define once and for all to whom such responsibilities extend—who counts or does not count as significant. . . . And ecological ethics awakens us to the wider more-than-human world . . . raising questions concerning the singular significance of beings other than animals, too: fungi, rivers, rocks" (*Against Ecological Sovereignty*, xix). Cary Wolfe makes a similarly eloquent argument about ethics, certainty, and responsibility in *Before the Law*; see especially the discussion of pragmatism in the face of the undecidability engendered by vast scale (such as that of factory farming and other incomprehensibly immense violences within contemporary biopolitics), 92–105.

65. Bringing the insights of the new materialism to a reinvigorated environmental humanities, Serenella Iovino and Serpil Oppermann compellingly argue for "rethink[ing] ontology, epistemology, and ethics—being, knowing, and acting—in terms of radical immanence" (Iovino, "Stories from the Thick of Things," 450). Serpil Oppermann, in the

second part of this diptych, offers an inspirational mission statement: "Material ecocriticism demonstrates a performative engagement with this world of becoming and meaning making, and attempts to form a unique materialist perspective which gives equal importance to discursive practices and the material parameters of the world through which meanings are enacted. It stands at the intersection of ecological and postmodern ideas that converge on the new ontologies of matter and agency, as well as on the new ethics that considers the mutuality between physical-nonphysical, technological-natural, and human-nonhuman aspects of life in contemporary reality" ("A Lateral Continuum," 469).

66. Where the new materialism and the Middle Ages meet is likely in posthumanism. See especially the essays gathered in the inaugural issue of *postmedieval*: Joy and Dionne, "When Did We Become Post/Human?" For a persuasive argument that, from the point of view of linguistics, thought and language are not equivalents (language possesses a materiality that thought cannot; it is also animated, "as much alive as it is dead," generative, and creative), see Chen, *Animacies*, 51–55 and 75–82.

67. Bogost, *Alien Phenomenology*, 7.

68. Latour, *We Have Never Been Modern*, 6. Timothy Morton makes a similar point throughout *The Ecological Thought*, arguing that modern nature is a kind of ghost or mirror of the human, so that even "the idea of pristine wilderness" is a version of our own obsession with private property (5). Of the ecological crisis Latour writes compellingly that the first step toward addressing its problems must be to comprehend the necessary failure of our terms: "Concern for the environment begins at the moment when there is no more environment, no zone of reality in which we could casually rid ourselves of the consequences of human political, industrial, and economic life. The historical importance of ecological crises stems not from a new concern with nature but, on the contrary, the impossibility of continuing to imagine politics on the one side and, on the other, a nature that would serve politics simultaneously as a standard, a foil, a reserve, a resource, and public dumping ground" (*Politics of Nature*, 58).

69. The conversation was about the work of Whitehead, who was fascinated by Cleopatra's Needle. See Latour, "Biography of an Inquiry," 17.

70. "All things equally exist, yet they do not exist equally" (Bogost, *Alien Phenomenology*, 11). In "The New Aesthetic Needs to Get Weirder" Bogost writes that, "if ontology is the philosophical study of existence, then object-oriented ontology puts things at the center of being. We humans are elements, but not the sole elements of philosophical interest. . . . OOO steers a path between scientific naturalism and social relativism, drawing attention to things at all scales and pondering their nature and relations with one another as much as ourselves." Flat ontology has sometimes been misconstrued as a denial of ethical relation or an objectification of humans, especially of humans who suffer. Alex Reid observes "I don't think that a flat ontology denies the existence of asymmetrical relations. It doesn't deny that humans are more important for humans than other objects or that

humans can, and often do, have asymmetrical roles in the networks in which they partici-pate. What a flat ontology does refute is the idea that the universe has some inherent great chain of being that puts humans at or near the top. What a flat ontology does critique, in a Latourian style, is the divide of humans and nonhumans in the modern world that puts ALL the agency on the human side" ("The Object Industry").

71. Levi Bryant's emphasis on systems theory (and particular his work on complex open systems, which inbuild a measure of closure but are still environmentally enmeshed) and the generative power of autopoeisis provide more conceptual flexibility; see *The De-mocracy of Objects*. Timothy Morton amply demonstrates the cogency of OOO-derived thinking to ecotheory in his supple work. For an overview of speculative realism and OOO that traces their genealogies and wrestles with the critical objections posed against both (especially by feminism and queer theory), see O'Rourke, "'Girls Welcome!!!'" Despite Harman's claims on the term, O'Rourke emphasizes that, like queer theory, OOO can-not be reduced to any single writer's works or to a well-delineated metatheory, stressing its "promissory nature," "provisionality," and "welcomeness to its own revisability" (279).

72. Morton, *The Ecological Thought*, 92.

73. Eileen Joy articulates the critical possibilities of OOO eloquently when she writes in a comment to Alex Reid's "The Object Industry": "turning one's attention to animals, objects, post/humanism and so on is precisely about thickening our capacity to imagine more capacious forms of 'living with'; it is precisely about developing more radical forms of welcoming and generosity to others . . . work in post/humanism, and in OOO, is at-tentive to the world, which includes and does not exile (or gleefully kill off) the human (although it certainly asks that we expand our angles of vision beyond just the human-centered ones); it is both political and ethical; and it is interested in what I would even call the 'tender' attention to and care of things, human and inhuman."

74. London Stone (@thelondonstone), Tweet, March 23, 2011, 5:19 AM. I am thank-ful to Tom Prendergast for sharing his ongoing research on the London Stone with me.

75. "Stones whiche no persone / Hath upon erthe," Gower, *Confessio Amantis*, 7.823–24.

76. Behind these withheld stones have been placed in the sun's crown gems better known from lithic lore, such as crystal and adamant (diamond). Russell Peck provides thorough notes referencing the appropriate lapidaries in his edition of Gower.

77. Bennett, *Vibrant Matter*, xviii.

78. Cf.: "If physical things are described as firm and hard, this is clearly the case only for whatever tries to move them" (Harman, *Prince of Networks*, 143).

79. Bennett, *Vibrant Matter*, 32.

80. Bennett glosses vitality as "the capacity of things—edibles, commodities, storms, metals—not only to impede or block the will and designs of humans but also to act as quasi agents or forces with trajectories, propensities, or tendencies of their own" (ibid., viii).

81. Ibid., 28. Bennett is not making an Augustinian argument for agency, even if both stress the dispersed and conflicted ways that volition unfolds. Bennett, like Latour, emphasizes the agency of the inhuman, stressing that "human intentionality can be agentic only when accompanied by a vast entourage of nonhumans" (108).

82. Ibid., 107. "A life thus names a restless activeness, a destructive-creative force-presence that does not coincide fully with any specific body" (54). Bennett is following Gilles Deleuze and Félix Guattari here in glossing the "great Alive" as a "pure immanence," as matter-movement, a "vitality proper not to any individual" (54). See Deleuze and Guattari, *A Thousand Plateaus,* 407. Though this formulation sounds a great deal like Lucretian atomism, medieval scholastic discussions of materiality tended to be Aristotelian, emphasizing that form gives identity to substance. Kellie Robertson has detailed how complicated this model was and emphasized that it was never abandoned once the Renaissance rediscovered Lucretius ("Medieval Materialism"). In this chapter—as, indeed, throughout this book—I am less interested in how theologians and other intellectuals worked out the precise relations between materiality and form as I am in mapping what a cluster of somewhat related texts (travel narratives, encyclopedias, and lapidaries) actually *do* with materiality and how materiality "moves" within texts where the imagination finds ample space to experiment.

83. The quotation is from Bennett, *Vibrant Matter,* 31. Bennett is reflecting upon Bernard Stiegler's *The Technics and Time,* vol. 1, where he suggests that consciousness itself may have arisen from human interaction with nonhuman forces.

84. Latour, "Morality and Technology," 249. See also J. Harris, *Untimely Matter in the Time of Shakespeare,* 3.

85. See Harman, *Tool-Being* and "The Well-Wrought Broken Hammer."

86. See, for example, Noah Heringman, who writes that, "as the basic inorganic solid substance, rock embodies the nonhuman and the type of the external object within a dualist epistemology" (*Romantic Rocks, Aesthetic Geology,* 54). While stone is clearly tasked to undertake such cultural work, it seldom does so in a way that enables it to remain a generalized category of "the most foreign" for long.

87. "Privee stoon" is Chaucer's description of the infinitely deferred philosopher's stone in The Canon's Yeoman's Tale, 8.1452. Gower speaks of the "philosophres ston" and its relation to alchemical learning in the *Confessio Amantis,* 4.2523.

88. For Augustine, for example, idols do not even merit the description of dead, since "lapides illi nunquam vixerunt," the stone from which they are fashioned was never alive (Plumpe, *"Vivum Saxum, Vivi Lapides,"* 9). Carolyn Dean examines how this Christian dismissal encouraged the denigration of intricate Inka relations to stone as idolatry—or even a puzzling "litholatry" (*A Culture of Stone,* 2). Dean traces a quick history of animated stone across several cultures in her introduction, mapping it against the Western tendency to see rock as "not to be noticed, and certainly not to be praised or worshipped" unless

carved by human hands into art (6). She articulates a project similar to my own: to see the lithic as "rocks yet to be remembered, as silence yet to be broken, and as action yet to be taken. So long as we understand the rocks of Inka ruins to be like the rocks of familiar metaphor—stone cold, stone deaf, stone silent—we deny Inka visuality and its interpretive possibilities" (178). We also deny rock its own power.

89. *Middle English Dictionary*, "domb."

90. Karl Steel's smart gloss in *How to Make a Human*, 6.

91. "Man, then, in that he has it in common with stones to be, with trees to live, with animals to feel, with angels to discern ["esse cum lapidibus, vivere cum arboribus, sentire et vivere cum animalibus, intelligere, id est rationabilitatem habere cum angelis"], is rightly represented by the title of the 'universe,' in whom after some sort the 'universe' itself is contained" (Gregory, *Moralia in Job*, 6.16, a commentary on Job 5:10; Migne, *Patrologia Latina*, 76.1214). The formulation was often repeated in the Middle Ages. Nature, for example, echoes Gregory's words in *Roman de la rose*, 19011–23.

92. Gervase of Tilbury, *Otia Imperialia*, 26: "In summa, homo mundus appellatur quia in se tocius mundi representat ymaginem, habens esse cum lapidibus, uiuere cum arboribus, sentire cum animalibus, et dicernere cum angelis." John Gower's articulation of this same chain is typical of the late medieval reception of Gregory's clear-cut, ascending scale: "Forthi Gregoire in his *Moral* / Seith that a man in special / The lasse world [microcosm] is properly, / And that he proeveth redely. / For man of soule resonable / Is to an angel resemblable, / And lich [like] to beste he hath fielinge, / And lich to trees he hath growinge; / The stones ben and so is he" (*Confessio Amantis*, Prol.945–53).

93. The quotation is from Lévinas, "Meaning and Sense," in *Basic Philosophical Writings*, 37. Lévinas takes the figure from K. Löwith, *Gesammelte Abhandlungen, Zur Kritik der geschichtlichen Existenz* (Stuttgart: Kohlhammer, 1960), 222.

94. Thus William Cronon writes of an outcrop in Aldrich Park, Irvine, where—despite the fact that each person encountering its geology perceives it differently—the rock remains itself: "this silent rock, this nature about which we argue so much, is also among the most important things we have in common" ("Introduction: In Search of Nature," 56).

95. Kellie Robertson's treatment of the activity of the stones in The Franklin's Tale is excellent: see "Exemplary Rocks" (quotation at 106). She writes that the moral of the tale is that "sometimes inanimate objects organize human communities (rather than the other way around) and that abstract notions of 'trouthe' are meaningless unless grounded in the matter of the natural world" (106).

96. See Daniell, *Death and Burial in Medieval England*, 165. Daniell suggests that the placement of the stone (in the mouth, atop the body) was less important than stone itself being included—though the significance of these grave goods is difficult to determine.

97. Joan Evans surveys these lists at length in *Magical Jewels of the Middle Ages and the*

Renaissance, 114–20. "Eagle stones" will be described in the concluding chapter. David Hinton gives an overview of earlier gem culture on the island and connects surviving jewelry with lapidary lore in *Gold and Gilt, Pots and Pins,* 187–92.

98. Abram, *Becoming Animal,* 29.

99. See especially Sobin, *Luminous Debris.* For a less poetic, more technical view of stone remains and human culture, see Kardulias and Yerkes, *Written in Stone,* and for work that combines the affective and the archeological, see Tilley, *Materiality of Stone.*

100. Levi Bryant argues that every object is also an event, a process, an activity: "Persistence is not a *static* feature of objects, but is rather an *activity* on the part of objects. Endurance is something that objects must do, not something that objects have as a default mode until perturbed from the outside in such a way as to be destroyed" ("Dynamic Life of Objects").

101. Shaviro, *Without Criteria,* 16.

102. Ibid., 17. Shaviro is expanding here upon the work of Alfred North Whitehead (the same work that spurred the conversation between Bruno Latour and Isabelle Stengers referenced earlier).

103. Bryant, "Dynamic Life of Objects."

104. Panthers run and humans ambulate because their bodies produce and enclose skeletons, calcified flesh at the heart of animal mobility. See De Landa, *A Thousand Years of Nonlinear History,* 26.

105. "We may be living creatures, but our aliveness is composed of geologic materials such as calcium, iron, and phosphorous. And the comparatively tiny living organisms that inhabit the earth's surface, be they humans, lichen or bacteria, are now seen to be key players in setting up and precipitating monumental geologic processes and planetary-scale chemical transformations in geologic materials. The earth would have a completely different geologic self if there were no life on it" (Ellsworth and Kruse, *Making the Geologic Now,* 17).

106. Alaimo, *Bodily Natures,* 11.

107. Robertson, "Exemplary Rocks," 97–98. Robertson continues: "Aquinas's meditation followed the Aristotelian 'intromission' model of perception, one that assumed an exterior object imprints itself on the percipient's sense faculty. Unlike later medieval and modern theories of cognition, the Aristotelian version did not assume the utter passivity of the object. These cognitive assumptions followed from an Aristotelian physical world where the elements (and those objects composed of them) were endowed with an inherent nature that directed the object's movements. Rocks did not fall to the ground from a height on account of gravity, but rather because their 'natural place' was earth and their natural habit to return to it."

108. Geoffrey of Monmouth, *History of the Kings of Britain,* ed. Reeve, trans. Wright. Citations by page numbers; here, 254–55.

109. Freed designed the United States Holocaust Memorial Museum in Washington D.C. and describes the structure as a "resonator of memory." Though externally fortress-like, the monolithic building's interior is a loose compilation of forms that are at once "open-ended" and "visceral," an "architecture of sensibility" designed to "take you in its grip" (United States Holocaust Memorial Museum, "Architecture and Art").

110. Deleuze and Guattari, *What Is Philosophy?*, 176–77.

111. As Elizabeth Grosz has argued, in a monument "the becomings of the earth couple with the becomings of life to produce intensities and sensations that in themselves summon up a new kind of life. . . . Artworks are not so much to be read, interpreted, deciphered as responded to, touched, engaged, intensified. . . . They make sensation real" (*Chaos, Territory, Art*, 79). Cf. Deleuze and Guattari, *What Is Philosophy?*, 164: "Sensations, percepts and affects are no longer feelings or affections: they are beings whose validity lies in themselves and exceeds any lived. They could be said to exist in the absence of man because man, as he is caught in stone, on the canvas, or by words is himself a compound of percepts and affects. The work of art is a being of sensation and nothing else: it exists in itself."

112. The whole quotation reads: "The success of a revolution resides only in itself, precisely in the vibrations, clinches and openings it gave to men and women at the moment of its making and that composes in itself a monument that is always in a process of becoming, like those tumuli to which each new traveler adds a stone" (Deleuze and Guattari, *What Is Philosophy?*, 177).

113. The tenon joints are shown piercing the tops of the lintels, even though in Stonehenge they do not actually go that far. Interestingly, the illustration shows four trilithons still standing; today only three remain upright. See Heck, "Histoire mythique et archéologie au quinzième siècle" and Kennedy, "Early Sketch of Stonehenge Found."

114. Many good definitions of "posthuman" exist, but I prefer the simplicity of Andrew Pickering's, since as he moves beyond the small ambit of traditional humanism he emphasizes the spatial: "*posthumanist* space [is] a space in which the human actors are still there but now inextricably entangled with the nonhuman, no longer at the center of action and no longer calling the shots" (*The Mangle of Practice*, 26). Cary Wolfe usefully stresses the challenges within the term: "when we talk about posthumanism, we are not just talking about the thematics of the decentering of the human in relation to either evolutionary, ecological, or technological coordinates . . . we are also talking about *how* thinking confronts that thematics, what thought has to become in the face of those challenges" (*What Is Posthumanism?*, xvi).

115. On the relation of things to human genesis and the uncertain future we have inherited as a result, see Fry, *Becoming Human by Design*.

116. Following Barry Cunliffe, Patricia Yaeger makes much of the heavy materiality of sea transport from its earliest days in "Sea Trash, Dark Pools and the Tragedy of the Commons," 523–24.

117. The hypothesis of Geoffrey Wainwright, who points out that the bluestones especially have always been a draw for pilgrims. The Amesbury Archer and his companion, who died ca. 2300 BCE, came from modern Switzerland.

118. Bjørnar Olsen surveys the burgeoning archeological bibliography on this topic in *In Defense of Things*, 85; quotation from same page.

119. Ibid.

120. I take the bulk of my examples in this chapter from Marbode of Rennnes, *De lapidibus*, the most influential source of rock knowledge in the Middle Ages; and the *Livre de Sydrac*, a popular later text derived in part from Marbode. I provide a full history of the genre in the concluding chapter, where I examine lapidaries at length.

121. A Franciscan, Bartholomaeus Anglicus was English by birth but wrote mostly in Paris as part of the academic community there. His encyclopedia *De proprietatibus rerum* was translated into English by John Trevisa. Although critical practice currently favors citation of Bartholomaeus from his original Latin, I quote in the book in Middle English (noting divergences from Bartholomaeus's Latin when appropriate; citation above is from *On the Properties of Things*, 16.48). Trevisa's translation is lively and weird, demonstrating well the vitality of the medieval text (a vitality obscured when a prejudice in favor of original texts freezes works into singular, originary moments and thereby misrepresents their medieval flourishing). Bartholomaeus's Latin is no more authoritative for the story of stone (and the story of how stone spurs story) that I am tracing than Trevisa's Middle English version.

122. Sarah Stanbury makes this point about ecological webs and the dangerous anthropocentricity of imagining human solitude in "Ecochaucer," 1.

123. David Williams, *Deformed Discourse*, 213–14. Williams writes that gems were identified as "cosmic monsters" in the lapidaries (213), but I have not been able to trace the reference. Rather than a kind of deformity arising from violation of the natural, lapidary stones quietly assert that the natural needs to be a more capacious category.

124. For an ecocritical examination of the medieval commonplace that this world is a transitory wilderness that can never offer a humane home, see Palti, "The Bound Earth in *Patience* and Other Middle English Poetry," especially 34–35.

125. Zalasiewicz, *Planet in a Pebble*, 7.

126. The quotation from Thomas Aquinas is found in Murphy, *Gemstone of Paradise*, 67.

127. The fourth book of Hildegard's *Physica* is a wide-ranging and creative lapidary (*De lapidibus*). The citation is from Murphy, *Gemstone of Paradise*, 55. Cf. Zalasiewicz in *Planet in a Pebble*, who writes "Our pebble is truly a microcosm of the Universe" (6).

128. Duckert, "Glacier," 76.

129. Morton, *The Ecological Thought*, 130.

130. On Isidore and T-O maps, see Biggs, "Isidore of Seville's Etymologies."

131. G. Ronald Murphy traces this paradisal origin for gems back to Augustine's commentary on Genesis; see *Gemstone of Paradise*, 41–48. Suzanne Conklin Akbari treats the theme in the *Book of John Mandeville* in *Idols in the East*, 60–62. These *preciouses pierres* tumble the waters of the four rivers of timeless Eden, sanctifying the land of Prester John.

132. Montgomery, *The Rocks Don't Lie*, 33.

Time

1. Burl, *Prehistoric Avebury*, 34–35.

2. Burl, *Stone Circles of Britain, Ireland and Brittany*, 317.

3. Donated upon its discovery to the Royal College of Surgeons, the barber-surgeon's skeleton was presumed destroyed when the institution was bombed in 1941. The remains were rediscovered in 1999 in a cardboard box stored in the basement of the Natural History Museum, and reexamined by Jackie McKinley. Though the "barber" may have been pinned by the falling rock, his bones were not crushed, making it impossible to know if he had fallen into the rock's pit while alive or been placed there when dead. See Denison, "Lost Skeleton of 'Barber-Surgeon' Found in Museum."

4. Gower, *Vox clamantis*, 1.Prol.1.

5. Jonathan Gil Harris gets at the provocation posed by time as active force and matter as agential in *Untimely Matter in the Time of Shakespeare*. Materiality, Harris argues, is polychronic, gathering multiple times into volatile concatenation.

6. Buridan's Aristotelian bent encouraged him to think about the world and infinity together. See Kaye, "(Re)Balance of Nature," 95. Robert Bartlett examines the conceptual problem a spherical earth composed of four elements of differing weights posed for medieval writers who struggled with the possibility of a globe covered by water as the earth's natural state: *The Natural and the Supernatural in the Middle Ages*, 44–50.

7. Martin J. S. Rudwick takes the phrase "deep time" from John McPhee's *Basin and Range*, remarking upon its analogy to astronomical deep space (Rudwick, *Scenes from Deep Time*, 255). He also employs the earth science term geohistory, "the immensely long and complex history of the earth, including the life on its surface (biohistory), as distinct from the extremely brief recent history that can be based on human records, or even the somewhat longer preliterate 'prehistory' of our species" (*Bursting the Limits of Time*, 2).

8. On resourcism and its imagining that the world is a lifeless "standing reserve" for human use, as well as alternative ethical modes that stress freeing the world from claims of human sovereignty, see M. Smith, *Against Ecological Sovereignty*, 102–3.

9. This "Cosmic Calendar" was famously calculated by Carl Sagan in his book *The Dragons of Eden*, 13–16.

10. Albertus Magnus, *Meteora*, 4.4.7, as quoted in *Book of Minerals*, 2.1.4n7.

11. An excellent account of the work of the Flood myth in the Middle Ages is Anlezark, *Water and Fire*. Anlezark emphasizes the adaptability over time of mythic modes

of dreaming prehistory. He argues that the Flood serves as an "archetype of the human experience of catastrophe," mixing a hope of human endurance with "the fear of collective extinction" (7). Anlezark also well demonstrates the parallels among and ultimate medieval convergence of classical, early Germanic, and biblical flood stories.

12. For a contemporary version of water and fire conveying time's restless, garrulous multiplicity while stone endures in silence, see Michel Serres's provocative account of elemental, auditory fury and the challenges posed by such sensuous disorder in his book *Genesis*.

13. Typically in this model humans live a blissful, garden-like life until they injure the earth through tilling and mining. Thus Chaucer in his poem "The Former Age" describes first cultivation as wounding of the ground through the plough (line 9), and with the unearthing of gems and metals comes covetousness (lines 29–30).

14. On the various dates for the age of the earth given in this paragraph, see Smail, *On Deep History and the Brain,* 22; Barney, *Penn Commentary on Piers Plowman,* 69; Rudwick, *Bursting the Limits of Time,* 116–17; Kaye, "(Re)Balance of Nature," 95. Robert Bartlett combs a variety of twelfth-century sources and gives the age of the world as "variously 3,948, 3,952, 4,182, 5,154, and 5,199" (*England under the Norman and Angevin Kings,* 655).

15. The phrase is used by Shryock and Smail in *Deep History* to describe the abandonment during the 1860s of a biblical "short chronology . . . in which history and geology are coeval" (5–6).

16. Rudwick, *Bursting the Limits of Time,* 2.

17. Robertson, "Medieval Materialism," 108. Robertson is speaking specifically of the chasm that is supposed to separate the Middle Ages from the early modern period, but her rich essay is generalizable beyond this specific focus. See also the work of Daniel Lord Smail, who traces how the Middle Ages and the Paleolithic are both put to work to maintain such gaps.

18. "And ye shal understonde that hit is the yldest toun of the worlde, for hit was makyd byfore Noeis floode. And ther beth bones of gyauntes sides that ben fourty foot long" (Mandeville, *Book,* ed. Kohanski and Benson, lines 400–401). Most versions of the "Defective" text contain a paradoxical assertion that the city is antediluvian and yet founded by Japheth, a son of Noah. The giants' bones are no doubt to be associated with the Flood itself.

19. Not that medieval authors alone found stories of the Flood in the fossilized remains of giants: see Montgomery, *The Rocks Don't Lie,* 82–88.

20. As Andrew Shryock and Daniel Lord Smail point out, short chronologies are not true to the bible itself, which does not contain calendar dates. Later interpreters "retroactively imposed" such frames to harness the narrative to differently organized contemporary chronicles, giving the Genesis story a "brittle precision" that snapped in the nineteenth century (*Deep History,* 6).

21. Evans and Serjeantson, *English Medieval Lapidaries,* 121.

22. For the classical language of the living root *(radix)* from which a mountain grows and its reception into Christian antiquity, see Plumpe, *"Vivum Saxum, Vivi Lapides,"* esp. 3.

23. See Elliott, "Landscape and Geography," 116. Elliott writes that the cave was once called Thurse Cave, "the giant's cave." The poem does not locate its action precisely, however, suggesting that the location is a suggestively composite expanse.

24. *Sir Gawain and the Green Knight,* line 2468.

25. See Virginia Zimmerman's excellent translation of the work of Jacques Derrida and Paul Ricoeur into a geological realm in *Excavating Victorians,* where she writes, "the geological trace is both the sign of the deep past (a past that theoretically stretches back towards beginnings and origin) and a sign that the past is passed. . . . The trace is not the past—this I do not dispute—but it is a material connection to the past, and while it shows erasure, it also preserves. Moreover it becomes the foundation for the new historiography that aims to present the past through narrative" (9).

26. I like David Abram's formulation, triggered as he contemplates a rock that forms a kind of "anchor" in his garden: "We say that the rock 'is' here, that the mountains 'are' over there; we use this little verb 'to be' countless times every day, and yet we forget that it is a *verb,* it names an *act*—that simply *to exist* is a very active thing to be doing" (*Becoming Animal,* 48–49).

27. Lubbock, *Pre-historic Times, as Illustrated by Ancient Remains, and the Manners and Customs of Modern Savages,* 1.

28. Manuel De Landa describes "nonlinear history" as a nonteleological, non-progressive, non-equilibrium-based mode in which "matter's inherent creativity" is evident (*A Thousand Years of Nonlinear History,* 15–17).

29. Andrew Shryock and Daniel Lord Smail have demonstrated how considering deep time alongside smaller-scale history leads to innovative analytical practices. Deep history opens historiography to the "realm of the imagination," creating a "shift in sensibilities" through which "intellectual endeavors" are not "prematurely sorted into separate boxes" (*Deep Time,* 15). Shryock and Smail go on to argue that this shift in scale—deep time *with* shallow time in a single field of analysis—enables us "to reconceive the human condition as the hominin one—that is, one that includes all the species in the genus *Homo* that are ancestrally as well as collaterally related to *Homo sapiens*" (15). I want to push this frame even further, though, to include time without human (or hominin) content, lithic aeons.

30. I am quoting from Shryock and Smail on the mission of paleohistory (ibid., 14), but believe the words hold just as true for the temporal spans imagined by medieval authors.

31. *Fossil* is an early modern Latin term for anything dug up from the ground. Martin J. S. Rudwick traces its narrowing of signification in "Fossil Objects," the opening chapter

of *The Meaning of Fossils*. There is no medieval word for fossil in the precise sense we use it today (the petrified remains of an organic creature). Fossils, gems, stones, and lithic architectures will often be treated as separate objects in my analysis, but they are deeply interconnected as manifestations of a singular, stony materiality. I am influenced as well by Quentin Meillassoux's idea of an "arche-fossil," an ancestral trace such as an isotope so ancient that it transports to "a past where both humanity and life are absent," a time-space he designates "the great outdoors" (*After Finitude*, 26). I find that this outdoors, though, is always knotted within and that the separation between matter and life Meillassoux assumes does not hold.

32. Caillois, *The Writing of the Stones*, 107.

33. See Duffin, "Lapis Judaicus or the Jews' Stone."

34. Joan Evans gives a thorough account, including references to the inventories from England and France, in *Magical Jewels of the Middle Ages and the Renaissance*, 114–15.

35. See Evershed, "A Bitorne's Clee." Evershed suggests that the "clee" is the same kind of fossil described in a will of 1253 as "meas linguas serpentinas," "my serpents's tongues" (226). Lydgate wrote a short poem on the creature, "Bycorne and Chychevache."

36. Dorothy Wyckoff's suggestion (since "some species [of trilobites] . . . have rather toad-like heads with bulging eyes"). See her translation of Albertus Magnus, *Book of Minerals*, 2.2.1, p. 75.

37. The episode is recounted in Boccaccio's *De genealogica deorum gentilium*, 4.68; see C. Cohen, *The Fate of the Mammoth*, 27. Cohen gives a quick and rather unnuanced overview of medieval and early modern fossils in the pages that follow.

38. Orchard, *Pride and Prodigies*, 286–87; Anlezark, *Water and Fire*, 326.

39. It is difficult to say when the fossil was worked into the church's structure, since St. John's has details dating from the twelfth, fourteenth, and seventeenth centuries and was restored in the nineteenth. The porch likely dates no later than 1624 (the date carved into it), and the floor may well be much earlier.

40. Amber *(electrum, succinus)* was not, however, a message from deep time for Albertus: he did not realize how ancient the material might be (Albertus Magnus, *Book of Minerals*, 2.2.17).

41. Albertus tells an elemental story of how a thundercloud might generate a thunder axe: "When this earthy dry smoke has been set afire in the viscous moisture in the cloud, it is baked into a stone, black or red in color, that falls from the cloud and splits beams and penetrates walls, and is called by the common people a 'thunder axe.'" The quotation is from his *Meteora*, 3.3.18 and is cited by Dorothy Wyckoff in the *Book of Minerals*, the introductory notes for *ceraurum* (2.2.3).

42. N. J. Higham writes of the ascription to Arthur as a "commonplace mechanism for explaining unnatural landscape features" in the "Brittonic world": *King Arthur*, 82.

43. Alfred K. Siewers calls it "an environmental textuality" (*Strange Beauty*, 40).

44. Chippindale, *Stonehenge Complete,* 28.

45. "Stanenges ubi lapides mire magnitudinis in modum portarum eleuati sunt" (Henry of Huntingdon, *Historia Anglorum,* 1.7). Henry describes the stones as "gateways upon gateways," an optical effect of looking through one trilithon at another; see Chippindale, *Stonehenge Complete,* 20–21. In his "Letter to Warin the Breton," written after he had access to the *History of the Kings of Britain,* Henry adds a small detail taken with small errors from Geoffrey of Monmouth: "Uther Pendragon, that is 'dragon's head,' a most distinguished young man, the son of Aurelius, brought a giants' circle from Ireland, which is now called Stonehenge." The letter is included in Diana Greenway's edition of the *Historia Anglorum,* quotation at 577.

46. Relevant here is the work on communication without traditional documents collected by Boone and Mignolo in *Writing without Words* and Mignolo, *The Darker Side of the Renaissance.*

47. See for example Mayor, "Geomythology."

48. The tomb remains magnificent to see today because, like Newgrange in Ireland, it is a fairly modern reconstruction, and perhaps a reenvisioning. See Burl, *Prehistoric Avebury,* 996–97. Though Burl does not mention this fact, the interior walls are likewise formed of stone with numerous fossils.

49. For these archeological discoveries, see Evans, *Magical Jewels of the Middle Ages and the Renaissance,* 13–14.

50. Suetonius, *Lives of the Caesars,* 72. Adrienne Mayor evocatively describes Augustus's villa as "the world's first paleontological museum" (*The First Fossil Hunters,* 143).

51. The quotation is from Rudwick's *Worlds before Adam,* 25.

52. Which is not to say that Augustine was uninterested in material objects, as the example that follows makes clear. Gary Wills observes that things confess (that is, testify) throughout Augustine's oeuvre: "*Confiteri* means, etymologically, to *corroborate,* to *confirm* testimony, and even inanimate things can do that—Augustine's fellow African Apuleius said that 'jewels confess [confirm the status of] the grande dame.' Augustine himself says that the inanimate universe confesses to (testifies to) God. The thing confessed does not have to be a moral truth—Augustine 'confesses' the fact that time is measurable. The term that best covers this range of meanings for *confession* is 'testimony'" (*Saint Augustine,* xiv).

53. Augustine discusses eternity and heaven in his *Confessions* 10.8 and 12.9. On Augustine's conceptualization of the "eternal present" and the challenge posed to it by other modes of thinking time, see Siewers, *Strange Beauty,* 48.

54. I realize that bone is not the same as stone, since it is organically produced, but would point out that (1) fossil calcium is indeed a major component of most stone, (2) bone might best be thought as stone produced within the body, and (3) stories of bone and stone are usually narratively inseparable. See especially De Landa, *A Thousand Years of Nonlinear History,* 26.

55. Claudine Cohen gives the episode a future-directed reading in *The Fate of the Mammoth,* 24–26, connecting the tooth to fossilized remains of elephants discovered throughout the Mediterranean since Greek and Roman days.

56. For a good overview of Augustine on time and human history, see Markus, *Saeculum.* This conception is given a vivid realization in the *Suite du Merlin,* where the prophet's entombment is horrific because for a while he seems to live outside of time, but time passes around him all the same.

57. The British Museum website description of the body, officially known as "Lindow II," reads like a crime report: "The man met a horrific death. He was struck on the top of his head twice with a heavy object, perhaps a narrow bladed axe. He also received a vicious blow in the back—perhaps from someone's knee—which broke one of his ribs. He had a thin cord tied around his neck which was used to strangle him and break his neck. By now he was probably dead, but then his throat was cut. Finally, he was placed face down in a pond in the bog" (http://www.britishmuseum.org/explore/highlights /highlight_objects/pe_prb/l/lindow_man.aspx). Like all the objects I have been examining in this essay, "Lindow II" is not an unmediated or "pure" intrusion of the ancient past into an alien present. Not only has the display of the corpse been carefully structured, but the body itself was freeze-dried after its discovery to prevent further deterioration.

58. "Past experiences become selectively conjoined with present perceptions and serve to colour them. Temporality is carried by the movements of the body into, out of, around and between places. We carry times to places through our movements and prior experiences, and direct contact with these places acts as a mnemonic trigger for stories and the construction of personal biographies" (Tilley, *Materiality of Stone,* 26).

59. Although not about prehistoric architectures, a rich explication of orientation devices, phenomenology, and queer effect may be found in Ahmed, *Queer Phenomenology.* Ahmed works against the freezing into singular temporalities that certain social and material formations foster, detailing the "openness of the future" that gets closed down and might be reactivated (82).

60. Olsen, *In Defense of Things,* 27–31.

61. "In the world of materials, humans figure as much within the context for stones as do stones within the context for humans. And these contexts, far from lying on disparate levels of being, respectively social and natural, are established as overlapping regions of the same world . . . the ever-unfolding world of materials in which the very being of humans, along with that of the non-humans they encounter, is bound up" (Ingold, *Being Alive,* 31).

62. For an examination of some of the complexities of Augustine's "now," see Dinshaw, *How Soon Is Now?,* 13–16.

63. See J. Harris, *Untimely Matter in the Time of Shakespeare,* 103.

64. As Quentin Meillassoux observes about what he calls the arche-fossil (traces of

the past so ancient their temporal transport brings us back to a time before life, a "great outdoors" of contingency and real possibility), "the arche-fossil enjoins us to *track thought by inviting us to discover the 'hidden passage' trodden by the latter in order . . . to get out of ourselves,* to grasp the in-itself, to know what is whether we are or not" (*After Finitude,* 27). See also Meillassoux's broadening of the arche-fossil beyond its initial and impossibly distant temporal parameters to "every discourse whose meaning includes a *temporal discrepancy* between thinking and being" (112). On Meillassoux's troubling (and unnecessary) antimedievalism, see Mitchell, "Cosmic Eggs," 155–56. Mitchell provides an essential critical survey of medieval ways of imagining beginnings that grant the materials their full complexity and challenge Meillassoux's reliance upon conventional periodizations.

65. Walter Stephens treats the passage and Augustine's reaction at length in *Giants in Those Days,* 90–92. Augustine knew the Vulgate version of Genesis (here quoted) but preferred the Vetus Latina (a translation of the Greek Septuagint), emphasizing that giants were continuously present before and after the Flood.

66. Earlier in my career I approached much of the material in this section through a psychoanalytic reading: *Of Giants.*

67. On these points, see the work of James Kugel, especially *Traditions of the Bible* and *How to Read the Bible.*

68. The standard edition remains *The Book of Enoch,* trans. Charles. This noncanonical book was well known to writers like Josephus, Tertullian, and Justin Martyr, and may have survived into Anglo-Saxon England. See Kaske, "*Beowulf* and the Book of Enoch" and Anlezark, *Water and Fire,* 320–21.

69. Not surprisingly the cleansing Flood was therefore typologically read as a prefiguration of Christian baptism and its power to wash away sin: Anlezark, *Water and Fire,* 38, 57–67.

70. Augustine, *City of God,* 15.23. In Augustine's account the offspring of Seth are the sons of God (*filii Dei*) who intermarry with the daughters of Cain (*filias hominum*), engendering prodigious but fully human offspring. Augustine's commentary on the Genesis passage and its medieval reception is considered in J. Dean, "The World Grown Old and Genesis," 560, and Stephens, *Giants in Those Days,* 79–85. Isidore of Seville will likewise write, "Some, inexperienced with Holy Scripture (i.e. Genesis 6:4), falsely suppose that apostate angels lay with the daughters of humans before the Flood, and that from this the Giants were born" (*Etymologies,* 11.14). Like Augustine, Isidore refutes the story only to embed it and pass it along to the future.

71. For a meditation on these lines from Lucan and their relation to stone, see Kerisel, *Of Stones and Man,* xiii.

72. Geologists refer to this Flood-derived model as catastrophism. It is important to note, however, that medieval writers also inherited from their classical forebears a model based upon gradualism. Structured around a Golden Age giving way to a debased era of

Iron, this human sorting of time through metals renders them lithic mediators of a slow human debasement.

73. For other instances of Christian glossing of marine fossils as evidence of the Flood, see Cohn, *Noah's Flood*, 73–93, and Mayor, *The First Fossil Hunters*, 210–11.

74. Daniel Lord Smail writes that "the Deluge made all prior history unknowable anyway, since it destroyed all the documents from which we could write such a history.... As an event that set the civilization clock back to zero, the Deluge marked an epistemological break with humanity's origin, which we cannot know, and the present stream of history, which we can" (*On Deep History and the Brain*, 13).

75. Ibid., 14.

76. Josephus, *Antiquities*, I.3.69–70.

77. For both the Irish "Poem of Fifty Questions" and the Cassian references, see Orchard, *Pride and Prodigies*, 67–68.

78. English translation from Gerald of Wales, *The History and Topography of Ireland*, 93–94. Gerald seems to be taking this story from the Lebor Gabála Érenn, where the granddaughter is named Cessair (and does not write her history in stone). I am grateful to Liza Blake for sharing her work on Gerald's narrative and its indigenous context with me. My thoughts on Caesura/Cessair were further catalyzed by Aisling Byrne's paper "The Archipelagic Otherworld: Geography and Identity in Medieval Ireland and Britain."

79. Gerald of Wales, *History and Topography of Ireland*, 93.

80. See especially the work of the archeologists Timothy Darvill and Geoffrey Wainwright.

81. The quotation—and much of my information about the bluestones—is taken from the excellent overview of recent archeological work on Stonehenge contained in Alexander, "If the Stones Could Speak," quotation at 53. For a recent news article on Craig Rhos-y-Felin, the outcropping in northern Pembrokeshire from which the bluestones originated, see Keys, "Scientists Discover Source of Rock Used in Stonehenge's First Circle."

82. Such collusion across the organic and the elemental may even have played a revolutionary role in human history. An archeologist studying the oldest monumental structure, the incised stones of Göbekli Tepe in Turkey, has argued that the construction of this temple that predates Stonehenge by six thousand years spurred the formation of the first cities, since building and maintaining the complex required the enduring stability of farming, domestication of animals, and urban collectives. Partnership with stone perhaps sparked the transformation that yielded Mesopotamian civilization. That, at least, is the thesis of Klaus Schmidt. See Symmes, "History in the Remaking" and the resources gathered at http://www.gobeklitepe.info/ and http://www.dainst.org/en/project /goebeklitepe?ft=all.

83. For one of many versions of the story, see Mandeville, *Book,* ed. Kohanski and Benson, 27.

84. A more modern version of this artistic address to the distant future is the "Letters of Utrecht" project, a poem being set in stone at the rate of one letter per week with a completion date of 12,012. See Hajer, "Long Poetry."

85. Frank Grady writes of the poem's literalizations in a way consonant with my argument here; see *Representing Righteous Heathens*, 38. D. Vance Smith describes the pagan judge's tomb as itself radiating a petrifying (and thereby deathly) effect: "the crypt outwards to the site of the living, who gaze back at the judge's corpse with a marmoreal quiescence. The work of metaphor transforms the living into memorial stone" ("Crypt and Decryption," 66). See Karl Steel's two excellent blog posts on Erkenwald as well: "Weeping with Erkenwald" and "Will Wonders Never Cease."

86. See Otter, *Inventiones*, 55, which relates the incident to an archeological impulse within Matthew's work.

87. Frederick Newmayer is quoted by R. C. Baker declaring that a language becomes "unintelligible to the descendants of the speakers after the passage of between 500 and 1000 years." See Baker, "Deep Time, Short Sight."

88. The interview was conducted by Geoff Manaugh of BLDGBLOG and published on November 2, 2009, as "One Million Years of Isolation." Van Luik describes the process of choosing Yucca and the goals of nuclear entombment there.

89. Baker, "Deep Time, Short Sight." See the similar circumstances surrounding New Mexico's Waste Isolation Pilot Plant (WIPP) examined by Julia Bryan-Wilson, "Building a Marker of Nuclear Warning."

90. "One can reasonably postulate that over a 10,000-year time frame, languages will be replaced or significantly modified, making any single language unreliable by itself as an effective device for communication" (Human Interference Task Force, "Reducing the Likelihood of Future Human Activities That Could Affect Geologic High-Level Waste Repositories," 11).

91. Ibid., 58.

92. Ibid., 75.

93. The exhibition is archived online at http://www.desertspace.org/wwwroot/warning_sign/index.html.

94. Baker "Deep Time, Short Sight." See also Bryan-Wilson, "Building a Marker of Nuclear Warning," 201n6, on the teams and Brill's artistic bent.

95. Bryan-Wilson, "Building a Marker of Nuclear Warning," 195.

96. On Bede's diluvian futurity, see Anlezark, *Water and Fire*, 44, 75–84.

97. De Landa, *A Thousand Years of Nonlinear History*, 267.

98. Manaugh, "One Million Years of Isolation."

99. Julia Bryan-Wilson emphasizes the inadequacy of most of the designs put forward to their actual task, since "there will be no upkeep of these grounds after 2030, once the

dump closes. . . . The EPA stipulates that the . . . marker must signify on its own, passively, with no guards or maintenance staff" ("Building a Marker of Nuclear Warning," 187).

100. I have examined the historical conditions for the erection of Norwich cathedral in *Hybridity, Identity and Monstrosity in Medieval Britain,* 129–34.

101. Zalasiewicz, *Planet in a Pebble,* 15.

102. Ibid., xii.

103. Ibid.

104. Ibid.

105. Ibid.

106. References to Geoffrey of Monmouth's *History of the Kings of Britain* are to the edition of Michael D. Reeve and the translation of Neil Wright and are given by page number (here, 28).

107. Rebecca R. Scott writes of this process in *Removing Mountains,* 210.

108. See, for example, the *Navigatio Sancti Brendani,* where the saint is first encountered in a *saltus virtutum,* an open field or meadow (1).

109. "eald enta geweorc idlu stodon," *The Wanderer,* 87. I explore the Old English trope of associating giants with ruins in *Of Giants,* 7–11.

110. On Geoffrey's confusion of these places, see the note in Thorpe's translation, p. 195.

111. See Heck, "Histoire mythique et archéologie au quinzième siècle," 256 and n15. Stephen Knight points out that this picture shows Merlin "as a mason, not a wizard" (*Merlin,* 29).

112. As Michelle Warren points out, with Stonehenge—as with every stone architecture in the text—Geoffrey also emphasizes that a history of the island is inherently, materially a history of multiple peoples (*History on the Edge,* 41).

113. The linking of Stonehenge and druids owes much to the antiquarians John Aubrey and William Stukeley; see the detailed explication in Chippindale, *Stonehenege Complete,* 66–95.

114. Typically enabled through an object that fosters temporal convergence, kinshipping is the forging of long connection "by means of relationship and exchange" that often extends into prehistory: Shryock, Trautmann, and Gamble, "Imagining the Human in Deep Time," in *Deep History,* 32.

115. Shryock and Smail, *Deep History,* 272. A kinshipping device is "a connecting tool that enables conceptual travel through time, using existing links to generate relationships to persons and places now absent." See Stiner et al., "Scale," in *Deep History,* 271.

116. It is possible that the bluestone was brought close to Stonehenge from what is now west Wales by the movement of glaciers (though evidence of glaciation in Wiltshire is thin). What matters most, though, is that the rocks are alien intrusions to their setting, no matter how they arrived; Stonehenge is not constructed of materials close at hand.

117. Stonehenge in the *History of the Kings of Britain* demonstrates that objects (in the words of Julian Yates) "obey their own temporalities, provide alternative chronologies or histories than those reckoned in terms of political or religious landmarks, and inscribe that knowledge in the texts they occasion" (*Error, Misuse, Failure,* xx). Like Gil Harris, Yates is inspired by the work of Michel Serres on the heterogeneous and nonlinear vectors of time. See especially Serres and Latour, *Conversations on Science, Culture, and Time,* 57. The stones' polychronicity continues today in the archeological stories being told about Stonehenge. Geoffrey's Merlin describes the stones as a source of healing, allying their powers with the lithotherapy evident in medieval lapidaries. Geoffrey Wainwright has been arguing that the bluestones of Stonehenge were revered for their curative powers. See Kennedy, "The Magic of Stonehenge."

118. The *Suite du Merlin* survives in three incomplete manuscripts. I worked with the Huth *Merlin* (London, British Library, Additional MS 38117) in *Merlin, roman en prose du XIIIe siècle,* ed. Paris and Ulrich. A good translation by Samuel N. Rosenberg of the section of the text I will be discussing may be found in *The Romance of Arthur.* Much background on the influence of the *Suite du Merlin* upon later Arthurian literature is contained in Wright, "'The Tale of King Arthur.'"

119. Lord, "Le Tombeau de Merlin."

120. Monika Otter eloquently explores the force of this word in *Inventiones.* See also Mary Carruthers on the relation between *inventio* and aesthetic experience: *The Experience of Beauty in the Middle Ages,* 25–26.

121. Sometimes stone takes the place of a relic, as in the *The Chronicle of Battle Abbey.* Eager to commemorate his victory at Hastings, William the Conqueror discovers the construction material he requires underneath the site of his proposed church and realizes that "the Lord had laid up a hidden treasure of stone there from the beginning of time for the predestined work." Monika Otter cites and analyzes the episode in *Inventiones,* 43 and 61, noting that the stones embody the temporality of forever *(ab euo)* in order to sanctify William's victory.

122. "Augustine finds the material appropriate in that clay is not simple dust but rather a mixture of water and earth, *limus enim aquae ac terrae commixtio est.* He then makes the comparison between the nature of human beings and clay" (Murphy, *Gemstone of Paradise,* 43).

123. For earth and human as "co-substantial bodies," see Feerick, "Economies of Nature in Shakespeare," 38.

124. Evans and Serjeantson, *English Medieval Lapidaries,* 129.

Force

1. I am grateful to Dan Remein for his inspirational meditation on wonder posted in the comments at my blog post "The Future of 'The Weight of the Past.'" Jane Bennett

glosses "wonder" with "enchantment," defined as transport away from the self when the strange is revealed within the quotidian. She cites Albertus Magnus on wonder as "shocked surprise" to make her point (*Enchantment of Modern Life*, 5). Bennett stresses "affective fascination" (12), plenitude, ethical generosity, and love of the world as essential to enchantment. Gillian Rudd richly details wonder and medieval worldedness in *Greenery*, 188–98.

2. On queer inducement to disorienting, productive perspective shift, see Sara Ahmed's groundbreaking *Queer Phenomenology*, esp. 170–72. Ahmed's detailing of the phenomenological and embodied effects of queer space has been essential to the framing of this chapter. Michael O'Rourke observes that the queer opens "new forms of being-in-the-world" and creates a space for "surprise, for wonder, for love, for happiness, for a world in which our very uncertainty about what it means to be human comes to be understood as definitive of the human condition" ("The Open," xvii, xviii).

3. For the ratiocination, mischievousness, amusement, and dread that constitute the "complex semantic field" of wonder in the Middle Ages, see Bynum, *Metamorphosis and Identity*, esp. 56–75.

4. Bogost, *Alien Phenomenology*, 131.

5. Thus Chaucer describes a dazed Pandarus, reeling from Troilus's rebuke, as rock-like: "This Pandarus . . . stant, astoned of thise causes tweye, / As stille as ston" (This Pandarus stood astonished for these two reasons, as still as a stone, *Troilus and Criseyde*, 5.1723, 1728–29).

6. See Thorndike, "The Latin Pseudo-Aristotle," 243.

7. See the excerpts from the *Lapidary of Aristotle* included by Dorothy Wyckoff in her edition of Albertus Magnus, *Book of Minerals*, 2.3.6 (n17).

8. I used *tectonic* in its triple meaning of "geological," "vast," and "constructed" or "composed." I am inspired here by the work of Nicholas Royle in *Veering*, who describes literature's work as a "twisted love story" (1) intimately bound to the "environment" (2)—a word likewise etymologically related to "to turn" through a shared origin in *virer*, to turn.

9. Jean-Pierre Vernant has written that the transformation of ancient Greek law from memorized form to a code inscribed on buildings in public spaces fixed the legal system into something that seemed as durable and pregiven as stone itself. See *The Origins of Greek Thought*, 52–60.

10. On the making of glass *(vitrum)*, see for example Isidore, *Etymologies*, 16.16. Isidore narrates a wonderful story about a craftsman of Tiberius Caesar who invents flexible, pliable, unbreakable glass. He is beheaded for the achievement because "if this skill became known, gold would be regarded as mud."

11. The later encyclopedist Bartholomaeus Anglicus distinguishes between the *calculus*, a smooth little stone that may be trodden without pain, and the *scrupulus*, a "litel

stoon" that is "rough and scharpe" that when stepped upon "grieueth ful sore" (*On the Properties of Things*, 16.21).

12. "Naturalcultural" is Donna Haraway's term for short-circuiting the fallacious divide between the two words and avoiding the Great Division they enact. See, for example, *When Species Meet*, 15–16.

13. Bennett, *Vibrant Matter*, vii.

14. Ibid., 58. Perhaps because she draws so heavily upon premodern materials, Jane Bennett's vibrant materialism amicably resonates with Isidore's articulation of the innate ability of *smaragdus, astrion, enhydros, galactitis,* and carbuncle to disrupt narratives of worldly rejection or reduction into utility.

15. Ibid., 59.

16. Caroline Walker Bynum has lucidly detailed the dynamism of medieval matter, "possessing power or desire" within Neoplatonic, Ovidian, and Aristotelian conceptualizations of substance, different as these frames could be (*Christian Materiality*, 239).

17. Kellie Robertson has rightly observed that "the basis of any time period's view of nature is based on its views of material substance" ("Medieval Materialism," 105).

18. The *Book*'s multiplicity is well stressed throughout Iain Macleod Higgins's magisterial *Writing East*, as well as his essay "Defining the Earth's Center in a Medieval 'Multi-Text.'" An excellent overview of recent scholarship on the *Book* may be found in Anthony Bale's comprehensive introduction to his fine translation of the *Book*, ix–xxxv.

19. The quotation comes from Hanna, "Mandeville," 123.

20. Kohanski and Benson give a good overview in the preface to their edition of the manuscript, Mandeville, *Book*, 14–15. All otherwise unattributed Middle English quotations are from this text.

21. I examine the bestiary as delectation of the forbidden in "Inventing with Animals in the Middle Ages." Such enjoyment often serves a culturally normalizing function, so that fantasies of the exotic buttress dominating identities: see Geraldine Heng's penetrating account of Mandeville's *Book* as panoptic device in *Empire of Magic*, 239–305.

22. Unanticipated, at least, in the *Liber de quisbusdam ultramarines partibus* of the German Dominican William of Boldensele, the foundation text for the *Book*'s narratives of Constantinople and travel to Palestine. Higgins writes of the Hippocrates's daughter episode and the necrophilia at Satalia (neither found in William) that they have in common a theme of "eros gone awry," that they derive from "the shadowy world where romance couples with folklore," and that—since they seem so out of place within the didactic narrative—they have a "crepuscular quality" (*Writing East*, 83).

23. "Ibi est anglus turris excelsissimae, ubi dominus ascendit et dixit ei is, qui temptabat eum, et ait ei dominus: non temptabis dominum deum tuum, sed illi soli seruies. Ibi est et lapis angularis mangus, de quo dictum est: lapidem, quem reprobauerunt aedificantes, hic factus est ad caput anguli" (*"Pilgrim of Bordeaux," Itinerarium Burdigalense*, 590).

24. On Mandeville's middles, Aristotle's *Nicomachean Ethics,* and intermediacy (as opposed to centrality), see Lochrie, "Provincializing Medieval Europe," 594.

25. A vivid example of such a souvenir may be found reproduced in Bagnoli et al, *Treasures of Heaven,* 37. A sixth-century painted wooden reliquary from Syria or Palestine is filled with an assortment of stones and a fragment of wood taken from the Holy Land. The central rock is labeled to announce that it derives from the Holy Sepulcher. I am grateful to Karen Overbey for sharing with me her own photographs of lithic pilgrimage relics.

26. According to M. C. Seymour, Satalia or Adalia is modern Antalya, where Paul sailed to Antioch. Seymour sees the story as a version of the Gorgon's head myth combined with that of Callimachus and Drusinia of Ephesus, but writes that "the immediate source is unknown" (Mandeville, *Defective Version,* 141). Though the tale does bear elements of both these narratives, it stands alone: this is not a story the Mandeville-author took wholesale from another known text.

27. A slightly earlier tomb holds the body of Hermogenes the Wise, discussed in the previous chapter. Disinterred at the building of Hagia Sophia in Constantinople, this two-thousand-year-old corpse was clutching a golden plaque on which was inscribed (in Hebrew, Greek, and Latin) the man's faith in messiah to come (228–34). This story is obviously similar to that narrated in the Middle English poem *St. Erkenwald* (see "Time," as well as Whatley, "Heathens and Saints," 346–47).

28. Iain Higgins observes that the narrative "is virtually unique among medieval travel writings in expanding the pilgrims' guide with a survey of the world beyond the Holy Land" ("Defining the Earth's Center in a Medieval 'Multi-Text,'" 40). He ties this movement somewhat counterintuitively to a desire to make Jerusalem the center of the entire text ("a consolation offered to a much shrunken Christendom and a challenge laid down to those Christians who, as the prologue puts it, have the wherewithal to undertake a holy voyage overseas," 45), but I am not so certain that Jerusalem's center is meant to hold.

29. For a thorough consideration of the Mandeville-author's sources, see Deluz, *Le Livre de Jehan de Mandeville,* 39–93, as well as the extensive table at 428–91.

30. On the circularity of the text, see Heng, *Empire of Magic,* 305, and Lomperis, "Medieval Travel Writing and the Question of Race," 152.

31. Thus Constantine is called "kyng of Ingelond that was that tyme called the Greet Brytayne" (152–53).

32. See Higgins, *Writing East,* 31.

33. Mary Baine Campbell describes its knightly narrator as a "hedonist of knowledge" who prizes beauty, forbearance, and understanding over critique (*The Witness and the Other World,* 141). Stephen Greenblatt argues that John Mandeville's "heterodox" position of generous curiosity possesses "lived consequences," such as the burning of a heretic who asserted that he learned his intolerable religious tolerance from reading the *Book*

(*Marvelous Possessions*, 46). Karma Lochrie finds in the text a laudable cosmopolitanism ("Provincializing Medieval Europe").

34. This remark does not, however, appear in the Defective version with which I have been working.

35. Andrew Colin Gow points out that only Mandeville and a few German sources identify the enclosed Gog and Magog as Jews: in most traditions (e.g., Matthew Paris) the enclosed peoples are Mongols/Tartars (*The Red Jews*, 53, 61–63). Suzanne Conklin Akbari contextualizes the episode in Mandeville well in *Idols in the East*, 135–40, emphasizing that the Jews in the *Book* are located at a "double place," within Christian cities and at the world's edge, "a spatial expression of their ontological status" (139). I wonder if the designation of the Jews as "Gog and Magog" is not meant to resonate simultaneously with "synagogue" and Geoffrey of Monmouth's naming of the aboriginal giant leader in *History of the Kings of Britain* as "Gogmagog," thus planting an English story far from home.

36. See Braude, "*Mandeville's* Jews among Others," 145. Braude explains this hatred through reference to Christian crusade and a desire to attain a Holy Land without coclaimants. Stephen Greenblatt describes this "ungenerous" attitude as the "most significant exception to the tolerance that is impressively articulated elsewhere" (*Marvelous Possessions*, 50). Iain Higgins writes that the *Book's* conspiracy theories might seem future-focused, but they are formulated "to incite ill-feeling against Jews in the present . . . a hostility verging on paranoia. . . . No other religious community . . . is so badly served in The Book as the Jews, who inhabit only the past and the future, and are depicted with a hostility bordering on paranoia" (*Writing East*, 42).

37. On this point, see especially Tomasch, "Postcolonial Chaucer and the Virtual Jew" and Krummel, *Crafting Jewishness in Medieval England*. Krummel articulates the complicated entwinement of Christian and Jew, hegemony and its imagined reversals, entrapment and apocalyptic escape in Mandeville's narrative at 69–88.

38. The passage had a long lifespan applied to the stony dullness of the "ungodly" and could be used of pagans or other figures of unbelief (see, for example, Werth, "A Heart of Stone"), but its use against the Jews was especially widespread.

39. *Petri Venerabilis adversus Iudeorum inveteratam duritiem*, 3, lines 564–70; cited in Abulafia, "Bodies in the Jewish-Christian Debate," 127. An excellent discussion of Peter and the Jews can be found in Flanagan, *Doubt in an Age of Faith*, 164–67.

40. See Akbari, *Idols in the East*, 114, and for a compelling Middle English visualization of this destruction in which "no fragment will remain as a locus for remembering a Jewish Jerusalem," 132. *The Siege of Jerusalem* imagines masons and miners who "hewen throw hard ston" and this "annihilation of the walls of the city, repeated in microcosm in the annihilation of the bodies of the Jewish men, is a visible manifestation of the erasure of Synagoga" (133).

41. "Dispute between the Virgin and the Cross," line 226.

42. David A. Hinton explores the history and architecture of these stone houses in "Medieval Anglo-Jewry." He writes that the only way to ascribe a house to a Jewish owner is through documentary evidence because "there is nothing about their plan or style to distinguish them from the properties of rich Gentiles" (98).

43. Bale, *The Jew in the Medieval Book,* 85.

44. Ibid., 86.

45. Yuval, *Two Nations in Your Womb.* I am giving Yuval the quickest of treatments here, and his argument has complicated ethical implications; see Hannah R. Johnson's nuanced study in *Blood Libel,* esp. 91–128. Yuval is far from alone in mapping the hybridities engendered through Christian-Jewish neighboring. For an extensive bibliography, see my essay "The Future of the Jews of York," from which some of the discussion of the geology of medieval anti-Judaism derives.

46. Morton glosses coexistentialism as "the entanglement of strangers" that leads to ethical interconnection rather than an attempt to abolish proximity and difference (*The Ecological Thought,* 47).

47. Yuval, *Two Nations in Your Womb,* 289.

48. Of this flow and ebb of stone Geraldine Heng astutely writes, "Readers may be forgiven if they do not recognize a description of the desert in this poetic description of a sandy sea, or if they should think they scent, minisculely, a whiff of resemblance to the imaginary worlds of science fiction narratives today" (*Empire of Magic,* 304).

49. Higgins, "Defining the Earth's Center in a Medieval 'Multi-Text,'" 32–33.

50. Zumthor, *Toward a Medieval Poetics;* see especially 40–76 and 407n.

51. Chaganti, "Choreographing *Mouvance,*" 77. Chaganti's approach innovatively maps *mouvance* through dance, performance, choreography, and bodies in motion.

52. Timothy Morton puts it well: "Yes, everything is interconnected. And it sucks" (*The Ecological Thought,* 33).

53. Quentin Meillassoux explores correlationism and its pitfalls in *After Finitude,* while coextension is a key term of Tim Ingold in *Being Alive.* See "Geophilia."

54. *Effusive* is an adjective adopted from geology, where it designates igneous rock that has poured out from the earth and taken a solid form in which movement has been both arrested and made manifest. *Radiance* captures the glimmer of a gem, its push into the world. Teeming with sensuousness, *allure* is a key term in the work of the philosopher Graham Harman, who uses the noun to indicate the seductive power of the inanimate.

55. The phrase is found in Weber's *Wissenschaft als Beruf,* 19, and its medieval significance is explored by Robert Bartlett in *The Natural and the Supernatural in the Middle Ages,* 32.

56. Bartlett, *The Natural and the Supernatural in the Middle Ages,* 33.

57. On this point, see especially Bennett's *Enchantment of Modern Life,* which dwells upon the environmental and political promise of magic's nondisappearance. Bennett's

eloquent "alter-tale" emphasizes that enchantment entails being "struck and shaken by the extraordinary that lives amid the familiar and the everyday"—to inhabit, that is, the medieval genre of romance: "even secular life houses extraordinary goings-on" (4).

58. The quotation is from Bennett, *Vibrant Matter,* 4, where she is describing "thing-power," the ability to provoke affects, reveal an "energetic vitality," and demonstrate an "excess" possessed beyond "association with human meanings." Bennett calls this quality vibrancy, to stress its energetic and excitative effects.

59. Isidore of Seville describes how amber *(sucinus),* which he recognized to be the sap of a tree, was called *electrum* in Greek because in myth "Phaeton was killed by a bolt of lightning [and] his sisters in their grief were turned into poplar trees, and they exude amber *(electrum)* as tears" (*Etymologies,* 16.8.6). He goes on to state that amber comes from pine rather than poplars and when rubbed becomes magnetized.

60. *Lancelot: Roman en prose,* 7.38. For the passage in translation, see *Lancelot-Grail,* 2.11.

61. "Aere contactus fit durior et lapidescit," Marbode of Rennes, *De lapidibus,* 314. Marbode's Latin poem is treated more fully in the following chapter.

62. See Marbode of Rennes, *De lapidibus,* 252–67, and John Riddle's note (p. 54) on jewel inventories.

63. Thus Stephen A. Walton, after a sensitive account of the medieval lapidary tradition, bluntly segregates the material he has collected by declaring in conclusion "Somewhere—and somehow—between the reign of Elizabeth I of England and the start of the Thirty Years' War, science was born" ("Theophrastus on *Lyngurium,*" 378).

64. Latour, "An Attempt at a Compositionist Manifesto," 471.

65. In John Trevisa's translation, "Carbunculus is a precious stoon and schyneþ as fure whos schynynge is not ouercome by night. It schyneþ in derke places, and it semeþ as it were flame" (Bartholomaeus Anglicus, *On the Properties of Things,* 16.25).

66. "more vertue is yhidde in a litel adamant wiþ colour of iren and derke" (Bartholomaeus Anglicus, *On the Properties of Things,* 16.47).

67. Mary Carruthers writes of the inseparability of medieval aesthetics from corporeal sensation and cognitive perception in *The Experience of Beauty in the Middle Ages:* "medieval aesthetic experience is bound into human sensation and . . . human knowledge is sense-derived, the agents of which are all corporeal" (8). Carruthers offers a corrective to the over-theologization of beauty in the Middle Ages, its reduction into allegories and lessons: "criticism of medieval arts . . . has become over-theologized and over-moralized to the point at where every flourish, every joke, every colour and ornament is said to conceal a lesson for the improvement of the viewer or listener. Since these putative lessons are often banal and repetitive, or obscure to the point of incoherence, it is no wonder that many in the modern audience who take great pleasure in medieval arts refuse to read criticism by medievalists or are put off by its religiosity. If a modern reader

finds something amusing in a medieval work composed before Chaucer it must be either unintentional or 'covering over' some sober doctrine in need of extraction" (8–9).

68. Graham Harman calls this surplus *withdrawal* and glosses the term as follows: "objects are not defined by their relations . . . objects are built of components, but exceed those components" (*Prince of Networks*, 132). Behind an object's manifold qualities, there will always be something more than can be described or known. Levi Bryant offers a similar definition of the withdrawal of objects in *The Democracy of Objects*, though he takes his inspiration from Lacan (262). Tim Morton offers this succinct summation: "I like to think that *withdrawal* means total *uniqueness*. Things withdraw from access, remember, which doesn't mean that they become vague haphazard blobs of whateverness. Withdrawal means 'unspeakable,' because unique. *Withdraw* doesn't mean *lose definition*, but be *so definite that all modes of access fail in some sense*" ("Withdrawal, What the Heck Is It?").

69. *Melion* in *"Melion" and "Bicarel,"* ed. and trans. Hopkins, 159, 164.

70. The spilled herbal potion is from Marie de France's lai *Les Deus Amanz.*

71. The storm gem appears in Chrétien de Troyes, *Le Chevalier au lion,* 419–50.

72. "Coparius is a stone þat is bred in þe eyre & some callen it fouldre; & he falleþ with tempest to þe erþe when gret tempest of þondres and lyʒtnyng fallen, & it falleþ in to þe erþe ix fote, & þe erþe reboundeþ aʒene by vertu of þe stone" (Evans and Serjeantson, *English Medieval Lapidaries*, 81).

73. Henry of Huntingdon was reading the ingenious work at the abbey of Le Bec in Normandy a few years after its completion. For Henry's account of his encounter with Geoffrey's work, see his "Letter to Warin the Breton" in *Historia Anglorum,* 558–59.

74. "The succession of names and languages traces the history of Britain's tenants, heirs to the stones' own colonial origins. As a monument to clever force, then, Stonehenge commemorates the achievements of whoever currently dominates the land" (Warren, *History on the Edge,* 149).

75. Olsen, *In Defense of Things,* 170. Olsen is working extensively here with Walter Benjamin's work; the quotation is from *Selected Writings,* 2:39.

76. Http://www.clonehenge.com.

77. Morton, "The Mesh," 28.

78. Bennett, *Vibrant Matter,* 31.

79. Pickering develops the terpsichorean metaphor most extensively, especially in *The Mangle of Practice,* 21 and 116–17. This "intertwining" of the human and the nonhuman into "free and forced moves in practice," he emphasizes, is not "optional" but the necessary unfolding of material agency over time. Cf. 144.

80. Marguerite Yourcenar articulates Caillois's beliefs well in her introduction to one of his last works, *The Writing of the Stones*: "he advocated an inverted anthropomorphism in which man, instead of attributing his emotions, sometimes condescendingly, to all other living beings, shares humbly, yet perhaps with pride, in everything contained or in-

nate in all three realms, animal, vegetable, and mineral" (xii). Anne Harris beautifully ties Caillois's work to the notion of "acheiropoieta, a principle that explores the 'madness' of things not made by human hands" ("Natural Beauty/Acheiropoieta").

81. Caillois, *The Writing of the Stones*, 1. For Caillois stone does not possess a particular agency. With its coils and convolutions, stone manifests an immanent aesthetic, a compulsion we share with the world itself to engender unnecessary works of allure. Stone is a durable recording device for this impulse.

82. Ibid., 1–2. On the medieval ardor for flecked, striped, patterned, and veined marble for just this innate artfulness, see Carruthers, *The Experience of Beauty in the Middle Ages*, 189–90. When the real material was too expensive or not available, plastered surfaces were sometimes painted to look like variegated stone, such as the faux marble columns of Saint-Savin-sur-Gartempe.

83. Mary Floyd-Wilson makes this point about the survival of vibrant and emanative stones into the early modern period and the discomfort "unseen but material effluvia" that "act on nearby bodies" might have—especially because (in her excellent formulation) "inhumans don't like to share." See "The Preternatural Ecology of 'A Lover's Complaint,'" quotations at 46 and 51.

84. See the work of R. R. Davies, Patricia Ingham, Rhonda Knight, Thorlac Turville-Petre, and Michelle Warren, among many others. Arthurian material emits resonant postcolonial reverberations, and detailing the agonistic layering of cultural differences within such texts (and the archipelago that becomes evident through such analysis) is an important project to which I also have contributed through collaborative publishing projects (see especially the collections *The Postcolonial Middle Ages* and *Cultural Diversity in the British Middle Ages*).

85. Some of my analysis of Geoffrey of Monmouth finds a tentative first expression in my book *Hybridity, Identity and Monstrosity in Medieval Britain*, 69–76.

86. On the ocean's salty relation to blood and the connection of both to an inhuman or blue ecology, see Mentz, "Shakespeare's Beach House," especially 89. Mentz's work throughout his book *At the Bottom of Shakespeare's Ocean* has been inspirational to me in framing what an inhuman ecology might include.

87. Monika Otter describes the episode in appropriately geologic language, observing that a tower built on shaky ground has the effect of "undermin[ing] . . . the substratum" of history that Geoffrey has so far constructed his narrative upon (*Inventiones*, 70).

88. Such moments of "magical," "generic," or "fictional" innovation have often been ascribed to vernacular writing, but as Monika Otter has made clear in her book *Inventiones*, Latin texts were just as capable of such sophisticated moments of creation, fabulation, discovery, and play.

89. Helen Cooper articulates Geoffrey's instigation to romance well when she writes "The larger story of romance begins with Geoffrey of Monmouth, and never quite leaves

him behind" (*The English Romance in Time,* 24). Romance comes from the word *romanz,* that is, French: unlike Geoffrey's Latin history, it is a vernacular genre of wide accessibility.

90. The agency of intratextual things, what Eileen Joy calls "the strange voluptuosity and singular tendencies of textual objects," means that literary texts may possess "propulsions of their own, as actants on the same ontological footing as everything else" ("Notes toward a Speculative Realist Literary Criticism").

91. The idea that Geoffrey opens that portal through which romance will quickly arrive is not new, but see its recent and forceful articulation in Helen Cooper's *English Romance in Time,* which begins its own narration of the genre with the appearance of the *History of the Kings of Britain* in about 1138. See also Wade, *Faeries in Medieval Romance,* 50–62, and Geraldine Heng's important linking of the birth of romance to the Crusades, colonization, and trauma in *Empire of Magic,* 17–61.

92. For an overview of the early romances, see Roberta L. Krueger's introduction to *The Cambridge Companion to Medieval Romance.*

93. On magic objects in Chrétien's works, see Carasso-Bulow, *The "Merveilleux" in Chrétien de Troyes' Romances,* esp. 67–69. Much is at stake, of course, in the romance imagination of a time when histories of peoples do not matter. The darker side of the genre is evident in the cultural dispossessions in which it participates.

94. "plus flanboianz et plus vermauz / que n'est au matin li solauz" (*Yvain,* 426–27).

95. Marbode of Rennes, *De lapidibus,* 420–27. For a demonstration of how lapidary knowledge infiltrated other types of narrative, see Schildgen, "Wonders on the Border."

96. Carasso-Bulow (*The "Merveilleux" in Chrétien de Troyes' Romances,* 76) describes this passage as written within Chrétien's "hyperbolic mode": fantastic objects trigger unexpected material and affective consequences. Timothy Morton gets it right when he insists that "the aesthetic dimension is the causal dimension" ("An Object-Oriented Defense of Poetry," 206).

97. I am quoting from the beautiful description of the material turn in ecological theory by Serenella Iovino and Serpil Oppermann in "Theorizing Material Ecocriticism," 450.

98. Frédéric Godefroy's influential *Dictionnaire de l'ancienne langue française* defined *aventure* as "ce qui arrive inopinément" (that which arrives unexpectedly). Godefroy aligned such unforeseen advent with *hasard, accident, risque, péril,* and *fortune.* These definitions are standard and uncontroversial. Cf., e.g., the entry for *aventure* in Pierre Kunstmann's in-progress *Dictionnaire Électronique de Chrétien de Troyes.*

99. Gervase of Tilbury makes this distinction in his preface to book 3 of the *Otia Imperialia.* Susan Crane details how worldly *aventure* and *merveille* structure Marie de France's *lai Bisclavret* in *Animal Encounters,* 57–63.

100. Citations of the French are from *Les Lais de Marie de France,* ed. Ewert; English translations are from *The Lais of Marie de France,* trans. Robert Hanning and Joan Ferrante. I am indebted to the excellent reading of Marie's *lais* by Cary Howie in *Claustrophilia,*

123–27, and to the magisterial work on her corpus by Sharon Kinoshita and Peggy McCracken in *Marie de France: A Critical Companion.*

101. Aligning the fairy monarch of the otherworld with Giorgio Agamben's idea of the sovereign who can create a "state of exception," James Wade describes the underground Fairy Realm as a space of arbitrariness "where the ordinary rules do not apply" (*Fairies in Medieval Romance,* 80). For Wade the "*unheimliche* strangeness" and "terrible beauty" (79) of this expanse is inexplicable, with no particular message to bear other than that of how power and the law can work.

Excursus

1. Abram, *Becoming Animal,* 4.
2. Ibid., 29.

Soul

1. See Quigley, "Holocaust Memorial."
2. The quotation is from the "Dispute between the Virgin and the Cross," line 226; see "Force."
3. Morton, *The Ecological Thought,* 4.
4. The definitive account of the denial of coevalness and its primitivizing effects is Fabian, *Time and the Other.*
5. Her name may even be derived from a rock: "Droguen," one of the rocks among the Rochers de Penmarch off Brittany's coast. See Tatlock and Mackaye, *Scene of the Franklin's Tale Visited,* 37–41.
6. Friedman, "Dorigen's 'Grisly Rokkes Blake' Again," 140.
7. For a fuller explication of Chaucer's use of Geoffrey of Monmouth and his figuring of Britons and the Welsh, see Lynch, "East Meets West in Chaucer's Squire's and Franklin's Tales" and my "Geographesis, or the Afterlife of Britain in Chaucer."
8. Patricia Ingham suggests this deployment of Fernandez-Armesto's description in relation to the Welsh in *Sovereign Fantasies* (see especially 11, 22–23, 39–40). See also Finke and Shichtman on "anachronistic humans," *King Arthur and the Myth of History,* 33–34.
9. "gens enim rudis et indomita bestiali more uiuens." Letter 87, John of Salisbury, *Letters,* 1:135.
10. Boethius, *Consolatio Philosophiae,* 2 meter 5.
11. For a sophisticated reading of the poem's complicated temporal and environmental entanglements that well contextualizes its sources, see Steel, "A Fourteenth-Century Ecology."
12. Pliny, *Natural History,* 1.1.
13. As has been my practice in this book, to emphasize the diversity and instability of medieval textuality I quote Bartholomaeus Anglicus, *De proprietatibus rerum* (here,

15.50) in the Middle English translation of John Trevisa (here, *On the Properties of Things*, 8.1). Suzanne Conklin Akbari examines the passage in *Idols in the East*, 145–46, focusing on the space it opens for bodily diversity and resolution of binarism in ways that undergird a system of subjugation.

14. On William of Newburgh's life and educational background, see Partner, *Serious Entertainments,* 51–56 and 99–100. I have explored William of Newburgh's relation to Geoffrey at much greater length in "Infinite Realms" and "Green Children from Another World, or The Archipelago in England."

15. "An alium orbem somniat infinita regna habentem?" William of Newburgh, *History of English Affairs,* 1.Prologue.

16. William of Malmesbury, *Gesta Regum Anglorum,* 2.169.

17. See Map, *De Nugis Curialium,* 26–31, and the analysis of the story in Wade, *Fairies in Medieval Romance,* 80, and Dinshaw, *How Soon Is Now?,* 60–63.

18. See Gerald's *Journey through Wales,* 78 in the Latin, 136 in the English translation. Monika Otter aptly describes the underground world as "of great scenic beauty and fruitfulness and possibility," relating its expanses to Gerald's own biography (*Inventiones,* 151). For a compelling reading of Gerald's story as a journey through the earth to the antipodes, see Goldie, *The Idea of the Antipodes,* 64–66.

19. See Siewers, *Strange Beauty* for a thorough (and beautiful) exploration of Irish and Welsh otherworlds (1–33); quotation in preceding sentence from 48. When their entrance opens in mounds, Siewers describes them as "portals of life and death" that offer an otherworld of "ancestral deities, older inhabitants, memory shaping identity with the land, and limits and ambiguities of mortality . . . [an] ecoregion that includes the nonhuman" (47).

20. William of Newburgh, *History of English Affairs,* 1.28. I have examined this moment of invitation at greater length in "Infinite Realms" (emphasizing its British resonance) and "The Future of the Jews of York" (where I dwell upon the feast's resemblance to a seder).

21. Monika Otter analyzes the cup's diminution into ordinariness well in *Inventiones,* where she writes that the cup "is merely traded back and forth between the kings . . . the kings involved do not know what to do with this intruder from another reality" (105).

22. Lynne Bruckner makes this point well in "Teaching Shakespeare in the Ecotone," 223.

23. I examine this process closely in my book *Hybridity, Identity and Monstrosity in Medieval Britain.*

24. I examine this story at greater length and provide a complete bibliography (and more thorough historical context) in "Green Children from Another World, or The Archipelago in England." The paragraphs that follow are a much condensed version of that argument.

25. On the Norman lithicization of the English landscape and postcoloniality, see Howe, "Anglo-Saxon England and the Postcolonial Void," esp. 27–28.

26. William writes that the Britons are relegated to "inviis montibus et saltibus," the last word suggesting rugged pastoral land. On relegating the Welsh to a nonagricultural, "primitive" identity (as opposed to England's field-clearing, cereal-based modernity), see Davies, *First English Empire*, 113–41.

27. For a sophisticated reading along these lines, see Ingham, "Pastoral Histories."

28. Cf. R. R. Davies: "In a world where the advance of bread-grains was much the dominant feature, these societies appeared to be culpably backward and underdeveloped" (*First English Empire*, 124). He then quotes William of Newburgh on the Irish: "The soil of Ireland would be fertile if it did not lack the industry of the dedicated farmer; but the country has an uncivilized and barbarous people, almost lacking in laws and discipline, lazy in agriculture, and thereby living more on milk than on bread" (*History of English Affairs*, 2.26).

29. As Monika Otter observes, the bishop's decision "to rebury the marvel and hide it forever only serves to highlight the stubbornness of such 'real toads.' Reversing the process of discovery does not undo it; covering up the object obviously does not make it go away" (*Inventiones*, 107).

30. See the title of chapter nine of Latour, *Pandora's Hope,* as well as p. 281, on being overtaken by action.

31. Newman, *From Virile Woman to WomanChrist,* 121. Juana realizes that many such stones contain souls, some of which had been imprisoned for centuries. She has them placed within her sickbed so that through her suffering and prayer they may be set free.

32. London, British Library, MS Royal 6 E VI, fol. 94v.

33. Zaleski, *Otherworld Journeys,* 51.

34. Carol Zaleski's review of the possibilities is thorough in *Otherworld Journeys,* 51.

35. On the changes to medieval clerical conceptualizations of matter and the "metaphysical worry" that Aristotle introduced—as well as the continuities with earlier, more Ovidian models—see Bynum, *Christian Materiality,* 234–37.

36. Robert Bartlett charts the challenges Aristotle's works posed, especially to conceptualizing nature, in *The Natural and the Supernatural in the Middle Ages,* 29–32.

37. Soul and body form, in the words of Caroline Walker Bynum, "a psychosomatic unity" (*The Resurrection of the Body in Western Christianity,* esp. 5, 11, 13, 135). On the implications of this model of embodied psyche, see especially Crane, *Performance of the Self,* 90–91.

38. "ioyned to þe body in twey maners, þat is to menynge, as mevere to þe þing þat is imeued, and also as a schipman is i-oned to þe schip" (Bartholomaeus Anglicus, *On the Properties of Things,* 3.3).

39. Bartholomaeus quotes extensively from the *Liber de spiritu et anima,* thought at the time to have been composed by Augustine.

40. *"vegetabilis þat ʒeueþ lif, sensibilis þat ʒeueþ felinge, racionalis þat ʒeueþ resoun"* (Bartholomaeus Anglicus, *On the Properties of Things,* 3.7).

41. See the excellent discussion of Aristotle and human "indistinction" in Feerick and Nardizzi, "Swervings," 2–4. This Aristotelian definition of soul corresponds to the third entry for "soule" in the *Middle English Dictionary.* The primary signification of the word was far more spiritual; it could also mean ghost, person, or capacity for religious experience, emotion, or imagination.

42. "clene withoute soule and withoute felyng, as alle thing that groweth undir grounde and is ygendrede in veynes of the erthe" (Bartholomaeus Anglicus, *On the Properties of Things,* 16.1).

43. Albertus Magnus, *Book of Minerals,* 1.1. Cf. "I have not seen the treatise of Aristotle [on stones], save for some excerpts, for which I have inquired assiduously in different parts of the world" (ibid., 3.1.1).

44. See Dorothy Wyckoff in the introduction to her translation of Albertus Magnus, *Book of Minerals,* xxx. Wyckoff writes that Aristotle is implying that he did compose a text on stones and minerals and that it did not survive, thus leading to Albertus's frustration at discovering only fragments (1.1.1, 2.3.6, 3.1.1). She suggests a date for Albertus's completion of his text of 1261–63 (xl).

45. See Thorndike, "Latin Pseudo-Aristotle," 243.

46. On Albertus and the inauguration of mineral science, see Riddle and Mulholland, "Albert on Stones and Minerals," 204. The geologist Dorothy Wyckoff made a similar argument for Albert's originality and influence in her edition of the *Book of Minerals.*

47. See Wyckoff's introduction to Albertus Magnus, *Book of Minerals,* xxxiv. Albertus distinguishes between two kinds of form, that which is connected to "the nature of the natural body" and that more closely related to the divine, which "is an incorporeal essence, moving and perfecting the body." See ibid., 1.1.6.

48. That is Albertus ventriloquizing Democritus: ibid., 1.1.4.

49. David Macauley examines Thales and souls in *Elemental Philosophy,* 51–52, where he writes that for Thales "what manifests the capacity to stir and change of its own accord is animated."

50. Cf. "no characteristics of life are found in stones" (Albertus Magnus, *Book of Minerals,* 1.1.6).

51. "virtus formans et efficiens lapides et producens ad formam lapidis hujus vel illius" (ibid., 1.1.5).

52. Allen, "Mineral Virtue," 130. *Virtus* is a medieval word intimate to the medieval elaboration of how the soul works, making the possession of *virtus* by rock an intriguing

problem for Albertus rather than (as in the lapidaries) an astonishing force to be cele-brated. I will discuss *virtus* at much greater length later in this chapter.

53. Ibid., 134.

54. Albertus Magnus, *Book of Minerals,* 2.3.6. Albertus is quoting while consider-ably expanding the *Lapidary of Aristotle,* which makes this claim only for magnetite. See Wyckoff's note in *Book of Minerals,* 150.

55. "druynesse [dryness], ouercomyng alle moisture, suffreþ noȝt erthe turne into sadness [solidity, permanence] of stone" (Albertus Magnus, *Book of Minerals,* 16.1); see also the entry for clay (16.2), where it is observed that through coldness water mixed with earth freezes so that "erthe turneþ to stone," while oily earth can be heated into petrification.

56. See Murphy, *Gemstone of Paradise,* 48.

57. Quoted ibid., 44.

58. Bennett, *Vibrant Matter,* 55.

59. Fol. 002r, upper left corner. Fairfax 3 is held by the Bodleian Library, Oxford (as BL 3883) and is contemporary with its author, who may have overseen the work's pro-duction. The image may be accessed online: http://bodley30.bodley.ox.ac.uk:8180/luna/servlet/detail/ODLodl~1~1~44662~113008:Confessio-Amantis—third-version—#.

60. For a compelling reading of Nebuchadnezzar in the *Confessio* as a figure for Islamic empire (in this dream) and later for England's own cultural hybridity, see Deanne Williams, "Gower's Monster." For a discussion of precious stones in Gower, see Heather, "Precious Stones in the Middle-English Verse of the Fourteenth Century."

61. Kellie Robertson captures this interconnection along the ladder of nature elo-quently: "Far from being 'worldless' [as Heidegger claimed], medieval stones were ir-repressibly vital: inner 'virtues' bestowed on them quasi-animate powers of motion and action, while 'mineral souls' linked them to the plants, animals, and humans further along the *scala naturae,* or ladder of nature. Lapidaries and encyclopedias documented the end-lessly entertaining charisma of ostensibly insensible stones . . . understanding of the inter-connectedness of all material bodies suggests that the allegorical reading of stones found in lapidaries were not mere analogies; rather, in a physical world where the rock and the human differ more by degree than by kind, where the divide between the material and the immaterial was not yet so indelible, the reciprocity of moral lessons was underwritten by an ontological connection manifest in the *scala naturae*" ("Exemplary Rocks," 92–93, 99).

62. Kerisel, *Of Stones and Man,* 2.

63. Ibid., 3.

64. Ibid., 4.

65. Notably, one of the first Vulcan "mind melds" is used to connect to the Horta and understand her maternal protectiveness: stone elicits affective connection, even in space.

66. See the *Middle English Dictionary,* "ston" 1g, with its numerous examples of "cold alse an ston" and "ded so ani ston."

67. *King of Tars,* line 585.

68. For example: "Thus for six successive years he [Thomas à Becket] lived in exile, afflicted with diverse and countless injustices. Like a living stone [1 Pet. 2:4–5] that is shaped for building the heavenly palace by many kinds of carving and compression [see Is. 28:16], so the greater the pressure on him to fall, the more firmly and immovably he was proved to stand. Nor indeed with such effort could assayed gold be burned up [see Wis. 3:5–6; Zech. 13:9] or a house built on solid rock be destroyed [Mt. 7:25]" (Head, *Medieval Hagiography,* 569). My thanks to Beth Sutherland for this reference. For a thorough examination of the "living stone" topos, see Plumpe, *"Vivum Saxi, Vivi Lapides"* (discussion of Peter and the church as collectivity of humans figured as building stones at 9).

69. Lupton, "Creature Caliban," 1. Lupton writes movingly of Caliban's loneliness as a spur to reconsidering possible human relations at 13.

70. Noreen Giffney and Myra J. Hird have similarly demonstrated that it is impossible to apply "a hermetic seal to the distinction between—however temporary and shifting—what gets to count as Human and nonhuman" ("Introduction," 5).

71. Braidotti, "Animals, Anomalies, and Inorganic Others," 528.

72. Quotation from Yaeger, "The Death of Nature and the Apotheosis of Trash," 324. Timothy Morton writes of mapping "the ways in which queerness, in its variegated forms, is installed in biological substance as such" ("Queer Ecology," 273–74). Morton's essay makes it clear throughout that the divisions between organic life and inorganic nonlife cannot be sustained. See also Morton's *Ecological Thought,* a project that frequently and inspirationally invokes the notion of a queer ecology. Somewhat perversely, I am also inspired in my thinking here by the work of Will Stockton, who ties the queer to human bodies yet materializes it through incommensurable objects that exist outside human time and will not adapt to linear histories, such as dirt and scatological matter (*Playing Dirty,* xix, 107).

73. Alaimo, *Bodily Natures,* 2. See also this book's introduction.

74. M. Smith, *Against Ecological Sovereignty,* 58.

75. "Utopian not because they exist in some pure form in a metaphysical beyond but precisely because they can offer some guidance to our worldly existence, which is always that of a being-in-the-world, never a purified being separable from the world. . . . Instead of looking for the divine in Man (the metaphysics of the anthropological machine), we might instead try to divine, sense something of (as a water-diviner does), the flows and depths of diverse worldly existences happening beneath their surface appearances" (ibid., 63–64).

76. Wolfe, *Before the Law,* 104.

77. Ibid., 92–93. Wolfe follows Derrida on this point.

78. Alaimo, *Bodily Natures,* 158.

79. "We *must* choose, and by definition we *cannot* choose everyone and everything at once. But this is precisely what ensures that, *in the future, we will have been wrong.* Our 'determinate' act of justice now will have been shown to be *too* determinate, revealed to have left someone or something out" (Wolfe, *Before the Law,* 103). Sobering but necessary knowledge: we always will have failed.

80. I am inspired in my use of the word "doing" here by the work of Anne Harris, in her brilliant essay "Pyromena" (mapping the activity of fire and its ethical wake).

81. "a.b.c. of þinges that ben ygendrede in þe erþe and in veynes þereof" (Albertus Magnus, *Book of Minerals,* 16.Prologue). The majority of lapidaries are alphabetical, but there are exceptions. Isidore of Seville, for example, arranged his discussion of gems around their colors.

82. In a description that fits medieval lapidaries as well as it does the litanies of diverse things for which actor network theory and object-oriented ontology are known, Ian Bogost writes that such collations of the various abandon "anthropocentric narrative coherence in favor of worldly detail," offering an "ontographic cataloguing" that resists reduction into purpose (*Alien Phenomenology,* 42). Comparing the frequent lists of strange items in the work of Bruno Latour and Graham Harman to medieval bestiaries, Bogost describes these "Latour litanies" as "provocations" to ontography ("uncover[ing] the repleteness of units and their interobjectivity . . . interaction through collocation," ibid., 39). Collation serves to emphasize difference and integrity.

83. "Smaragdus virens nimium / Dat lumen oleaginum; / Est fides integerrima, / Ad omne bonum patula, / Quae nunquam scit deficere / A pietatis opere." The text of the lapidary is reproduced as an appendix to Marbode of Renne's *De lapidibus,* 119–21.

84. These pagan materials tended to be serenely absorbed into the storehouse of Christian knowledge: the best way to make use of them, it seems, was not to acknowledge the challenge they often posed. A different model is offered by the Hebrew lapidary of Berakhyah Ben Natronai ha-Nakdan *(Sefer Ko'aḥ ha-Avanim).* Basing his text on a French translation of Marbode's lapidary, Berakhyah purified his materials by eliminating references to pagan mythology.

85. Derived mainly from Bede and Isidore, the brief "Old English Lapidary" names twelve stones from Revelations and is the oldest surviving vernacular example of the genre. The lapidary may be found in Evans and Serjeantson, *English Medieval Lapidaries,* 13–15.

86. The best discussion of Marbode and his lasting influence is John M. Riddle's introduction to *De lapidibus.* Riddle reiterates a traditional division of the lapidaries into three groups: the scientific, the magical, and the Christian. Most lapidaries, however, overlap

these categories significantly. Nichola Erin Harris argues for six lapidary types in "The Idea of Lapidary Medicine," 11–14: mineralogical studies deriving from Theophrastus's *De lapidibus* and culminating in works like Albertus Magnus's *Book of Minerals* and Georgius Agricola's *De natura fossilium*; encyclopedic works like those by Pliny the Elder, Isidore of Seville, Arnold of Saxony, Bartholomaeus Anglicus, Thomas of Cantimpré, and Vincent of Beauvais, all of which contain sections on stones and their properties; verse lapidaries such as Marbode's poem; various prose lapidaries composed in Latin and the vernacular; texts on various subjects that contain an excursus on medicinal properties of stones; and printed popular advice manuals. All the works within Harris's taxonomy, however, contain a common store of information about stones and their powers, and most Western lapidary knowledge derives (as Harris demonstrates) from a total of twelve classical and medieval sources. Quotations from Marbode in my own discussion are from the edition of John M. Riddle and the translation of C. W. King, cited by line numbers and silently emended for clarity.

87. See Evans, *Magical Jewels of the Middle Ages and the Renaissance,* 35.

88. "Quot species lapidum, que nomina, quive colores / Quae sit his region, vel quanta potentia cuique." Quotation from the prologue of Marbode of Rennes, *De lapidibus.*

89. Riddle, "Lithotherapy in the Middle Ages," 50.

90. See "virtus" in Niermeyer, *Mediae Latinitatis Lexicon Minus,* 1111–12, and "vertu" in the *Middle English Dictionary* and the *Anglo-Norman Dictionary*. Having migrated to nonhumans like gems *virtus* then returns to the human through figures like Dante's *donnapetra,* who radiates her lapidary virtue like a diamond. See Durling and Martinez, *Time and the Crystal,* 32.

91. See the *Middle English Dictionary,* "vertu" 3a, "vital force," and the General Prologue of the *Canterbury Tales,* 1.4.

92. "Naturae lapis humanae servire creatus," writes Marbode of Rennes, *De lapidibus,* 468.

93. "Some ben yfounde in veynes of þe erþe and ben ymynede wiþ metalles. [fro] þe inner parties some ben caste vp out of þe grete see and þe place of here generacion is vnknowe. And always suche precious stones ben yfounde in cliffs of þe see and in sonde and in grauel of ryueres. And some breeden in bodyes of foules and of crepyng bestes. But whennes euere þei come þey ben yfounde yhiȝte þer, by þe grace of God, in passyng gret virtue whan þey ben noble and verrey" (Bartholomaeus Anglicus, *On the Properties of Things,* 16.47).

94. "Omnium inferiorum virtutes a superioribus descendere" (Albertus Magnus, *Book of Minerals,* 2.1.3).

95. "For Albert, God was not in each rock, but he had put certain powers into them through secondary causes, including the celestial bodies. Those powers, whatever they

are, can be discovered only by observation of their effects" (Riddle and Mulholland, "Albert on Stones and Minerals," 214).

96. Of this holy matter Derek Krueger writes, "More than ordinary souvenirs, these items conveyed and contained the blessings of the holy places where they were gathered" ("The Religion of Relics," 10), and his essay surveys some of the key texts and provides illustrations of the materials and containers used. A vivid example of the gathering of matter as relics is a sixth-century painted wooden reliquary with an assortment of stones and a fragment of wood taken from the Holy Land. The interior of the box's lid depicts Christ's nativity, baptism, crucifixion, tomb, and ascension; the relics correspond to the depictions. The box was displayed as part of the *Treasures of Heaven* exhibit and an image is reproduced in the catalog twice: p. 37 (Krueger's analysis) and p. 219 (in a discussion of the contemporary collection of rocks as art, especially in Robert Smithson's "Non-sites"). I am grateful to Karen Overbey for sharing her images of lithic relics with me.

97. See Shoham-Steiner, "Jews and Healing at Medieval Saints' Shrines," 114–15. As Shoham-Steiner observes, "This exemplum demonstrates that Jews, especially in dire need, did indeed consider employing Christian relics in domestic medical care or exploring non-Jewish methods of faith healing" (115).

98. For a picture of the Middleham Jewel and a contextualization that includes some similar amulets, see Robinson, "From Altar to Amulet," 114–15, who suggests that the pendant was a birth amulet.

99. By "nontheologized" I do not mean antitheological, but paratheological. That is, *virtus* is in no way dissonant with church teaching; indeed, it is mainly explicated in texts composed by clerics. But it does not necessarily work as allegory, or as a pedagogical tool, and it does not necessarily bring the texts in which it appears back to meditation upon the divine. Medieval Christian theology is generally nonanthropocentric, in that it urges a contempt for this world and for human accomplishments, urging attention upon a heaven to come, God's providence, and eternity. *Virtus* quietly opens a space for the contemplation of the mundane, and the wonders that unfold both outside and within mortal time, without the necessity of making a larger statement about a life to come.

100. Marbode of Rennes, *De lapidibus*, 98. Hildegard of Bingen therefore recommended that pregnant women carry jasper constantly. See her *Liber Quartus: De lapidibus*, 10 (col. 1237); and Riddle's note on p. 41 of his edition of Marbode's *De lapidibus*.

101. The Sloane Lapidary is included in Evans and Serjeantson, *English Medieval Lapidaries*. Quotation from 120.

102. See the version of the medical lapidary in Riddle's edition of Marbode of Rennes, *De lapidibus*, p. 124: "Amethistus, si aqua lavetur, et sterili mulieri detur, continuo concipit."

103. Grosz, *Chaos, Territory, Art*, 63.

104. Ibid., 71, 62.

105. "Art enables matter to become expressive, to not just satisfy but also to inten-sify—to resonate and become more than itself" (ibid., 4). For a more collaborative model of making monuments in which supposedly lifeless objects like stone actually shape human thought and memory as epistemological collaborators, see Flusser and Bec, *Vampyroteuthis Infernalis*, 62–63.

106. Grosz describes the process as a "calling to attention, this making of one's own body into a spectacle" (*Chaos, Territory, Art*, 66).

107. Benjamin, *The Arcades Project*, 8, 79.

108. The quotation is from Morton, "Queer Ecology," 273.

109. Nichola Harris writes that these stones were later identified as "*aëtites* or eagle-stones," offering that they might be geodes ("The Idea of Lapidary Medicine," 47), but Theophrastus does not provide any information that would allow such a naturalization. Pliny says of Theophrastus in his *Natural History* only that the Greek philosopher believed some stones give birth to other stones ("aliquos lapides qui pariant"; see Harris, "The Idea of Lapidary Medicine," 36).

110. Marbode of Rennes, *De lapidibus*, 493–95. Cf. Bartholomaeus Anglicus, who says that he is quoting Damigeron ("Dyascorides") even though the extant text of Damigeron does not have an entry for the stone: "Pionites est lapis qui dicitur esse feminei sexus. Nam certo tempore concipit et parit cum simile lapidem et confert pregnantibus ut dicit Dyas(corides)" (*De proprietatibus rerum*, 16.79). See Riddle's edition of Marbode's *De lapidibus*, 113. The Peterborough Lapidary lists as its penultimate entry *proinces*, which it describes as "stone of femal kend, as it is seyd, for somtyme he conceueþ & bereþ such anoþer stone." See Evans and Serjeantson, *English Medieval Lapidaries*, 118.

111. The quotation is from Riddle's commentary in his edition of Marbode's *De lapidibus* (p. 72), but Wyckoff makes the same observation in her edition of Albertus Magnus (*Book of Minerals*, 2.2.14), as does Nichola Harris ("The Idea of Lapidary Medi-cine," 47).

112. *Physiologus*, trans. Curley, 6.

113. For a good example of fire stones as clothed couple, see Cambridge, St. John's Col-lege, MS A.15, fol. 103v.

114. Kellie Robertson acutely observes, "These anthropomorphizing accounts of fire-producing stones suggest a natural world motivated by recognizably human desires and behaviors. The habit of moralizing rocks in this way seems to reduce the inanimate object to a screen on which the human is projected in grainy but recognizable form" ("Exem-plary Rocks," 93). Robertson argues against such reductive reading (rocks are more than humans in "petric drag") by pointing out that "this allegorized world is one of mutual, rather than unidirectional, influence" (94): both rocks and humans are changed by their proximity and relations.

115. Although fully a part of the *Physiologus* tradition from which the Aberdeen Besti-

ary derives, *adamas* is also a transition to the lapidary that follows. Vellum quality changes at this point, and it is possible the *adamas* portrait is unfinished.

116. Debra Hassig describes the peaceful illustration as almost a landscape portrait: *Medieval Bestiaries*, 117. The illustration is reproduced in her book as figure 120.

117. Cambridge, Gonville and Caius College, MS 384/604, fol. 174. Hassig describes the illustration as conveying "the somewhat distressed, white faces of a man and a woman, each placed in the center of a dark brown, flowerlike rock with orange flames emanating from all sides," an illustration that genders the stones without "sacrificing their rockiness" (*Medieval Bestiaries*, 117). I was unable to obtain permission to reproduce the image.

118. Robertson, "Exemplary Rocks," 106.

119. Some of my thinking here is inspired by Peggy McCracken's breathtaking analysis of the challenges of vegetal identity (as "being and sharing") in the *Roman d'Alexandre;* see "The Floral and the Human."

120. See Albertus Magnus, *Book of Minerals*, 4.2. Valerie Allen explicates the emanative principle lucidly in "Mineral Virtue," 132–33. Rocks for Albertus provide the perfect "wombs" for gestating metals, concentrating the earthly exhalations that form their base. See also Durling and Martinez, *Time and the Crystal,* who write, "Striking in Albert's theory is the projection onto the cosmic scale of the principles of sexual reproduction, the influence of the heavens being parallel to the pouring of seed into the womb of the earth. In essence, this is a version of the ancient myth of the *hieròs gamós,* the marriage of sky and earth. At another level it is interesting as an effort to devise a theory that will give a certain autonomy to earthly process, thought of as initiated by the first causes but proceeding in some sense on its own" (41).

121. "whanne it þondreþ horriblich þe fire eire li3teneþ; whan clowdes smyten togyderes þis stone falleþ" (Bartholomaeus Anglicus, *On the Properties of Things,* 16.31).

122. As Stephen A. Walton points out ("Theophrastus on *Lyngurium*," 365), sexual difference among stones does not originate with Theophrastus, since Babylonian and Egyptian sources allude to the phenomena. Theophrastus is, however, the gateway through which this idea passed to Roman authors and thence to the Middle Ages.

123. Studer and Evans publish the text as the "Second Anglo-Norman Prose Lapidary," where the diamond is described as "a culur de cristal": *Anglo-Norman Lapidaries,* 119.

124. "And it is double, as Isider seiþ, male and female. And always tweyne ben yfounde in þe egles nest: and þe egle may nought breede wiþoute þese stones. . . . Þe male þerof is hard and is liche to a gomme þat is ycleped galle. And þis male is somdel blasynge, and the female is neisshe" (Bartholomaeus Anglicus, *On the Properties of Things,* 16.38).

125. India was in fact the sole source of diamonds in the west until their discovery in Brazil in 1730. See Levinson, "Diamond Sources and Their Discovery," 73.

126. From Mandeville, *Defective Version*, 61. This account is a much amplified meditation on the diamonds of the *Speculum Naturale* of Vincent of Beauvais (8.40), who writes of pearls giving birth via gestation ("quanto mulier foetum gestat in utero suo," 8.107). Mandeville was the popular conduit through which amorous diamonds passed into more widespread medieval knowledge; no writer offers anything like his vision of lithic procreation.

127. I quote from the lively translation of Ian McLeod Higgins, 99. For the French, see Mandeville, *Le Livre des merveilles du monde*, 306.

128. The Latin commandment from Genesis will be quoted shortly after this episode, on the island of Lamory: Mandeville, *Le Livre des merveilles du monde*, 332.

129. "Qe multiplient et engroisent touz les aunz"; "ils croistent touz les aunz visiblement, et ly petitz deviegnent bien grantz": ibid., 306.

130. Many of these diamond traits derive from Pliny the Elder on *adamas* (*Natural History*, 37.15). Pliny called *adamas* "the most highly valued of human possessions."

131. On the lunar orientation of the English—as well as Mandeville's Englishness more generally—see Akbari, *Idols in the East*, 37, 53, 64.

132. "þe worchinges of þe planetis is liche to þat ston magnas *[lapidi magneti]*, adamaunt, & to iren." John Trevisa, cited in the *Middle English Dictionary*, "adama(u)nt" 2.

133. Isidore of Seville, *Etymologies*, 3.29. Robert Bartlett quotes and translates the passage to illustrate the medieval idea that the four constituent elements of the cosmos (earth, air, fire, water) are always in motion, a restless *machina mundi*: *The Natural and the Supernatural in the Middle Ages*, 38.

134. I quote Valerie Allen's apt description of Aristotelian matter in Albertus Magnus from her essay "Mineral Virtue," 129–30.

135. Gregory of Nyssa, *De opificio hominis*, 13.1; PG 44.165A. Mary Carruthers quotes the passage in *The Experience of Beauty in the Middle Ages* and relates it to the fundamental flux of all created matter and to the porous, humoral composition of the body, 32–33.

136. Stones, that is, possess a vibrancy that escapes category and constraint (including human time scales). Within their native temporality they demonstrate what Gilles Deleuze calls *une vie*, an impersonal life ("Immanence"). See also Jane Bennett's inspirational chapter "A Life of Metal," in *Vibrant Matter*, 52–61, where she writes: "As the indefinite article suggests, this is an indeterminate vitality. . . . A life thus names a restless activity, a destructive-creative force that does not coincide fully with any specific body. A life tears the fabric of the actual without ever coming fully 'out' in a person, place or thing. . . . A life is a-subjective" (53–54).

137. See the *Middle English Dictionary* entry for "ston," section 10.

138. See Walton, "Theophrastus on *Lyngurium*," 372.

139. Aelred of Rievaulx, *Spiritual Friendship*, 1.53–54. I thank Travis Neel who in friendship brought this passage to my attention.

140. Bennett, "Earthling, Now and Forever?," 245, 246.

Afterword

1. See John Trevisa's translation of Bartholomaeus Anglicus's *De proprietatibus rerum,* 16.74. In describing stones as the bones of earth's body, Bartholomaeus is directly following Ambrose, but the trope is ubiquitous.

2. Latour, "Why Has Critique Run Out of Steam?," 233.

3. Bartholomaeus Anglicus, *On the Properties of Things,* 15.173. Only polar bears ("white beeres mooste huge and moost fers") seem strong enough to break through this frozen landscape to reveal the movement of water—and fish—nearby. Bartholomaeus describes the generation of crystal through freezing at 16.30.

BIBLIOGRAPHY

The Aberdeen Bestiary. http://www.abdn.ac.uk/bestiary/index.hti.

Abram, David. *Becoming Animal: An Earthly Cosmology.* New York: Vintage, 2010.

Abulafia, Anna Sapir. "Bodies in the Jewish-Christian Debate." In *Framing Medieval Bodies,* ed. Sarah Kay and Miri Rubin, 123–37. Manchester: Manchester University Press, 1994.

———. *Christian-Jewish Relations, 1000–1300: Jews in the Service of Medieval Christendom.* Harlow: Longman, 2011.

Adam of Eynsham. *Magna Vita Sancti Hugonis: The Life of Saint Hugh of Lincoln.* Ed. and trans. Decima L. Douie and Hugh Farmer. London: Thomas Nelson and Sons, 1961.

Aelred of Rievaulx. *Spiritual Friendship.* Ed. Marsha L. Dutton. Trans. Lawrence C. Braceland. Trappist, Ky.: Cistercian Publications, 2010.

Ahmed, Sara. "Open Forum Imaginary Prohibitions: Some Preliminary Remarks on the Founding Gestures of the 'New Materialism.'" *European Journal of Women's Studies* 15 (2008): 23–39.

———. *Queer Phenomenology: Orientations, Objects, Others.* Durham, N.C.: Duke University Press, 2006.

Akbari, Suzanne Conklin. "Becoming Human." *postmedieval* 1 (2010): 272–89.

———. *Idols in the East: European Representations of Islam and the Orient, 1100–1450.* Ithaca: Cornell University Press, 2009.

Alaimo, Stacy. *Bodily Natures: Science, Environment, and the Material Self.* Bloomington: Indiana University Press, 2010.

———. "States of Suspension: Trans-Corporeality at Sea." *Interdisciplinary Studies in Literature and the Environment* 19 (2012): 476–93.

Alaimo, Stacy, and Susan Hekman, eds. *Material Feminisms.* Bloomington: Indiana University Press, 2008.

Alan of Lille. *De Planctu Naturae.* Ed. N. M. Häring. *Studie Medievali,* 3rd series, 19, no. 2 (1978): 797–879.

———. *The Plaint of Nature.* Trans. J. J. Sheridan. Toronto: Pontifical Institute of Mediaeval Studies, 1980.

Albertus Magnus. *Book of Minerals.* Trans. Dorothy Wyckoff. Oxford: Clarendon Press, 1967.

———. *De anima.* In *Alberti Magni opera omnia,* ed. Auguste Borgnet and E. Borgnet, 5:117–443. Paris: L. Vives, 1890. http://arts.uwaterloo.ca/~albertus/PDFs/Borgnet-volumen%2005.pdf.

———. *De mineralibus.* In *Alberti Magni opera omnia,* ed. Auguste Borgnet and E. Borgnet, 5:1–115. Paris: L. Vives, 1890. http://arts.uwaterloo.ca/~albertus/PDFs/Borgnet-volumen%2005.pdf .

———. *De natura locorum.* Trans. Jean Paul Tilmann. In Jean Paul Tilmann, *An Appraisal of the Geographical Works of Albertus Magnus and His Contributions to Geographical Thought.* Ann Arbor: University of Michigan Press, 1971.

Alexander, Caroline. "If the Stones Could Speak: Searching for the Original Meaning of Stonehenge." *National Geographic,* June 2008, 34–59.

Allen, Valerie. "Mineral Virtue." In *Animal, Vegetable, Mineral: Ethics and Objects,* ed. Jeffrey Jerome Cohen, 123–52. Washington, D.C.: Oliphaunt, 2011.

Anglo-Norman Dictionary. http://www.anglo-norman.net/.

Anlezark, Daniel. *Water and Fire: The Myth of the Flood in Anglo-Saxon England.* Manchester: Manchester University Press, 2006.

Appadurai, Arjun, ed. *The Social Life of Things: Commodities in a Cultural Perspective.* Cambridge: Cambridge University Press, 1986.

Aquinas, Thomas. *Summa Theologica.* In *Opera Omnia,* vols. 1–4. New York: Musurgia, 1948–50.

Arnold, John H. *Belief and Unbelief in Medieval Europe.* London: Hodder Arnold, 2005.

Augustine of Hippo. *Concerning the City of God against the Pagans.* Trans. Henry Bettenson. London: Penguin Books, 2003.

———. *The Confessions of Saint Augustine.* Trans. F. J. Sheed. New York: Sheed and Ward, 1943.

———. *Sancti Augustini Opera: De Genesi Contra Manichaeos.* Ed. Dorothea Weber. Vienna: Österreichische Akademie der Wissenschaften, 1998.

Avicenna [Ibn Sīnā]. "On the Formation of Stones and Mountains." In *A Sourcebook in Medieval Science,* ed. Edward Grant, 615–20. Cambridge, Mass.: Harvard University Press, 1974.

Bachelard, Gaston. *Earth and Reveries of the Will: An Essay on the Imagination of Matter.* Trans. Kenneth Haltman. Dallas: Dallas Institute Publications, 2002.

Bagnoli, Martina. "The Stuff of Heaven: Materials and Craftsmanship in Medieval Reliquaries." In *Treasures of Heaven: Saints, Relics, and Devotion in Medieval Europe,* ed. Martina Bagnoli, Holger A. Klein, C. Griffith Mann, and James Robinson, 137–47. New Haven: Yale University Press, 2010.

Bagnoli, Martina, Holger A. Klein, C. Griffith Mann, and James Robinson, eds. *Treasures of Heaven: Saints, Relics, and Devotion in Medieval Europe.* New Haven: Yale University Press, 2010.

Baisier, Léon. *The Lapidaire Chrétien, Its Composition, Its Influence, Its Sources.* Washington, D.C.: Catholic University of America, 1936.

Baker, R. C. "Deep Time, Short Sight: Bracing for Yucca Mountain's Nuclear Forever." *Village Voice,* May 28, 2002. http://www.villagevoice.com/2002-05-28/news/deep -time-short-sight/.

Bale, Anthony. *Feeling Persecuted: Christians, Jews and Images of Violence in the Middle Ages.* London: Reaktion Books, 2010.

———. "Fictions of Judaism in England before 1290." In *The Jews in Medieval Britain: Historical, Literary and Archaeological Perspectives,* ed. Patricia Skinner, 129–44. Woodbridge: Boydell, 2003.

———. *The Jew in the Medieval Book: English Antisemitisms, 1350–1500.* Cambridge: Cambridge University Press, 2006.

Barad, Karen. *Meeting the Universe Halfway: Quantum Physics and the Entanglement of Matter and Meaning.* Durham, N.C.: Duke University Press, 2007.

———. "Posthumanist Performativity: Toward an Understanding of How Matter Comes to Matter." *Signs* 28 (2003): 801–31.

Barndt, Kerstin. "Layers of Time: Industrial Ruins and Exhibitionary Temporalities." *PMLA* 125 (2010): 134–41.

Barney, Stephen A. *The Penn Commentary on Piers Plowman.* Vol. 5. Philadelphia: University of Pennsylvania Press, 2006.

Bartholomaeus Anglicus. *De proprietatibus rerum.* Frankfurt, 1601; reprint, Frankfurt: Minerva, 1964.

———. *De proprietatibus rerum.* Vol. 1, *Introduction génerale, Prohemium, and Libri I–IV.* Ed. B. van den Abeele, H. Meyer, M. W. Twomey, B. Roling, and R. J. Long. Turnhout: Brepols, 2007.

———. *De proprietatibus rerum.* Vol. 6, *Liber XVIII.* Ed. I. Ventura. Turnhout: Brepols, 2007.

———. *On the Properties of Things: John Trevisa's Translation of Bartholomaeus Anglicus "De Proprietatibus Rerum."* Ed. M. C. Seymour. 3 vols. Oxford: Clarendon Press, 1975–89.

Bartlet, Suzanne. "Women in the Medieval Anglo-Jewish Community." In *The Jews in Medieval Britain: Historical, Literary and Archaeological Perspectives,* ed. Patricia Skinner, 113–27. Woodbridge: Boydell, 2003.

Bartlett, Robert. *England under the Norman and Angevin Kings, 1075–1225.* Oxford: Clarendon Press, 2000.

———. *The Natural and the Supernatural in the Middle Ages.* Cambridge: Cambridge University Press, 2008.

Bayless, Martha. "The Story of the Fallen Jew and the Iconography of Jewish Unbelief." *Viator* 34 (2003): 142–56.

Benjamin, Walter. *The Arcades Project.* Cambridge, Mass.: Harvard University Press, 1999.

———. *Selected Writings.* Cambridge, Mass.: Belknap Press, 2002.

Bennett, Jane. "Earthling, Now and Forever?" In *Making the Geologic Now: Responses to the Material Conditions of Contemporary Life,* ed. Elizabeth Ellsworth and Jamie Kruse, 244–46. Brooklyn: Punctum Books, 2012.

———. *The Enchantment of Modern Life: Crossings, Energetics, and Ethics.* Princeton: Princeton University Press, 2001.

———. "Systems and Things: A Response to Graham Harman and Timothy Morton." *New Literary History* 43 (2012): 225–33.

———. *Vibrant Matter: A Political Ecology of Things.* Durham, N.C.: Duke University Press, 2010.

Berakhyah Ben Natronai ha-Nakdan. *Sefer Ko'aḥ ha-Avanim (On the Virtue of the Stones).* Ed. and trans. Gerrit Bos and Julia Zwink. Leiden: Brill, 2010.

Bereton, Georgina, ed. *Des Grantz Geanz: An Anglo-Norman Poem.* Oxford: Basil Blackwell, 1937.

Bernau, Anke. "Beginning with Albina: Remembering the Nation." *Exemplaria* 21 (2009): 247–73.

———. "'Britain': Originary Myths and the Stories of Peoples." In *Oxford Handbook of Medieval Literature in English,* ed. Elaine Treharne and Greg Walker, 629–48. Oxford: Oxford University Press, 2010.

Biale, David. *Blood and Belief: The Circulation of a Symbol between Jews and Christians.* Berkeley: University of California Press, 2007.

Biddick, Kathleen. *The Typological Imaginary: Circumcision, Technology, History.* Philadelphia: University of Pennsylvania Press, 2003.

Biggs, Sarah J. "Isidore of Seville's Etymologies: Who's Your Daddy?" *Medieval Manuscripts Blog.* September 13, 2012. British Library. http://britishlibrary.typepad.co.uk /digitisedmanuscripts/2012/09/isidore-of-sevilles-etymologies.html.

Bishop, Louise M. *Words, Stone and Herbs: The Healing Word in Early Modern England.* Syracuse: Syracuse University Press, 2007.

Boethius. *Consolatio Philosophiae.* Ed. James J. O'Donnell. Bryn Mawr Latin Commentaries 1–2. Bryn Mawr: Bryn Mawr College, 1984; 1990. http://faculty.georgetown.edu /jod/boethius/jkok/list_t.htm.

Bogost, Ian. *Alien Phenomenology, or, What It's Like to Be a Thing.* Minneapolis: University of Minnesota Press, 2012.

——. "The New Aesthetic Needs to Get Weirder." *The Atlantic,* April 13, 2012. http:// www.theatlantic.com/technology/archive/2012/04/the-new-aesthetic-needs-to -get-weirder/255838/.

——. *Unit Operations: An Approach to Videogame Criticism.* Cambridge, Mass.: MIT Press, 2006.

Bohak, Gideon. *Ancient Jewish Magic: A History.* Cambridge: Cambridge University Press, 2008.

The Book of Enoch, or I Enoch. Trans. R. H. Charles. Oxford: Clarendon Press, 1912.

Boone, Elizabeth Hill, and Walter D. Mignolo, eds. *Writing without Words: Alternative Literacies in Mesoamerica and the Andes.* Durham, N.C.: Duke University Press, 1994.

Boswell, James. *The Life of Samuel Johnson.* Ed. Christopher Hibbert. London: Penguin, 1986.

Bowers, John M. *An Introduction to the Gawain Poet.* Gainesville: University Press of Florida, 2012.

Boyarin, Daniel. *Border Lines: The Partition of Judaeo-Christianity.* Philadelphia: University of Pennsylvania Press, 2004.

——. *Dying for God: Martyrdom and the Making of Christianity and Judaism.* Berkeley: University of California Press, 1999.

Boyle, T. Coraghessan. *Descent of Man: Stories.* New York: Penguin, 1990.

Braidotti, Rosi. "Animals, Anomalies, and Inorganic Others." *PMLA* 124 (2009): 526–32.

Brand, Stewart. *The Clock of the Long Now.* New York: Basic Books, 1999.

Braude, Benjamin. "*Mandeville*'s Jews among Others." In *Pilgrims and Travelers to the Holy Land,* ed. Bryan F. Le Beau and Menachem Mor, 133–58. Omaha, Neb.: Creighton University Press, 1996.

Brayton, Dan. *Shakespeare's Ocean.* Charlottesville: University of Virginia Press, 2012.

Brayton, Dan, and Lynne Bruckner. "Introduction: Warbling Invaders." In *Ecocritical Shakespeare,* ed. Lynne Bruckner and Dan Brayton, 1–9. Farnham: Ashgate, 2011.

Brook, G. L., ed. *The Harley Lyrics: The Middle English Lyrics of M.S. Harley 2253.* Manchester: Manchester University Press, 1956.

Brown, Bill. "Objects, Others, and Us (the Refabrication of Things)." *Critical Inquiry* 36, no. 2 (2010): 183–217.

——. "Thing Theory." In *Things,* ed. Bill Brown, 1–22. Chicago: University of Chicago Press, 2004.

——, ed. "Things." Special issue, *Critical Inquiry* 28, no. 1 (2001).

Bruckner, Lynne. "Teaching Shakespeare in the Ecotone." In *Ecocritical Shakespeare,* ed. Lynne Bruckner and Dan Brayton, 223–37. Farnham: Ashgate, 2011.

Bryant, Levi R. *The Democracy of Objects.* Ann Arbor: Open Humanities Press, 2011.

———. "The Dynamic Life of Objects." *Larval Subjects* (blog). January 12, 2012. http://larvalsubjects.wordpress.com/2012/01/12/the-dynamic-life-of-objects/.

———. "Social Constructivism Again: What SR Means to Me." *Larval Subjects* (blog). May 9, 2012. http://larvalsubjects.wordpress.com/2012/05/09/social-constructivism-again-what-sr-means-to-me/.

———. "Speculative Realist Literary Criticism." *Larval Subjects* (blog). December 23, 2011. http://larvalsubjects.wordpress.com/2011/12/23/speculative-realist-literary-criticism/.

Bryant, Levi, Graham Harman, and Nick Srnicek, eds. *The Speculative Turn: Continental Materialism and Realism.* Melbourne: re.press, 2011.

Bryan-Wilson, Julia. "Building a Marker of Nuclear Warning." In *Monuments and Memory, Made and Unmade,* ed. Robert S. Nelson and Margaret Olin, 183–204. Chicago: University of Chicago Press, 2003.

Buell, Lawrence. *The Future of Environmental Criticism: Environmental Crisis and Literary Imagination.* Oxford: Blackwell, 2005.

Burger, Glenn, and Steven Kruger. "Introduction." In *Queering the Middle Ages,* ed. Glenn Burger and Steven Kruger, xi–xxiii. Minneapolis: University of Minnesota Press, 2001.

Burl, Aubrey. *Prehistoric Avebury.* 2nd ed. New Haven: Yale University Press, 2002.

———. *The Stone Circles of Britain, Ireland and Brittany.* New Haven: Yale University Press, 2000.

Burns, E. Jane. *Sea of Silk: A Textile Geography of Women's Work in Medieval French Literature.* Philadelphia: University of Pennsylvania Press, 2009.

Butler, Judith. *Bodies That Matter: On the Discursive Limits of "Sex."* New York: Routledge, 1993.

Bynum, Caroline Walker. *Christian Materiality: An Essay on Religion in Late Medieval Europe.* New York: Zone Books, 2011.

———. *Metamorphosis and Identity.* New York: Zone Books, 2001.

———. *The Resurrection of the Body in Western Christianity, 200–1336.* New York: Columbia University Press, 1995.

Byrne, Aisling. "The Archipelagic Otherworld: Geography and Identity in Medieval Ireland and Britain." Paper presented at the New Chaucer Society Biennial Congress, Siena, 2010.

Caillois, Roger. *The Writing of the Stones.* Trans. Barbara Bray. Charlottesville: University of Virginia Press, 1985.

Campbell, Mary Baine. *The Witness and the Other World: Exotic European Travel Writing, 400–1600.* Ithaca: Cornell University Press, 1988.

Carasso-Bulow, Lucienne. *The "Merveilleux" in Chrétien de Troyes' Romances.* Geneva: Librairie Droz, 1976.

Carley, James P., and Julia Crick, eds. "Constructing Albion's Past: An Annotated Edition of *De origine gigantum.*" In *Arthurian Literature,* vol. 13, ed. James Carley and Felicity Riddy, 41–114. Cambridge: D. S. Brewer, 1995.

Carruthers, Mary. *The Experience of Beauty in the Middle Ages.* Oxford: Oxford University Press, 2013.

Cavell, Stanley. *The Claim of Reason: Wittgenstein, Skepticism, Morality, and Tragedy.* Oxford: Oxford University Press, 1979.

Chaganti, Seeta. "Choreographing *Mouvance*: The Case of the English Carol." *Philological Quarterly* 87 (2008): 77–103.

———. "Vestigial Signs: Inscription, Performance, and *The Dream of the Rood.*" *PMLA* 125 (2010): 48–72.

Champion, Matthew. *Seahenge: A Contemporary Chronicle.* Norfolk: Barnwell's Printing, 2000.

Chaucer, Geoffrey. *The Riverside Chaucer.* Gen. ed. Larry D. Benson. 3rd ed. New York: Houghton Mifflin, 1987.

Chayes, Evelien. *L'Éloquence des Pierres précieuses: De Marbode de Rennes à Alard d'Amsterdam et Rémy Belleau. Sur quelques lapidaires du XVIe siècle.* Paris: Honoré Champion, 2010.

Chazan, Robert. *Reassessing Jewish Life in Medieval Europe.* Cambridge: Cambridge University Press, 2010.

Chen, Mel Y. *Animacies: Biopolitics, Racial Mattering, and Queer Affect.* Durham, N.C.: Duke University Press, 2012.

Chenu, Marie-Dominique. *Nature, Man and Society in the Twelfth Century.* Trans. Jerome Taylor and Lester K. Little. Toronto: University of Toronto Press, 1997.

Chippindale, Christopher. *Stonehenge Complete.* Rev. ed. London: Thames & Hudson, 1994.

Chrétien de Troyes. Paris, Bibliothèque Nationale de France, MS Français 794. http://gallica.bnf.fr/ark:/12148/btv1b84272526/f13.item.

———. *Romans: suivis des Chansons, avec un appendice Philomena, sous la direction de Michel Zink. éd. et trad. de J.M.Fritz pour Erec et Enide; Ch. Méla et O. Collet pour Cligès; Ch. Méla pour Le Chevalier de la charette et le Conte du Graal; D.F. Hult pour Le Chevalier au lion; M.-Cl. Zai pour les chansons; O.Collet pour Philomena.* Paris: Librairie générale française, 1994.

"Cleanness." In *The Gawain Poet: Complete Works,* trans. Marie Borroff. New York: W. W. Norton, 2011.

"Cleanness." In *The Poems of the Pearl Manuscript: "Pearl," "Cleanness," "Patience," "Sir*

Gawain and the Green Knight," 5th ed., ed. Malcolm Andrew and Ronald Waldron. Exeter: University of Exeter Press, 2007.

Cohen, Claudine. *The Fate of the Mammoth: Fossils, Myth, and History.* Trans. William Rodarmor. Chicago: University of Chicago Press, 2002.

Cohen, Jeffrey Jerome. "An Abecedarium for the Elements." *postmedieval* 2 (2011): 291–303.

———, ed. *Animal, Vegetable, Mineral: Ethics and Objects.* Washington, D.C.: Oliphaunt, 2011.

———, ed. *Cultural Diversity in the British Middle Ages: Archipelago, Island, England.* New York: Palgrave Macmillan, 2008.

———. "The Future of the Jews of York." In *Christians and Jews in Medieval England: Narratives and Contexts for the York 1190 Massacre,* ed. Sarah Rees Jones and Sethina Watson, 278–93. Suffolk: Boydell and Brewer, 2013.

———. "The Future of 'The Weight of the Past.'" *In the Middle* (blog). February 8, 2009. http://www.inthemedievalmiddle.com/2009/02/future-of-weight-of-past.html.

———. "Geographesis, or The Afterlife of Britain in Chaucer." Forthcoming.

———. "Green Children from Another World, or The Archipelago in England." In *Cultural Diversity in the British Middle Ages: Archipelago, Island, England,* ed. Jeffrey Jerome Cohen, 75–94. New York: Palgrave Macmillan, 2008.

———. *Hybridity, Identity and Monstrosity in Medieval Britain: On Difficult Middles.* New York: Palgrave, 2006.

———. "Introduction: Infinite Realms." In *Cultural Diversity in the British Middle Ages: Archipelago, Island, England,* ed. Jeffrey Jerome Cohen, 1–16. New York: Palgrave Macmillan, 2008.

———. "Inventing with Animals in the Middle Ages." In *Engaging with Nature: Essays on the Natural World in Medieval and Early Modern Europe,* ed. Barbara A. Hanawalt and Lisa J. Kiser, 39–62. Notre Dame: University of Notre Dame Press, 2008.

———. *Of Giants: Sex, Monsters and the Middle Ages.* Minneapolis: University of Minnesota Press, 1999.

———, ed. *The Postcolonial Middle Ages.* New York: Palgrave, 2000.

———, ed. *Prismatic Ecologies: Ecotheory beyond Green.* Minneapolis: University of Minnesota Press, 2013.

Cohen, Jeffrey Jerome, and Lowell Duckert, eds. "Ecomaterialism." Special issue, *postmedieval* 4 (2013).

———, eds. *Elemental Ecocriticism.* Minneapolis: University of Minnesota Press, forthcoming.

Cohen, Jeremy. *Living Letters of the Law: Ideas of the Jew in Medieval Christianity.* Berkeley: University of California Press, 1999.

———. *Sanctifying the Name of God: Jewish Martyrs and Jewish Memories of the First Crusade.* Philadelphia: University of Pennsylvania Press, 2006.

Cohn, Norman. *Noah's Flood: The Genesis Story in Western Thought.* New Haven: Yale University Press, 1996.

Collingwood, R. G. *The Idea of Nature.* Oxford: Clarendon Press, 1945.

Connolly, William E. "Materialities of Experience." In *New Materialisms: Ontology, Agency, and Politics,* ed. Diana Coole and Samantha Frost, 178–200. Durham, N.C.: Duke University Press, 2010.

Coole, Diana, and Samantha Frost. "Introducing the New Materialisms." In *New Materialisms: Ontology, Agency, and Politics,* ed. Diana Coole and Samantha Frost, 1–43. Durham, N.C.: Duke University Press, 2010.

———, eds. *New Materialisms: Ontology, Agency, and Politics.* Durham, N.C.: Duke University Press, 2010.

Coomans, Thomas. "'Produits du terroir' et 'appellations contrôlées': Le role des pierres à bâtir dans le definition des écoles regionals d'architecture medieval en Belgique." In *Ex Quadris Lapidibus: La pierre et sa mise en oeuvre dans l'art medieval: mélanges d'histoire de l'art offerts à Éliane Vergnolle,* ed. Yves Gallet, 221–32. Turnhout: Brepols, 2011.

Cooper, Helen. *The English Romance in Time: Transforming Motifs from Geoffrey of Monmouth to the Death of Shakespeare.* Oxford: Oxford University Press, 2004.

The Corpus of Anglo Saxon Stone Sculpture. http://www.ascorpus.ac.uk/index.php.

Crane, Susan. *Animal Encounters: Contacts and Concepts in Medieval Britain.* Philadelphia: University of Pennsylvania Press, 2013.

———. *Gender and Romance in Chaucer's "Canterbury Tales."* Princeton: Princeton University Press, 1994.

———. *Performance of the Self: Ritual, Clothing, and Identity during the Hundred Years War.* Philadelphia: University of Pennsylvania Press, 2002.

Cronon, William. "Introduction: In Search of Nature." In *Uncommon Ground: Toward Reinventing Nature,* ed. William Cronon, 23–56. New York: Norton, 1995.

Cruikshank, Julie. *Do Glaciers Listen? Local Knowledge, Colonial Encounters, and Social Imagination.* Vancouver: University of British Columbia Press, 2005.

Cuomo, Chris J. *Feminism and Ecological Communities: An Ethic of Flourishing.* London: Routledge, 1998.

Cutler, Alan. *The Seashell on the Mountaintop: A Story of Science, Sainthood, and the Humble Genius Who Discovered a New History of the Earth.* New York: Penguin, 2003.

Dales, Richard C. "Marius 'On the Elements' and the Twelfth-Century Science of Matter." *Viator* 3 (1972): 191–218.

Damigeron. *De Virtutibus Lapidum.* Ed. Joel Radcliffe. Trans. Patricia P. Tahil. Seattle: Ars Obsura, 1989.

Daniell, Christopher. *Death and Burial in Medieval England: 1066–1550.* London: Routledge, 1997.

Darvil, Timothy, and Geoffrey Wainwright. "Stonehenge Excavations 2008." *Antiquaries Journal* 89 (2009): 1–19.

Davies, Daniel. "Lithographia." *The Oyster's Earrings* (blog). May 23, 2013. http://theoysters earrings.wordpress.com/2013/05/23/lithographia/.

Davies, R. R. *The First English Empire: Power and Identity in the British Isles, 1093–1343.* Oxford: Oxford University Press, 2000.

Dean, Carolyn. *A Culture of Stone: Inka Perspectives on Rock.* Durham, N.C.: Duke University Press, 2010.

Dean, James. "The World Grown Old and Genesis in Middle English Historical Writings." *Speculum* 57 (1982): 548–68.

De Landa, Manuel. *A New Philosophy of Society: Assemblage Theory and Social Complexity.* London: Continuum, 2006.

———. *A Thousand Years of Nonlinear History.* New York: Serve Editions, 2000.

Delaney, Sheila. *Chaucer and the Jews: Sources, Contexts, Meanings.* New York: Routledge, 2002.

Deleuze, Gilles. "Immanence: A Life. . . ." *Theory, Culture & Society* 14, no. 2 (1997): 3–7.

Deleuze, Gilles, and Félix Guattari. *A Thousand Plateaus: Capitalism and Schizophrenia.* Trans. Brian Massumi. Minneapolis: University of Minnesota Press, 1987.

———. *What Is Philosophy?* Trans. Hugh Tomlinson and Graham Burchell. New York: Columbia University Press, 1991.

Deluz, Christiane. *Le Livre de Jehan de Mandeville: Une "géographie" au XIVe siècle.* Louvain-la-Neuve: Institut d'Études Médiévales de l'Université Catholique de Louvain, 1988.

Denison, Simon, ed. "Lost Skeleton of 'Barber-Surgeon' Found in Museum." *British Archaeology* 48 (1999). http://www.archaeologyuk.org/ba/ba48/ba48news.html.

Derrida, Jacques. *L'animal que donc je suis.* Ed. Marie-Louise Mallet. Paris: Galilée, 2006.

———. *The Animal That Therefore I Am.* Trans. David Wills. New York: Fordham University Press, 2008.

Dictionnaire Électronique de Chrétien de Troyes. LFA/Université d'Ottawa ATILF/Université de Lorraine. http://www.atilf.fr/dect.

Dinshaw, Carolyn. *How Soon Is Now? Medieval Texts, Amateur Readers, and the Queerness of Time.* Durham, N.C.: Duke University Press, 2012.

———. "Theorizing Queer Temporalities." *GLQ* 13 (2007): 177–95.

"The Dispute between the Virgin and the Cross." In *The Minor Poems of the Vernon Manuscript,* part 2, ed. F. J. Furnivall, EETS 117. London: Kegan Paul, Trench, Trübner, 1901; reprint, 1987.

Dobson, Barrie. *The Jews of Medieval York and the Massacre of March 1190.* York: University of York, 1974; rev. 1996.

———. "The Medieval York Jewry Reconsidered." In *The Jews in Medieval Britain: Histori-*

cal, Literary and Archaeological Perspectives, ed. Patricia Skinner, 145–56. Woodbridge: Boydell, 2003.

Donadio, Rachel. "The Closest Reader." *New York Times Review of Books,* December 10, 2006. http://www.nytimes.com/2006/12/10/books/review/Donadio.t.html.

Duckert, Lowell. "Glacier." *postmedieval* 4 (2013): 68–79.

———. "Speaking Stones, John Muir, and a Slower (Non)humanities." In *Animal, Vegetable, Mineral: Ethics and Objects,* ed. Jeffrey Jerome Cohen, 273–79. Washington, D.C.: Oliphaunt, 2011.

Duffin, Christopher J. "Lapis Judaicus or the Jews' Stone: The Folklore of Fossil Echinoid Spines." *Proceedings of the Geologists' Association* 117 (2006): 265–75.

Dundes, Alan, ed. *The Flood Myth.* Berkeley: University of California Press, 1988.

Durling, Robert M., and Ronald L. Martinez. *Time and the Crystal: Studies in Dante's Rime Petrose.* Berkeley: University of California Press, 1990. http://publishing.cdlib.org /ucpressebooks/view?docId=ft8s200961&brand=ucpress.

Economou, George. *The Goddess Natura in Medieval Literature.* Cambridge, Mass.: Harvard University Press, 1972.

Edmondson, George. "Naked Chaucer." In *The Post-Historical Middle Ages,* ed. Elizabeth Scala and Sylvia Federico, 139–60. New York: Palgrave Macmillan, 2009.

———. *The Neighboring Text: Chaucer, Boccaccio, Henryson.* Notre Dame: University of Notre Dame Press, 2011.

———. "*Pearl*: The Shadow of the Object, the Shape of the Law." *Studies in the Age of Chaucer* 26 (2004): 29–63.

Edwards, John. "The Church and the Jews in Medieval England." In *The Jews in Medieval Britain: Historical, Literary and Archaeological Perspectives,* ed. Patricia Skinner, 85–95. Woodbridge: Boydell, 2003.

Eidelberg, Shlomo. *The Jews and the Crusaders: The Hebrew Chronicles of the First and Second Crusades.* Madison: University of Wisconsin Press, 1977.

Einbinder, Susan L. *Beautiful Death: Jewish Poetry and Martyrdom in Medieval France.* Princeton: Princeton University Press, 2002.

———. *No Place of Rest: Jewish Literature, Expulsion, and the Memory of Medieval France.* Philadelphia: University of Pennsylvania Press, 2009.

Elliott, Ralph. "Landscape and Geography." In *A Companion to the Gawain-Poet,* ed. Derek Brewer and Jonathan Gibson, 105–17. Cambridge: D. S. Brewer, 1997.

Ellsworth, Elizabeth, and Jamie Kruse, eds. *Making the Geologic Now: Responses to the Material Conditions of Contemporary Life.* Brooklyn: Punctum Books, 2012.

Elrington, C. R., ed. "Parishes: Tredington." *A History of the County of Gloucester.* Vol. 8. British History Online. http://www.british-history.ac.uk/report.aspx?compid=66406.

Epstein, Steven A. *The Medieval Discovery of Nature.* Cambridge: Cambridge University Press, 2012.

Evans, Joan. *Magical Jewels of the Middle Ages and the Renaissance, Particularly in England.* London: Oxford University Press, 1921.

Evans, Joan, and Mary S. Serjeantson, eds. *English Medieval Lapidaries.* London: Oxford University Press, 1933.

Evershed, S. "A Bitorne's Clee." In *Sussex Archaeological Collections Relating to the History and Antiquities of the County,* 20:226–27. Lewes: George P. Bacon, 1868.

Fabian, Johannes. *Time and the Other: How Anthropology Makes Its Object.* New York: Columbia University Press, 1983.

Feerick, Jean E. "Economies of Nature in Shakespeare." *Shakespeare Studies* 39 (2011): 32–42.

Feerick, Jean E., and Vin Nardizzi. "Swervings: On Human Indistinction." In *The Indistinct Human in Renaissance Literature,* ed. Jean E. Feerick and Vin Nardizzi, 1–12. New York: Palgrave Macmillan, 2012.

Finke, Laurie A., and Martin B. Shichtman. *King Arthur and the Myth of History.* Gainesville: University Press of Florida, 2004.

Flanagan, Sabrina. *Doubt in an Age of Faith: Uncertainty in the Long Twelfth Century.* Turnhout: Brepols, 2008.

Floyd-Wilson, Mary. *English Ethnicity and Race in Early Modern Drama.* Cambridge: Cambridge University Press, 2003.

———. "The Preternatural Ecology of 'A Lover's Complaint.'" *Shakespeare Studies* 39 (2011): 43–53.

Floyd-Wilson, Mary, and Garrett Sullivan, eds. *Embodiment and Environment in Early Modern England.* London: Palgrave, 2007.

Flusser, Vilém, and Louis Bec. *Vampyroteuthis Infernalis: A Treatise, with a Report by the Institut Scientifique de Recherche Paranaturaliste.* Trans. Valentine A. Palis. Minneapolis: University of Minnesota Press, 2012.

Foucault, Michel. "The Masked Philosopher." In *Ethics, Subjectivity and Truth: The Essential Works of Michel Foucault 1954–1984,* ed. James D. Faubion, trans. Robert Hurley et al., 1:321–28. Harmondsworth: Penguin, 1997.

Fradenburg, L. O. Aranye. "Criticism, Anti-Semitism, and the *Prioress's Tale.*" *Exemplaria* 1 (1989): 69–115.

———. "Simply Marvellous." *Studies in the Age of Chaucer* 26 (2004): 1–27.

Freeman, Elizabeth. "Time Binds, or, Erotohistory." *Social Text* 23 (2005): 57–68.

Friedman, John B. "Dorigen's 'Grisly Rokkes Blake' Again." *Chaucer Review* 31 (1996): 133–44.

Frojmovic, Eva. "Early Ashkenazic Prayer Books and Their Christian Illuminators." In *Crossing Borders: Hebrew Manuscripts as a Meeting-Place of Cultures,* ed. Piet van Boxel and Sabine Arndt, 45–56. Oxford: Bodleian Library, 2009.

Frow, John. "A Pebble, a Camera, a Man Who Turns into a Telegraph Pole." In *Things*, ed. Bill Brown, 346–61. Chicago: University of Chicago Press, 2004.

Fry, Tony. *Becoming Human by Design*. London: Berg, 2012.

Gallet, Yves, ed. *Ex Quadris Lapidibus: La pierre et sa mise en oeuvre dans l'art medieval: mélanges d'histoire de l'art offerts à Éliane Vergnolle*. Turnhout: Brepols, 2011.

Garland-Thomson, Rosemarie. "Misfits: A Feminist Materialist Disability Concept." *Hypatia* 26 (2011): 591–609.

Garrett, R. M. *Precious Stones in Old English Literature*. Münchener Beitrage zur Romanischen und Englischen Philologie 47 (Leipzig: A. Deichert nachf. [G. Böhme], 1909)

Geary, Patrick. *Phantoms of Remembrance: Memory and Oblivion at the End of the First Millennium*. Princeton: Princeton University Press, 1994.

Geoffrey of Monmouth. *The Historia Regum Britannie*. Vol. 1, *Bern, Bürgerbibliothek MS 568 (the 'Vulgate' Version)*. Ed. Neil Wright. Cambridge: D. S. Brewer, 1984.

———. *The History of the Kings of Britain*. Trans. Lewis Thorpe. London: Penguin, 1966.

———. *The History of the Kings of Britain: An Edition and Translation of the "De gestis Britonum"* (Historia regum Britanniae). Ed. Michael D. Reeve. Trans. Neil Wright. Woodbridge: Boydell & Brewer, 2007.

Gerald of Wales. *Giraldi Cambrensis Opera*. Ed. J. S. Brewer. London, 1862.

———. *The History and Topography of Ireland*. Trans. John J. O'Meara. London: Penguin Books, 1982.

———. *Itinerarium Kambriae [Journey Through Wales]*. Vol. 6 of *Giraldi Cambrensis Opera*, ed. J. S. Brewer, J. F. Dimock, and G. F. Warner, 8 vols., Rolls Series 21. London, 1861–91.

———. *The Jewel of the Church*. Trans. John J. Hagen. Leiden: E. J. Brill, 1979.

———. *The Journey through Wales and The Description of Wales*. Trans. Lewis Thorpe. London: Penguin Books, 1978.

Gervase of Tilbury. *Otia Imperialia: Recreation for an Emperor*. Ed and trans. S. E. Banks and J. W. Binns. Oxford: Clarendon Press, 2002.

Giffney, Noreen, and Myra J. Hird. "Introduction: Queering the Non/Human." In *Queering the Non/Human*, ed. Noreen Giffney and Myra J. Hird, 1–16. Aldershot: Ashgate, 2008.

Glacken, Clarence. *Traces on the Rhodian Shore: Nature and Culture in Western Thought from Ancient Times to the End of the Eighteenth Century*. Berkeley: University of California Press, 1967.

Glotfelty, Cheryll, and Harold Fromm, eds. *The Ecocriticism Reader: Landmarks in Literary History*. Athens: University of Georgia Press, 1996.

Godard, Gaston. "The Fossil Proboscideans of Utica (Tunisia), A Key to the 'Giant' Controversy, from Saint Augustine (424) to Peiresc (1632)." *Geological Society, London, Special Publications* 310, no. 1 (2009): 67–76.

Godefroy, Frédéric. *Dictionnaire de l'ancienne langue française et de tous ses dialectes du IXème au XVème siècle.* 10 vols. 1880–95. http://www.micmap.org/dicfro/.

Goldberg, Jonathan. *The Seeds of Things: Theorizing Sexuality and Materiality in Renaissance Representations.* New York: Fordham University Press, 2009.

Goldie, Matthew Boyd. *The Idea of the Antipodes: Place, People, and Voices.* New York: Routledge, 2010.

Gould, Stephen Jay. *Time's Arrow, Time's Cycle: Myth and Metaphor in the Discovery of Geological Time.* Cambridge, Mass.: Harvard University Press, 1987.

Gow, Andrew Colin. *The Red Jews: Antisemitism in an Apocalyptic Age, 1200–1600.* Leiden: E. J. Brill, 1995.

Gower, John. *Confessio Amantis.* Vol. 1. Ed. Russell A. Peck, with Latin translations by Andrew Galloway. Kalamazoo: Medieval Institute Publications, 2000; 2nd ed., 2006. http://d.lib.rochester.edu/teams/publication/peck-confessio-amantis-volume-1.

———. *Vox clamantis.* In *The Complete Works of John Gower,* ed. G. C. Macaulay. Oxford: Clarendon Press, 1899–1902; reprint, Grosse Pointe, Mich.: Scholarly Press, 1968.

Grady, Frank. *Representing Righteous Heathens in Late Medieval England.* New York: Palgrave Macmillan, 2005.

Grant, George. *The Foundations of Modern Science in the Middle Ages: Their Religious, Institutional, and Intellectual Contexts.* Cambridge: Cambridge University Press, 1996.

———. *God and Reason in the Middle Ages.* Cambridge: Cambridge University Press, 2001.

Greenblatt, Stephen. *Marvelous Possessions: The Wonder of the New World.* Chicago: University of Chicago Press, 1991.

Greene, Virginia, Sarah Kay, Sharon Kinoshita, Peggy McCracken, and Zrinka Stahuljak. *Thinking Through Chrétien de Troyes.* Woodbridge: Boydell & Brewer, 2011.

Gregory. *Moralia in Job S. Gregorii Magni.* Ed. Mark Adriaen. 3 vols. Corpus Christianorum Series Latina 143–143B. Turnhout: Brepols, 1979.

———. *Morals on the Book of Job.* Trans. in *A Library of Fathers of the Holy Catholic Church,* vols. 18, 21, 23, and 31. Oxford: J. H. Parker, 1844–50. http://www.lectionarycentral.com/GregoryMoraliaIndex.html.

Gross, Kenneth. *The Dream of the Moving Statue.* University Park: Pennsylvania State University Press, 2006.

———. *Puppet: An Essay on Uncanny Life.* Chicago: University of Chicago Press, 2011.

Grosz, Elizabeth. *Chaos, Territory, Art: Deleuze and the Framing of the Earth.* New York: Columbia University Press, 2008.

Guyénot, Laurent. *La Mort Féerique: Anthropologie du Merveilleux XIIe–XVe Siècle.* Paris: Gallimard, 2011.

Hache, Émilie, and Bruno Latour. "Morality or Moralism? An Exercise in Sensitization." Trans. Patrick Camiller. *Common Knowledge* 16, no. 2 (2010): 311–30.

Hacking, Ian. *The Social Construction of What?* Cambridge, Mass.: Harvard University Press, 1999.

Hajer, Charlotte. "Long Poetry: The Letters of Utrecht." The Long Now Foundation. March 29, 2012. http://blog.longnow.org/02012/03/29/long-poetry-the-letters-of-utrecht/.

Hamilton, G. L. "Storm-Making Springs: Studies on the Sources of *Yvain.*" *Romantic Review* 2, no. 4 (1911): 355–75.

Hanawalt, Barbara A., and Lisa J. Kiser. "Introduction." In *Engaging with Nature: Essays on the Natural World in Medieval and Early Modern Europe,* ed. Barbara A. Hanawalt and Lisa J. Kiser, 1–10. Notre Dame: University of Notre Dame Press, 2008.

Hanna, Ralph. "Mandeville." In *Middle English Prose: A Critical Guide to Major Authors and Genres,* ed. A. S. G. Edwards, 121–32. New Brunswick: Rutgers University Press, 1984.

Hanning, Robert. *The Vision of History in Early Britain: From Gildas to Geoffrey of Monmouth.* New York: Columbia University Press, 1966.

Hansen, Abby Jane Dubman. "Shakespeare and the Lore of Precious Stones." *College Literature* 4 (1977): 210–19.

Haraway, Donna. *Crystals, Fabrics and Fields: Metaphors of Organicism in Twentieth-Century Developmental Biology.* New Haven: Yale University Press, 1976.

———. *Simians, Cyborgs, and Women: The Reinvention of Nature.* New York: Routledge, 1991.

———. *When Species Meet.* Minneapolis: University of Minnesota Press, 2008.

Harman, Graham. *Circus Philosophicus.* Ropley: Zer0 Books, 2010.

———. "On the Mesh, the Strange Stranger and Hyperobjects: Morton's Ecological Ontology." *tarp: Architecture Manual,* 2012, 16–19.

———. *Prince of Networks: Bruno Latour and Metaphysics.* Melbourne: re.press, 2009.

———. *The Quadruple Object.* Ropley: Zer0 Books, 2011.

———. *Tool-Being: Heidegger and the Metaphysics of Objects.* Peru, Ill.: Open Court, 2002.

———. "The Well-Wrought Broken Hammer: Object-Oriented Literary Criticism." *New Literary History* 43 (2012): 183–203.

Harris, Anne. "Natural Beauty/Acheiropoieta." *Medieval Meets World* (blog). February 2013. http://medievalmeetsworld.blogspot.com/2013/02/natural-beautyacheiropoieta.html.

———. "Pyromena: Fire's Doing." In *Elemental Ecocriticism,* ed. Jeffrey Jerome Cohen and Lowell Duckert. Minneapolis: University of Minnesota Press, forthcoming.

Harris, Anne F., and Karen Eileen Overbey. "Field Change / Discipline Change." In *Burn after Reading,* vol. 2: *The Future We Want,* ed. Jeffrey Jerome Cohen, 127–43. Brooklyn: Punctum Books, 2014.

Harris, Jonathan Gil. *Untimely Matter in the Time of Shakespeare.* Philadelphia: University of Pennsylvania Press, 2009.

Harris, Nichola Erin. "The Idea of Lapidary Medicine: Its Circulation and Practical

Applications in Medieval and Early Modern England: 1000–1750." PhD diss., Rutgers, State University of New Jersey, 2009.

Hassig, Deborah. *Medieval Bestiaries: Text, Image, Ideology.* Cambridge: Cambridge University Press, 1995.

Hawkes, Jane. "Reading Stone." In *Theorizing Anglo-Saxon Stone Sculpture,* ed. Catherine E. Karkov and Fred Orton, 5–30. Morgantown: West Virginia University Press, 2003.

Head, Thomas F., ed. *Medieval Hagiography: An Anthology.* New York: Garland, 2000.

Heather, P. J. "Precious Stones in the Middle-English Verse of the Fourteenth Century." *Folklore* 42 (1931): 217–64, 345–404.

Heck, Christian. "*Erexit lapidem in titulum:* Dresser ou tailler la pierre de Béthel? Réinterpretations romanes d'un récit fondateur." In *Ex Quadris Lapidibus: La pierre et sa mise en oeuvre dans l'art medieval: mélanges d'histoire de l'art offerts à Éliane Vergnolle,* ed. Yves Gallet, 23–34. Turnhout: Brepols, 2011.

———. "Histoire mythique et archéologie au quinzième siècle: Une représentation inédite de Stonehenge." In *Tributes in Honor of James H. Marrow: Studies in Painting and Manuscript Illumination of the Late Middle Ages and Northern Renaissance,* ed. Jeffrey F. Hamburger and Anne S. Korteweg, 253–60. Turnhout: Brepols, 2006.

Heidegger, Martin. *The Fundamental Concepts of Metaphysics: World, Finitude, Solitude.* Trans. William McNeill and Nicholas Walker. Bloomington: Indiana University Press, 2001.

Heng, Geraldine. *Empire of Magic: Medieval Romance and the Politics of Cultural Fantasy.* New York: Columbia University Press, 2003.

Henry of Huntingdon. *De gemmis preciosis.* Ed. Winston Black. "Henry of Huntingdon's Lapidary Rediscovered and his *Anglicanus Ortus* Reassembled." *Mediaeval Studies* 68 (2006): 43–87.

———. *Historia Anglorum: The History of the English People.* Ed. and trans. Diana Greenway. Oxford: Clarendon Press, 1996.

Heringman, Noah. *Romantic Rocks, Aesthetic Geology.* Ithaca: Cornell University Press, 2004.

Herzogenrath, Bernd. *Deleuze/Guattari & Ecology.* New York: Palgrave Macmillan, 2009.

Higgins, Iain Macleod. "Defining the Earth's Center in a Medieval 'Multi-Text': Jerusalem in *The Book of John Mandeville.*" In *Text and Territory: Geographical Imagination in the European Middle Ages,* 29–53. Philadelphia: University of Pennsylvania Press, 1998.

———. *Writing East: The "Travels" of Sir John Mandeville.* Philadelphia: University of Pennsylvania Press, 1997.

Higham, N. J. *King Arthur: Myth-Making and History.* London: Routledge, 2002.

Hildegard of Bingen. *Liber Quartus: De lapidibus.* In *Physica sive subtilitates diversarum naturarum creaturarum, Patrologia Latina,* ed. Jacques-Paul Migne, 197, cols. 1247–66. Paris: Migne, 1844.

Hillaby, Joe. "Jewish Colonisation in the Twelfth Century." In *The Jews in Medieval Britain: Historical, Literary and Archaeological Perspectives,* ed. Patricia Skinner, 15–40. Woodbridge: Boydell, 2003.

Hinton, David A. *Gold and Gilt, Pots and Pins: Possessions and People in Medieval Britain.* Oxford: Oxford University Press, 2005.

———. "Medieval Anglo-Jewry: The Archaeological Evidence." In *The Jews in Medieval Britain: Historical, Literary and Archaeological Perspectives,* ed. Patricia Skinner, 97–111. Woodbridge: Boydell, 2003.

Hoffmann, Richard C. "*Homo et Natura, Homo in Natura*: Ecological Perspectives on the European Middle Ages." In *Engaging with Nature: Essays on the Natural World in Medieval and Early Modern Europe,* ed. Barbara A. Hanawalt and Lisa J. Kiser, 11–38. Notre Dame: University of Notre Dame Press, 2008.

Holler, William M. "Unusual Stone Lore in the Thirteenth-Century *Lapidary of Sydrac.*" *Romance Notes* 20 (1979): 135–42.

Holsinger, Bruce. "Of Pigs and Parchment: Medieval Studies and the Coming of the Animal." *PMLA* 124 (2009): 616–23.

Howe, Nicholas. "Anglo-Saxon England and the Postcolonial Void." In *Postcolonial Approaches to the European Middle Ages: Translating Cultures,* ed. Ananya Jahanara Kabir and Deanne Williams, 25–47. Cambridge: Cambridge University Press, 2005.

Howie, Cary. *Claustrophilia: The Erotics of Enclosure in Medieval Literature.* New York: Palgrave Macmillan, 2007.

Howlett, Richard, ed. *Chronicles of the Reigns of Stephen, Henry II and Richard I.* Rolls Series 82. London, 1884–89.

Human Interference Task Force. "Reducing the Likelihood of Future Human Activities That Could Affect Geologic High-Level Waste Repositories." Prepared for the Office of Nuclear Waste Isolation, May 1984. International Atomic Energy Agency. http://www.iaea.org/inis/collection/NCLCollectionStore/_Public/16/010/16010246.pdf.

Hyams, Paul. "The Jewish Minority in Mediaeval England, 1066–1290." *Journal of Jewish Studies* 25 (1974): 270–93.

Imperial College London. "From Cotton Candy to Rock: New Evidence about Beginnings of the Solar System." *Science Daily,* March 28, 2011.

Ingham, Patricia Clare. "Amorous Dispossessions: Knowledge, Desire, and the Poet's Dead Body." In *The Post-Historical Middle Ages,* ed. Elizabeth Scala and Sylvia Federico, 13–35. New York: Palgrave Macmillan, 2009.

———. "Introductory Note: Premodern Things." *Exemplaria* 22 (2010): 97–98.

———. "Pastoral Histories: Utopia, Conquest, and the Wife of Bath's Tale." *Texas Studies in Literature and Language* 44 (2002): 34–46.

———. *Sovereign Fantasies: Arthurian Romance and the Making of Britain.* Philadelphia: University of Pennsylvania Press, 2001.

Ingold, Tim. *Being Alive: Essays on Movement, Knowledge and Description.* London: Routledge, 2011.

Iovino, Serenella. "Book Review: Steps to a Material Ecocriticism. The Recent Literature about the 'New Materialisms' and Its Implications for Ecocritical Theory." *Ecozon@* 3 (2012): 134–45.

———. "Stories from the Thick of Things: Introducing Material Ecocriticism." Part I of Serenella Iovino and Serpil Oppermann, "Theorizing Material Ecocriticism: A Diptych," *Interdisciplinary Studies in Literature and the Environment* 19 (2012): 449–60.

Iovino, Serenella, and Serpil Oppermann. "Material Ecocriticism: Materiality, Agency, and Models of Narrativity." *Ecozon@* 3 (2012): 75–91.

———. "Theorizing Material Ecocriticism: A Diptych." *Interdisciplinary Studies in Literature and the Environment* 19 (2012): 449–75.

Isidore of Seville. *Etymologies (Isidori Hispalensis Episcopi Etymologiarum sive Originum Libri XX).* Ed. William Lindsay. 2 vols. 1911; reprint, Oxford: Oxford University Press, 1989.

———. *The Etymologies of Isidore of Seville.* Trans. Stephen A. Barney, W. J. Lewis, J. A. Beach, and Oliver Berghof. Cambridge: Cambridge University Press, 2006.

Jacks, Philip. "Restauratio and Reuse: The Afterlife of Roman Ruins." *Places* 20 (2008): 10–20.

Jaeger, Stephen C. *Ennobling Love: In Search of a Lost Sensibility.* Philadelphia: University of Pennsylvania Press, 1999.

John of Salisbury, *Letters of John of Salisbury.* Vol. 1, *The Early Letters (1153–1161).* Ed. W. J. Millor, H. E. Butler, and C. N. L. Brooke. Oxford: University of Oxford Press, 1986.

Johnson, Barbara. *Persons and Things.* Cambridge, Mass.: Harvard University Press, 2008.

Johnson, Hannah R. *Blood Libel: The Ritual Murder Accusation and at the Limit of Jewish History.* Ann Arbor: University of Michigan Press, 2012.

Josephus, Flavius. *Antiquities.* Cambridge, Mass.: Harvard University Press, 1998.

Joy, Eileen A. "Notes toward a Speculative Realist Literary Criticism: #STU09." Svenska Twitteruniversitetet. December 21, 2011. http://svtwuni.wordpress.com/2011/12/21/eileen-a-joy-stu09/.

Joy, Eileen A., and Craig Dionne, eds. "When Did We Become Post/Human?" Special issue, *postmedieval* 1 (2010).

Kardulias, P. Nick, and Richard W. Yerkes, eds. *Written in Stone: The Multiple Dimensions of Lithic Analysis.* Lanham, Md.: Lexington Books, 2003.

Karkov, Catherine E. "Naming and Renaming: The Inscription of Gender in Anglo-Saxon Sculpture." In *Theorizing Anglo-Saxon Stone Sculpture,* ed. Catherine E. Karkov and Fred Orton, 31–64. Morgantown: West Virginia University Press, 2003.

Kaske, R. E. "*Beowulf* and the Book of Enoch." *Speculum* 46 (1971): 421–31.

Kaye, Joel. "The (Re)Balance of Nature, ca. 1250–1350." In *Engaging with Nature: Essays on the Natural World in Medieval and Early Modern Europe,* ed. Barbara A. Hanawalt and Lisa J. Kiser, 85–113. Notre Dame: University of Notre Dame Press, 2008.

Kennedy, Maev. "Early Sketch of Stonehenge Found." *The Guardian,* November 27, 2006.

———. "The Magic of Stonehenge: New Dig Finds Clues to Power of Bluestones." *The Guardian,* September 23, 2008.

Kerisel, Jean. *Of Stones and Man: From the Pharaohs to the Present Day.* Trans. Philip Cockle. London: Taylor & Francis, 2005.

———. *Pierres et Hommes, des Pharaons à nos jours.* Paris: Presses de l'ENPC, 2004.

Keys, David. "Scientists Discover Source of Rock Used in Stonehenge's First Circle." *The Independent.* December 18, 2011. http://www.independent.co.uk/news/science /archaeology/news/scientists-discover-source-of-rock-used-in-stonehenges-first -circle-6278894.html.

The King of Tars. Ed. Judith Perryman. Heidelberg: Carl Winter, 1980.

Kinoshita, Sharon. *Medieval Boundaries: Rethinking Difference in Old French Literature.* Philadelphia: University of Pennsylvania Press, 2006.

Kinoshita, Sharon, and Peggy McCracken. *Marie de France: A Critical Companion.* Woodbridge: Boydell and Brewer, 2012.

Kiser, Lisa. "Alain de Lille, Jean de Meun, and Chaucer: Ecofeminism and Some Medieval Lady Natures." In *Mediaevalitas: Reading the Middle Ages,* ed. Piero Boitani and Anna Torti, 1–14. Cambridge: D. S. Brewer, 1996.

———. "Chaucer and the Politics of Nature." In *Beyond Nature Writing: Expanding the Boundaries of Ecocriticism,* ed. Kathleen R. Wallace and Karla Armbruster, 41–56. Charlottesville: University of Virginia Press, 2001.

Kitson, Peter. "Lapidary Traditions in Anglo-Saxon England: Part I, the Background; the Old English Lapidary." *Anglo-Saxon England* 7 (1978): 9–60.

———. "Lapidary Traditions in Anglo-Saxon England: Part II, Bede's *Explanatio Apocalypsis* and Related Works." *Anglo-Saxon England* 12 (1983): 73–123.

Klaver, Irene J. "Phenomenology on (the) Rocks." In *Eco-Phenomenology: Back to the Earth Itself,* ed. Charles S. Brown and Ted Toadvine, 155–69. Albany: State University of New York Press, 2003.

Knight, Rhonda. "Stealing Stonehenge: Translation, Appropriation, and Cultural Identity in Robert Mannyng of Brunne's *Chronicle." Journal of Medieval and Early Modern Studies* 32 (2002): 41–58.

Knight, Stephen. *Merlin: Knowledge and Power through the Ages.* Ithaca: Cornell University Press, 2009.

Kolbert, Elizabeth. "Enter the Anthropocene." In *Making the Geologic Now: Responses to the Material Conditions of Contemporary Life,* ed. Elizabeth Ellsworth and Jamie Kruse, 28–32. Brooklyn: Punctum Books, 2012.

Kordecki, Lesley. *Ecofeminist Subjectivities: Chaucer's Talking Birds*. New York: Palgrave Macmillan, 2011.

Kornbluth, Geneva. *Engraved Gems of the Carolingian Empire*. University Park: Pennsylvania State University Press, 1995.

Krueger, Derek. "The Religion of Relics in Late Antiquity and Byzantium." In *Treasures of Heaven: Saints, Relics, and Devotion in Medieval Europe,* ed. Martina Bagnoli, Holger A. Klein, C. Griffith Mann, and James Robinson, 5–17. New Haven: Yale University Press, 2010.

Krueger, Roberta L., ed. *The Cambridge Companion to Medieval Romance*. Cambridge: Cambridge University Press, 2000.

Kruger, Stephen. *The Spectral Jew: Conversion and Embodiment in Medieval Europe*. Minneapolis: University of Minnesota Press, 2006.

Krummel, Miriamne. *Crafting Jewishness in Medieval England: Legally Absent, Virtually Present*. New York: Palgrave Macmillan, 2011.

Kruse, Jamie, and Elizabeth Ellsworth. *Geologic City: A Field Guide to the GeoArchitecture of New York*. New York: Smudge Studios, 2011.

Kugel, James. *How to Read the Bible: A Guide to Scripture, Then and Now*. Cambridge, Mass.: Harvard University Press, 2007.

———. *Traditions of the Bible: A Guide to the Bible as It Was at the Start of the Common Era*. Cambridge, Mass.: Harvard University Press, 1999.

Lampert, Lisa. *Gender and Jewish Difference from Paul to Shakespeare*. Philadelphia: University of Pennsylvania Press, 2004.

Lancelot: Roman en prose de XIIIe siècle. Ed. Alexandre Micha. 9 vols. Geneva: Librarie Droz, 1978–83.

Lancelot-Grail: The Old French Arthurian Vulgate and Post-Vulgate in Translation. Ed. Norris J. Lacy. 5 vols. New York: Garland, 1993–96.

Langland, William. *Piers Plowman: An Edition of the C-Text*. Ed. Derek Pearsall. Berkeley: University of California Press, 1978.

Langmuir, Gavin I. *History, Religion, and Antisemitism*. Berkeley: University of California Press, 1993.

———. "The Knight's Tale of Young Hugh of Lincoln." *Speculum* 47 (1972): 459–82.

———. *Toward a Definition of Antisemitism*. Berkeley: University of California Press, 1996.

Latham, R. E., et al., eds. *Dictionary of Medieval Latin from British Sources*. 2 vols. Oxford: Oxford University Press, 1975–2013.

Latour, Bruno. "An Attempt at a Compositionist Manifesto." *New Literary History* 41 (2010): 471–90.

———. "Biography of an Inquiry: On a Book about Modes of Existence." Trans. by Cathy Porter. http://www.bruno-latour.fr/sites/default/files/126-KARSENTI-AIME-BIO -GB.pdf. 20 pages.

———. "Morality and Technology: The End of the Means." Trans. Couze Venn. *Theory, Culture & Society* 19, nos. 5–6 (2002): 247–60.

———. *On the Modern Cult of the Factish Gods.* Durham, N.C.: Duke University Press, 2010.

———. *Pandora's Hope: Essays on the Reality of Sciences Studies.* Cambridge, Mass.: Harvard University Press, 1999.

———. *Politics of Nature: How to Bring the Sciences into Democracy.* Trans. Catherine Porter. Cambridge, Mass.: Harvard University Press, 2004.

———. *Reassembling the Social.* Oxford: Oxford University Press, 2005.

———. *We Have Never Been Modern.* Trans. Catherine Porter. Cambridge, Mass.: Harvard University Press, 1993.

———. "Why Has Critique Run Out of Steam? From Matters of Fact to Matters of Concern." In *Things,* ed. Bill Brown, 225–48. Chicago: University of Chicago Press, 2004.

Lavezzo, Kathy. "The Minster and the Privy: Rereading the Prioress's Tale." *PMLA* 126 (2011): 363–82.

Leopold, Aldo. *A Sand County Almanac and Sketches Here and There.* New York: Oxford University Press, 1948.

Lévinas, Emmanuel. *Basic Philosophical Writings.* Ed. Adriaan T. Peperzak, Simon Critchley, and Robert Bernasconi. Bloomington: Indiana University Press, 2008.

Levinson, Alfred A. "Diamond Sources and Their Discovery." In *The Nature of Diamonds,* ed. George E. Harlow, 72–104. Cambridge: Cambridge University Press, 1998.

Liberles, Robert. *Salo Wittmayer Baron: Architect of Jewish History.* New York: New York University Press, 1995.

Lindberg, David C. *The Beginnings of Western Science: The European Scientific Tradition in Philosophical, Religious, and Institutional Context, 600 BC to AD 1450.* Chicago: University of Chicago Press, 1992.

Lochrie, Karma. "Provincializing Medieval Europe: Mandeville's Cosmopolitan Utopia." *PMLA* 124 (2009): 592–99.

Lomperis, Linda. "Medieval Travel Writing and the Question of Race." *JMEMS* 31 (2001): 149–64.

Lord, David Nash. "Le Tombeau de Merlin." Early British Kingdoms. 2001. http://www.earlybritishkingdoms.com/archaeology/tombeaum.html.

Lubbock, John. *Pre-historic Times, as Illustrated by Ancient Remains, and the Manners and Customs of Modern Savages.* London: Williams and Norgate, 1865.

Lupton, Julia. "Creature Caliban." *Shakespeare Quarterly* 51, no. 1 (2000): 1–23.

Lurio, Melissa Belleville. "An Educated Bishop in an Age of Reform: Marbode, Bishop of Rennes, 1092–1123." PhD diss., Boston University, 2004.

Lydgate, John. "Bycorne and Chychevache." In *Mummings and Entertainments,* ed. Claire Sponsler. Kalamazoo: Medieval Institute Publications, 2010. http://d.lib.rochester

.edu/teams/text/sponsler-lydgate-mummings-and-entertainments-bycorne-and
-chychevache.

Lynch, Kathryn L. "East Meets West in Chaucer's Squire's and Franklin's Tales." *Speculum*
70 (1995): 530–51.

Macauley, David. *Elemental Philosophy: Earth, Air, Fire, and Water as Environmental Ideas.*
Albany: State University of New York Press, 2010.

Malkiel, David. *Reconstructing Ashkenaz: The Human Face of Franco-German Jewry, 1000–*
1250. Stanford: Stanford University Press, 2009.

Manaugh, Geoff. "One Million Years of Isolation: An Interview with Abraham Van Luik."
BLDGBLOG. November 2, 2009. http://bldgblog.blogspot.com/2009/11/million
-years-of-isolation-interview.html.

Mandeville, Jean de. *Le Livre des merveilles du monde.* Ed. Christiane Deluz. Paris: CNRS,
2000.

Mandeville, John. *The Book of John Mandeville.* Ed. Tamarah Kohanski and C. David
Benson. Kalamazoo: Medieval Institute Publications, 2007.

———. *The Book of John Mandeville.* Ed. and trans. Iain Macleod Higgins. Indianapolis:
Hackett Publishing, 2011.

———. *The Book of Marvels and Travels.* Ed. and trans. Anthony Bale. Oxford: Oxford
University Press, 2012.

———. *The Defective Version of Mandeville's Travels.* Ed. M. C. Seymour. Oxford: Oxford
University Press, 2002.

Mansell, Darrel. "Metaphor as Matter." *Language and Literature* 17 (1992): 109–20.

Map, Walter. *De Nugis Curialium: Courtiers' Trifles.* Ed. and trans. M. R. James. Rev. C. N. L.
Brooke and R. A. B. Mynors. Oxford: Clarendon Press, 1983.

Marbode of Rennes. *Marbode of Rennes' "De lapidibus" Considered as a Medical Treatise*
with Text, Commentary, and C. W. King's Translation Together with Text and Translation
of Marbode's Minor Works on Stones. Ed. John M. Riddle. Wiesbaden: Franz Steiner
Verlag, 1977.

Marcus, Ivan G. "A Jewish-Christian Symbiosis: The Culture of Early Ashkenaz." In *Cul-*
tures of the Jews: A New History, ed. David Biale, 449–516. New York: Schocken Books,
2002.

———. *Rituals of Childhood: Jewish Acculturation in Medieval Europe.* New Haven: Yale
University Press, 1996.

Marian. "Firestones." *Mostly Medieval: Images and Reflections* (blog). October 28, 2012.
http://mostlymedievalimagesreflections.blogspot.com/2012/10/firestones.html.

———. "Monolithically." *Mostly Medieval: Images and Reflections* (blog). December 19, 2012.
http://mostlymedievalimagesreflections.blogspot.com/2012/12/monolithically.html.

Marie de France. *L'Espergatoire Seint Patriz: Nouvelle édition critique accompagnée du De*

Purgatorio Sancti Patricii (éd de Warnke). Ed. Yolande de Pontfarcy. Louvain: Peeters, 1995.

———. *Lais.* Ed. Alfred Ewert. London: Bristol Classics Press, 1995.

———. *The Lais of Marie de France.* Trans. Robert Hanning and Joan Ferrante. Durham, N.C.: Labyrinth Press, 1978.

Markus, R. A. *Saeculum: History and Society in the Theology of St. Augustine.* Cambridge: Cambridge University Press, 1970.

Mayor, Adrienne. *The First Fossil Hunters: Paleontology in Greek and Roman Times.* Princeton: Princeton University Press, 2000.

———. "Geomythology." In *Encyclopedia of Geology,* ed. Richard Selley, Robin Cocks, and Ian Palmer. Oxford: Elsevier, 2004. http://www.stanford.edu/dept/HPS/Mayor Geomythology.pdf.

McCracken, Peggy. *The Curse of Eve, the Wound of the Hero: Blood, Gender, and Medieval Literature.* Philadelphia: University of Pennsylvania Press, 2003.

———. "The Floral and the Human." In *Animal, Vegetable, Mineral: Ethics and Objects,* ed. Jeffrey Jerome Cohen, 65–90. Washington, D.C.: Oliphaunt, 2011.

McPhee, John. *Basin and Range.* New York: Macmillan, 1981.

Meillassoux, Quentin. *After Finitude.* Trans. Ray Brassier. London: Continuum, 2008.

"Melion" and "Bicarel": Two Old French Werwolf Lays. Ed. and trans. Amanda Hopkins. Liverpool Online Series: Critical Editions of French Texts 10. Liverpool: University of Liverpool, Department of French, 2005. http://www.liv.ac.uk/media/livacuk /cultures-languages-and-area-studies/liverpoolonline/Werwolf.pdf.

Mentz, Steve. "After Sustainability." *PMLA* 127 (2012): 586–92.

———. *At the Bottom of Shakespeare's Ocean.* London: Continuum, 2009.

———. "Shakespeare's Beach House, or The Green and the Blue in *Macbeth.*" *Shakespeare Studies* 39 (2011): 84–93.

Merlin, roman en prose du XIIIe siècle. Ed. Gaston Paris and Jacob Ulrich. Paris: Société des Anciens Textes Français, 1886.

Middle English Dictionary. University of Michigan. http://quod.lib.umich.edu/m/med/.

Migne, J.-P., ed. *Patrologia cursus completus, series Latina.* 221 vols. Paris, 1844–64.

Mignolo, Walter D. *The Darker Side of the Renaissance: Literacy, Territoriality, & Colonization.* Ann Arbor: University of Michigan Press, 2003.

Mitchell, J. Allen. "Cosmic Eggs, or Events before Anything." In *Speculative Medievalisms: Discography,* ed. Petropunk Collective [Eileen Joy, Anna Kłosowska, Nicola Masciandaro, and Michael O'Rourke], 143–58. Brooklyn: Punctum Books, 2012.

———. *Ethics and Eventfulness in Middle English Literature.* New York: Palgrave Macmillan, 2009.

———. "In the Event." In *Dark Chaucer: An Assortment,* ed. Myra Seaman, Eileen A. Joy, and Nicola Masciandaro, 89–100. New York: Punctum Books, 2012.

———. "The Middle English *Pearl*: Figuring the Unfigurable." *Chaucer Review* 35 (2000): 86–111.

Montgomery, David R. *The Rocks Don't Lie: A Geologist Investigates Noah's Flood.* New York: W. W. Norton, 2012.

Morton, Timothy. *The Ecological Thought.* Cambridge, Mass.: Harvard University Press, 2010.

———. *Ecology without Nature: Rethinking Environmental Aesthetics.* Cambridge, Mass.: Harvard University Press, 2009.

———. "Guest Column: Queer Ecology." *PMLA* 125 (2010): 273–82.

———. "The Mesh." In *Environmental Criticism for the Twenty-First Century,* ed. Stephanie LeMenager, Teresa Shewry, and Ken Hiltner, 19–30. New York: Routledge, 2011.

———. "An Object-Oriented Defense of Poetry." *New Literary History* 43 (2012): 205–24.

———. "The Oedipal Logic of Ecological Awareness." *Environmental Humanities* 1 (2012): 7–21.

———. "Sublime Objects." *Speculations* 2 (2011): 207–27.

———. "Thinking Ecology: The Mesh, the Strange Stranger, and the Beautiful Soul." *Collapse* 6 (2010): 265–93.

———. "Withdrawal, What the Heck Is It?" *Ecology without Nature* (blog). January 20, 2012. http://ecologywithoutnature.blogspot.com/2012/01/withdrawal-what-heck-is-it.html.

Muecke, Stephen. "Motorcycles, Snails, Latour: Criticism without Judgment." *Cultural Studies Review* 18 (2012): 40–58.

Mundill, Robin R. "Edward I and the Final Phase of Anglo-Jewry." In *The Jews in Medieval Britain: Historical, Literary and Archaeological Perspectives,* ed. Patricia Skinner, 56–70. Woodbridge: Boydell, 2003.

Murphy, G. Ronald, S. J. *Gemstone of Paradise: The Holy Grail in Wolfram's Parzival.* Oxford: Oxford University Press, 2010.

Nagel, Alexander. "The Afterlife of the Reliquary." In *Treasures of Heaven: Saints, Relics, and Devotion in Medieval Europe,* ed. Martina Bagnoli, Holger A. Klein, C. Griffith Mann, and James Robinson, 211–22. New Haven: Yale University Press, 2010.

Nardizzi, Vin. "Felling Falstaff in Windsor Park." In *Ecocritical Shakespeare,* ed. Lynne Bruckner and Dan Brayton, 123–38. Farnham: Ashgate, 2011.

———. "Shakespeare's Globe and England's Woods." *Shakespeare Studies* 39 (2011): 54–63.

———. "The Wooden Matter of Human Bodies: Prosthesis and Stump in *A Larum for London.*" In *The Indistinct Human in Renaissance Literature,* ed. Jean E. Feerick and Vin Nardizzi, 119–36. New York: Palgrave Macmillan, 2012.

———. *Wooden Os: Shakespeare's Theatres and England's Trees.* Toronto: University of Toronto Press, 2013.

———. "Wooden Slavery." *PMLA* 126 (2011): 313–15.

Navigatio Sancti Brendani abbatis. Ed. Carl Selmer. Notre Dame: University of Notre Dame Press, 1959.

Newman, Barbara. *From Virile Woman to WomanChrist: Studies in Medieval Religion and Literature.* Philadelphia: University of Pennsylvania Press, 1995.

———. *God and the Goddesses: Vision, Poetry, and Belief in the Middle Ages.* Philadelphia: University of Pennsylvania Press, 2005.

Niermeyer, J. F. *Mediae Latinitatis Lexicon Minus.* Leiden: Brill, 1976.

Nirenberg, David. *Communities of Violence: Persecution of Minorities in the Middle Ages.* Princeton: Princeton University Press, 1996.

Nolan, Maura. "Historicism after Historicism." In *The Post-Historical Middle Ages,* ed. Elizabeth Scala and Sylvia Federico, 63–85. New York: Palgrave Macmillan, 2009.

Oatman-Stanford, Hunter. "Read My Rings: The Oldest Living Tree Tells All." *Collectors Weekly.* November 13, 2012. http://www.collectorsweekly.com/articles/oldest-living-tree-tells-all/.

O'Dair, Shannon. "'To Fright the Animals and to Kill Them Up': Shakespeare and Ecology." *Shakespeare Studies* 39 (2011): 74–83.

Olsen, Bjørnar. *In Defense of Things: Archaeology and the Ontology of Objects.* Lanham: Altamira Press, 2010.

Oppermann, Serpil. "Ecocriticism's Theoretical Discontents." *Mosaic* 44 (2011): 154–69.

———. "A Lateral Continuum: Ecocriticism and Postmodern Materialism." Part II of Serenella Iovino and Serpil Oppermann, "Theorizing Material Ecocriticism: A Diptych." *Interdisciplinary Studies in Literature and the Environment* 19 (2012): 460–75.

Orchard, Andy. *Pride and Prodigies: Studies in the Monsters of the Beowulf Manuscript.* Cambridge: D. S. Brewer, 1995.

O'Rourke, Michael. "'Girls Welcome!!!': Speculative Realism, Object Oriented Ontology and Queer Theory." *Speculations* 2 (2011): 275–312.

———. "The Open." In *Queering the Non/Human,* ed. Noreen Giffney and Myra J. Hird, xvii–xxi. Aldershot: Ashgate, 2008.

Otter, Monika. *Inventiones: Fiction and Referentiality in Twelfth-Century English Historical Writing.* Chapel Hill: University of North Carolina Press, 1996.

Overbye, Dennis. "Finland's 100,000-Year Plan to Banish Its Nuclear Waste." *New York Times,* May 10, 2010. http://www.nytimes.com/2010/05/11/science/11nuclear.html.

Ovid. *Metamorphoses.* Trans. Mary M. Innes. Harmondsworth: Penguin, 1955.

Palti, Kathleen. "The Bound Earth in *Patience* and Other Middle English Poetry." *Interdisciplinary Studies in Literature and Environment* 20 (2013): 31–51.

Paris, Matthew. *Chronica majora.* Ed. Henry Richards Luard. Rolls Series 57. 7 vols. London: Longman, 1872–73.

————. *Matthew Paris's English History from the Year 1235 to 1272*. Trans. J. A. Giles. London: Henry G. Bohn, 1854.

Partner, Nancy. *Serious Entertainments: The Writing of History in Twelfth-Century England*. Chicago: University of Chicago Press, 1977.

Patterson, Lee. "The Living Witness of Our Redemption: Martyrdom and Imitation in Chaucer's Prioress's Tale." *Journal of Medieval and Early Modern Studies* 31 (2001): 507–60.

Pearl. In *The Poems of the Pearl Manuscript: "Pearl," "Cleanness," "Patience," "Sir Gawain and the Green Knight,"* 5th ed., ed. Malcolm Andrew and Ronald Waldron. Exeter: University of Exeter Press, 2007.

Pearson, Mike Parker. *Stonehenge: A New Understanding: Solving the Mysteries of the Greatest Stone Age*. New York: The Experiment, 2013.

Perniola, Mario. *Sex Appeal of the Inorganic*. Trans. Massimo Verdicchio. London: Continuum, 2004.

Physiologus: A Medieval Book of Nature Lore. Trans. Michael J. Curley. Chicago: University of Chicago Press, 1979.

Physiologus Latinus versio Y. Ed. Francis J. Carmody. Berkeley: University of California Press, 1941.

Pickering, Andrew. *The Mangle of Practice: Time, Agency and Science*. Chicago: University of Chicago Press, 1995.

"Pilgrim of Bordeaux," *Itinerarium Burdigalense [Pilgrimage to Jerusalem of the Anonymous Pilgrim of Bordeaux]*. Ed. Aubrey Stewart. Palestine Pilgrim's Text Society, 1887. http://www.christusrex.org/www1/ofm/pilgr/bord/10Bord01MapEur.html.

Pliny. *Natural History*. Trans. H. Rackham et al. Loeb Classical Library. 10 Vols. Cambridge, Mass.: Harvard University Press, 1940–63.

Plumpe, J. C. "*Vivum Saxum, Vivi Lapides*: The Concept of 'Living Stone' in Classical and Christian Antiquity." *Traditio* 1 (1943): 1–14.

Povinelli, Elizabeth A. "Do Rocks Listen? The Cultural Politics of Apprehending Australian Aboriginal Labor." *American Anthropologist* 97 (1995): 505–18.

Prendergast, Thomas, and Stephanie Trigg. "The Negative Erotics of Medievalism." In *The Post-Historical Middle Ages*, ed. Elizabeth Scala and Sylvia Federico, 117–37. New York: Palgrave Macmillan, 2009.

"The Prose Merlin and The Suite du Merlin (episodes)." Trans. Samuel N. Rosenberg. In *The Romance of Arthur: An Anthology of Medieval Texts in Translation*, ed. James J. Wilhelm, 348–63. New York: Garland, 1994.

Provost, William. "Chaucer's 'Kynde Nature.'" In *Man and Nature in the Middle Ages*, ed. Susan J. Ridyard and Robert G. Benson, 185–98. Sewanee, Tenn.: University of the South Press, 1995.

Pugh, Tison. *Queering Medieval Genres*. New York: Palgrave Macmillan, 2004.

Quigley, Sarah. "Holocaust Memorial: Architect Peter Eisenman, Berlin 2005." Polynational War Memorial. September 21, 2005. http://www.war-memorial.net/Holocaust-Memorial--Architect-Peter-Eisenman,-Berlin-2005-2.66.

Quinn, Jill Sisson. "Metamorphic: Notes on Love, Geology, and the Limits of Language." *Orion* 32 (2013): 38–47.

Ralph of Coggeshall. *Chronicon Anglicanum.* Ed. Joseph Stevenson. Rolls Series 6. London, 1875.

Randall, Margaret. *Stones Witness.* Tucson: University of Arizona Press, 2007.

Reid, Alex. "The Object Industry." *Digital Digs: An Archeology of the Future* (blog). May 29, 2012. http://www.alex-reid.net/2012/05/the-object-industry.html.

Richardson, H. G. *The English Jewry under Angevin Kings.* London: Methuen, 1960.

Richmond, Colin. "Englishness and Medieval Anglo-Jewry." In *Chaucer and the Jews: Sources, Contexts, Meanings,* ed. Sheila Delany, 213–27. New York: Routledge, 2002.

Riddle, John M. "Lithotherapy in the Middle Ages: Lapidaries Considered as Medical Texts." In *Quid Pro Quo: Studies in the History of Drugs,* 39–50. Aldershot: Ashgate, 1992.

Riddle, J. M., and J. A. Mulholland. "Albert on Stones and Minerals." In *Albertus Magnus and the Sciences: Commemorative Essays 1980,* ed. James A. Weisheipel, 203–34. Toronto: Pontifical Institute of Mediaeval Studies, 1980.

Rider, Jeff. "The Other Worlds of Romance." In *The Cambridge Companion to Medieval Romance,* ed. Roberta L. Krueger, 115–31. Cambridge: Cambridge University Press, 2000.

Roberts, Lawrence D., ed. *Approaches to Nature in the Middle Ages.* Binghamton: Center for Medieval and Renaissance Studies, 1982.

Robertson, Kellie. "Exemplary Rocks." In *Animal, Vegetable, Mineral: Ethics and Objects,* ed. Jeffrey Jerome Cohen, 91–121. Washington, D.C.: Oliphaunt, 2011.

———. "Medieval Materialism: A Manifesto." *Exemplaria* 22 (2010): 99–118.

———. "Medieval Things: Materiality, Historicity and the Premodern Object." *Literature Compass* 5 (2008): 1060–80.

Robinson, James. "From Altar to Amulet: Relics, Portability, and Devotion." In *Treasures of Heaven: Saints, Relics, and Devotion in Medieval Europe,* ed. Martina Bagnoli, Holger A. Klein, C. Griffith Mann, and James Robinson, 111–16. New Haven: Yale University Press, 2010.

Roman de la Rose par Guillaume de Lorris et Jean de Meun. Ed. Ernest Langlois. 5 vols. Paris: Librairie Ancienne Édouard Champion, 1914–24.

Roser, Sandrine. "La pierre dans le chantier de l'abbaye de Baume-les-Messieurs (premiere quart du XVe siècle)." In *Ex Quadris Lapidibus: La pierre et sa mise en oeuvre dans l'art medieval: mélanges d'histoire de l'art offerts à Éliane Vergnolle,* ed. Yves Gallet, 153–61. Turnhout: Brepols, 2011.

Rossi, Paolo. *The Dark Abyss of Time: The History of the Earth and the History of Nations from Hooke to Vico.* Trans. Lydia G. Cochrane. Chicago: University of Chicago Press, 1984.

Roth, Cecil. "A Hebrew Elegy of the York Martyrs of 1190." *Transactions of the Jewish Historical Society of England* 16 (1945–51): 213–20.

———. *A History of the Jews in England.* 3rd ed. Oxford: Clarendon Press, 1964.

Royle, Nicholas. *Veering: A Theory of Literature.* Edinburgh: University of Edinburgh Press, 2012.

Rubin, Miri. *Gentile Tales: The Narrative Assault on Late Medieval Jews.* New Haven: Yale University Press, 1999.

Rudd, Gillian. *Greenery: Ecocritical Readings of Late Medieval English Literature.* Manchester: Manchester University Press, 2007.

Rudwick, Martin J. S. *Bursting the Limits of Time: The Reconstruction of Geohistory in the Age of Revolution.* Chicago: University of Chicago Press, 2005.

———. *The Meaning of Fossils: Episodes in the History of Palaeontology.* 2nd ed. Chicago: University of Chicago Press, 1976.

———. *Scenes from Deep Time: Early Pictorial Representations of the Prehistoric World.* Chicago: University of Chicago Press, 1992.

———. *Worlds before Adam: The Reconstruction of Geohistory in the Age of Reform.* Chicago: University of Chicago Press, 2008.

Sagan, Carl. *The Dragons of Eden: Speculations on the Evolution of Human Intelligence.* New York: Ballantine Books, 1986.

Saint Erkenwald. Ed. Clifford Peterson. Philadelphia: University of Pennsylvania Press, 1977.

Sallis, John. *Stone.* Bloomington: Indiana University Press, 1994.

Salter, David. *Holy and Noble Beasts: Encounters with Animals in Medieval Literature.* Woodbridge: D. S. Brewer, 2001.

Saunders, Corinne. *Magic and the Supernatural in Medieval English Romance.* Woodbridge: D. S. Brewer, 2010.

Scala, Elizabeth. *Absent Narratives, Manuscript Textuality, and Literary Structure in Late Medieval England.* New York: Palgrave Macmillan, 2002.

———. "The Texture of *Emaré*." *Philological Quarterly* 85 (2006): 223–46.

Scarry, Elaine. *On Beauty and Being Just.* Princeton: Princeton University Press, 2001.

Scheil, Andrew P. *The Footsteps of Israel: Understanding Jews in Anglo-Saxon England.* Ann Arbor: University of Michigan Press, 2004.

Scherb, Victor A. "Assimilating Giants: The Appropriation of Gog and Magog in Medieval and Early Modern England." *Journal of Medieval and Early Modern Studies* 32 (2002): 59–84.

Schiff, Randy. "Cross-Channel Becomings-Animal: Primal Courtliness in Guillaume de Palerne and William of Palerne." *Exemplaria* 21 (2009): 418–38.

———. "The Instructive Other Within: Secularized Jews in *The Siege of Jerusalem*." In *Cultural Diversity in the British Middle Ages: Archipelago, Island, England*, ed. Jeffrey Jerome Cohen, 135–51. New York: Palgrave Macmillan, 2008.

———. "The Loneness of the Stalker: Poaching and Subjectivity in *The Parlement of the Thre Ages*." *Texas Studies in Literature and Language* 51 (2009): 263–93.

———. "Sovereign Exception: Pre-National Consolidation in *The Taill of Rauf Coilyear*." In *The Anglo-Scottish Border and the Shaping of Identity, 1300–1600*, ed. Mark Bruce and Katherine Terrell, 33–50. New York: Palgrave Macmillan, 2012.

Schildgen, Brenda Deen. "Wonders on the Border: Precious Stones in the *Comedy*." *Dante Studies* 113 (1995): 131–50.

Scholey, Anna. "Magical Rings in Middle English Romance: An Interdisciplinary Study in Medieval Literature and Material Culture." Master's thesis, University of Birmingham, 2009.

Scott, Michael W. "The Matter of Makira: Colonialism, Competition, and the Production of Gendered Peoples in Contemporary Solomon Islands and Medieval Britain." *History and Anthropology* 23 (2012): 115–48.

Scott, Rebecca R. *Removing Mountains: Extracting Nature and Identity in the Appalachian Coalfields*. Minneapolis: University of Minnesota Press, 2010.

Serres, Michel. *Biogea*. Trans. Randolph Burks. Minneapolis: Univocal, 2012.

———. *Genesis*. Trans. Geneviève James and James Nielson. Ann Arbor: University of Michigan Press, 1995.

———. *Statues: Le second livre des fondations*. Paris: Éditions François Bourin, 1987.

Serres, Michel, and Bruno Latour. *Conversations on Science, Culture, and Time*. Trans. Roxanne Lapidus. Ann Arbor: University of Michigan Press, 1995.

Shaviro, Steven. *Without Criteria: Kant, Whitehead, Deleuze, and Aesthetics*. Cambridge, Mass.: MIT Press, 2009.

Shoham-Steiner, Ephraim. "Jews and Healing at Medieval Saints' Shrines: Participation, Polemics, and Shared Cultures." *Harvard Theological Review* 103 (2010): 111–29.

Shryock, Andrew, and Daniel Lord Smail. *Deep History: The Architecture of Past and Present*. Berkeley: University of California Press, 2011.

Siewers, Alfred K. *Strange Beauty: Ecocritical Approaches to Early Medieval Landscape*. New York: Palgrave Macmillan, 2009.

Simpson, James R. *Troubling Arthurian Histories: Court Culture, Performance and Scandal in Chrétien de Troyes's Erec et Enide*. Bern: Peter Lang, 2007.

Sir Gawain and the Green Knight. In *The Gawain Poet: Complete Works*, trans. Marie Borroff. New York: W. W. Norton, 2011.

Sir Gawain and the Green Knight. In *The Poems of the Pearl Manuscript: "Pearl," "Cleanness," "Patience," "Sir Gawain and the Green Knight,"* 5th ed., ed. Malcolm Andrew and Ronald Waldron. Exeter: University of Exeter Press, 2007.

Sir Orfeo. In *The Middle English Breton Lays,* ed. Anne Laskaya and Eve Salisbury, 15–59. Kalamazoo: TEAMS, 1995.

Skinner, Patricia. "Introduction: Jews in Medieval Britain and Europe." In *The Jews in Medieval Britain: Historical, Literary and Archaeological Perspectives,* ed. Patricia Skinner, 1–11. Woodbridge: Boydell, 2003.

Smail, Daniel Lord. *On Deep History and the Brain.* Berkeley: University of California Press, 2008.

———. "The Original Subaltern." *postmedieval* 1 (2010): 180–86.

Smith, Barbara Herrnstein. *Scandalous Knowledge: Science, Truth and the Human.* Durham, N.C.: Duke University Press, 2005.

Smith, Bruce R. "Shakespeare @ the Limits." *Shakespeare Studies* 39 (2011): 104–13.

Smith, D. Vance. "Crypt and Decryption: Erkenwald Terminable and Interminable." *New Medieval Literatures* 5 (2002): 59–85.

Smith, Mick. *Against Ecological Sovereignty: Ethics, Biopolitics, and Saving the Natural World.* Minneapolis: University of Minnesota Press, 2011.

Sobin, Gustaf. *Luminous Debris: Reflecting on Vestige in Provence and Languedoc.* Berkeley: University of California Press, 1999.

Spiegel, Gabrielle M. "Geneaology: Form and Function in Medieval Historical Narrative." *History and Theory* 22 (1983): 43–53.

Stacey, Robert C. "Crusades, Martyrdoms and the Jews of Norman England, 1096–1190." In *Juden und Christen zur Zeit der Kreuzzüge,* ed. Alfred Haverkamp, 233–51. Sigmaringen: Jan Thorbeke Verlag, 1999.

———. "The English Jews under Henry III." In *The Jews in Medieval Britain: Historical, Literary and Archaeological Perspectives,* ed. Patricia Skinner, 41–55. Woodbridge: Boydell, 2003.

———. "Jews and Christians in Twelfth-Century England: Some Dynamics of a Changing Relationship." In *Jews and Christians in Twelfth-Century Europe,* ed. Michael A. Signer and John Van Engen, 340–54. Notre Dame: University of Notre Dame Press, 2011.

Stanbury, Sarah. "Ecochaucer: Green Ethics and Medieval Nature." *Chaucer Review* 39 (2004): 1–16.

———. "The *Man of Law's Tale* and Rome." *Exemplaria* 22 (2010): 119–37.

———. *The Visual Object of Desire in Late Medieval England.* Philadelphia: University of Pennsylvania Press, 2008.

Steel, Karl. "A Fourteenth-Century Ecology: 'The Former Age' with Dindimus." In *Rethinking Chaucerian Beasts,* ed. Carolynn Van Dyke, 185–99. New York: Palgrave Macmillan, 2012.

———. *How to Make a Human: Animals and Violence in the Middle Ages.* Columbus: Ohio State University Press, 2011.

———. "Weeping with Erkenwald, or, Complicit with Grace." *In the Middle* (blog).

October 14, 2008. http://www.inthemedievalmiddle.com/2008/10/weeping-with -erkenwald-or-complicit.html.

———. "Will Wonders Never Cease: St. Erkenwald with Claustrophilia." *In the Middle* (blog). November 17, 2009. http://www.inthemedievalmiddle.com/2009/11/will -wonders-never-cease-st-erkenwald_17.html.

———. "With the World, or Bound to Face the Sky: The Postures of the Wolf-Child of Hesse." In *Animal, Vegetable, Mineral: Ethics and Objects,* ed. Jeffrey Jerome Cohen, 9–34. Washington, D.C.: Oliphaunt, 2011.

Stein, Robert M. *Reality Fictions: Romance, History and Governmental Authority, 1025– 1180.* Notre Dame: University of Notre Dame Press, 2006.

Stephens, Walter. *Giants in Those Days: Folklore, Ancient History, and Nationalism.* Lincoln: University of Nebraska Press, 1989.

Stewart, Kathleen. "Weak Theory in an Unfinished World." *Journal of Folklore Research* 45 (2008): 71–82.

Stockton, Will. *Playing Dirty: Sexuality and Waste in Early Modern Comedy.* Minneapolis: University of Minnesota Press, 2011.

Strickland, Deborah. *Saracens, Demons and Jews: Making Monsters in Medieval Art.* Princeton: Princeton University Press, 2003.

Studer, Paul, and Joan Evans, eds. *Anglo-Norman Lapidaries.* Paris: Édouard Champion, 1924.

Suetonius. *Lives of the Caesars.* Trans. Catharine Edwards. Oxford: Oxford University Press, 2000.

Symmes, Patrick. "Turkey: Archeological Dig Reshaping Human History." February 18, 2010. http://www.newsweek.com/turkey-archeological-dig-reshaping-human-history -75101?piano_d=1.

Szymborska, Wislawa. *Poems, New and Collected, 1957–1997.* Trans. Stanislaw Baranczak and Clare Cavanagh. New York: Harcourt, 1998.

Tatlock, J. S. P., and P. Mackaye. *The Scene of the Franklin's Tale Visited.* London: K. Paul, Trench, Trübner, 1914.

Taylor, Joseph. "'Me longeth sore to Bernysdale': Centralization, Resistance and the Bare Life of the Greenwood in *A Gest of Robyn Hode.*" *Modern Philology* 110 (2013): 313–39.

Thacker, Eugene. *In the Dust of This Planet: Horror of Philosophy.* Vol. 1. Winchester: Zer0 Books, 2011.

Theophrastus. *On Stones.* Ed. and trans. Earle R. Caley and John F. C. Richards. Columbus: Ohio State University Press, 1956.

Thomas, Keith. *Man and the Natural World: Changing Attitudes in England, 1500–1800.* Harmondsworth: Penguin, 1983.

Thorndike, Lynn. "The Latin Pseudo-Aristotle and Medieval Occult Science." *Journal of English and Germanic Philology* 21 (1922): 229–58.

Tilley, Christopher. *The Materiality of Stone: Explorations in Landscape Phenomenology.* Oxford: Berg, 2004.

Tomasch, Sylvia. "Postcolonial Chaucer and the Virtual Jew." In *The Postcolonial Middle Ages,* ed. Jeffrey Jerome Cohen, 243–60. New York: Palgrave, 2000.

Travis, Peter W. *Disseminal Chaucer: Rereading "The Nun's Priest's Tale."* Notre Dame: University of Notre Dame Press, 2010.

Trigg, Stephanie. *Shame and Honor: A Vulgar History of the Garter.* Philadelphia: University of Pennsylvania Press, 2012.

———. *Congenial Souls: Reading Chaucer from Medieval to Postmodern.* Minneapolis: University of Minnesota Press, 2002.

Turville-Petre, Thorlac. *England the Nation: Language, Literature, and National Identity, 1290–1340.* Oxford: Clarendon Press, 1996.

United States Holocaust Memorial Museum. "Architecture and Art." http://www.ushmm .org/information/about-the-museum/architecture-and-art/.

Venarde, Bruce L. *Robert of Arbrissel: A Medieval Religious Life.* Washington, D.C.: Catholic University of America Press, 2003.

Vernant, Jean-Pierre. *The Origins of Greek Thought.* Ithaca: Cornell University Press, 1982.

Vincent of Beauvais. *Speculum quadruplex sive, Speculum maius, naturale, doctrinale, morale, historiale.* Graz: Akademische Druck Verlagsanstalt, 1964.

Wace. *Roman de Brut: A History of the British.* Ed. and trans. Judith Weiss. Exeter: University of Exeter Press, 2003.

Wade, James. *Fairies in Medieval Romance.* New York: Palgrave Macmillan, 2011.

Waldron, Jennifer. "Of Stones and Stony Hearts: Desdemona, Hermione, and the Post-Reformation Theater." In *The Indistinct Human in Renaissance Literature,* ed. Jean E. Feerick and Vin Nardizzi, 205–27. New York: Palgrave Macmillan, 2012.

Wallace, David. *Premodern Places: Calais to Surinam, Chaucer to Aphra Behn.* Oxford: Blackwell, 2004.

Walton, Stephen A. "Theophrastus on *Lyngurium*: Medieval and Early Modern Lore from the Classical Lapidary Tradition." *Annals of Science* 58 (2001): 357–79.

The Wanderer. Ed. R. F. Leslie. Manchester: Manchester University Press, 1966.

Warner, Marina. "The Writing of Stones." *Cabinet* 29 (2008): 34–41.

Warren, Michelle. *History on the Edge: Excalibur and the Borders of Britain, 1100–1300.* Minneapolis: University of Minnesota Press, 2000.

Weber, Max. *Wissenschaft als Beruf.* Leipzig: Reclam, 1995.

Werth, Tiffany. "A Heart of Stone: The Ungodly in Early Modern England." In *The Indistinct Human in Renaissance Literature,* ed. Jean E. Feerick and Vin Nardizzi, 181–203. New York: Palgrave Macmillan, 2012.

Westrem, Scott. "Against Gog and Magog." In *Text and Territory: Geographical Imagination in the European Middle Ages,* 54–75. Philadelphia: University of Pennsylvania Press, 1998.

Whatley, Gordon. "Heathens and Saints: *St. Erkenwald* in its Legendary Context." *Speculum* 61 (1986): 330–63.

White, Lynn, Jr. "The Historical Roots of Our Ecological Crisis." In *The Ecocriticism Reader: Landmarks in Literary Ecology,* ed. Cheryll Glotfelty and Harold Fromm, 3–14. Athens: University of Georgia Press, 1996.

Wilbur, Richard. *Collected Poems 1943–2004.* Orlando: Harcourt, 2004.

William of Malmesbury. *Gesta Regum Anglorum: The History of the English Kings.* Ed. and trans. R. A. B. Mynors. Completed by R. M. Thomson and M. Winterbottom. 2 vols. Oxford: Clarendon Press, 1998.

William of Newburgh. *Historia de rebus anglicis.* In *Chronicles of the Reigns of Stephen, Henry II and Richard I,* ed. Richard Howlett, 2 vols. Rolls Series 82. London, 1884–89.

———. *The History of English Affairs,* Book 1. Ed. and trans. P. G. Walsh and M. J. Kennedy. Wilthsire: Aris and Phillips, 1988.

———. *The History of William of Newburgh.* Trans. Joseph Stevenson. Felinfach: Llanerch Publishers, 1996.

Williams, David. *Deformed Discourse: The Function of the Monster in Mediaeval Thought and Literature.* Montreal: McGill-Queen's University Press, 1996.

Williams, David B. *Stories in Stone: Travels through Urban Geology.* New York: Walker & Company, 2009.

Williams, Deanne. "Gower's Monster." In *Postcolonial Approaches to the European Middle Ages: Translating Cultures,* ed. Ananya Jahanara Kabir and Deanne Williams, 127–50. Cambridge: Cambridge University Press, 2005.

Wills, Gary. *Saint Augustine.* New York: Penguin, 2005.

Wilson, E. O. *Biophilia.* Cambridge, Mass.: Harvard University Press, 1984.

Witmore, Michael. "We Have Never Not Been Inhuman." *postmedieval* 1 (2010): 208–14.

Wolfe, Cary. *Before the Law: Humans and Other Animals in a Biopolitical Frame.* Chicago: University of Chicago Press, 2012.

———. *What Is Posthumanism?* Minneapolis: University of Minnesota Press, 2010.

Wood, Ian. "Ruthwell: Contextual Searches." In *Theorizing Anglo-Saxon Stone Sculpture,* ed. Catherine E. Karkov and Fred Orton, 104–30. Morgantown: West Virginia University Press, 2003.

Wright, Thomas L. "'The Tale of King Arthur': Beginnings and Foreshadowings." In *Malory's Originality: A Critical Study of "Le Morte Darthur,"* ed. R. M. Lumiansky, 9–66. Baltimore: Johns Hopkins University Press, 1964.

Wrightson, Keith. "'The Decline of Neighbourliness' Reconsidered." In *Local Identities in Late Medieval and Early Modern England,* ed. Norman L. Jones and Daniel Woolf, 19–49. New York: Palgrave Macmillan, 2007.

Wylie, John. "Landscape, Absence and the Geographies of Love." *Transactions of the Institute of British Geographers* 34 (2009): 275–89.

Yaeger, Patricia. "Editor's Column: The Death of Nature and the Apotheosis of Trash; or, Rubbish Ecology." *PMLA* 123 (2008): 321–39.

———. "Editor's Column: Sea Trash, Dark Pools, and the Tragedy of the Commons." *PMLA* 125 (2010): 523–45.

Yates, Julian. *Error, Misuse, Failure: Object Lessons from the English Renaissance.* Minneapolis: University of Minnesota Press, 2003.

———. "It's (for) You; or, The Tele-t/r/opical Post-human." *postmedieval* 1 (2010): 223–34.

Yates, Julian, and Garrett Sullivan. "Introduction: Shakespeare and Ecology." *Shakespeare Studies* 39 (2011): 23–31.

Yuval, Israel Jacob. *Two Nations in Your Womb: Perceptions of Jews and Christians in Late Antiquity and the Middle Ages.* Trans. Barbara Harshav and Jonathan Chipman. Berkeley: University of California Press, 2006.

Ywain and Gawain. In *Sir Perceval of Galles and Ywain and Gawain,* ed. Mary Flowers Braswell. Kalamazoo: Medieval Institute Publications, 1995. http://d.lib.rochester.edu/teams/text/braswell-ywain-and-gawain.

Zalasiewicz, Jan. *The Earth after Us: What Legacy Will Humans Leave in the Rocks?* Oxford: Oxford University Press, 2008.

———. *The Planet in a Pebble: A Journey into Earth's Deep History.* Oxford: Oxford University Press, 2010.

Zaleski, Carol. *Otherworld Journeys: Accounts of Near-Death Experience in Medieval and Modern Times.* Oxford: Oxford University Press, 1988.

Zimmerman, Virginia. *Excavating Victorians.* Albany: SUNY Press, 2008.

Zoellner, Tom. "Five Myths about Diamonds." *Washington Post,* July 4, 2010.

Zumthor, Paul. *Toward a Medieval Poetics.* Trans. Philip Bennett. Minneapolis: University of Minnesota Press, 1992.

INDEX

Jeffrey Jerome Cohen is professor of English and director of the Medieval and Early Modern Studies Institute at George Washington University. He is the author and editor of numerous books, including *Medieval Identity Machines*; *Of Giants: Sex, Monsters, and the Middle Ages*; *Monster Theory: Reading Culture*; and *Prismatic Ecology: Ecotheory beyond Green,* all from the University of Minnesota Press.

36911061R00229

Made in the USA
Lexington, KY
18 April 2019